Foundation Mathematics

For Class X

Part-1 of 2

NoMoreClass™

AF670161

NOTION PRESS

NOTION PRESS

India. Singapore. Malaysia.

ISBN xxx-x-xxxxx-xx-x

Dedicated to our Beloved Prime Minister Shree Narendra Modi ji, whose life gives the Inspiration to every Individual

If a Man ***Decides*** *to achieve something in his life nothing is Impossible*

कर्मण्येवाधिकारस्ते मा फलेषु कदाचन।

मा कर्मफलहेतुर्भूर्मा ते सङ्गोऽस्त्वकर्मणि॥ २-४७

Karmanye vadhikaraste Ma Phaleshu Kadachana,

Ma Karmaphalaheturbhurma Te Sangostvakarmani

You have the right to work only but never to its fruits.

Let not the fruits of action be your motive, nor let your attachment be to inaction.

CONTENT

TOPIC NAME	PAGE NO.

3. PAIR OF LINEAR EQUATIONS IN TWO VARIABLES

4. INTRODUCTION TO TRIGONOMETRY

TOPIC NAME	PAGE NO.

5. SIMILAR TRIANGLES

TOPIC NAME PAGE NO.

6. STATISTICS

1 REAL NUMBERS

THEORY

1.1 INTRODUCTION :

KEY CONCEPT

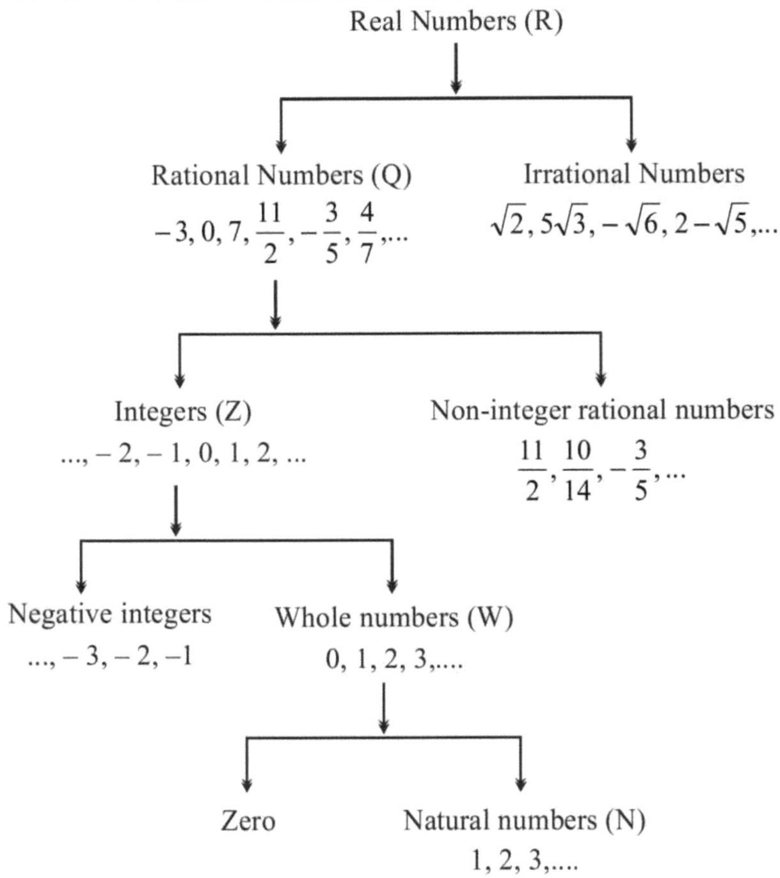

- **Natural numbers :** The counting numbers 1,2,3..... are called natural numbers. It is denoted by N.

  N = {1,2.3..........}

- **Whole numbers :** In the set of natural number if we include the number 0, the resulting set is known as the set of whole numbers.

  It is represented by W.

  W = {0,1,2.......}

- **Integers :** Natural numbers along with 0 and their negatives are called integers and the set of integers is denoted by I

$$I = \{.........-4, -3, -2, -1, 0, 1, 2, 3.........\}$$

- **Rational numbers :** A rational number is a number which can be expressed in the form of p/q, where p and q are integers and q is not zero.

- **Irrational numbers :** A number is called irrational if it can not be written in the form of p/q, where p and q are integers and $q \neq 0$

  The system R of real numbers includes rational as well irrational numbers.

  In this chapter we will begin with a brief recall of divisibility of integers as well state some important properties of integers.

1.2 RATIONAL NUMBERS

Decimal Representation of Rational Numbers :

KEY CONCEPT

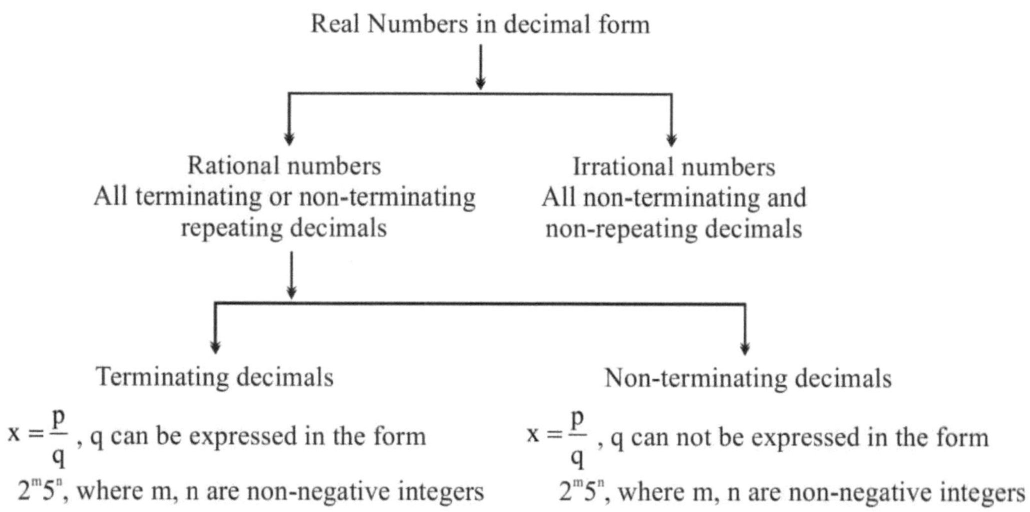

(i) **Finite or Terminating Decimal :** Every fraction p/q can be expressed as a decimal, if the decimal expression of p/q terminates, i.e. comes to an end, then the decimal so obtained is called a terminating decimal.

e.g,. $1/4 = 0.25$, $5/8 = 0.625$, $2\frac{3}{5} = \frac{13}{5} = 2.6$

Thus, each of the numbers $\frac{1}{4}, \frac{5}{8}$ and $2\frac{3}{5}$ can be expressed in the form of a terminating decimal.

Important : A fraction p/q is a terminating decimal only, when prime factors of q are 2 and 5 only.

e.g. Each one of the fractions $\frac{1}{2}, \frac{3}{4}, \frac{7}{20}, \frac{13}{25}$ is a terminating decimal, since the denominator of each has no prime factor other than 2 and 5.

(ii) Repeating (or Recurring) Decimals: A decimal in which a digit or a set of digits repeats periodically, is called a repeating or a recurring decimal.
In a recurring decimal, we place a bar over the first block of the repeating part and omit the other repeating blocks.

e.g. (i) $\frac{2}{3} = 0.666 \ldots\ldots\ldots\ldots\ldots\ldots = 0.\overline{6}$

(ii) $\frac{15}{7} = 2.142857142857 \ldots\ldots\ldots\ldots = 2.\overline{142857}$

REMEMBER

Special Characteristics of Rational Numbers :

(i) Every rational number is expressible either as a terminating decimal or as a repeating decimal.
(ii) Every terminating decimal is a rational number.
(iii) Every repeating decimal is a rational number.

Fractions :

(a) Common fraction : Fractions whose denominator is not 10.

(b) Decimal fraction : Fractions whose denominator is 10 or any power of 10.

(c) Proper fraction : Numerator < Denominator i.e. $\frac{2}{7}$

(d) Improper fraction : Numerator > Denominator i.e. $\frac{7}{2}$

(e) Mixed fraction : Consists of integral as well as fractional part i.e. $5\frac{2}{9}$

(f) Compound fraction : Fraction whose numerator and denominator themselves are fractions. i.e. $\frac{4/5}{3/7}$.

(g) Continued fraction : Fraction consists of the fractional denominators.

i.e., $1+\cfrac{1}{2-\cfrac{3}{5+\cfrac{4}{7}}}$

Illustrations

Illustration 1 : Simplify: $$3+\cfrac{2}{1+\cfrac{1}{4-\cfrac{2}{3}}}$$

Sol. $$3+\cfrac{2}{1+\cfrac{1}{\left(\frac{4}{1}-\frac{2}{3}\right)}} = 3+\cfrac{2}{1+\cfrac{1}{\left(\frac{10}{3}\right)}} = 3+\cfrac{2}{\left(1+\frac{3}{10}\right)} = 3+\cfrac{2}{\left(\frac{13}{10}\right)}$$

$$= 3 + 2\times\frac{10}{13} = 3+\frac{20}{13} = \frac{39+20}{13} = \frac{59}{13}.$$

- **Prime numbers :** All natural numbers that have one and itself only as their factors are called prime numbers i.e. prime numbers are exactly divisible by 1 and themselves.
Example : 2, 3, 5, 7, 11, 13, 17, 19, 23 ....etc.

- **Twin Primes :** The term twin primes is used for a pair of odd prime numbers that differ by two.
Example : 3 and 5 are twin primes.

- **Co-prime numbers :** If the H.C.F. of the given numbers (not necessarily prime) is 1 then they are known as co-prime numbers.
Example : 5, 6, are co-prime as H.C.F. of (5, 6) = 1.

IMPORTANT

Note : (i) 1 is neither prime nor composite number.
(ii) 2 is the only prime number which is even.
(iii) Any two consecutive numbers will always be co-prime.

- **Composite numbers :** All natural numbers that have more than two different factors are called composite numbers. If C is the set of composite numbers then C = {4,6,8,9,10,12,.....}.

- **Perfect Number :** If the sum of all factors of a number is twice the number then this number is called perfect number.
If $2^k - 1$ = Prime number, then $(2^k - 1)(2^{k-1})$ is a perfect number.
Example : 6, 28, etc.

- **Imaginary Numbers:** All the numbers whose square is negative are called imaginary numbers.
Example : 2i, – 7i, i, ... where $i = \sqrt{-1}$ $(i^2 = -1)$.

- **Complex Numbers :** The combined form of real and imaginary numbers is known as complex numbers. It is denoted by Z = a + ib where a is real part and b is imaginary part of Z and a, b $\in$ R.
The set of complex numbers is the super set of all the sets of numbers.

Illustrations

Illustration 2 : Express $\frac{2157}{625}$ in the decimal form.

Sol. We have,

$$
\begin{array}{r|l}
625 & 2157.0000 \,(3.4512 \\
 & \underline{1875} \\
 & \;\;2820 \\
 & \;\;\underline{2500} \\
 & \;\;\;\;3200 \\
 & \;\;\;\;\underline{3125} \\
 & \;\;\;\;\;\;750 \\
 & \;\;\;\;\;\;\underline{625} \\
 & \;\;\;\;\;\;\;\;1250 \\
 & \;\;\;\;\;\;\;\;\underline{1250} \\
 & \;\;\;\;\;\;\;\;\;\;\;\;0
\end{array}
$$

$\therefore \quad \frac{2157}{625} = 3.4512$ **Ans.**

Illustration 3 : Find the decimal representation of $\frac{-16}{45}$.

Sol. By long division, we have

$$
\begin{array}{r|l}
45 & 160 \,(0.3555 \\
 & \underline{135} \\
 & \;\;250 \\
 & \;\;\underline{225} \\
 & \;\;\;\;250 \\
 & \;\;\;\;\underline{225} \\
 & \;\;\;\;\;\;250 \\
 & \;\;\;\;\;\;\underline{225} \\
 & \;\;\;\;\;\;\;\;25
\end{array}
$$

$\therefore \quad \frac{16}{45} = 0.355 \ldots = 0.3\bar{5}$

Hence, $\frac{-16}{45} = -0.3\bar{5}$. **Ans.**

Conversion of Decimal Numbers into Rational Numbers of the form p/q :

(i) Procedure for terminating decimal :

Step. 1 : Count the number of numerals to the right of the decimal point. Let it be m.

Step. 2 : Drop the decimal point and in the denominator write 1 followed by m zeros.

Step. 3 : Simplify the fraction.

Illustrations

Illustration 4 : Convert 6.225 to the form p/q.

Sol. 1. Number of numerals to the right of decimal is 3 i.e. m = 3.

2. Write $6.225 = \frac{6225}{1000}$

3. Simplify (divide the numerator and denominator by 25) $= 6.225 = \frac{249}{40}$

(ii) Conversion of Pure Recurring Decimal to the form p/q.

Step.1 : Obtain the repeating decimal and put it equal to x.

Step 2 : Write the number in decimal form by removing bar from the top of repeating digits and listing repeating digits at least twice :

e.g. write $x = 0.\bar{8}$ as $x = 0.888$ ....

Step 3 : Determine the no. of digits having bar on their heads.

Step 4 : If the repeating decimal has 1 place repetition, multiply by 10, a two place repetition, multiply by 100, a three place repetition, multiply by 1000 and so on.

Step 5 : Subtract the number in step II from the numbers obtained in step IV.

Step 6 : Divide both sides of the equation by the coefficient of x.

Step 7 : Write the rational number in its simplest form.

Illustrations

Illustration 5 : Express $0.\overline{585}$ in the form p/q.

Sol. Let $x = 0.\overline{585}$

$x = 0.585585585$ ....(i)

Here, we have 3 repeating digits after the decimal point. So, we multiply both sides of (i) by 10^3=1000 to get

$1000\,x = 585.585585$ ....(ii)

Subtracting (i) from (ii), we get

$1000\,x - x = (585.585585 \text{ ....}) - (0.585585\ldots)$

$999\,x = 585 \quad \Rightarrow \quad x = \frac{585}{999}$

(iii) Conversion of a Mixed Recurring Decimal to the form p/q.

Step 1 : Obtain the mixed recurring decimal and write it equal to x.

Step 2 : Determine the number of digits after the decimal point which do not have bar on them. Let there be n digits without bar just after the decimal point.

Step 3 : Multiply both sides of x by 10^n, so that only the repeating decimal is on the right side of the decimal point.

Step 4 : Use the method of converting pure recurring decimal to the form p/q and obtain the value of x.

Illustrations

Illustration 6 : Express $0.22\bar{5}$ in the form p/q.

Sol. Let $x = 0.22\bar{5}$ ....(i)

The no of digits after the decimal point which do not have bar on them is 2.

$\therefore$ Multiply both sides of x by 10^2.

$100\,x = 22.\bar{5}$ ....(ii)

Here, we have 1 repeating digit after the decimal point. So, multiply both sides of (ii) by 10 to get.

$1000\,x = 225.55$ ....(iii)

Subtracting (ii) from (iii)

$1000\,x - 100\,x = (225.55\ldots\ldots) - (22.55\ldots\ldots)$

$900\,x = 203 \Rightarrow x = \frac{203}{900}$.

1.3 IRRATIONAL NUMBERS :

A number is an irrational number, if it has a non terminating and non-repeating decimal representations. A number that cannot be put in the form p/q where p, q are integers and $q \neq 0$ is called irrational number.

e.g. $\sqrt{2}$, $\sqrt{3}$, $\sqrt{11}$, π etc.

Illustration 7 : Prove that $\sqrt{5}$ is an irrational number.

Sol. Let us assume on the contrary that $\sqrt{5}$ is a rational number. Then, there exist co-prime positive integers a and b such that

$\sqrt{5} = \frac{a}{b} \Rightarrow 5b^2 = a^2$

$\Rightarrow$ $5 \mid a^2$ $[\because 5 \mid 5b^2]$

$\Rightarrow$ $5 \mid a$ ......(i)

$\Rightarrow$ $a = 5c$ for some positive integer c

$\Rightarrow$ $a^2 = 25c^2$

$\Rightarrow$ $5b^2 = 25c^2$ $[\because a^2 = 5c^2]$

$\Rightarrow$ $b^2 = 5c^2$

$\Rightarrow$ $5 \mid b^2$ $[\because 5 \mid 5c^2]$

$\Rightarrow$ $5 \mid b$ ....(ii)

From (i) and (ii), we find that a and b have at least 5 as a common factor. This contradicts the fact that a and b are co-prime.

Hence, $\sqrt{5}$ is an irrational number.

Illustration 8 : Prove that $\sqrt{3} - \sqrt{2}$ is an irrational number.

Sol. If possible, let $\sqrt{3} - \sqrt{2}$ be a rational number equal to x.

Then, $x = \sqrt{3} - \sqrt{2}$

$\Rightarrow$ $x^2 = (\sqrt{3} - \sqrt{2})^2$

$\Rightarrow$ $x^2 = 3 + 2 - 2\sqrt{3}\sqrt{2}$

$\Rightarrow$ $x^2 = 5 - 2\sqrt{6}$

$\Rightarrow$ $x^2 - 5 = -2\sqrt{6}$

$\Rightarrow$ $\frac{5 - x^2}{2} = \sqrt{6}$

Now, x is rational

$\Rightarrow$ x^2 is rational

$\Rightarrow$ $\frac{5 - x^2}{2}$ is rational

$\Rightarrow$ $\sqrt{6}$ is rational.

But, $\sqrt{6}$ is irrational.

Thus, we arrive at a contradiction. So, our supposition that $\sqrt{3} - \sqrt{2}$ is rational, is wrong.

Hence, $\sqrt{3} - \sqrt{2}$ is an irrational number. **Ans.**

REMEMBER

Some Properties of irrational numbers :

(a) The –ve of an irrational number is an irrational number.

(b) The sum of a rational and an irrational number is an irrational number.

(c) The product of a non–zero rational number with an irrational number is always an irrational number.

1.4 REAL NUMBERS :

The collection of real numbers consists of all the rational and irrational numbers and is denoted by R. Every real number corresponds to a point on the line and conversely, every point on the number line represents a real number.

REMEMBER

Properties of all real numbers :

(a) Closure property of addition :

The sum of two real numbers is always a real number.

(b) Commutative law for addition :

$a + b = b + a$, $\forall$ real numbers 'a' and 'b'.

(c) Associative law for addition :

$(a + b) + c = a + (b + c)$,

$\forall$ real numbers a, b and c.

(d) Existence of additive identity :

Zero is the additive identity.

$a + 0 = 0 + a = a$, $\forall$ real numbers a.

(e) Existence of addition inverse :

For each real number 'a', there exists a real number '–a' such that $a + (-a) = (-a) + a = 0$.

(f) Closure property for multiplication :

The product of two real numbers is a real number.

(g) Commutative law of multiplication :

$ab = ba$, $\forall$ real numbers a and b.

(h) Associative law of multiplication :

$(ab)c = a(bc)$, $\forall$ real numbers a, b and c.

(i) Existence of multiplicative identity :

1 is called the multiplicative identity.

$1.a = a.1 = a$, $\forall$ real numbers a.

(j) Existence of multiplicative inverse :

Every non–zero real number 'a' has its multiplicative inverse $\frac{1}{a}$.

(k) Distributive law of multiplication over addition :

$a(b + c) = ab + ac$, $\forall$ real numbers a, b and c.

Important

"Zero is a real number which has no multiplicative inverse".

KEY CONCEPT

1.5 TEST OF DIVISIBILITY :

Divisibility by	Divisibility Rule
2	The unit digit of the number must be even
3	The sum of digits of the number must be divisible by 3
4	The number formed by last two digits of the given number must be divisible by 4
5	The unit digit of the number must be 0 or 5.
6	The given number must be divisible by 2 and 3.
7	Subtract two times of the unit digit from the number formed by excluding the unit digit from the given number, then the result obtained must be 0 or divisible by 7.
8	The number formed by last three digits of given number must be divisible by 8
9	The sum of digits of the given number must be divisible by 9
11	The difference between the sums of the digits at even and odd places must be zero or multiple of 11
12	The number must be divisible by 3 & 4.
13	Add four times of the unit digit to the given number formed by excluding unit digit, then the result obtained must be divisible by 13.
17	Subtract five times of the unit digit from the number formed by excluding the unit digit from the given number then the result must be 0 or divisible by 17.
19	Add two times of the unit digit to the given number formed by excluding unit digit, then the result obtained must be divisible by 19.

1.6 RADICALS :

An expression written under a radical sign is called a radical expression. The **radicand** is the number under the radical.

A surd is the simplest type of irrational number, one whose radicand is a rational number.

e.g. $\sqrt{5}$, $3\sqrt{7}$ and $\frac{1}{\sqrt{3}}$ are surds whereas $3\sqrt{5-\sqrt{2}}$ and $\sqrt{\sqrt{3}}$ are not surds.

The order of a surd is indicated by its index.

The order of a radical is the denominator of its fractional exponent.

e.g., $\sqrt[n]{a}$ is the surd of nth order.

(i) Pure surd : A surd in which the whole of the rational number is under the radical sign. & makes the **radicand**, is called pure surd.

e.g. $\sqrt{8}$, $\sqrt[3]{15}$, $\sqrt[4]{11}$ etc.

(ii) Mixed surd : If some part of the quantity under the radical sign is taken out of it then it makes the surd mixed.

e.g. $3\sqrt[4]{2}$, $4\sqrt{2}$ etc.

(iii) Like surds (Similar surds) : The surds having the same irrational factor are called similar surds.

e.g. $\sqrt{3}, 5\sqrt{3}, \frac{2}{5}\sqrt{3}$ are like surds.

(iv) Unlike surds : The surds having different irrational factor are called dissimilar surds.

e.g. $\sqrt{2}, 2\sqrt{3}, 2\sqrt{5}$ are unlike surds.

KEY CONCEPT

Laws of Radicals :

If a, b are positive rational numbers and m, n, p are positive integers, then

(i) $a^0 = 1$

(ii) $(\sqrt[n]{a})^n = a$, $\sqrt[n]{a^n} = a = (\sqrt[n]{a})^n$

(iii) $(\sqrt[n]{a})(\sqrt[n]{b}) = \sqrt[n]{ab}$

(iv) $\frac{\sqrt[n]{a}}{\sqrt[n]{b}} = \sqrt[n]{\frac{a}{b}}$

(v) $\sqrt[m]{\sqrt[n]{a}} = \sqrt[mn]{a} = \sqrt[n]{\sqrt[m]{a}}$

(vi) $\sqrt[n]{a^p} = (a^p)^{1/n} = \sqrt[mn]{a^{pm}}$

(vi) $a^{-n} = \frac{1}{a^n}$

Illustration 9 : Convert :

(i) $\sqrt[4]{1875}$ into mixed surd. (ii) $3\sqrt[5]{7}$ into pure surd.

Sol. (i) We have $1875 = 5^4 \times 3$

$$\sqrt[4]{1875} = \sqrt[4]{5^4 \times 3} = 5\sqrt[4]{3}$$

(ii) $$3\sqrt[5]{7} = \sqrt[5]{3^5 \times 7} = \sqrt[5]{243 \times 7} = \sqrt[5]{1701}$$

Illustration 10 : Simplify : $\left(\frac{81}{16}\right)^{-3/4} \times \left[\left(\frac{25}{9}\right)^{-3/2} \div \left(\frac{5}{2}\right)^{-3}\right]$

Sol. We have,

$$\left(\frac{81}{16}\right)^{-3/4} \times \left[\left(\frac{25}{9}\right)^{-3/2} \div \left(\frac{5}{2}\right)^{-3}\right] = \left(\frac{3^4}{2^4}\right)^{-3/4} \times \left[\left(\frac{5^2}{3^2}\right)^{-3/2} \div \left(\frac{5}{2}\right)^{-3}\right]$$

$$= \left[\left(\frac{3}{2}\right)^4\right]^{-3/4} \times \left[\left(\frac{5}{3}\right)^2\right]^{-3/2} \div \left[\left(\frac{5}{2}\right)^{-3}\right] = \left(\frac{3}{2}\right)^{4\times-3/4} \times \left[\left(\frac{5}{3}\right)^{2\times-3/2} \div \left(\frac{5}{2}\right)^{-3}\right]$$

$$= \left(\frac{3}{2}\right)^{-3} \times \left[\left(\frac{5}{3}\right)^{-3} \div \left(\frac{5}{2}\right)^{-3}\right] = \left(\frac{2}{3}\right)^3 \times \left[\left(\frac{3}{5}\right)^3 \div \left(\frac{2}{5}\right)^3\right] = \frac{2^3}{3^3} \times \left[\frac{3^3}{5^3} \div \frac{2^3}{5^3}\right]$$

$$= \frac{2^3}{3^3} \times \left[\frac{3^3}{5^3} \times \frac{5^3}{2^3}\right] = 1. \textbf{ Ans.}$$

Illustration 11 : If x, y, z are positive real numbers show that :

$$\sqrt{x^{-1}y} \cdot \sqrt{y^{-1}z} \cdot \sqrt{z^{-1}x} = 1$$

Sol. We have,

$$\sqrt{x^{-1}y} \cdot \sqrt{y^{-1}z} \cdot \sqrt{z^{-1}x}$$

$$= \sqrt{\frac{y}{x}} \cdot \sqrt{\frac{z}{y}} \cdot \sqrt{\frac{x}{z}} = \left(\frac{y}{x}\right)^{1/2} \left(\frac{z}{y}\right)^{1/2} \left(\frac{x}{z}\right)^{1/2} = \frac{y^{1/2}}{x^{1/2}} \cdot \frac{z^{1/2}}{y^{1/2}} \cdot \frac{x^{1/2}}{z^{1/2}} = 1. \textbf{ Ans.}$$

1.7 RATIONALISATION OF DENOMINATOR :

Sometimes we come across expressions containing square root in their denominators. Addition, subtraction, multiplication and division of such expressions is convenient if their denominators are free from square roots. To make the denominators free from square roots, we multiply the numerator and denominator by an irrational number. Such a number is called rationlisation factor.

Illustrations

Illustration 12 : Rationalise the denominator of $\frac{1}{3+\sqrt{2}}$

Sol. We have,

$$\frac{1}{3+\sqrt{2}} = \frac{1}{3+\sqrt{2}} \times \frac{3-\sqrt{2}}{3-\sqrt{2}} = \frac{3-\sqrt{2}}{9-2} = \frac{3-\sqrt{2}}{7}$$

Illustration 13 : If both a and b are rational numbers, find the values of a and b.

$$\frac{\sqrt{5}+\sqrt{3}}{\sqrt{5}-\sqrt{3}} = a + b\sqrt{15}$$

Sol. Rationalising the denominator, we get

$$\frac{\sqrt{5}+\sqrt{3}}{\sqrt{5}-\sqrt{3}} = \frac{\sqrt{5}+\sqrt{3}}{\sqrt{5}-\sqrt{3}} \times \frac{\sqrt{5}+\sqrt{3}}{\sqrt{5}+\sqrt{3}} = \frac{(\sqrt{5}+\sqrt{3})^2}{(\sqrt{5})^2-(\sqrt{3})^2}$$

$$\Rightarrow \frac{\sqrt{5}+\sqrt{3}}{\sqrt{5}-\sqrt{3}} = \frac{(\sqrt{5})^2+(\sqrt{3})^2+2\sqrt{5}\times\sqrt{3}}{(\sqrt{5})^2-(\sqrt{3})^2}$$

$$\Rightarrow \frac{\sqrt{5}+\sqrt{3}}{\sqrt{5}-\sqrt{3}} = \frac{5+3+2\sqrt{5\times 3}}{5-3} = \frac{8+2\sqrt{15}}{5-3} = 4+\sqrt{15}$$

$$\therefore \frac{\sqrt{5}+\sqrt{3}}{\sqrt{5}-\sqrt{3}} = a+b\sqrt{15} \Rightarrow 4+\sqrt{15} = a+b\sqrt{15} \Rightarrow a = 4 \text{ and } b = 1.$$ **Ans.**

Illustration 14 : If $x = 3 - 2\sqrt{2}$, find $x^2 + \frac{1}{x^2}$.

Sol. We have, $x = 3 - 2\sqrt{2}$

$$\therefore \frac{1}{x} = \frac{1}{3-2\sqrt{2}} = \frac{1}{3-2\sqrt{2}} \times \frac{3+2\sqrt{2}}{3+2\sqrt{2}} = \frac{3+2\sqrt{2}}{3^2-(2\sqrt{2})^2} = \frac{3+2\sqrt{2}}{9-8} = 3+2\sqrt{2}.$$

Thus, $x^2+\frac{1}{x^2} = (3-2\sqrt{2})^2+(3+2\sqrt{2})^2$

$$\Rightarrow x^2+\frac{1}{x^2} = 3^2+(2\sqrt{2})^2 - 2\times 3\times 2\sqrt{2} + 3^2 + (2\sqrt{2})^2 + 2\times 3\times 2\sqrt{2}$$

$$\Rightarrow x^2+\frac{1}{x^2} = 9+8-12\sqrt{2}+9+8+12\sqrt{2} = 34.$$ **Ans.**

Illustration 15 : Show that : $\frac{1}{1+x^{b-a}+x^{c-a}} + \frac{1}{1+x^{a-b}+x^{c-b}} + \frac{1}{1+x^{b-c}+x^{a-c}} = 1$

Sol. We have,

$$= \frac{1}{1+x^{b-a}+x^{c-a}} + \frac{1}{1+x^{a-b}+x^{c-b}} + \frac{1}{1+x^{b-c}+x^{a-c}}$$

$$= \frac{x^a}{x^a+x^{b-a+a}+x^{c-a+a}} + \frac{x^b}{x^b+x^{a-b+b}+x^{c-b+b}} + \frac{x^c}{x^c+x^{b-c+c}+x^{a-c+c}}$$

[Multiplying N^r and D^r of three terms by x^a, x^b and x^c respectively]

$$= \frac{x^a}{x^a+x^b+x^c} + \frac{x^b}{x^b+x^a+x^c} + \frac{x^c}{x^c+x^b+x^a}$$

$$= \frac{x^a+x^b+x^c}{x^a+x^b+x^c} = 1$$

Illustration 16 : Simplify : $\frac{3\sqrt{2}}{\sqrt{6}-\sqrt{3}}-\frac{4\sqrt{3}}{\sqrt{6}-\sqrt{2}}+\frac{2\sqrt{3}}{\sqrt{6}+2}$

Sol. $\frac{3\sqrt{2}}{\sqrt{6}-\sqrt{3}}-\frac{4\sqrt{3}}{\sqrt{6}-\sqrt{2}}+\frac{2\sqrt{3}}{\sqrt{6}+2}=T_1-T_2+T_3$ (say)

$$T_1=\frac{3\sqrt{2}}{\sqrt{6}-\sqrt{3}}\times\frac{\sqrt{6}+\sqrt{3}}{\sqrt{6}+\sqrt{3}}=\frac{3\sqrt{2}(\sqrt{6}+\sqrt{3})}{6-3}$$

$$=\sqrt{2}(\sqrt{6}+\sqrt{3})$$

$$=2\sqrt{3}+\sqrt{6}$$

$$T_2=\frac{4\sqrt{3}}{\sqrt{6}-\sqrt{2}}\times\frac{\sqrt{6}+\sqrt{2}}{\sqrt{6}+\sqrt{2}}=\frac{4\sqrt{18}+4\sqrt{6}}{6-2}$$

$$=\frac{4(3\sqrt{2}+\sqrt{6})}{4}=3\sqrt{2}+\sqrt{6}$$

$$T_3=\frac{2\sqrt{3}}{\sqrt{6}+2}\times\frac{\sqrt{6}-2}{\sqrt{6}-2}=\frac{2\sqrt{3}\left(\sqrt{6}-2\right)}{6-4}=3\sqrt{2}-2\sqrt{3}$$

$\therefore$ Given expression $=T_1-T_2+T_3$

$$=2\sqrt{3}+\sqrt{6}-3\sqrt{2}-\sqrt{6}+3\sqrt{2}-2\sqrt{3}=0$$

Illustration 17 : If $x=\frac{\sqrt{a+2b}+\sqrt{a-2b}}{\sqrt{a+2b}-\sqrt{a-2b}}$, then show that $bx^2-ax+b=0$

Sol. $x=\frac{\sqrt{a+2b}+\sqrt{a-2b}}{\sqrt{a+2b}-\sqrt{a-2b}}\times\frac{\sqrt{a+2b}+\sqrt{a-2b}}{\sqrt{a+2b}+\sqrt{a-2b}}$

$$=\frac{\left(\sqrt{a+2b}+\sqrt{a-2b}\right)^2}{(a+2b)-(a-2b)}=\frac{a+2b+a-2b+2\sqrt{(a+2b)(a-2b)}}{4b}$$

$$x=\frac{2(a+\sqrt{(a^2-4b^2)})}{2\times 2b}$$

$2bx=a+\sqrt{(a^2-4b^2)}\quad\Rightarrow\quad 2bx-a=\sqrt{(a^2-4b^2)}$

On squaring both sides, we get :

$\Rightarrow 4b^2x^2+a^2-4abx=a^2-4b^2$

or $4b^2x^2-4abx+4b^2=0$

Dividing by 4b , we get, $bx^2-ax+b=0$

Hence the result.

Illustration 18 : Find the square root of $2+\sqrt{3}$.

Sol. Let $\sqrt{2+\sqrt{3}} = \sqrt{x}+\sqrt{y}$

$2+\sqrt{3} = x+y+2\sqrt{xy}$ (By squaring both sides.)

Now comparing the parts of both sides,

$x+y=2$ .... (1)

$2\sqrt{xy} = \sqrt{3}$ .... (2)

or $4xy = 3$ .... (3) (By squaring both sides of equation 2.)

we know that

$(x-y)^2 = (x+y)^2 - 4xy$

$(x-y)^2 = 4-3$

$(x-y)^2 = 1$

$x-y = 1$ .... (4)

On solving equations (1) and (4), we get

$$x = \frac{3}{2},\ y = \frac{1}{2}$$

Since $\sqrt{2+\sqrt{3}} = \sqrt{x}+\sqrt{y}$

$$= \pm\left[\sqrt{\frac{3}{2}}+\sqrt{\frac{1}{2}}\right]$$

$$= \pm\left[\frac{1}{\sqrt{2}}\left(\sqrt{3}+1\right)\right]$$

$$\sqrt{2+\sqrt{3}} = \pm\frac{1}{\sqrt{2}}\left(1+\sqrt{3}\right)$$

1.8 TO FIND THE NUMBER OF DIVISORS OF A COMPOSITE NUMBER :

IMPORTANT FORMULAE

Let N denotes a natural number such that

$N = a^p b^q c^r$ ...., where a, b, c, ... are different prime numbers and p, q, r, ... are positive integers, then

(i) n = The number of divisors of $N = (p+1)(q+1)(r+1)$ ....

Note : This includes as divisors, both unity and the number itself.

(ii) The sum of divisors of $N = \left(\frac{a^{p+1}-1}{a-1}\right)\left(\frac{b^{q+1}-1}{b-1}\right)\left(\frac{c^{r+1}-1}{c-1}\right)$ ......

(iii) The product of divisors of $N = (N)^{\frac{n}{2}}$, where n is the total number of divisors of N.

Illustrations

Illustration 19 : If a number N = 30 then, find
(i) The number of divisors of N
(ii) The sum of divisors of N
(iii) The product of divisors of N

Sol. Prime factorisation of $30 = 2^1 \times 3^1 \times 5^1$

(i) Let n = the number of divisors of 30 = $(1 + 1)(1 + 1)(1 + 1) = 2 \times 2 \times 2 = 8$.
and these divisors are : 1, 2, 3, 5, 6, 10, 15, 30

(ii) The sum of divisors of 30 $= \left(\frac{2^{1+1}-1}{2-1}\right)\left(\frac{3^{1+1}-1}{3-1}\right)\left(\frac{5^{1+1}-1}{5-1}\right)$

$$= \left(\frac{2^2-1}{1}\right)\left(\frac{3^2-1}{2}\right)\left(\frac{5^2-1}{4}\right)$$

$$= 3 \times \frac{8}{2} \times \frac{24}{4}$$

$$= 9 \times 8 = 72.$$

(iii) Product of divisors of 30 $= (N)^{n/2} = (30)^{8/2} = (30)^4 = 810000$.

1.9 ABSOLUTE VALUE OR MODULUS OF A RATIONAL NUMBER :

1. The absolute value of a rational number is the number without any regard to its sign.
Thus, for any rational number x,

The absolute value of $x = |x| = \begin{cases} x, \text{if } x > 0 \\ 0, \text{if } x = 0 \\ -x, \text{if } x < 0 \end{cases}$

2. $|x + y| \le |x| + |y|$, where x and y are rational numbers.
3. $|x \times y| = |x| \times |y|$, where x and y are rational numbers.
4. $|x - y| \ge |x| - |y|$, where x and y are rational numbers.

REMEMBER

5. Modulus of a real number given by $|x|$.

(i)	If	$\lvert x\rvert = a$	$\Rightarrow$	$x = \pm a$
(ii)	If	$\lvert x\rvert < a$	$\Rightarrow$	$-a < x < a$
(iii)	If	$\lvert x\rvert > a$	$\Rightarrow$	$x > a$ or $x < -a$
(iv)	If	$\lvert x - a\rvert < l$	$\Rightarrow$	$a - l < x < a + l$
(v)	If	$\lvert x - a\rvert > l$	$\Rightarrow$	$x > a + l$ or $x < a - l$

Illustration 20 : Find the value of x, when $x - 3|x| = -4$ is simplified

Sol.

(i) If $x \geq 0$, then $|x| = x$ and given equation becomes $x - 3x = -4$ or $-2x = -4$.

$x = +2$.

(ii) If $x < 0$, then $|x| = -x$ and given equation becomes,

$$x - 3(-x) = -4$$
$$x + 3x = -4$$
$$4x = -4$$
$$x = -1.$$

Therefore, $x = 2$ or -1. **Ans.**

1.10 HCF AND LCM OF FRACTIONS :

Note : Make sure that the fractions are in the most reducible form.

(1) HCF of fractions $= \dfrac{\text{HCF of their numerators}}{\text{LCM of their denominators}}$.

Illustration 21 : Find HCF of $\frac{9}{2}, \frac{3}{4}$ and $\frac{6}{7}$.

Sol. $\text{HCF}\left(\frac{9}{2}, \frac{3}{4}, \frac{6}{7}\right) = \frac{\text{HCF }(9, 3, 6)}{\text{LCM }(2, 4, 7)} = \frac{3}{28}$.

---

(2) LCM of fractions $= \dfrac{\text{LCM of their numerators}}{\text{HCF of their denominators}}$.

Illustration 22 : Find LCM of $\frac{9}{2}, \frac{3}{4}$ and $\frac{6}{7}$.

Sol. $\text{LCM}\left(\frac{9}{2}, \frac{3}{4}, \frac{6}{7}\right) = \frac{\text{LCM }(9, 3, 6)}{\text{HCF }(2, 4, 7)} = \frac{18}{1} = 18$.

1.11 TO FIND UNIT DIGIT IN EXPONENTIAL EXPRESSION :

Cyclicity : In number system, every number repeats its unit digit after some definite number of powers.

For example

1 repeat its unit digit after every consecutive power. So the cyclicity of 1 is 1.

2 repeat its unit digit after every four powers. So the cylicity of of 2 is 4.

REMEMBER

Cyclicity chart :

Unit digit in the number x	Possible unit digit in the number x^n (where n is positive integer)	Cyclicity of unit digit in the number x
0	0	1
1	1	1
2	2, 4, 8, 6	4
3	3, 9, 7, 1	4
4	4, 6	2
5	5	1
6	6	1
7	7, 9, 3, 1	4
8	8, 4, 2, 6	4
9	9, 1	2

Illustrations

Illustration 23 : Find the unit digit in 3^{47}.

Sol. Cyclicity of 3 is 4,

Remainder of $\frac{47}{4}$ is 3.

In cyclicity chart, the possible unit digit in 3^n at 3rd place is 7, so the unit digit in 3^{47} is 7.

1.12 DIVISIBILITY :

A non zero integer 'a' is said to divide an integer 'b' if there exists an integer 'c' such that b = ac

The integer 'b' is called the dividend, integer 'a' is known as the divisor and integer 'c' is known as the quotient. For example, 3 divides 36 because there is an integer 12 such that 36 = 3 × 12. However, 3 does not divide 35 because there do not exist an integer 'c' such that 35 = 3 × c. In other words, 35 = 3 × c is not true for any integer 'c'.

Note: If a non zero integer 'a' divides an integer 'b', then we write a | b. This is read as "a divides b". When a | b, we say that 'b is divisible by a' or 'a is a factor of b' or 'b is a multiple of a' or 'a is divisor of b'.

REMEMBER

Some Properties of Divisibility

(i) ± 1 divides every non-zero integer.

(ii) 0 does not divide any integer.

(iii) If a is a non zero integer and b is any integer, then $a \mid b \Rightarrow a \mid -b, -a \mid b$ and $-a \mid -b$.

(iv) If a and b are non-zero integers, then

$a \mid b$ and $b \mid a \quad \Rightarrow a = \pm b$

(v) If a is a non-zero integer and b,c are any two integers, then

$$a \mid b \text{ and } a \mid c \Rightarrow \begin{cases} a \mid b \pm c \\ a \mid bc \\ a \mid bx \text{ for any integer } x \end{cases}$$

(vi) If a and c are non zero integers and b,d are any two integers, then

(a) $a \mid b$ and $c \mid d \Rightarrow ac \mid bd$

(b) $ac \mid bc \Rightarrow a \mid b$

IMPORTANT

1.13 EUCLID'S DIVISION LEMMA

(a) **Euclid's division Lemma:** Let *a* and *b* be any two positive integers. Then, there exist unique *q* and *r* such that :

$$a = bq + r, 0 \leq r < b$$

If $b \mid a$, then $r = 0$, otherwise, r satisfies the strict inequality.

$$0 < r < b$$

Highest Common Factor (HCF) : HCF of two or more numbers is the largest number that divides all the given numbers completely.

It is also called the Greatest Common Divisor (GCD).

Lowest or least Common Multiple (LCM) : The LCM of two or more numbers is the smallest number which is multiple of each of the numbers or in other words the LCM of two or more numbers is the smallest number which is divisible by all the given numbers.

Illustrations

Illustration 24 : Show that any positive odd integer is of the form 6q + 1 or, 6q + 3 or, 6q + 5, where q is some integer.

Sol. Let 'a' be any positive integer and b = 6. Then, by Euclid's division lemma there exists integers 'a' and 'r' such that

$$a = 6q + r, \text{ where } 0 \leq r < 6.$$

$\Rightarrow$ a = 6q or, a = 6q + 1 or, a = 6q + 2 or, a = 6a + 3 or, a = 6q + 4 or, a = 6q + 5.

$[\therefore 0 \leq r < 6 \Rightarrow r = 0, 1,2,3,4,5]$

$\Rightarrow$ a = 6q + 1 or, a = 6q + 3 or, a = 6q + 5.

$[\because$ a is an odd integer, $\therefore$ 6q, $a \neq 6q + 2, a \neq 6q + 4]$

Hence, any odd integer is of the form 6q + 1 or, 6q + 3 or, 6q + 5.

Illustration 25 : Use Euclid's division algorithm to find the HFC of 4052 and 12576.

Sol. Given integers are 4052 and 12576 such that 12576 > 4052. Applying Euclid's division lemma to 12576 and 4052.

$\Rightarrow \quad 12576 = 4052 \times 3 + 420$

$\Rightarrow \quad 4052 = 420 \times 9 + 272$

$\Rightarrow \quad 420 = 272 \times 1 + 148$

$\Rightarrow \quad 272 = 148 \times 1 + 124$

$\Rightarrow \quad 148 = 124 \times 1 + 24$

$\Rightarrow \quad 124 = 24 \times 5 + 4$

$\Rightarrow \quad 24 = 4 \times 6 + 0$

We observe that the remainder at this stage is zero. Therefore, the divisor at this stage i.e. 4(or the remainder at the earlier stage) is the HCF of 4052 and 12576.

REMEMBER

Properties of HCF and LCM of given numbers

(i) The HCF of given numbers is *not greater than* any of two numbers.

(ii) The LCM of given numbers is *not less than* any of given numbers.

(iii) The HCF of given numbers is always factor of their LCM

(iv) The HCF of two coprime numbers is 1.

(v) The LCM of two or more coprime numbers is equal to their product.

IMPORTANT FORMULAE

(i) If a and b are two positive integers then

$$a \times b = \text{HCF}(a, b) \times \text{LCM}(a, b)$$

(ii) If a, b, c are positive integers

$$\text{LCM}(a, b, c) = \frac{a.b.c.\text{HCF}(a,b,c)}{\text{HCF}(a,b).\text{HCF}(b,c).\text{HCF}(c,a)}$$

$$\text{HCF}(a, b, c) = \frac{a.b.c.\text{LCM}(a,b,c)}{\text{LCM}(a,b).\text{LCM}(b,c).\text{LCM}(c,a)}$$

Illustrations

Illustration 26 : If the HCF of 210 and 55 is expressible in the form $210 \times 5 + 55y$, find y.

Sol. Applying Euclid's division lemma on 210 and 55, we get

$\Rightarrow \quad 210 = 55 \times 3 + 45$

$\Rightarrow \quad 55 = 45 \times 1 + 10$

$\Rightarrow \quad 45 = 4 \times 10 + 5$

$\Rightarrow \quad 10 = 5 \times 2 + 0$

We observe that the remainder at this stage is zero. So, the last divisor i.e. 5 is the HCF of 210 and 55.

$\therefore \quad 5 = 210 \times 5 + 55y$

$\Rightarrow \quad 55y = 5 - 210 \times 5 = 5 - 1050$

$\Rightarrow \quad 55y = -1045$

$\Rightarrow \quad y = \frac{1045}{55} = -19.$

Illustration 27 : Find the largest number which divides 245 and 1029 leaving remainder 5 in each case.

Sol. Given that the required number which divides 245 and 1029, the remainder is 5 in each case. This means $245 - 5 = 240$ and $1029 - 5 = 1024$ are completely divisible by the required number. Now is common factor of 240 and 1024,

Let us now find the HCF of 240 and 1024 by Euclid's algorithm.

3	240 192	1024 960	4
3	48 48	64 48	1
	0 (Remainder)	(16) (HCF)	

Clearly, HCF of 240 and 1024 is the last divisor i.e., 16.

Hence, required number = 16.

- **Prime factorization method to find HCF**

  Step–1 : Find prime factorisation of each of the given number.

  Step–2 : Identify common prime factors.

  Step–3 : Find the product of all the common prime factors, using each common prime factor the least number of times it appears in the prime factorisation of any of the given numbers. The product so obtained is the required HCF.

- **Prime factorization method to find LCM**

  Step–1 : Write the prime factorisation of each of the given numbers.

  Step–2 : Find the product of all different prime factors of the numbers using each common prime factor the highest number of times it appears in the prime factorisation of any of the numbers. The product so obtained is the required LCM of the given number.

KEY CONCEPT

Euclid's Division Alogrithm :

Algorithm: An algorithm is a series of well defined steps which provide a procedure of calculation repeated successively on the results of earlier steps till the desired result is obtained.
Euclid's division algorithm is an algorithm to compute the highest common factor (HCF) of two given positive integers.

IMPORTANT

Some Important Results

(i) If b is a factor of a, then HCF of (a,b) = b which is simply written as (a,b) = b.
(ii) If a = q.b+r, r < b then HCF of (a,b) = HCF of (b, r) or (a,b) = (b,r)
(iii) If (a,b) = 1 and bc is divisible by a, then c is divisible by a. This is known as Gauss's Theorem.
(iv) If a and b are primes and a | bc ⇒ a | c
(v) The HCF(d) of two positive integers a and b can be expresed as a linear combination of a and b i.e.d = xa + yb for some integers x and y. Also this representation is not unique.

Illustrations

Illustration 28 : Determine the prime factorization of the number 13915.

Sol. Using the prime factorization tree, we have

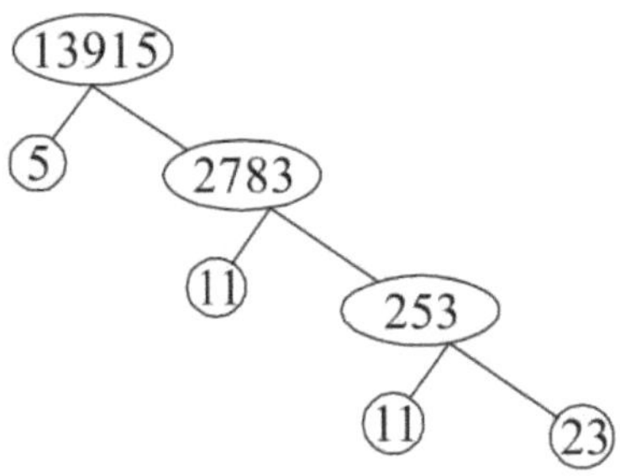

∴ $13915 = 5 \times 11 \times 11 \times 23 = 5 \times 11^1 \times 23$. Ans.

Illustration 29 : Prove that there is no natural number for which 4^n ends with the digit zero.

Sol. We know that any positive integer ending with the digit zero is divisible by 5 and so its prime factorization must contain the prime 5.

We have,

$4^n = (2^2)^n = 2^{2n}$

⇒ The only prime in the factorization of 4^n is 2.

⇒ There is no other primes in the factorization of $4^n = 2^{2n}$

⇒ 5 does not occur in the prime factorization of 4^n for any.

⇒ 4^n does not end with the digit zero for any natural number.

1.14 THE FUNDAMENTAL THEOREM OF ARITHMETIC :

REMEMBER

Theorem (Fundamental Theorem of Arithmetic) :

Every composite number can be expressed (factorised) as a product of primes and this factorisation is unique, apart from the order in which the prime factors occurs.

The prime factorisation of a natural number is unique except the order of its factors.

Let x be a composite number we factorise it as $x = p_1 \times p_2 \times p_3....p_n$, where $p_1, p_2...p_n$ are primes and written in ascending order i.e. $p_1 \leq p_2 \leq p_3...p_n$. If we combine we will get powers of primes.

Theorem :

Let p be a prime number and a be positive integer. If p divides a^2 then p also divides a

1.15 DETERMINING THE NATURE OF THE DECIMAL EXPANSION OF RATIONAL NUMBERS :

We have studied that the decimal expansion of a rational number is either terminating or non terminating repeating (or recurring) without knowing when it is terminating and when it is non-terminating repeating. Here in this section we will explore exactly when the decimal expansion of a rational number is terminating and when it is non terminating repeating.

REMEMBER

Theorem :

Let x be a rational number whose decimal expansion terminates. Then x can be expressed in the form p/q where p and q are coprimes and the prime factorisation of q is of the form $2^m \times 5^n$ where m and n are non negative integers.

Theorem :

Let $x = p/q$ be a rational number such that the prime factorization of q is the form of $2^m \times 5^n$ where m and n are non-negative integers. Then x has a decimal expansion which terminates.

Theorem :

Let $x = p/q$ be a rational number such that prime factorization of q ***is not*** of the form $2^m \times 5^n$ where m and n are non negative integers. Then x has a decimal expansion which is non-terminating repeating.

Illustration 30 : Find the HCF and LCM of 144, 180 and 192 by prime factorization method.

Sol. Using the factor tree for the prime factorization of 144, 180 and 192, we have

$144 = 2^4 \times 3^2$, $180 = 2^2 \times 3^2 \times 5$ and $192 = 2^6 \times 3$

Common prime factors and their smallest exponents in 144, 180 and 192 as follows :

Common prime factors	**Least exponents**
2	2
3	1

$\therefore$ HCF $= 2^2 \times 3^1 = 12$

Prime factors of 144, 180, 192 and their greatest exponents as follows :

Prime factors of 144, 180 and 192	**Greatest exponents**
2	6
3	2
5	1

$\therefore$ LCM $= 2^6 \times 3^2 \times 5^1 = 64 \times 9 \times 5 = 2880$.

Illustration 31 : In a seminar, the number of participants in Hindi, English and Mathematics are 60, 84 and 108 respectively. Find the minimum number of rooms required if in each rooms required if in each room the same number of participlants are to be seated and all of them being in the same subject.

Sol. The number of participants in each room must be the HCF of 60, 84 and 108

Prime factorizations of 60, 84 and 108

$60 = 2^2 \times 3 \times 5$, $84 = 2^2 \times 3 \times 7$ and $108 = 2^2 \times 3^3$

$\therefore$ HCF of 60, 80 and 108 is $2^2 \times 3 = 12$

Therefore, in each room 12 participants can be seated.

$\therefore$ Number of rooms required $= \dfrac{\text{Total number of participants}}{12} = \dfrac{60+84+108}{12} = \dfrac{252}{12} = 21.$

Illustration 32 : Without actually performing the long division, state whether the following rational numbers will have terminating decimal expansion or a non-terminating repeating decimal expansion. Also, find the number of places of decimals after which the decimal expansion terminates.

(i) $\dfrac{13}{3125}$ (ii) $\dfrac{23}{2^3 5^2}$

Sol.

(i) We have, $\dfrac{13}{3125} = \dfrac{13}{2^0 \times 5^5}$

This shows that the prime factorization of the denominator of $\dfrac{13}{3125}$ is of the form $2^m \times 5^n$.

Hence, it has terminating decimal expansion which terminates after 5 places of decimals.

(ii) Prime factorization of the denominator of $\dfrac{23}{2^3 \times 5^2}$ is of the form $2^m \times 5^n$. So, it has terminating decimal expansion which terminates after 3 places of decimals.

SOLVED EXAMPLES

Example 1

Find two irrational number between 0.12 and 0.13

Solution

0.1201001000100001............., 0.12101001000100001............

Example 2

If $\frac{9^n \times 3^2 \times 3^n - (27)^n}{(3^3)^5 \times 2^3} = \frac{1}{27}$. Find the value of 'n'.

Solution

$\frac{3^{2n+2+n} - 3^{3n}}{3^{15} \times 2^3} = \frac{1}{27} \Rightarrow \frac{3^{3n}(9-1)}{3^{15} \times 2^3} = \frac{1}{27} \Rightarrow 3^{3n-15} = 3^{-3}$

$\Rightarrow 3n - 15 = -3 \Rightarrow 3n = 12 \Rightarrow n = 4$

Example 3

A-5 digit number abcde is such that the 6-digit number abcde1 is the product of the 6-digit number 1abcde and 3. The sum of the digits of the number abcde is -

Solution

A.T.Q.

abcde1 = 1abcde × 3

i.e.

$a \times 10^5 + b \times 10^4 + c \times 10^3 + d \times 10^2 + e \times 10 + 1 = 3 \times [1 \times 10^5 + a \times 10^4 + b \times 10^3 + c \times 10^2 + d \times 10 + e]$

$a \times 10^4 (10-3) + b \times 10^3(10-3) + c \times 10^2(10-3) + d \times 10(10-3) + e(10-3) + 1 - 3 \times 10^5 = 0$

$a \times 10^4 + b \times 10^3 + c \times 10^2 + d \times 10^1 + e = \frac{3 \times 10^5 - 1}{7}$

abcde = 42857

$\therefore \quad a + b + c + d + e = 4 + 2 + 8 + 5 + 7 = 26$

Example 4

Seven Oranges weigh the same as four Apples and five Apples weigh the same as six Guava. Which of the following gives the description of the fruits in increasing order of weights ?

Solution

7Or = 4A = k

5A = 6G

$Or = \frac{k}{7}$

$A = \frac{k}{4}$

$G = \frac{5}{6}A = \frac{5}{6} \times \frac{k}{4} = \frac{5k}{24}$

LCM of 7, 4, 24 is 168

Or : A : G

$\frac{k}{7} : \frac{k}{4} : \frac{5k}{24}$

= 24k : 42k : 35k

= 24 : 42 : 35

$\therefore O < G < A$

Example 5

What least number must be subtracted from 16160 to get a perfect square ? Also find the square root of this perfect square.

Solution

Let us try to find the square root of 16160.

$$\begin{array}{r|l} & \quad 127 \\ \hline 1 & \overline{1}\ \overline{61}\ \overline{60} \\ & 1 \\ \hline 22 & \ \ 61 \\ & \ \ 44 \\ \hline 247 & \ \ 1760 \\ & \ \ 1729 \\ \hline & \quad 31 \end{array}$$

This shows that $(127)^2$ is less than 16160 by 31. So in order to get a perfect square, 31 must be subtracted from the given number.

$\therefore$ Required perfect square number = (16160 – 31) = 16129

Also, $\sqrt{16129} = 127$

Example 6

Find the square root of $3 + \sqrt{2}$.

Solution

Let $\sqrt{3+\sqrt{2}} = \sqrt{p} + \sqrt{q}$

$3 + \sqrt{2} = p + q + 2\sqrt{pq}$ [By squaring both sides]

by equating the parts

$p + q = 3$ ...(i)

$\Rightarrow \quad 2\sqrt{pq} = \sqrt{2}$ ...(ii)

$\Rightarrow \quad 4pq = 2$ ...(iii) [By squaring both sides of (ii)]

$\Rightarrow \quad (p-q)^2 = (p+q)^2 - 4pq$

$\therefore \quad (p-q)^2 = 9 - 2$

$\Rightarrow \quad (p-q)^2 = 7$

$\Rightarrow \quad p - q = \sqrt{7}$ ...(iv)

$\because \quad p + q = 3$ [By eq^n (i)]

$\Rightarrow \quad p = \frac{1}{2}(3+\sqrt{7})$ [On adding (i) & (iv)]

$\Rightarrow \quad q = \frac{1}{2}(3-\sqrt{7})$ [On subtracting (i) & (iv)]

$\therefore \sqrt{3+\sqrt{2}} = \pm\frac{1}{\sqrt{2}}\left(\sqrt{3+\sqrt{7}} + \sqrt{3-\sqrt{7}}\right)$

Example 7

Find the least number which must be subtracted from 2509 to make it a perfect square.

Solution

Let us find the square root of 2509.

	50
5	25 09
	− 25
100	00 09
	− 00 00
100	09

So 2509 is 9 more than the square of 50 so 09 must be substracted to make it. a perfect square.

Example 8

If the number 357 * 25 * is divisible by both 3 and 5, then the missing digit in the unit's place and the thousandth place respectively are :

Solution

Let the required number be 357y25x.

Then, for divisibility by 5, we must have x = 0 or x = 5.

Case I When x = 0.

Then, sum of digits = (22 + y). For divisibility by 3, (22 + y) must be divisible by 3.

$\therefore$ y = 2 or 5 or 8.

$\therefore$ Number are (0, 2) or (0, 5) or (0, 8)

Case II When x = 5.

Then, sum of digits = (27 + y). For divisibility by 3, we must have y = 0 or 3 or 6 or 9.

$\therefore$ Numbers are (5, 0) or (5, 3) or (5, 6) or (5, 9).

Example 9

Which of the following numbers $\sqrt{\pi^2}, \sqrt[3]{0.8}, \sqrt[4]{0.00016}, \sqrt[3]{-1}, \sqrt{0.001}$ is/are rational ?

Solution

(A) $\sqrt{\pi^2} = \pi$ (irrational no.)

(B) $\sqrt[3]{0.8}$

(C) $\sqrt[4]{0.00016}$

(D) $\sqrt[3]{-1} = -1$ (rational no.)

(E) $\sqrt{0.001} = \sqrt{1/1000} = 0.1/\sqrt{10}$ (irrational no.)

Example 10

If $\frac{5+\sqrt{3}}{7-4\sqrt{3}} = 47a + \sqrt{3}\,b$ then find the value of 'a' and 'b'.

Solution

Taking L.H.S

$$= \frac{5+\sqrt{3}}{7-4\sqrt{3}} \times \frac{7+4\sqrt{3}}{7+4\sqrt{3}} = \frac{(5+\sqrt{3})(7+4\sqrt{3})}{49-48} = 35 + 12 + 20\sqrt{3} + 7\sqrt{3}$$

$$= 47 + 27\sqrt{3} = 47a + 27\sqrt{3} \quad \text{[Given]}$$

Hence a = 1 and b = 27

Example 11

Find the value of :

$$\frac{1}{3-\sqrt{8}}-\frac{1}{\sqrt{8}-\sqrt{7}}+\frac{1}{\sqrt{7}-\sqrt{6}}-\frac{1}{\sqrt{6}-\sqrt{5}}+\frac{1}{\sqrt{5}-2}.$$

Solution

$$\left(\frac{1}{3-\sqrt{8}}\times\frac{3+\sqrt{8}}{3+\sqrt{8}}\right)-\left(\frac{1}{\sqrt{8}-\sqrt{7}}\times\frac{\sqrt{8}+\sqrt{7}}{\sqrt{8}+\sqrt{7}}\right)+\left(\frac{1}{\sqrt{7}-\sqrt{6}}\times\frac{\sqrt{7}+\sqrt{6}}{\sqrt{7}+\sqrt{6}}\right)-\left(\frac{1}{\sqrt{6}-\sqrt{5}}\times\frac{\sqrt{6}+\sqrt{5}}{\sqrt{6}+\sqrt{5}}\right)+\left(\frac{1}{\sqrt{5}-2}\times\frac{\sqrt{5}+2}{\sqrt{5}+2}\right)$$

$$=\left(\frac{3+\sqrt{8}}{9-8}\right)-\left(\frac{\sqrt{8}+\sqrt{7}}{8-7}\right)+\left(\frac{\sqrt{7}+\sqrt{6}}{7-6}\right)-\left(\frac{\sqrt{6}+\sqrt{5}}{6-5}\right)-\left(\frac{\sqrt{5}+2}{5-4}\right)$$

$$=3+\sqrt{8}-\sqrt{8}-\sqrt{7}+\sqrt{7}+\sqrt{6}-\sqrt{6}-\sqrt{5}+\sqrt{5}+2$$

$$=5.$$

Example 12

Three pieces of cakes of weights $4\frac{1}{2}$ Ibs, $6\frac{3}{4}$ Ibs and $7\frac{1}{5}$ Ibs respectively are to be divided into parts of equal weights. Further, each must be as heavy as possible. If one such part is served to each guest, then what is the maximum number of guests that could be entertained ?

Solution

$$\text{HCF}\left(\frac{9}{2},\frac{27}{4},\frac{36}{5}\right)=\frac{\text{HCF}(9,27,36)}{\text{LCM}(2,4,5)}=\frac{9}{20}\text{ Ibs} \quad = \text{weight of each piece.}$$

$$\text{Total weight}=\frac{9}{2}+\frac{27}{4}+\frac{36}{5}=18.45$$

$$\text{Maximum no. of guests}=\frac{18.45\times 20}{9}=41.$$

CONCEPT APPLICATION LEVEL - I [NCERT Questions]

Q.1 Use Euclid's division algorithm to find the HCF of 196 and 38220.

Sol. $38220 = 196 \times 195 + 0$

Therefore, HCF (196, 38220) = 196. **Ans.**

Q.2 Find the HCF and LCM of 6, 72 and 120, using the prime factorization method.

Sol.

$$\begin{array}{c|c} 2 & 6 \\ \hline 3 & 3 \\ \hline & 1 \end{array} \qquad \begin{array}{c|c} 2 & 72 \\ \hline 3 & 36 \\ \hline 2 & 18 \\ \hline 3 & 9 \\ \hline 3 & 3 \\ \hline & 1 \end{array} \qquad \begin{array}{c|c} 2 & 120 \\ \hline 2 & 60 \\ \hline 2 & 30 \\ \hline 3 & 15 \\ \hline 5 & 5 \\ \hline & 1 \end{array}$$

$6 = 2 \times 3$

$72 = 2 \times 2 \times 2 \times 3 \times 3$

$120 = 2 \times 2 \times 2 \times 3 \times 5$

HCF (6, 72, 120) $= 2 \times 3 = 6$.

LCM (6, 72, 120) $= 2 \times 2 \times 2 \times 3 \times 3 \times 5 = 360$. **Ans.**

Q.3 Express each number as a product of its prime factors :
(i) 3825 (ii) 5005

Sol. Prime factorization of 3825 & 5005 are :

(i) $$\begin{array}{c|c} 3 & 3825 \\ \hline 3 & 1275 \\ \hline 5 & 425 \\ \hline 5 & 85 \\ \hline 17 & 17 \\ \hline & 1 \end{array}$$

$3825 = 3 \times 3 \times 5 \times 5 \times 17$ **Ans.**

(ii) $$\begin{array}{c|c} 5 & 5005 \\ \hline 7 & 1001 \\ \hline 11 & 143 \\ \hline 13 & 13 \\ \hline & 1 \end{array}$$

$5005 = 5 \times 7 \times 11 \times 13$. **Ans.**

Q.4 Find the LCM and HCF of the following integers by applying the prime factorization method 17, 23 and 29

Sol. LCM $= 17 \times 23 \times 29 = 11339$

HCF = 1. **Ans.**

Q.5 Given that HCF (306, 657) = 9, find LCM (306, 657).

Sol. HCF = (306, 657) × LCM (306, 657) = 306×657

or $9 \times$ LCM (306, 657) $= 306 \times 657$

LCM (306, 657) $= \dfrac{306 \times 657}{9} = 22338$. **Ans.**

Q.6 Check whether 6^n can end with the digit 0 for any natural number n.

Sol. Let for any natural number n. Then number 6^n ends with 0, then 6^n will be divisible by 5.

But $6^n = (2 \times 3)^n$

The prime factors of 6 are 2 and 3.

In prime factorisation of 6^n, there is no factor 5. Therefore 6^n is not divisible by 5 and there does not exist any natural number n for which 6^n ends with zero. **Ans.**

Q.7 Explain why $7 \times 11 \times 13 + 13$ and $7 \times 6 \times 5 \times 4 \times 3 \times 2 \times 1 + 5$ are composite numbers.

Sol.

$$7 \times 11 \times 13 + 13 = 13(7 \times 11 \times 1 + 1)$$
$$= 13 \times (77 + 1)$$
$$= 13 \times 78$$
= It is a composite number.

$$7\ 6 \times 5 \times 4 \times 3 \times 2 \times 1 + 5 = 5\,(7 \times 6 \times 4 \times 3 \times 2 \times 1 + 1)$$
$$= 5 \times (1008 + 1)$$
$= 5 \times 1009 =$ It is a composite number. **Ans.**

Q.8 Prove that $3+2\sqrt{5}$ is irrational.

Sol. Let us assume, to the contrary, that $3+2\sqrt{5}$ is a rational number.

Now, $3+2\sqrt{5} = \frac{a}{b}$, (where a and b are integers, $b \neq 0$ and a and b are coprime.)

$\Rightarrow \quad 2\sqrt{5} = \frac{a}{b} - 3$

$\sqrt{5} = \frac{a}{2b} - \frac{3}{2}$

$\because$ a and b are integers

$\therefore \quad \frac{a}{2b} - \frac{3}{2}$ is a rational number.

$\Rightarrow \quad \sqrt{5}$ is rational number.

But $\sqrt{5}$ is an irrational number. This shows that our assumption is incorrect. Therefore, $3+2\sqrt{5}$ is irrational number. **Ans.**

Q.9 Without actually performing the long division, state whether the following rational numbers will have a terminating decimal expansion or a non-terminating repeating decimal expansion:

(i) $\frac{13}{3125}$ **(ii)** $\frac{23}{2^3\,5^2}$ **(iii)** $\frac{129}{2^2\,5^7 7^5}$ **(iv)** $\frac{77}{210}$

Sol. (i) $\frac{13}{3125}$

we have, denominator $= 3125 = 5 \times 5 \times 5 \times 5 \times 5 = 5^5 = 2^0 \times 5^5 = 2^m \times 5^n.$

Therefore, $\frac{13}{3125}$ must have a terminating decimal expansion.

(ii) $\frac{23}{2^3\,5^2}$ = denometor $= 2^3\ 5^2 = 2^m \times 5^n$

Therefore, $\frac{23}{2^3 5^2}$ must have a terminating.

(iii) $\frac{129}{2^2\,5^7 7^5}$ denominator $= 2^2\,5^7\,7^5 \neq 2^m \times 5^n$. (Non-terminating).

(iv) $\frac{77}{210} = \frac{11}{30}$ denominator $= 30 = 2 \times 3 \times 5 \times 7 \neq 2^m \times 5^n$ (Non-terminating). **Ans.**

CONCEPT APPLICATION LEVEL - II [Previous Year Questions]

Multiple Choice Questions with one correct answer :

Q.1 The product of the additive inverse and multiplication inverse of 6 is :

(A) –6 (B) 1 (C) –1 (D) $\frac{1}{6}$

Q.2 The value of $\sqrt{3\sqrt{3\sqrt{3\sqrt{3\sqrt{3.......}}}}}$ is :

(A) 0 (B) 3 (C) Both 0 and 3 (D) Can't be determined

Q.3 Which of the following statements is correct?

(A) 0 is called the additive identity for rational numbers.

(B) 1 is called the multiplicative identity for rational numbers.

(C) The additive inverse of 0 is zero itself.

(D) All the above.

Q.4 The value of $\sqrt{80}-\sqrt{45}$ is :

(A) $\sqrt{35}$ (B) $\sqrt{5}$ (C) $4\sqrt{5}$ (D) $4(\sqrt{5}-\sqrt{3})$

Q.5 The number $3^{11}-3^{8}$ is divisible by prime numbers:

(A) 2 and 3 only (B) 2, 3 and 11 only (C) 3^{11} only (D) 2, 3 and 13 only

Q.6 Find the unit digit in $132^{74}-(3498)^{49}$:

(A) 6 (B) 0 (C) 4 (D) 2

Q.7 Which of the following alternatives is wrong? Given that :

(i) Difference of two rational numbers is a rational number.

(ii) Subtraction is commutative on rational numbers

(iii) Addition is not commutative on rational numbers.

(A) (ii) & (iii) (B) (i) only (C) (i) & (iii) (D) All the above

Q.8 The average of the middle two rational numbers if $\frac{2}{5},\frac{1}{2},\frac{3}{4},\frac{5}{7}$ are arranged in ascending order is :

(A) $\frac{5}{4}$ (B) $\frac{9}{10}$ (C) $\frac{39}{35}$ (D) $\frac{17}{28}$

Q.9 Which is smallest among :

$10-3\sqrt{11}$, $18-5\sqrt{13}$ and $51-10\sqrt{26}$

(A) $10-3\sqrt{11}$ (B) $18-5\sqrt{13}$ (C) $51-10\sqrt{26}$ (D) All are equal

Q.10 The greater between $\sqrt{19}-\sqrt{14}$ and $\sqrt{12}-\sqrt{7}$

(A) $\sqrt{19}-\sqrt{14}$ (B) $\sqrt{12}-\sqrt{7}$ (C) Both are equal (D) Can't say

Q.11 The smallest among $\sqrt[2]{2}$, $\sqrt[3]{4}$ and $\sqrt[4]{3}$ is :

(A) $\sqrt[2]{2}$ (B) $\sqrt[4]{3}$ (C) $\sqrt[3]{4}$ (D) Can't compare

Q.12 A number that has to be added to 9247653140 in order to make it divisible by 8 is :
(A) 2 (B) 8 (C) 6 (D) 4

Q.13 In order that the six digit number 1x0x3x be divisible by 11, the digit x should be :
(A) 2 (B) 1 (C) 4 (D) 5

Q.14 What are the values of x and y if 15x 0468913y is divisible by 8 and 11, where x and y are single digit integers?
(A) x = 3, y = 6 (B) x = 6, y = 9 (C) x = 9, y = 12 (D) x = 0, y = 3

Q.15 What is the complete solution to the equation :
$|3 - 4x| = 13$?
(A) $x = \frac{5}{2}, x = 4$ (B) $x = \frac{5}{2}, x = -4$ (C) $x = -\frac{5}{2}, x = 4$ (D) $x = -\frac{5}{2}, x = -4$

Q.16 If $x^{p^q} = (x^p)^q$, then p = **[Harayana NTSE Stage-1_2013]**
(A) $q^{\frac{1}{q}}$ (B) 1 (C) q^q (D) $q^{\frac{1}{q-1}}$

Q.17 The rationalizing factor of $\sqrt[n]{\frac{a}{b}}$ is **[Karnataka NTSE Stage-1_2014]**
(A) $ab\sqrt[n]{\frac{a}{b}}$ (B) $\sqrt[n]{\frac{a}{b}}$ (C) $\sqrt[n]{\frac{a^{n-1}}{b^{n-1}}}$ (D) $\sqrt[n]{\frac{a^{n+1}}{b^{n+1}}}$

Q.18 The value of $\left(\frac{x^b}{x^c}\right)^{\frac{1}{bc}} \cdot \left(\frac{x^c}{x^a}\right)^{\frac{1}{ca}} \cdot \left(\frac{x^a}{x^b}\right)^{\frac{1}{ab}}$ on simplifying is **[Rajasthan NTSE Stage-1_2015]**
(A) x (B) $\frac{1}{x}$ (C) 1 (D) –1

Q.19 Which real number lies between 2 and 2.5 **[Chandigarh NTSE Stage-1_2014]**
(A) $\sqrt{11}$ (B) $\sqrt{8}$ (C) $\sqrt[3]{7}$ (D) $\sqrt[3]{9}$

Q.20 The HCF of any two prime numbers a and b is **[Rajasthan NTSE Stage-1_2015]**
(A) a (B) ab (C) b (D) 1

Q.21 The traffic lights at three different singals change after 48 seconds, 72 seconds and 108. If they change at 7 a.m. simultaneously. How many times they will change between 7 a.m. to 7.30 a.m. simultaneously?
[Harayana NTSE Stage-1_2015]
(A) 3 (B) 4 (C) 5 (D) 2

Q.22 Which of the following is rational number? **[IMO-2016]**
(A) Sum of $(2+\sqrt{3})$ and its reciprocal (B) Square root of 18
(C) Square root of $7+4\sqrt{3}$ (D) None of these

Q.23 Expressing $0.\overline{23} + 0.2\overline{3}$ as a single decimal, we get **[NTSE-2016]**
(A) $0.46\overline{5}$ (B) $0.4\overline{65}$ (C) $0.\overline{465}$ (D) $0.465\overline{4}$

CONCEPT APPLICATION LEVEL - III

SECTION-A

Subjective Type Questions :

Q.1 Find the largest number that will divide 398, 436 and 542 leaving remainders 7, 11 and 15 respectively.

Q.2 Find the largest number that divides 2053 and 967 and leaves a remainder of 5 and 7 respectively.

Q.3 In a seminar, the number of participants in Hindi, English and Mathematics are 60, 84 and 108, respectively. Find the minimum number of rooms required if in each room the same number of participants are to be seated and all of them being in the same subject.

Q.4 Three sets of English, Hindi and Mathematics books have to be stacked in such a way that all the books are stored topic wise and the height of each stack is the same. The number of English books is 96, the number of Hindi books is 240 and the number of Mathematics books is 336. Assuming that the books are of the same thickness, determine the number of stacks of English, Hindi and Mathematics books.

Q.5 Prove that $\sqrt{2}+\sqrt{5}$ is irrational.

Q.6 Find the missing number in the following factorisation sequence.

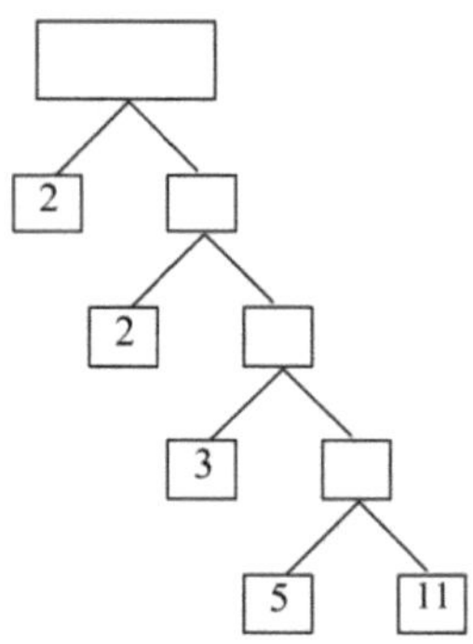

Q.7 Find the largest number that divides 2053 and 967 leaves remainder of 5 and 7 respectively.

Q.8 Two tankers contains 850 litres and 680 litres of petrol respectively. Find the maximum capacity of a container which can measure the petrol of either tank in exact number of times.

Q.9 The length, breadth and height of a room are 8 m 25 cm, 6 m 75 cm and 4m 50 cm respectively. Determine the longest rod which can measure the three dimensions of the room exactly.

Q.10 If a number N= 126, then

Find : (i) The number of divisors of N. (ii) The sum of divisors of N.

(iii) The product of divisors of N. (iv) The number of distinct prime divisors.

(v) The number of proper divisors of N.

Q.11 Find the HCF of $\frac{2}{3},\frac{3}{4}$ and $\frac{6}{7}$.

Q.12 Find the LCM of $\frac{5}{6},\frac{10}{17}$ and $\frac{15}{16}$.

SECTION-B

Multiple choice questions with one correct answer :

Q.1 If the LCM of a and 18 is 36 and the HCF of a and 18 is 2, then a =
(A) 2 (B) 3 (C) 4 (D) 1

Q.2 The number of decimal places after which the decimal expansion of the rational number $\frac{23}{2^2 \times 5}$ will terminate, is
(A) 1 (B) 2 (C) 3 (D) 4

Q.3 If n is a natural number, then $9^{2n} - 4^{2n}$ is always divisible by
(A) 5 (B) 13 (C) both 5 and 13 (D) None of these

Q.4 If $x^{1/8} = m$ and $x^{1/4} = n$ and $n = 4m$, then find the value of $\sqrt{x}$.
(A) 512 (B) 216 (C) 324 (D) 256

Q.5 The LCM of two numbers is 567 and their HCF is 9. If the difference between the two numbers is 18, find the two numbers :
(A) 36 and 18 (B) 78 and 60 (C) 63 and 81 (D) 52 and 34

Q.6 If n is any natural number, then $6^n - 5^n$ always ends with
(A) 1 (B) 3 (C) 5 (D) 7

Q.7 The smallest number by which $\sqrt{27}$ should be multiplied so as to get a rational number is
(A) $\sqrt{27}$ (B) $3\sqrt{3}$ (C) $\sqrt{3}$ (D) 3

Q.8 If $a = 2^3 \times 3$, $b = 2 \times 3 \times 5$ and LCM (a, b, c) $= 2^3 \times 3^2 \times 5$, then c =
(A) 1 (B) 9 (C) 3 (D) 4

Q.9 Which of the following is a pair of coprimes?
(A) (14, 35) (B) (18,25) (C) {31,93} (D) (32,62)

Q.10 HCF of $2^3 \times 3^2 \times 5$, $2^3 \times 3^3 \times 5^2$ and $2^2 \times 3 \times 5^3 \times 7$ is
(A) 30 (B) 48 (C) 60 (D) 105

Q.11 The product of two numbers is 2160 and their GCD is 12. The numbers are
(A) 72, 30 (B) 36, 60 (C) 96, 25 (D) None

Q.12 LCM of two numbers is 14 times their HCF. The sum of LCM and HCF is 600. If one number is 280, then the other is
(A) 40 (B) 60 (C) 80 (D) 100

Q.13 The ratio of two numbers is 3 : 4 and their HCF is 4. Then LCM is
(A) 12 (B) 16 (C) 24 (D) 48

Q.14 The HCF of $(4a^2b^3 - 9b)$ and $(2a^2b^2 - ab - 3)$ is
(A) (2a – 3) (B) (2ab – 3) (C) (2b – 3a) (D) None of these

Q.15 What is the greatest number which shall divide 305 and 629 and leave a remainder 8 in each case?
(A) 24 (B) 36 (C) 27 (D) 35

SECTION-C

Multiple choice Questions with one or more than one correct answers :

Q.1 If n is a natural number, then $\sqrt{n}$ can be

(A) a natural number (B) always an rational number
(C) an irrational number (D) always a natural number

Q.2 Which of the following statements for natural numbers a, b and c is/are true

(A) If a is divisible by b and b is divisible by c, then a must be divisible by c.
(B) If a is a factor of both b and c, then a must be a factor of b+c
(C) If a is a factor of both b and c then a must be a factor of b–c.
(D) If a is a factor of b and b anc c are coprime, then a,c must also be coprimers.

Q.3 Which of the following rational numbers have terminating decimal expansion

(A) 64/455 (B) 29/343 (C) 13/325 (D) 1/308

Q.4 The number $\sqrt{14+6\sqrt{5}}+\sqrt{14-6\sqrt{5}}$ is,

(A) is a rational numbers (B) is not a rational number
(C) simplifies to 5 (D) simplifies to 6

Q.5 The number $\sqrt{3+2\sqrt{2}}-\sqrt{3-2\sqrt{2}}$ can be

(A) rational number (B) natural number (C) prime number (D) irrational number

Q.6 Simplify: $1+\dfrac{6}{5+\dfrac{4}{3-\dfrac{1}{2}}}$

(A) $\frac{14}{45}$ (B) $\frac{63}{33}$ (C) $\frac{13}{19}$ (D) $\frac{21}{11}$

SECTION-D

Match the following (one to one) :

Column-I and **column-II** contain **four** entries each. One entry of column-I is to be matched with one entry of column-II.

Q.1

Column I		**Column II**
(i)	–10	(P) Natural number
(ii)	π	(Q) Integer but not a natural number
(iii)	3	(R) Rational number but not an integer
(iv)	5/2	(S) Irrational

Q.2

	Column I		**Column II**
(i)	Every odd integer is of the form 2m – 1 where m is	(P)	Rational
(ii)	$3.\overline{27}$ is	(Q)	Equal
(iii)	The LCM and HCF of two rational numbers are equal then the numbers must be	(R)	Integer
(iv)	$\sqrt{2}+\sqrt{5}$ is	(S)	Irrational

Q.3

	Column I		**Column II**
(i)	$\frac{-10}{15}$	(P)	1
(ii)	$3+2\sqrt{5}$	(Q)	Prime number
(iii)	$\left(\frac{2p^2q}{xy}\right)^0$	(R)	Irrational
(iv)	2	(S)	Fractional but not natural number

Match the following (one to many) :

Column-I and **column-II** contains **four** entries each. Entries of column-I are to be matched with some entries of column-II. One or more than one entries of column-I may have the matching with the some entries of column-II and one entry of column-II may have one or more than one matching with entries of column-I

Q.4

	Column I		**Column II**
(i)	If two irrational numbers are added then sum may be	(P)	Irrational number
(ii)	Division of a natural number by another natural number gives	(Q)	Rational number
(iii)	Natural number	(R)	Neither rational nor irrational
(iv)	Every real number	(S)	None of these

Q.5

	Column I		**Column II**
(i)	The sum of two prime numbers	(P)	Natural number
(ii)	The product of three consecutive natural numbers is	(Q)	Even number
(iii)	Sum of two even numbers	(R)	Odd number
(iv)	Sum of two odd numbers	(S)	None of these

ANSWER KEY

CONCEPT APPLICATION LEVEL - II

Multiple Choice Questions with one correct answer :

Q.1	C	Q.2	B	Q.3	D	Q.4	B	Q.5	D
Q.6	A	Q.7	A	Q.8	D	Q.9	B	Q.10	B
Q.11	B	Q.12	D	Q.13	D	Q.14	A	Q.15	C
Q.16	D	Q.17	C	Q.18	C	Q.19	D	Q.20	D
Q.21	B	Q.22	A	Q.23	B				

CONCEPT APPLICATION LEVEL - III

SECTION-A

Q.1 17 Q.2 64 Q.3 12 Q.4 14

Q.6 Going upwards 55, 165, 330, 660

Q.7 64

Q.8 170 litres

Q.9 75 cm

Q.10 (i) 12 (ii) 312 (iii) 126^6 (iv) 3 (v) 10

Q.11 $\frac{1}{84}$

Q.12 30

SECTION-B

Q.1	C	Q.2	B	Q.3	C	Q.4	D	Q.5	C
Q.6	A	Q.7	C	Q.8	B	Q.9	B	Q.10	C
Q.11	B	Q.12	C	Q.13	D	Q.14	B	Q.15	C

SECTION-C

Q.1	A,C	Q.2	A,B,C,D	Q.3	C	Q.4	A,D
Q.5	A, B, C	Q.6	B,D				

SECTION-D

Q.1 (i)-(Q), (ii)-(S), (iii)-(P), (iv)-(R)

Q.2 (i)-(R), (ii)-(P), (iii)-(Q), (iv)-(S)

Q.3 (i)-(S), (ii)-(R), (iii)-(P), (iv)-(Q)

Q.4 (i)-(P,Q), (ii)-(Q), (iii)-(Q), (iv)-(P,Q)

Q.5 (i)-(PQR), (ii)-(PQ), (iii)-(Q), (iv)-(Q)

2 POLYNOMIALS

THEORY

2.1 INTRODUCTION :

In earlier classes, we have learnt about polynomials in one variable, their degrees, factors, multiples and zeros (or roots). In this chapter, we will study about the geometrical representation of linear quadratic and cubic polynomials and geometrical meaning of their zeros. We will also study about the relationship between the zeros and coefficients of a polynomial. LCM and HCF of two or more polynomials, rational expressions, basic operation on polynomials and concept of square root of polynomials.

2.2 POLYNOMIALS :

An algebraic expression f(x) of the form $f(x) = a_0 + a_1x + a_2x^2 + \ldots\ldots\ldots + a_nx^n$; where $a_0, a_1, a_2, \ldots\ldots, a_n$ are real numbers and all the indices of variable x are non-negative integers, is called a polynomial in variable x and the highest indices n is called the degree of the polynomial, if $a_n \neq 0$. Here, a_0, a_1x, $a_2x^2, \ldots\ldots$ and a_nx^n are called the terms of the polynomial and $a_0, a_1, a_2 \ldots\ldots\ldots\ldots a_n$ are called various coefficients of the polynomial f(x). A polynomial in x is said to be in standard form when the terms are written either in increasing order or in decreasing order of the indices of x in various terms.

For example : $x^2 - a^2$, $ax^2 + bx + c, x^3 + 3x^2 + 3x + 1$, $y^3 - 7y + 6$ etc. are the polynomials written in their standard form.

Illustrations

Illustration 1 : Which of the following expressions are polynomials?

(i) $\dfrac{1}{x^{-2}} + \dfrac{1}{x^{-1}} + \dfrac{1}{2}$ **(ii)** $\dfrac{1}{x}(x-1)(x-2)$

(iii) $\dfrac{(x^2+x+1)(x+1)}{(1+x)}$ **(iv)** $x^2 + \dfrac{1}{x^2}$

Solution :

(i) $\dfrac{1}{x^{-2}} + \dfrac{1}{x^{-1}} + \dfrac{1}{2} = x^2 + x^1 + \dfrac{1}{2}x^0$ [It is a polynomial]

(ii) $\dfrac{1}{x}(x-1)(x-2) = x^{-1}(x^1 - 1)(x^1 - 2)$

$= x^{-1}(x^2 - 3x + 2)$

$= x - 3 + 2x^{-1}$

$= x^1 - 3x^0 + 2x^{-1}$ [It is not a polynomial]

(iii) $\dfrac{(x^2+x+1)(x+1)}{(x+1)} = x^2 + x + 1 = x^2 + x^1 + 1 \cdot x^0$ [It is a polynomial]

(iv) $x^2 + \dfrac{1}{x^2} = x^2 + x^{-2}$ [It is not a polynomial]

Illustration 2. **Rewrite the following polynomials in the standard form :**

(i) $x - 7 + 8x^2 + 9x^3$ (ii) $-5x^2 + 6 - 3x^3 + 4x$

Solution : **(i)** $9x^3 + 8x^2 + x - 7$ is the standard form of $x - 7 + 8x^2 + 9x^3$.

(ii) $-3x^3 - 5x^2 + 4x + 6$ is the standard form of $-5x^2 + 6 - 3x^3 + 4x$.

- **Degree of a Polynomial in One Variable :** In case of a polynomial in one variable, the highest power of the variable is called the degree of the polynomial.
For example : the degree of $9x^3 + 8x^2 + x - 7$ is 3.

- **Degree of a Polynomial in Two or More Variables :** In case of polynomials in more than one variable, the sum of the powers of the variables in each term is taken up and the highest sum so obtained is called the degree of the polynomial.
For example : the degree of $5x^3 + 6x^2y^2 + 12y^3$ is $2 + 2 = 4$. Because the power of the variables in first and third terms is 3 but the sum of power of variables in second term is 4 and $4 > 3$. Hence the degree is 4.

- **Additive Inverse of a Polynomial :** A polynomial Q is the additive inverse of a polynomial P if the sum of Q and P is zero, e.g. $3x^2 - 5x + 7$ is the additive inverse of $-3x^2 + 5x - 7$.
The additive inverse of a polynomial is obtained by reversing the sign of each of the coefficients of the polynomial.

- **Value of a polynomial :** The value of a polynomial f(x) at x = a is obtained by substituting x = a in the given polynomial and is denoted by f(a).
Consider the polynomial : $p(x) = 6x^2 + 7x - 2$
If we replace x by 1 everywhere in p(x), we get
$$p(1) = 6(1)^2 + 7(1) - 2$$
$$= 6 + 7 - 2 = 11$$
So, we say that the value of p(x) at x = 1 is 11.

- **Zero(es) / Root(s) of polynomials :** x = r is a root or zero of a polynomial p(x), if p(r) = 0.
In other words, x = r is a root or zero of a polynomial p(x), if it is a solution to the equation p(x) = 0.
The process of finding the zeros of p(x) is nothing more than solving to the equation p(x) = 0.

- **Geometrical meaning of the zero(es) of a polynomial :** Zero(es) of a polynomial is/are the x-coordinate of the point(s) where the graph of y = f(x) intersects the x-axis.

- **Graphs of polynomial :** In algebraic language the graph of a polynomial f(x) is the collection of all points (x,y), where y = f(x). In geometrical or in graphical language the graph of a polynomial f(x) is a smooth free hand curve passing through point (x_1, y_1), (x_2, y_2), (x_3, y_3)...........etc, where y_1, y_2, y_3 .... are the values of the polynomial f(x) at x_1, x_2, x_3 ....respectively. In order to draw the graph of a polynomial f(x), we may follow the following algorithm.

Algorithm

Step - 1:- Find the values $y_1, y_2 ...... y_n$ of polynomial f(x) at different points $x_1, x_2 ...... x_n$ and prepare a table that gives values of y or f(x) for various values of x.

Step - 2:- Plot the points $(x_1 y_1), (x_2, y_2), (x_3, y_3) .... (x_n, y_n)$ on rectangular coordinate system. In plotting these points we may use different scales on the x and y axes.

Step -3:- Draw a free hand smooth curve passing through points plotted in step 2 to get the graph of the polynomial f(x).

x	x_1	x_2	....	x_n
y = f(x)	$y_1 = f(x_1)$	$y_2 = f(x_2)$	....	$y_n = f(x_n)$

- **Graph of a Linear Polynomial :-** Consider a linear polynomial f(x) = ax + b, a ≠ 0. We know that the graph of polynomial y = ax + b is a straight line, so it is called a linear polynomial. Since a straight line can be determined by two points, so only two points need to be poltted to draw the graph of y = ax +b. The graph of y = ax + b crosses the x axis at exactly one point namely $\left(\frac{-b}{a}, 0\right)$.

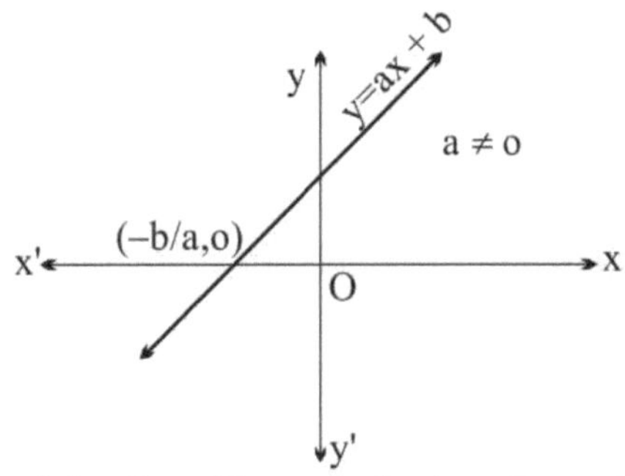

- **Graph of a Quadratic Polynomial :-** Consider a quadratic polynomial $f(x) = y = ax^2 + bx + c$. Where a, b and c be real numbers and a ≠ 0. We know that the graph of quadratic polynomial is a cup shaped graph known as parabola.
In order to draw the graph of a quadratic polynomial f(x), we may follow the following algorithm.

Algorithm to draw the graph of quadratic polynomial :

Step -1 : Write the given quadratic polynomial $f(x) = y = ax^2 + bx + c$.

Step -2 : Determine the zero of the polynomial , if they exist. This can be done by putting y = 0 i.e. $ax^2 + bx + c = 0$.

Step -3 : Calculate the discriminant $D = b^2 - 4ac$

Step - 4 : Determine the point where the curve intersects y - axis. This can be done by putting x = 0 in the given function and calculating the value of y.

Step - 5 : Determine the vertex i.e., $\left(\frac{-b}{2a}, \frac{-D}{4a}\right)$.

Step - 6 : Prepare a table of selected values of x and corresponding values of y (generally two or three points on the left and two or three points on the right of the vertex.)

Step - 7 : Draw a smooth curve, through these points.

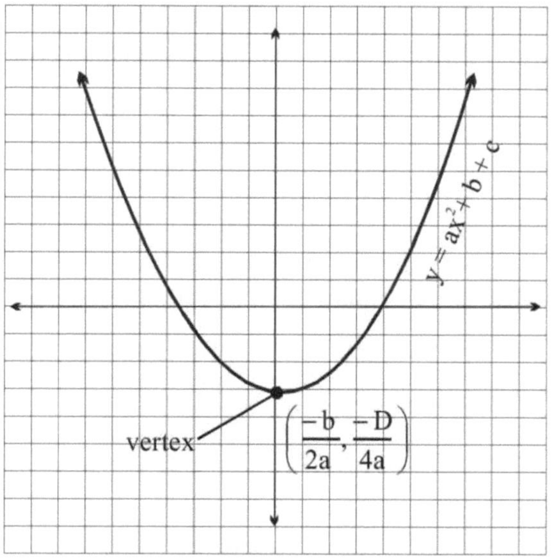

Graph of Quadratic Polynomial : The graph of a quadratic polynomial $ax^2 + bx + c$, $a \neq 0$ is a parabola which opens upward or downward as $a > 0$ or $a < 0$, we have the following possibilities :-

Case-I : If $\mathbf{a > 0}$, then graph of a quadratic polynomial looks similar to one of the graphs in Figure (i), (ii) and (iii). In these figures parabola is opening upward.

(i) When $b^2 - 4ac > 0$ $\Rightarrow$

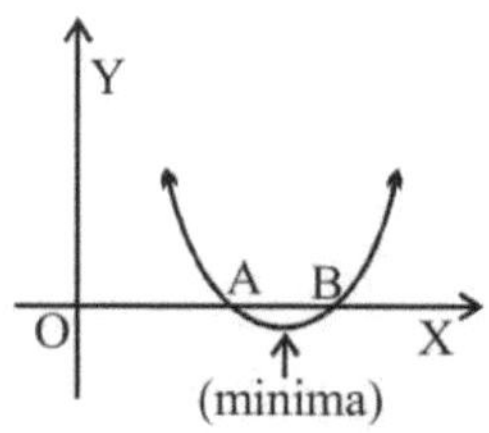

The graph $y = ax^2 + bx + c$, $a \neq 0$ cuts the x-axis at two distinct points A and B. The x-coordinates of these points are the two zeroes of the polynomial $y = ax^2 + bx + c$, $a \neq 0$.

(ii) When $b^2 - 4ac = 0$ $\Rightarrow$

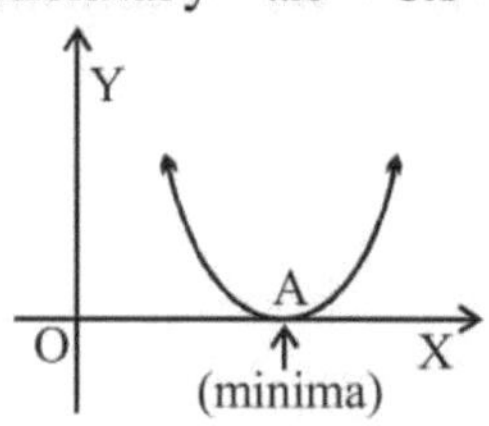

In this case, the graph of polynomial $y = ax^2 + bx + c$, $a \neq 0$, touches the x-axis at exactly one point A and whose coordinates are $\left(\frac{-b}{2a}, 0\right)$. So, in this case the x-coordinates of point A gives two equal zeros of the polynomial $y = ax^2 + bx + c$, $a \neq 0$.

(iii) When $b^2 - 4ac < 0$ (In this case polynomial $ax^2 + bx + c$ is not factorizable.)

$\Rightarrow$

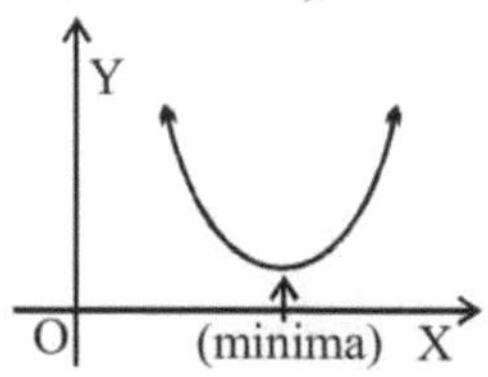

The graph of polynomial $y = ax^2 + bx + c$, $a \neq 0$ does not cut or touch x-axis. The curve of parabola remains completely above the x-axis.

Case-II : If $\mathbf{a < 0}$, then graph of the quadratic polynomial looks similar to one of the graphs in Figure (iv), (v) and (vi). In these figures parabola is opening downwards.

(iv) When $b^2 - 4ac > 0$ $\Rightarrow$

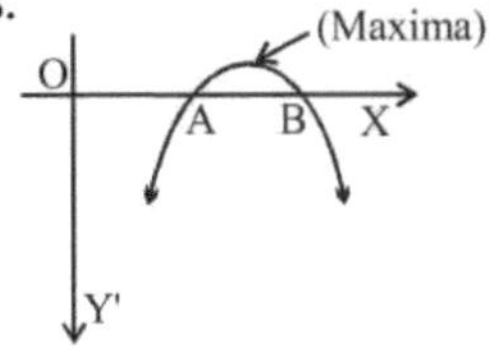

The graph $y = ax^2 + bx + c,\ a \neq 0$ cuts the x-axis at two distinct points A and B. The x-coordinates of these points are the two zeroes of the polynomial $y = ax^2 + bx + c,\ a \neq 0$.

(v) When $b^2 - 4ac = 0$ $\Rightarrow$

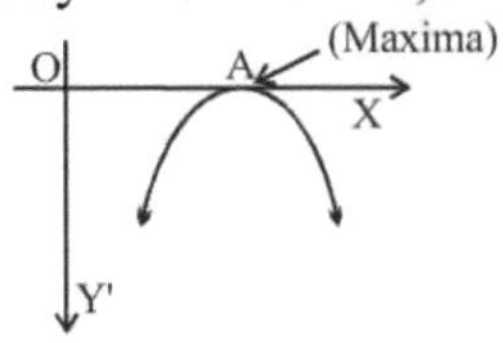

In this case, the graph of polynomial $y = ax^2 + bx + c,\ a \neq 0$, touches the x-axis at exactly one point A and whose coordinates are $\left(\frac{-b}{2a}, 0\right)$. So, in this case the x-coordinates of point A gives two equal zeros of the polynomials $y = ax^2 + bx + c,\ a \neq 0$.

(vi) When $b^2 - 4ac < 0$ (In this case polynomial $ax^2 + bx + c$ is not factorizable.)

$\Rightarrow$

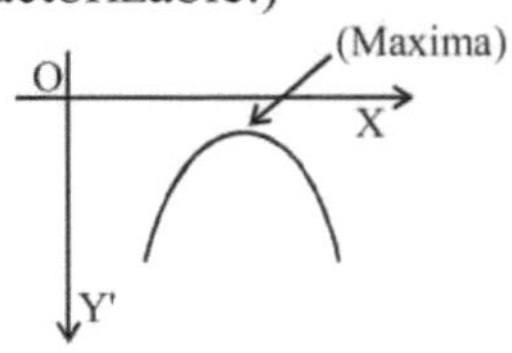

The graph of polynomial $y = ax^2 + bx + c,\ a \neq 0$ does not cut or touch x-axis. The curve of parabola remains completely below the x-axis.

Illustrations

Illustration 3 : Draw the graph of quadratic polynomial $x^2 - 2x + 3$ & read off zeros from the graph.

Solution : Let $y = x^2 - 2x + 3$

Put $y = 0$ $\Rightarrow$ $x^2 - 2x + 3 = 0$

Now, $D = b^2 - 4ac = (-2)^2 - 4 \times 1 \times 3 = 4 - 12 = -8 < 0$. Hence no real zeros :

Now vertex of the parabola $= \left(-\frac{b}{2a}, -\frac{D}{4a}\right) = \left(-\frac{(-2)}{2 \times 1}, -\frac{(-8)}{4 \times 1}\right) = (1, 2)$

Required table for $y = x^2 - 2x + 3$

x	$y = x^2 - 2x + 3$			y
	x^2	– 2x	3	
1	1	– 2	3	2
2	4	– 4	3	3
0	0	0	3	3
3	9	– 6	3	6
4	16	– 8	3	11
– 1	1	2	3	6
– 2	4	4	3	11

Now, we have ordered pairs : (1,2) (2,3) (0,3) (3,6) (–1,6) (–2,11) and (4,11)

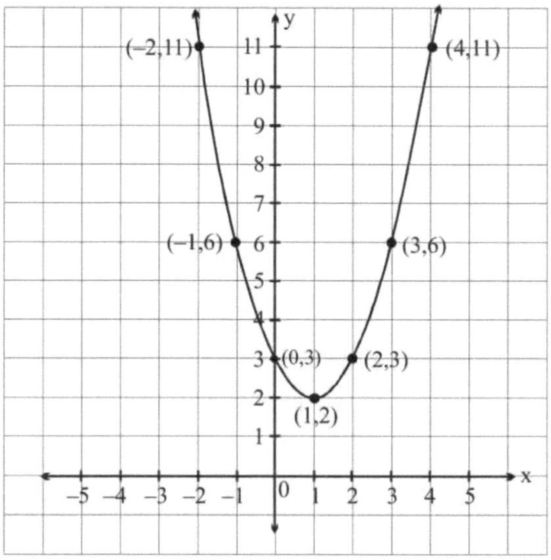

Since the graph of the polynomial does not meet or intersect the x-axis at all, therefore the given polynomial has no real zeros.

▶ **Graph of a cubic polynomial :**

A cubic polynomial is a function of the form $y = ax^3 + bx^2 + cx + d$.

where $a \neq 0$, and a, b, c and d are real constants.

Case-I : If **a > 0**, then graph of a cubic function looks similar to one of the graphs in Figure (i), (ii) and (iii).

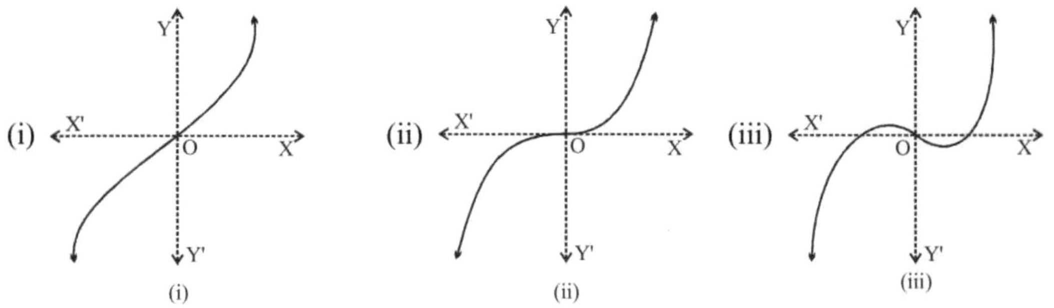

(i) (ii) (iii)

Case-II : If **a < 0**, then graph of the cubic function looks similar to one of the graphs in Figure (iv), (v) and (vi).

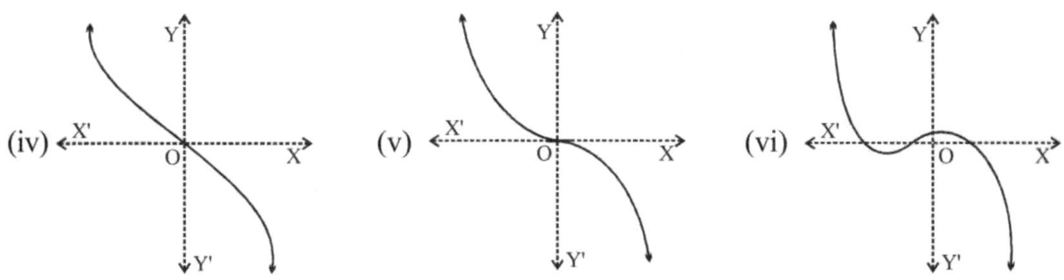

(iv) (v) (vi)

Illustrations

Illustration 4 : Look at the graphs given below. Each is the graph of y = p(x) where p(x) is a polynomial. For each of the following graphs, find the number of zeroes of p(x).

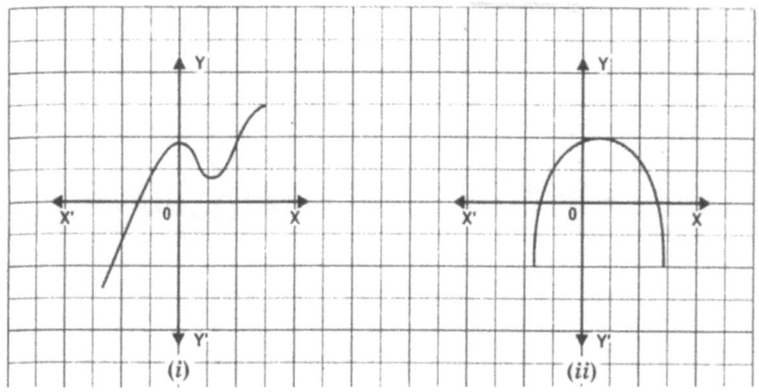

Solution :

(i) Since the graph intersects the x-axis at one point only, the polynomial p(x) has only one zero.

(ii) Since the graph intersects the x-axis at two points, the polynomial p(x) has two zeroes.

KEY CONCEPT

▶ **Relation Between Zero(es) and Coefficient of a polynomial :**

(a) Zero of a linear polynomial ax + b, is $x = -\dfrac{b}{a}$

(b) If quadratic polynomial $ax^2 + bx + c = k(x - \alpha)(x - \beta)$. where k is any real constant ; then α and β are zeroes of quadratic polynomial $ax^2 + bx + c$
where a, b, c, $\in$ R and $a \neq 0$

$$\alpha + \beta = -\frac{\mathbf{b}}{\mathbf{a}}$$

i.e., sum of zeros $= \dfrac{-\text{coefficient of } x}{\text{coefficient of } x^2}$

and $\alpha.\beta = \dfrac{\mathbf{c}}{\mathbf{a}}$

i.e., Product of zeros $= \dfrac{\text{constant term}}{\text{coefficient of } x^2}$

(c) If cubic polynomial $ax^3 + bx^2 + cx + d = k(x-\alpha)(x-\beta)(x-\gamma)$ where k is any real constant, then α, β, and γ are zeroes of cubic polynomial.
$ax^3 + bx^2 + cx + d$ where a, b, c, d $\in$R and a $\neq 0$

$$\text{sum of zeros} = -\frac{\text{coefficient of } x^2}{\text{coefficient of } x^3}$$

$$\text{i.e. } \alpha + \beta + \gamma = -\frac{\mathbf{b}}{\mathbf{a}};$$

$$\text{sum of the product of the zeros taken two at a time} = \frac{\text{coefficient of } x}{\text{coefficient of } x^3}$$

$$\text{i.e. } \alpha\beta + \beta\gamma + \gamma\alpha = \frac{\mathbf{c}}{\mathbf{a}};$$

$$\text{and product of the zeros} = -\frac{\text{constant term}}{\text{coefficient of } x^3}$$

$$\text{i.e. } \alpha\beta\gamma = \frac{-\mathbf{d}}{\mathbf{a}}.$$

2.3 HCF OF GIVEN POLYNOMIALS :

For two given polynomials, f(x) and g(x), r(x) can be taken as the Highest Common Factor, if

(i) r(x) is a common factor of f(x) and g(x) and

(ii) Every common factor of f(x) and g(x) is also a factor of r(x).
Highest common factor is generally referred to as HCF.

▶ **Method for finding HCF of the given polynomials :**

Step 1 : Express each polynomial as a product of powers of irreducible factors which also requires the numerical factors to be expressed as the product of the powers of primes.

Step 2 : If there is no common factor then HCF is 1 and if there are common irreducible factors, we find the least exponent of these irreducible factors in the factorized form of the given polynomials.

Step 3 : Raise the common irreducible factors to the smallest or the least exponents found in step 2 and take their product to get the HCF.

Illustrations

Illustration 5 : Find the HCF of $(x^2 - 6x + 5)$ and $(x^2 + 9x - 10)$.

Solution. : Factorising each expression

$$x^2 - 6x + 5 = (x-1)(x-5)$$

$$x^2 + 9x - 10 = (x-1)(x+10)$$

Since, the common factor of $x^2 - 6x + 5$ and $x^2 + 9x - 10$ is $(x - 1)$
therefore, HCF of $(x^2 - 6x + 5)$ and $(x^2 + 9x - 10)$ is $(x - 1)$.

2.4 LCM OF GIVEN POLYNOMIALS :

Least Common Multiple or the Lowest Common Multiple is the product of all the factors (taken once) of the polynomials given with their highest exponents respectively.

▶ **Method for finding LCM of the given polynomials :**

Step 1 : First express each polynomial as a product of powers of irreducible factors.

Step 2 : Consider all the irreducible factors (only once) occurring in the given polynomials. For each of these factors, consider the greatest exponent in the factorized form of the given polynomials.

Step 3 : Now raise each irreducible factor to the greatest exponent and multiply them to get the LCM.

Illustrations

Illustration 6 : Find the LCM of $(x^2 - 6x + 5)$ and $(x^2 + 9x - 10)$.

Solution : Factorising each expression

$x^2 - 6x + 5 = (x - 1)(x - 5)$

$x^2 + 9x - 10 = (x - 1)(x + 10)$

Now, LCM of $(x^2 - 6x + 5)$ and $(x^2 + 9x - 10)$ is

$(x - 1)(x - 5)(x + 10)$

Remember

Relation between the HCF, the LCM and the product of polynomials :

If f(x) and g(x) are two polynomials then we have the relation,

[HCF of f(x) and g(x)] × [LCM of f(x) and g(x)] = ± [f(x) × g(x)].

Illustrations

Illustration 7 : Let $f(x) = (x+3)^2(x-1)(x+2)^3$ and $g(x) = (x+3)(x-1)^2(x+2)^2$ be two polynomials. Verify that

[f(x) × g(x)] = [HCF of f(x) and g(x)] × [LCM of f(x) and g(x)]

Solution : The common factors with the least exponents are $(x + 3)$, $(x - 1)$, $(x + 2)^2$.

$\Rightarrow$ HCF $= (x - 1)(x + 3)(x + 2)^2$

All the factors (taken only once) with the highest exponents are $(x + 3)^2$, $(x - 1)^2$, $(x + 2)^3$.

$\Rightarrow$ LCM $= (x - 1)^2 (x + 2)^3 (x + 3)^2$

Now $f(x) \times g(x) = \{(x+3)^2(x-1)(x+2)^3\} \times \{(x+3)(x-1)^2(x+2)^2\}$

$= (x - 1)^3 (x + 2)^5 (x + 3)^3$

$= [(x - 1)(x + 2)^3 (x + 3)^2]\,[(x - 1)(x + 2)^2 (x + 3)]$

$=$ [LCM of f(x) and g(x)] × [HCF of f(x) and g(x)]

2.5 RATIONAL EXPRESSIONS :

Rational expression is 'an algebraic expression which is of the form $\frac{f(x)}{g(x)}$, where f(x) and g(x) are polynomials and g(x) is not a zero polynomial.

For any rational number of the form $\frac{p}{q}$, where $p, q \in z$ and $q \neq 0$. p and q are called numerator and denominator respectively. Eventhough p and q are integers $\frac{p}{q}$ need not to be an integer. Similarly for any rational expression $\frac{f(x)}{g(x)}$, f(x) is called numerator and g(x) is called denominator.

Eventhough f(x) and g(x) are polynomials $\frac{f(x)}{g(x)}$ need not to be a polynomial.

For Example :

1. $\frac{2x-1}{x^2-3x+1}$ is rational expression.
2. $\frac{x^3+5x^2-\sqrt{3}x+\sqrt{5}}{2x^2-\sqrt{5}x+8}$ is a rational expression.
3. $\frac{x^2-5\sqrt{x}-1}{3x-5}$ is not a rational expression as the numerator is not a polynomial.

IMPORTANT

Note : 1. Every polynomial is a rational expression as f(x) can be written as $\frac{f(x)}{1}$.

2. $\frac{f(x)}{g(x)}$ is not a rational expression if either numerator f(x) or denominator g(x) or both f(x) and g(x) are not polynomials.

▶ **Rational expressions in lowest terms :**

Let f(x) and g(x) have integer coefficients and HCF of f(x) and g(x) is 1, then the rational expression $\frac{f(x)}{g(x)}$ is said to be in its lowest terms.

▶ Addition/subtraction of rational expressions :

The sum of any two rational expressions $\frac{f(x)}{g(x)}$ and $\frac{h(x)}{p(x)}$ is written as

$$\frac{f(x)}{g(x)}+\frac{h(x)}{p(x)}=\frac{f(x)p(x)+h(x)g(x)}{g(x)\,p(x)}$$

If the denominators g(x) and p(x) are equal then $\frac{f(x)}{g(x)}+\frac{h(x)}{p(x)}=\frac{f(x)+h(x)}{g(x)}=\frac{f(x)+h(x)}{p(x)}$.

The difference of the above rational expressions can be written as $\frac{f(x)}{g(x)}-\frac{h(x)}{p(x)}=\frac{f(x)p(x)-h(x)g(x)}{g(x)\,p(x)}$

IMPORTANT

Note : 1. Sum or difference of two rational expressions is also a rational expression.

2. For any rational expressions $\frac{f(x)}{g(x)}$, $\frac{-f(x)}{g(x)}$ is called the additive inverse of $\frac{f(x)}{g(x)}$.

i.e., $\frac{f(x)}{g(x)}+\left(\frac{-f(x)}{g(x)}\right)=0$

Illustrations

Illustration 8 : Simplify $\frac{3x-1}{x+2}+\frac{2x-1}{x+1}$

Solution : $\frac{3x-1}{x+2}+\frac{2x-1}{x-1}=\frac{(3x-1)(x-1)+(2x-1)(x+2)}{(x+2)(x-1)}$

$$=\frac{3x^2-3x-x+1+2x^2+4x-x-2}{x^2-x+2x-2}=\frac{5x^2-x-1}{x^2+x-2}$$

▶ Multiplication of rational expressions :

The product of two rational expressions $\frac{f(x)}{g(x)}$ and $\frac{h(x)}{p(x)}$ is given by $\frac{f(x)}{g(x)}\times\frac{h(x)}{p(x)}=\frac{f(x).h(x)}{g(x).p(x)}$

KEY CONCEPT

Note : 1. The process of finding the

(i) product of two rational expressions is similar to the process of finding the product of two rational numbers.

(ii) product of two rational expressions is also a rational expression.

2. After finding the product of two rational expressions the resultant rational expression must be put in its lowest terms.

Illustrations

Example 9 : Find the product of $\frac{x^2-6x+5}{x+10}$ and $\frac{x^2+12x+20}{x^2-1}$

Solution : $\frac{x^2-6x+5}{x+10} \times \frac{x^2+12x+20}{x^2-1} = \frac{(x-1)(x-5)}{(x+10)} \times \frac{(x+2)(x+10)}{(x-1)(x+1)}$

$$= \frac{(x-5)(x+2)}{(x+1)} = \frac{x^2-3x-10}{x+1}$$

▶ **Division of rational expressions :**

Let $\frac{f(x)}{g(x)}$ and $\frac{h(x)}{p(x)}$ be two non-zero rational expressions, then $\frac{f(x)}{g(x)} \div \frac{h(x)}{p(x)} = \frac{f(x)}{g(x)} \times \frac{p(x)}{h(x)}$

i.e., $\frac{f(x)\cdot p(x)}{g(x)\cdot h(x)}$ which is also a rational expression.

Note : The process of dividing two rational expressions is similar to the process of dividing two rational numbers.

Illustrations

Illustration 10 : Express $\frac{(x^2+6x+5)}{(x^2-4x+3)} \div \frac{(x^2+9x+20)}{(x^2-3x+2)}$ as a rational expression in its lowest terms.

Solution : $\frac{(x^2+6x+5)}{(x^2-4x+3)} \div \frac{(x^2+9x+20)}{(x^2-3x+2)}$

Factorising quadratic expression,

$$= \frac{(x+1)(x+5)}{(x-3)(x-1)} \div \frac{(x+4)(x+5)}{(x-2)(x-1)}$$

$$= \frac{(x+1)(x+5)}{(x-3)(x-1)} \times \frac{(x-2)(x-1)}{(x+4)(x+5)} = \frac{(x+1)(x-2)}{(x-3)(x+4)} = \frac{x^2-x-2}{x^2+x-12}$$

2.6 BASIC OPERATIONS ON POLYNOMIALS :

(i) **Sum and Difference of two polynomials :** The sum and difference of two polynomials can be found by grouping like terms, taking the variable with same index common if any and then taking algebraic sum of the coefficient of like terms.

Illustration 11 : Add $p(x) = 4x^3 + 5x^2 + 2x - 1$ and $q(x) = 3x^3 - 6x^2 + 7$

Solution : $p(x) + q(x) = (4x^3 + 5x^2 + 2x - 1) + (3x^3 - 6x^2 + 7)$

$= 4x^3 + 3x^3 + 5x^2 - 6x^2 + 2x - 1 + 7$

$= 7x^3 - x^2 + 2x + 6$

Illustration 12 : Subtract $p(x) = 8x^4 - 3x^2 + x + 9$ from $q(x) = 10x^4 + 5x^3 - 2x^2 - 6x + 4$.

Solution : $q(x) - p(x) = (10x^4 + 5x^3 - 2x^2 - 6x + 4) - (8x^4 - 3x^2 + x + 9)$

$= 10x^4 - 8x^4 + 5x^3 - 2x^2 + 3x^2 - 6x - x + 4 - 9$

$= 2x^4 + 5x^3 + x^2 - 7x - 5$

(ii) Multiplication of Monomials :

Product of monomials = (Product of their numerical coefficients) × (Product of their variable parts)

Illustration 13 : Find the product of $4x^2yz^3$ and $3xy^2$.

Solution : $(4x^2yz^3) \times (3xy^2) = (4 \times 3) \times (x^2yz^3 \times xy^2)$

$= 12 . x^{2+1} . y^{1+2} . z^3 = 12\, x^3 y^3 z^3$

(iii) Multiplication of Two Polynomials :

Multiply each term of the multiplicand by each term of the multiplier and take the algebraic sum of theses products.

Illustration 14 : Find the product of $2x^2 + 5x + 6$ and $x - 1$.

Solution : $(2x^2 + 5x + 6)(x - 1) = 2x^2(x - 1) + 5x(x - 1) + 6(x - 1)$

$= 2x^3 - 2x^2 + 5x^2 - 5x + 6x - 6$

$= 2x^3 + 3x^2 + x - 6$

(iv) Division of Polynomials :

On dividing a polynomial p(x) by a polynomial d(x), let the quotient be q(x) and the remainder be r(x), then p(x) = d(x). q(x) + r(x), where either r(x) = 0 or deg. r(x) < deg. d (x).

Here, Dividend = p(x), Divisor = d(x), Quotient = q (x) and Remainder = r(x).

Note : Division algorithm helps in determining the other two zeroes of a cubic polynomial when one zero is known.

Division algorithm of a polynomial by a polynomial :

Step 1 : Arrange the terms of the dividend and the divisor in descending order of their degrees.

Step 2 : Divide the first term of the dividend by the first term of the divisor to obtain the first term of the quotient.

Step 3 : Multiply all the terms of the divisor by the first term of the quotient and subtract the result from the dividend.

Step 4 : Consider the remainder as new dividend and proceed as before.

Step 5 : Repeat this process till we obtain a remainder which is either 0 or a polynomial of degree less than that of the division.

Illustrations

Illustration 15 : Divide $p(x) = x^3 - 3x^2 + 5x - 3$ by the polynomial $g(x) = x + 2$, find the quotient and the remainder.

Solution :

$$
\begin{array}{r|l}
 & x^2 - 5x + 15 \\
\hline
x+2 & x^3 - 3x^2 + 5x - 3 \\
 & \underline{\overset{-}{x^3} \overset{-}{+} 2x^2} \\
 & \quad -5x^2 + 5x - 3 \\
 & \quad \underline{\underset{+}{-}5x^2 \underset{+}{-} 10x} \\
 & \qquad\quad 15x - 3 \\
 & \qquad\quad \underline{\overset{-}{15x} \overset{-}{+} 30} \\
 & \qquad\qquad -33
\end{array}
$$

Thus quotient $= x^2 - 5x + 15$ and remainder $= -33$.

Illustration 16 : Find the integral zero of the polynomial : $f(y) = 4y^3 - 8y^2 - y + 2$

Solution : Suppose K is an integral zero of the polynomial $f(y) = 4y^3 - 8y^2 - y + 2$

Thus K is a factor of constant term 2, then possible values of k are $1, -1$ and $2, -2$

Now, $f(1) = 4(1)^3 - 8(1)^2 - 1 + 2$

$= 4 - 8 - 1 + 2 = -3 \neq 0$

$\because f(1) \neq 0$

$\therefore$ 1 is not a zero of f(y).

$f(-1) = 4(-1)^3 - 8(-1)^2 - (-1) + 2$

$= -4 - 8 + 1 + 2 = -9 \neq 0$

Since $f(-1) \neq 0$, therefore -1 is not a zero of f(y)

$f(2) = 4(2)^3 - 8(2)^2 - (2) + 2$

$= 32 - 32 - 2 + 2 = 0$

$\because f(2) = 0$, therefore 2 is zero of f(y).

$f(-2) = 4(-2)^3 - 8(-2)^2 - (-2) + 2$

$= -32 - 32 + 2 + 2 = -60 \neq 0$

Since $f(-2) \neq 0$, therefore -2 is not a zero of f(y).

The only integral zero of f(y) is 2. If there are other zeroes then they are not integers.

2.7 CONCEPT OF SQUARE ROOTS :

If x is any variable then x^2 is called the square of the variable and for x^2, x is called the square root.

Square root of x^2 can be denoted as $\sqrt{x^2}$.
x and –x can both be considered as the square roots of x^2 because $(x)(x) = x^2$ and $(-x)(-x) = x^2$.

In this study we restrict $\sqrt{x^2}$ to x, i.e., + ve value of x.

▶ **Methods of finding the square roots of algebraic expression other than monomials :**
Here we are discussing two methods to find the square root of an algebraic expression which is not a monomial. They are :
(i) Method of division.
(ii) Method of undetermined coefficients.

(i) Method of division : We discuss the method of division to find the square root of an algebraic expression using the following example :

Illustrations

Illustration 17 : Find the square root of $x^2 - 4x + 4$.

Solution :

Divisor	
	$x^2 - 4x + 4$
x	x^2
	$-$
	$-4x + 4$
$2x - 2$	$-4x + 4$
	$+ \quad -$
	0

therefore, $\sqrt{x^2 - 4x + 4} = (x - 2)$

Step 1 : Arrange the given expression in the descending powers of the variable x.

Step 2 : Then the square root of the first term in the expression is calculated. In the above problem first term is x^2 whose square root is x. This is now the first term of the square root of the expression.

Step 3 : Then the square of x i.e., x^2 is written below the first term of the expression and subtracted. The difference is zero. Then the next two terms in the expression $-4x + 4$ are brought down as the dividend for the next step. Double the first term of the square root and put it down as the first term of the next divisor i.e., $2(x) = 2x$ is to be written as the first term of the next divisor. Now the first term $-4x$ of the dividend $-4x + 4$ is to be divided by the first term 2x (of the new divisor). Here we get –2 which is the second term of the square root of the given expression and the second term of the new divisor.

Step 4 : Thus the new divisor becomes $2x - 2$. Multiply $(2x - 2)$ by (-2) and the product $-4x + 4$ is to be brought down under the second dividend $-4x + 4$ and subtracted where we get 0.

Step 5 : Thus $x - 2$ is the square root of the given expression $x^2 - 4x + 4$.

Illustration 18 : Find the square root of $4x^6 - 12x^5 + 9x^4 + 8x^3 - 12x^2 + 4$.

Solution : Follow the steps indicated in the previous example.

$$
\begin{array}{r|l}
 & 4x^6 - 12x^5 + 9x^4 + 8x^3 - 12x^2 + 4 \\
2x^3 & 4x^6 \\
 & - \\ \hline
4x^3 - 3x^2 & -12x^5 + 9x^4 \\
 & -12x^5 + 9x^4 \\
 & + \quad - \\ \hline
4x^3 - 6x^2 + 2 & 8x^3 - 12x^2 + 4 \\
 & 8x^3 - 12x^2 + 4 \\
 & + \quad - \\ \hline
 & 0
\end{array}
$$

$$\therefore \sqrt{4x^6 - 12x^5 + 9x^4 + 8x^3 - 12x^2 + 4} = 2x^3 - 3x^2 + 2.$$

(ii) Method of undetermined coefficients : The method of undetermined coefficient to find the square root of an algebraic expression is explained in the following example.

Illustration 19 : Find the square root of $x^4 + 4x^3 + 10x^2 + 12x + 9$

Solution : The degree of the given expression is 4, its square root will hence be an expression of degree 2.

Let the expression $ax^2 + bx + c$ to be the square root of $x^4 + 4x^3 + 10x^2 + 12x + 9$

Therefore, $\sqrt{x^4 + 4x^3 + 10x^2 + 12x + 9} = ax^2 + bx + c$

$\Rightarrow$ $x^4 + 4x^3 + 10x^2 + 12x + 9 = (ax^2 + bx + c)^2$

We know that $(p + q + r)^2 = p^2 + q^2 + r^2 + 2pq + 2qr + 2rp$

Here, $p = ax^2$, $q = bx$, $r = c$

$\Rightarrow$ $x^4 + 4x^3 + 10x^2 + 12x + 9$

$= (ax^2)^2 + (bx)^2 + c^2 + 2(ax^2)(bx) + 2(bx)(c) + 2(c)(ax^2)$

$\Rightarrow$ $x^4 + 4x^3 + 10x^2 + 12x + 9 = a^2x^4 + b^2x^2 + 2abx^3 + 2cax^2 + 2bcx + c^2$

Now equating the like terms on either sides of the equality, we have

$x^4 = a^2x^4$

$\Rightarrow$ $a^2 = 1$ $\Rightarrow a = 1$

and $4x^3 = 2abx^3$ $\Rightarrow 2ab = 4$

$ab = 2$, but $a = 1$

$\Rightarrow b = 2$

and $b^2 + 2ca = 10$ $\Rightarrow 2^2 + 2c(1) = 10$ $(\because a = 1, b = 2)$

$2c = 6$

$\Rightarrow c = 3$

$\therefore$ The square root of the given expression is

$ax^2 + bx + c$ i.e., $x^2 + 2x + 3$.

IMPORTANT FORMULAE

Algebraic Identities :

(i) $(x + y)^2 = x^2 + y^2 + 2xy$

(ii) $(x - y)^2 = x^2 + y^2 - 2xy$

(iii) $(x + y + z)^2 = x^2 + y^2 + z^2 + 2xy + 2yz + 2zx$

(iv) $(x + y)^3 = x^3 + y^3 + 3xy\,(x + y)$

(v) $(x - y)^3 = x^3 - y^3 - 3xy\,(x - y)$

(vi) $(x^2 - y^2) = (x + y)\,(x - y)$

(vii) $x^3 + y^3 = (x + y)\,(x^2 - xy + y^2)$

(viii) $x^3 - y^3 = (x - y)\,(x^2 + xy + y^2)$

(ix) $(x^3 + y^3 + z^3 - 3xyz) = (x + y + z)\,(x^2 + y^2 + z^2 - xy - yz - zx)$

(x) Conditional Identity : if $(x + y + z) = 0$, then $x^3 + y^3 + z^3 = 3xyz$

SOLVED EXAMPLES

Example 1

Factorise :

(i) $8a^3 + b^3 + 12a^2b + 6ab^2$ **(ii)** $a^4 + \frac{1}{a^4} - 3$

(iii) $4x^2 + \frac{1}{4x^2} + 2 - 9y^2$ **(iv)** **Factorise :** $y^4 + y^2 - 2ay + 1 - a^2$

Solution

(i) $8a^3 + b^3 + 12a^2b + 6ab^2 = (2a)^3 + b^3 + 6ab(2a + b)$

$= (2a + b)(4a^2 + b^2 - 2ab) + 6ab(2a + b)$

$= (2a + b)(4a^2 + b^2 + 4ab)$

$= (2a + b)(2a + b)^2$

$= (2a + b)^3$

(ii) $(a^2)^2 + \left(\frac{1}{a^2}\right)^2 - 2.(a^2)\left(\frac{1}{a^2}\right) - 1 = \left(a^2 - \frac{1}{a^2}\right)^2 - (1)^2 = \left(a^2 - \frac{1}{a^2} + 1\right)\left(a^2 - \frac{1}{a^2} - 1\right)$

(iii) $4x^2 + \frac{1}{4x^2} + 2 - 9y^2 = (2x)^2 + 2.(2x).\left(\frac{1}{2x}\right) + \left(\frac{1}{2x}\right)^2 - (3y)^2$

$= \left(2x + \frac{1}{2x}\right)^2 - (3y)^2 = \left(2x + \frac{1}{2x} + 3y\right)\left(2x + \frac{1}{2x} - 3y\right)$

(iv) We arrange the expression in powers of a.

We have the given expression.

$= -a^2 - 2ay + 1 + y^2 + y^4$

$= -[a^2 + 2ay - y^2 - y^4 - 1]$

$= -[a^2 + 2ay + y^2 - 2y^2 - y^4 - 1]$

$= -[(a + y)^2 - (y^2 + 1)^2]$

$= -[y^2 + 1 + a + y][-y^2 - 1 + a + y]$

$= [y^2 + 1 + a + y][y^2 + 1 - a - y]$

Example 2

If $f(x) = x^4 - 2x^3 + 3x^2 - ax + b$ is a polynomial such that when it is divided by $(x - 1)$ and $(x + 1)$ the remainders are respectively 5 and 19. Determine the remainder when f(x) is divided by $(x - 2)$.

Solution

When f(x) is divided by $(x - 1)$ and $(x + 1)$ the remainders are 5 and 19 respectively.

$\therefore$ $f(1) = 5$ and $f(-1) = 19$

$\Rightarrow$ $1^4 - 2(1)^3 + 3(1)^2 - a(1) + b = 5$

and $(-1)^4 - 2(-1)^3 + 3(-1)^2 - a(-1) + b = 19$

$\Rightarrow$ $1 - 2 + 3 - a + b = 5$

and $1 + 2 + 3 + a + b = 19$

$\Rightarrow$ $-a + b = 3$ ...(i)

and $a + b = 13$ ...(ii)

From equation (i) and (ii)

We have $a = 5$ and $b = 8$

So, $f(x) = x^4 - 2x^3 + 3x^2 - 5x + 8$

The remainder when f(x) is dividing by $(x - 2)$ is equal to

$= f(2) = 2^4 - 2(2^3) + 3(2)^2 - 5(2) + 8 = 16 - 16 + 12 - 10 + 8 = 10$

Example 3

If both $x - 2$ and $x - \frac{1}{2}$ are factors of $px^2 + 5x + r$, show that $p = r$.

Solution

Let $f(x) = px^2 + 5x + r$ be the given polynomial. Since $x - 2$ and $x - \frac{1}{2}$ are factors of f(x).

$\therefore \quad f(2) = 0$ and $f\left(\frac{1}{2}\right) = 0 \qquad [\because x - 2 = 0 \Rightarrow x = 2$ and $x - \frac{1}{2} = 0 \Rightarrow x = \frac{1}{2}]$

$\Rightarrow \quad p \times 2^2 + 5 \times 2 + r = 0$ and $p\left(\frac{1}{2}\right)^2 + 5 \times \frac{1}{2} + r = 0$

$\Rightarrow \quad 4p \times 10 + r = 0$ and $\frac{p}{4} + \frac{5}{2} + r = 0$

$\Rightarrow \quad 4p + r = -10$ and $\frac{p + 4r + 10}{4} = 0$

$\Rightarrow \quad 4p + r = -10$ and $p + 4r + 10 = 0$

$\Rightarrow \quad 4p + r = -10$ and $p + 4r = -10$

$\Rightarrow \quad 4p + r = p + 4r \qquad [\because$ RHS of the two equations are equal]

$\Rightarrow \quad 3p = 3r$

$\Rightarrow \quad p = r$

Example 4

What must be subtracted from $8x^4 + 14x^3 - 2x^2 + 7x - 8$ so that the resulting polynomial is exactly divisible by $4x^2 + 3x - 2$.

Solution

We know that

Dividend = Quotient × Divisor + Remainder

$\Rightarrow$ Dividend – Remainder = Quotient × Divisor

Clearly, RHS of the above result is divisible by the divisor.

Therefore, LHS is also divisible by the divisor. Thus, if we subtract remainder from the dividend, then it will be exactly divisible by the divisor.

Dividing $8x^4 + 14x^3 - 2x^2 + 7x - 8$ by $4x^2 + 3x - 2$, we get

$$
\begin{array}{r|l}
 & 2x^2 + 2x - 1 \\
4x^2 + 3x - 2 & 8x^4 + 14x^3 - 2x^2 + 7x - 8 \\
 & 8x^4 + 6x^3 - 4x^2 \\
 & - \quad - \quad + \\
\hline
 & 8x^3 + 2x^2 - 7x - 8 \\
 & 8x^3 + 6x^2 - 4x \\
 & - \quad - \quad + \\
\hline
 & -4x^2 + 11x - 8 \\
 & -4x^2 - 3x + 2 \\
 & + \quad + \quad - \\
\hline
 & 14x - 10
\end{array}
$$

$\therefore$ Quotient $= 2x^2 + 2x - 1$ and Remainder $= 14x - 10$

Thus, if we subtract the remainder $14x - 10$ from $8x^4 + 14x^3 - 2x^2 + 7x - 8$, it will be divisible by $4x^2 + 3x - 2$.

Example 5

Find the zeros of the quadratic polynomial $f(x) = abx^2 + (b^2 - ac)x - bc$, and verify the relationship between the zeros and its coefficients

Solution

We have,

$f(x) = abx^2 + (b^2 - ac)x - bc$

$\Rightarrow \quad f(x) = abx^2 + b^2x - acx - bc$

$\Rightarrow \quad f(x)\ bx(ax + b) - c(ax + b)$

$\Rightarrow \quad f(x) = (ax + b)(bx - c)$

The zeros of f(x) are given by

$f(x) = 0$

$\Rightarrow \quad (ax + b)(bx - c) = 0$

$\Rightarrow \quad ax + b = 0$ or, $bx - c = 0$

$\Rightarrow \quad x = -\frac{b}{a}$ or, $x = \frac{c}{b}$

Thus, the zeros of (x) are : $\alpha = -\frac{b}{a}$ and $\beta = \frac{c}{b}$

Now, $\alpha + \beta = -\frac{b}{a} + \frac{c}{b} = \frac{ac - b^2}{ab}$ and $\alpha\beta = -\frac{b}{a} \times \frac{c}{b} = -\frac{c}{a}$

Also, $-\frac{\text{Coefficient of } x}{\text{Coefficient of } x^2} = -\left(\frac{b^2 - ac}{ab}\right) = \frac{ac - b^2}{ab}$

And, $\frac{\text{Constant trem}}{\text{Coefficient of } x^2} = -\frac{bc}{ab} = -\frac{c}{a}$

Hence, Sum of the zeros $= -\frac{\text{Coefficient of } x}{\text{Coefficient of } x^2}$

And, Product of the zeros $= \frac{\text{Constant term}}{\text{Coefficient of } x^2}$

Example 6

Draw the graph of the polynomial $f(x) = -4x^2 + 4x - 1$. Also, find the vertex of this parabola.

Solution

Let $y = f(x)$ or, $y = -4x^2 + 4x - 1$

The following table gives the values of y for various values of x.

x	– 2	–3/2	–1	–1/2	0	1/2	1	3/2	2	5/2	3
$y = -4x^2 + 4x - 1$	– 25	–16	–9	–4	–1	0	–1	–4	–9	–16	–25

Thus the following points lie on the graph of $y = -4x^2 + 4x - 1$:

(– 2, 25), (–3/2, – 16), (– 1, – 9), (– 1/2, – 4), (0, – 1), (1/2, 0), (1, – 1), (3/2, – 4), (2, – 9), (5/2, –16), (3, – 25) etc.

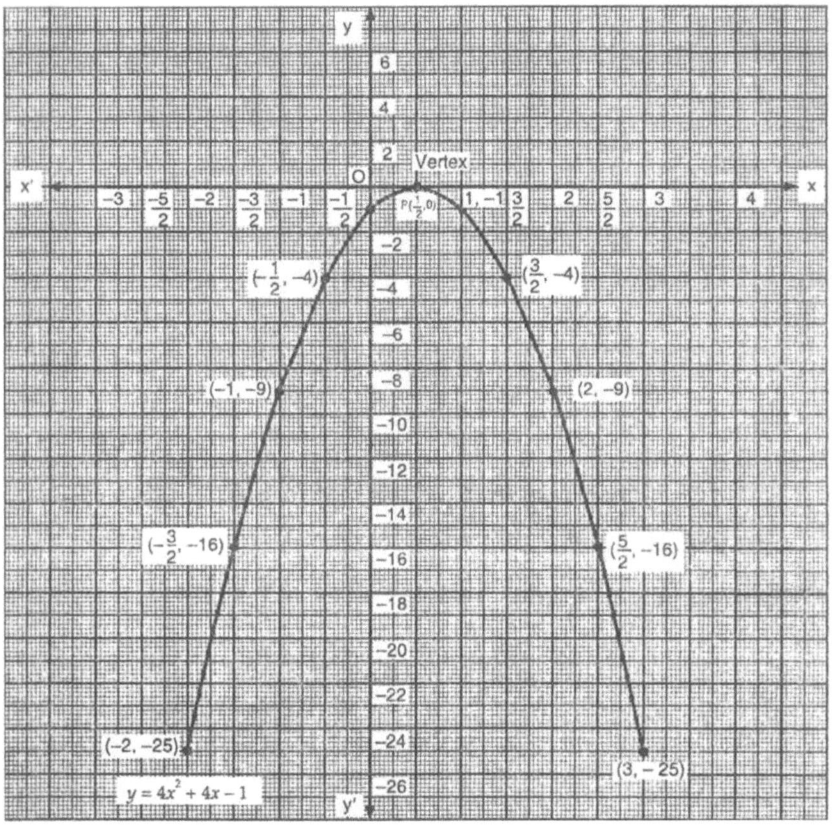

Observations : From the graph of the polynomial $f(x) = -4x^2 + 4x - 1$, we make the following observations

(i) The coefficient of x^2 in $f(x) = -4x^2 + 4x - 1$ is -4m a negative real number and so the parabola opens downwards.

(ii) The polynomial $f(x) = -4x^2 + 4x - 1 = -(2x - 1)^2$ is factorizable into two equal factors equal to $2x - 1$. So, the parabola cuts X-axis at two coincident points having coordinates (1/2, 0).

(iii) The polynomial $f(x) = -4x^2 + 4x - 1$ has two equal roots each equal to 1/2. So, the parabola touches X-axis at one point (1/2, 0) only i.e. it cuts X-axis at coincident points.

(iv) On comparing the polynomial $-4x^2 + 4x - 1$ with $ax^2 + bx + c$, we get $a = -4$, $b = 4$ and $c = 1$.

The vertex of the parabola has the coordinates (1/2, 0) i.e. $\left(\frac{-b}{2a}, \frac{-D}{4a}\right)$,

where $D = b^2 - 4ac$.

(v) $d = b^2 - 4ac = 4 - 4 = 0$. So, the parabola touches X-axis.

Example 7

Obtain all the zeros of $3x^4 + 6x^3 - 2x^2 - 10x - 5$, if two of its zeros are $\sqrt{\frac{5}{3}}$ and $-\sqrt{\frac{5}{3}}$.

Solution

$f(x) = 3x^4 + 6x^2 - 2x^2 - 10x - 5$

Given : $\sqrt{\frac{5}{3}}$ and $-\sqrt{\frac{5}{3}}$ are the zeros of f (x).

$\therefore$ $\left(x - \sqrt{\frac{5}{3}}\right)\left(x + \sqrt{\frac{5}{3}}\right)$ are the factors of f (x).

$\left(x^2 - \frac{5}{3}\right)$ are the factor of f (x) or $(3x^2 - 5)$ are the factor of f (x).

$$\begin{array}{r|l} & x^2 + 2x + 1 \\ \hline 3x^2 - 5 & 3x^4 + 6x^3 - 2x^2 - 10x - 5 \\ & \underset{-}{3x^4} \quad \underset{+}{-} 5x^2 \\ \hline & 6x^3 + 3x^2 - 10x - 5 \\ & \underset{-}{6x^3} \quad \underset{+}{-} 10x \\ \hline & 3x^2 - 5 \\ & \underset{-}{3x^2} \underset{+}{-} 5 \\ \hline & 0 \end{array}$$

So, $3x^4 + 6x^3 - 2x^2 - 10x - 5 = (3x^2 - 5)(x^2 + 2x + 1)$

$$= 3\left(x^2 - \frac{5}{3}\right)(x + 1)^2 = 3\left(x - \sqrt{\frac{5}{3}}\right)\left(x + \sqrt{\frac{5}{3}}\right)(x + 1)^2$$

$\therefore$ Zeros are $\sqrt{\frac{5}{3}}, -\sqrt{\frac{5}{3}}, -1$ and -1.

Example 8

If α, β are zeros of quadratic polynomial $kx^2 + 4x + 4$, find the value of k such that $(\alpha + \beta)^2 - 2\alpha\beta = 24$.

Solution

$f(x) = kx^2 + 4x + 4$

$\alpha + \beta = -\frac{4}{k}, \alpha\beta = \frac{4}{k}$

Now, $(\alpha + \beta)^2 - 2\alpha\beta = 24$

$\Rightarrow \left(-\frac{4}{k}\right)^2 - 2\left(\frac{4}{k}\right) = 24 \qquad \Rightarrow \frac{16}{k^2} - \frac{8}{k} = 24$

$\Rightarrow 24k^2 + 8k - 16 = 0 \qquad \Rightarrow 3k^2 + k - 2 = 0$

$\Rightarrow 3k^2 + 3k - 2k - 2 = 0 \qquad \Rightarrow 3k(k + 1) - 2(k + 1) = 0$

$\Rightarrow (k + 1)(3k - 2) = 0 \qquad \Rightarrow k = -1 \text{ or } k = \frac{2}{3}$.

Example 9

The polynomials $ax^3 + 3x^2 - 3$ and $2x^3 - 5x + a$ when divided by $(x - 4)$ leaves remainders R_1 & R_2 respectively then value of 'a' if $2R_1 - R_2 = 0$.

Solution

$R_1 = a(4)^3 + 3(4)^2 - 3$

$R_1 = 64a + 45$

$R_2 = 2(4)^3 - 5(4) + a = 128 - 20 + a = 108 + a$

Given: $2R_1 - R_2 = 0$

$2(64a + 45) - (108 + a) = 0$

$128a + 90 - 108 - a = 0$

$127a = 18 \qquad \Rightarrow \qquad a = \frac{18}{127}$

CONCEPT APPLICATION LEVEL - I [NCERT Questions]

Q.1 **The graphs of $y = p(x)$ are given in figure for some polynomials $p(x)$. Find the number of zeroes of $p(x)$, in each case.**

(i) 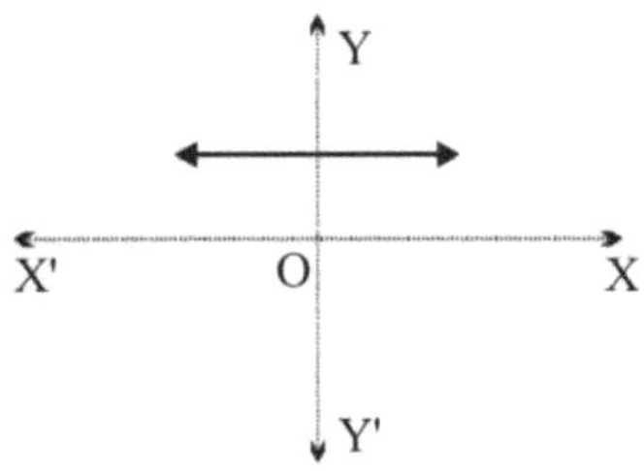

(ii) 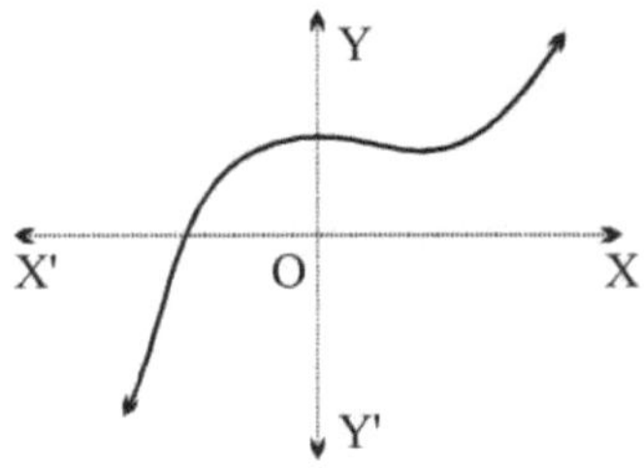

(iii) 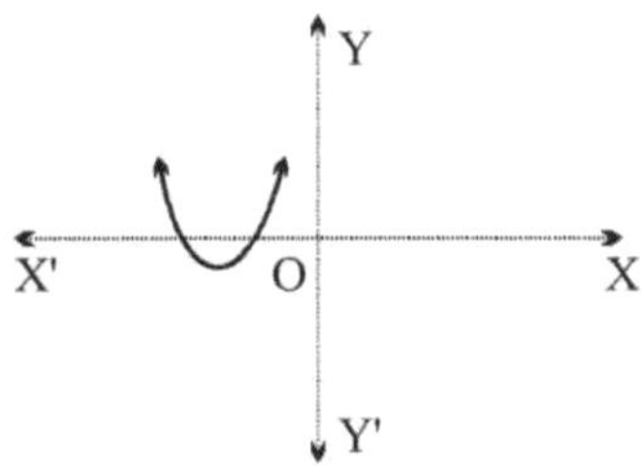

(iv) 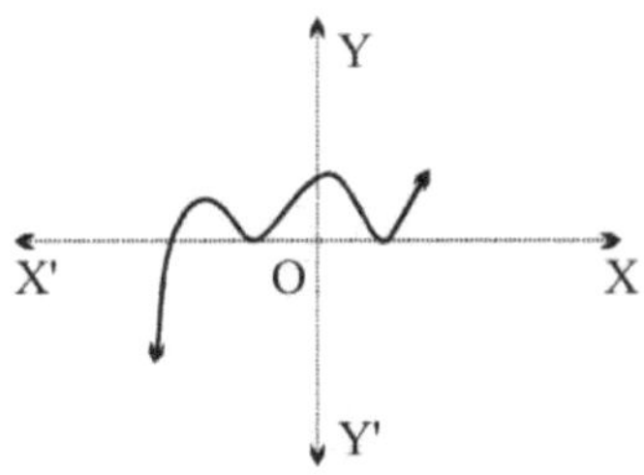

Sol. (i) no zero (ii) one zeroe (iii) two zeroes (iv) three zeroes

Q.2 **Find the Zeroes of the quadratic polynomial $6x^2 - 3 - 7x$ and verify the relationship between the zeroes and the coefficients.**

Sol. $6x^2 - 7x - 3 = 6x^2 - 9x + 2x - 3$

$= 3x(2x - 3) + 1(2x - 3)$

$= (2x - 3)(3x + 1)$

$\because$ $(2x - 3)$ and $(3x + 1)$ are the factors of $6x^2 - 7x - 3$ therefore, $\frac{3}{2}$ and $-\frac{1}{3}$ are the zeroes of $6x^2 - 7x - 3$,

Now, relationship between the zeroes and the coefficients :

(i) Sum of zeroes $= \frac{3}{2} + \left(-\frac{1}{3}\right) = \frac{3}{2} - \frac{1}{3} = \frac{9-2}{6} = \frac{7}{6} = \frac{-(-7)}{6}$

Sum of zeroes $= \frac{-\text{coefficient of } x}{\text{coefficient of } x^2}$

(ii) product of zeroes $= \left(\frac{3}{2}\right)\left(-\frac{1}{3}\right) = -\frac{1}{2} = \frac{-3}{6}$

product of zeroes $= \frac{\text{constant term}}{\text{coefficient of } x^2}$

Q.3 Find a quadratic polynomial with $\frac{1}{4}$ and –1 as the sum and product of its zeroes respectively.

Sol. sum of zeroes $= \frac{1}{4}$

product of zeroes $= -1$

quadratic polynomial $= x^2 - (\text{sum of zeroes})\,x + \text{product of zeroes}$

$$= x^2 - \left(\frac{1}{4}\right)x + (-1) = x^2 - \frac{1}{4}x - 1$$

$$= \frac{4x^2 - x - 4}{4} = \frac{1}{4}(4x^2 - x - 4)$$

or quadratic polynomial $= 4x^2 - x - 4$

Q.4 Divide the polynomial p(x) by the polynomial g(x) and find the quotient and remainder in the following :

$p(x) = x^4 - 3x^2 + 4x + 5, \qquad g(x) = x^2 + 1 - x$

Sol.

$$
\begin{array}{r|l|l}
x^2 - x + 1 & x^4 - 3x^2 + 4x + 5 & x^2 + x - 3 \\
 & x^4 + x^2 \quad\quad -x^3 & \\
 & - \quad - \quad\quad\quad + & \\ \hline
 & x^3 - 4x^2 + 4x + 5 & \\
 & x^3 - x^2 + x & \\
 & - \quad + \quad - & \\ \hline
 & -3x^2 + 3x + 5 & \\
 & -3x^2 + 3x - 3 & \\
 & + \quad - \quad + & \\ \hline
 & 8 & \\ \hline
\end{array}
$$

quotient $= x^2 + x - 3$

remainder $= 8$

Q.5 Check whether the first polynomial is a factor of the second polynomial by dividing the second polynomial by the first polynomial : $x^3 - 3x + 1,\ x^5 - 4x^3 + x^2 + 3x - 1$

Sol.

$$
\begin{array}{r|l|l}
x^3 - 3x + 1 & x^5 - 4x^3 + x^2 + 3x - 1 & x^2 - 1 \\
 & x^5 - 3x^3 + x^2 & \\
 & - \quad + \quad - & \\ \hline
 & -x^3 + 3x - 1 & \\
 & -x^3 + 3x - 1 & \\
 & + \quad - \quad + & \\ \hline
 & 0 & \\ \hline
\end{array}
$$

$\because$ remainder is 0 therefore, $x^3 - 3x + 1$ is a factor of $x^5 - 4x^3 + x^2 + 3x - 1$

Q.6 Obtain all other zeroes of $3x^4 + 6x^3 - 2x^2 - 10x - 5$, if two of its zeroes are $\sqrt{\frac{5}{3}}$ and $-\sqrt{\frac{5}{3}}$.

Sol. Two zeroes are $\sqrt{\frac{5}{3}}$ and $-\sqrt{\frac{5}{3}}$ therefore, $\left(x-\sqrt{\frac{5}{3}}\right)$ and $\left(x+\sqrt{\frac{5}{3}}\right)$ are two factors of $3x^4 + 6x^3 - 2x^2 - 10x - 5$.

now $\left(x-\sqrt{\frac{5}{3}}\right)\left(x+\sqrt{\frac{5}{3}}\right) = x^2 - \left(\sqrt{\frac{5}{3}}\right)^2 = x^2 - \frac{5}{3} = \frac{1}{3}(3x^2 - 5)$

Now dividing $3x^4 + 6x^3 - 2x^2 - 10x - 5$ by $(3x^2 - 5)$,

$$
\begin{array}{r|l|l}
3x^2-5 & 3x^4 + 6x^3 - 2x^2 - 10x - 5 & x^2+2x+1 \\
 & 3x^4 \quad\quad - 5x^2 & \\
 & - \quad\quad\quad + & \\
\hline
 & +6x^3 + 3x^2 - 10x - 5 & \\
 & +6x^3 \quad\quad - 10x & \\
 & - \quad\quad\quad + & \\
\hline
 & 3x^2 - 5 & \\
 & 3x^2 - 5 & \\
 & - \quad + & \\
\hline
 & 0 &
\end{array}
$$

Quotient $= x^2 + 2x + 1 = (x + 1)^2 = (x + 1)(x + 1)$
therefore, other two zeroes are $-1, -1$.

Q.7 On dividing $x^3 - 3x^2 + x + 2$ by a polynomial g(x), the quotient and remainder were $x - 2$ and $-2x + 4$, respectively. Find g(x).

Sol. Division algorithm:

dividend = quotient × divisor + remainder

$x^3 - 3x^2 + x + 2 = (x - 2) \times g(x) + (-2x + 4)$

or $g(x) = \dfrac{x^3 - 3x^2 + x + 2 + 2x - 4}{x - 2}$

or $g(x) = \dfrac{x^3 - 3x^2 + 3x - 2}{x - 2} = \dfrac{(x^2 - x + 1)(x - 2)}{(x - 2)} = x^2 - x + 1$

Q.8 Find a cubic polynomial with the sum, sum of the product of its zeroes taken two at a time, and the product of its zeroes as 2, –7, – 14 respectively.

Sol. Sum of zeroes = 2

Sum of the product of the zeroes taken two at a time = – 7

product of zeroes = –14

Cubic polynomial

$= x^3 -$ (sum of zeroes) $x^2 +$ (sum of the product of the zeroes taken two at a time) $x -$ product of zeroes

$= x^3 - 2x^2 + (-7)x - (-14)$

$= x^3 - 2x^2 - 7x + 14$

Q.9 If the zeroes of the polynomial $x^3 - 3x^2 + x + 1$ **are** $a - b, a, a + b$**, find a and b.**

Sol. $(a - b)$, a and $(a + b)$ are zeroes of $x^3 - 3x^2 + x + 1$

or $x^3 - 3x^2 + x + 1 = x^3 - [(a - b) + (a) + (a + b)]\,x^2 + [(a - b)(a) + (a)(a + b) + (a + b)(a - b)]x$
$- (a-b)(a)(a + b)$

$= x^3 - (3a)\,x^2 + (a^2 - ab + a^2 + ab + a^2 - b^2)\,x - a(a^2 - b^2)$

or $x^3 - 3x^2 + x + 1 = x^3 - 3ax^2 + (3a^2 - b^2)x - a(a^2 - b^2)$

Comparing both sides, we get.

$-3a = -3$

$\Rightarrow$ $a = 1$ [on comparing coefficients of x^2]

and $3a^2 - b^2 = 1$ [on comparing coefficients of x]

$\Rightarrow$ $3(1)^2 - b^2 = 1 \Rightarrow 3 - b^2 = 1 \Rightarrow b = \pm\sqrt{2}$

$a = 1, b = \pm\sqrt{2}$ Ans.

Q.10 If the polynomial $x^4 - 6x^3 + 16x^2 - 25x + 10$ **is divided by another polynomial** $x^2 - 2x + K$**, the remainder comes out to be** $x + a$**, find K and a.**

Sol.

$$
\begin{array}{l|l|l}
x^2 - 2x + K & x^4 - 6x^3 + 16x^2 - 25x + 10 & x^2 - 4x + (8 - K) \\
 & x^4 - 2x^3 + Kx^2 & \\
 & - \quad + \quad - & \\
\hline
 & -4x^3 + (16 - K)\,x^2 - 25x + 10 & \\
 & -4x^3 + 8x^2 \qquad - 4Kx & \\
 & + \quad - \qquad + & \\
\hline
 & (8-K)\,x^2 + (4K - 25)\,x + 10 & \\
 & (8-K)\,x^2 - 2(8 - K)\,x + K(8 - K) & \\
 & - \quad + \quad - & \\
\hline
 & (-25 + 16 + 2K)\,x + 10 - 8K + K^2 &
\end{array}
$$

Remainder $= (-9 + 2K)\,x + (K^2 - 8K + 10)$

or $(-9 + 2K)x + (K^2 - 8K + 10) = x + a$ (given)

Comparing both sides,

$-9 + 2K = 1$ (on comparing coefficients of x)

$2K = 10$

or $K = 5$

and $K^2 - 8K + 10 = a$ (On comparing constant terms)

$(5)^2 - 8 \times 5 + 10 = a$

or $a = 25 - 40 + 10$

$a = 35 - 40$ or $a = -5$

CONCEPT APPLICATION LEVEL - II [Previous Year Questions]

Multiple choice questions with one correct answer.(From Q.1 to Q. 13)

Q.1 Which polynomial represents $(3x^2 + x - 4)(2x - 5)$?
(A) $6x^3 - 13x^2 - 13x - 20$ (B) $6x^3 - 13x^2 - 13x + 20$
(C) $6x^3 - 13x^2 + 13x - 20$ (D) $6x^3 + 13x^2 + 3x + 20$ **(IMO, 2011)**

Q.2 $2x + 7 \overline{\big) 2x^4 + 21x^3 + 35x^2 - 37x + 46}$ =

(A) $x^3 - 7x^2 - 7x + 6 - \dfrac{4}{2x+7}$ (B) $2x^3 + 14x^2 - 14x + 12 - \dfrac{4}{2x+7}$

(C) $x^3 - 7x^2 + 7x - 6 + \dfrac{4}{2x+7}$ (D) $x^3 + 7x^2 - 7x + 6 + \dfrac{4}{2x+7}$ **(IMO, 2011)**

Q.3 If α and β are the zeros of the polynomial $f(x) = x^2 - 5x + K$ such that $\alpha - \beta = 1$, then find the value of K.
(A) 5 (B) 6 (C) 7 (D) 2 **(IMO, 2012)**

Q.4 When $6x^3 + 11x^2 - 39x - 65$ is divided by $(x^2 - 1 + x)$ then the remainder is :
(A) $-38x - 60$ (B) $-40x + 5$ (C) $-21x - 20$ (D) $31x + 60$ **(IMO, 2012)**

Q.5 Find a quadratic polynomial whose zeroes are $(2\alpha + 1)$ and $(2\beta + 1)$ if α and β are the zeroes of the polynomial $f(t) = 2t^2 - 7t + 6$. **(IMO, 2012)**
(A) $2t^2 - 9t + 10$ (B) $t^2 - 9t + 20$ (C) $t^2 - 7t + 10$ (D) $2t^2 - 7t + 10$

Q.6 Simplify : $\dfrac{3}{(x-1)} - \dfrac{2}{x} + \dfrac{(x-3)}{(x-1)(x-1)}$ **(NIMO, Level-I)**

(A) $\dfrac{2x^2 + 6x + 2}{x^3 - x}$ (B) $\dfrac{2x^2 + 6x + 2}{x - 1}$ (C) $\dfrac{2x^2 + 6x}{x - 1}$ (D) None of these

Q.7 The zeroes of the polynomial $f(x) = 3x^2 - x - 4$ are : **(NIMO 2011)**

(A) $-\dfrac{4}{3}, \dfrac{-4}{3}$ (B) $\dfrac{4}{3}, -1$ (C) $\dfrac{-4}{3}, \dfrac{4}{3}$ (D) $\dfrac{-4}{3}, -1$

Q.8 The cubic polynomial whose three roots are 4, –2 and –4 is : **(NIMO 2011)**
(A) $x^3 + 2x^2 - 16x - 32$ (B) $x^3 + 2x^2 + 16x + 32$
(C) $x^3 + 2x^2 - 16x + 32$ (D) $x^3 + 2x^2 + 16x - 32$

Q.9 Divide the polynomial $g(x) = x^3 - 3x^2 + 3x - 5$ by the polynomial $h(x) = x^2 + x + 1$ and the quotient and remainder are : **(NIMO 2011)**
(A) $(x - 4, 6x - 1)$ (B) $(x + 4, 6x + 1)$ (C) $(x^2 + 1, 3x + 2)$ (D) $(x^2 + 1, x - 2)$

Q.10 If a quadratic polynomial of the form $x^2 + ax + b$ has no linear term and the constant term is negative, then: **(5th NIMO Level-I)**

(A) one of the zeroes is reciprocal of the other (B) one of the zeroes is negative of the other.
(C) one of the zeroes is twice of the other (D) one of the zeroes is half of the other

Q.11 If $x = \sqrt{7} - \sqrt{5}$, $y = \sqrt{5} - \sqrt{3}$ and $z = \sqrt{3} - \sqrt{7}$, then the value of $x^3 + y^3 + z^3 - 2xyz$ is :

(A) $-4\sqrt{5} - 12\sqrt{3} + \sqrt{7}$ (B) $-4\sqrt{5} + 2\sqrt{3} + 2\sqrt{7}$
(C) $4\sqrt{5} + 12\sqrt{3} + 2\sqrt{7}$ (D) $4\sqrt{5} - 12\sqrt{3} + \sqrt{7}$ **(5th NIMO Level-I)**

Q.12 If x, y and z are real numbers such that $x + y + z = 5$ and $xy + yz + zx = 3$, what is the largest value that x can have ? **(5th NIMO Level-I)**

(A) $\frac{5}{3}$ (B) $\sqrt{19}$ (C) $\frac{13}{3}$ (D) None of these

Q.13 Graph drawn from the equation $y = x^2 - 3x - 4$ will be : **(NTSE 2013)**

(A) Circle (B) Parabola (C) Straight Line (D) Hyperbola

Q.14 Let $p_1(x) = ax^2 - bx - c$, $p_2(x) = bx^2 - cx - a$, $p_3(x) = cx^2 - ax - b$ be three quadratic polynomials where a, b, c are non-zero real numbers. Suppose there exists a real number such that $p_1(\alpha) = p_2(\alpha) = p_3(\alpha)$. Prove that $a = b = c$. **(RMO 2010)**

Q.15 If the zero of the polynomial $f(x) = k^2x^2 - 17x + k + 2 (k > 0)$ are reciprocal of each other, then the value of k is **[Delhi NTSE Stage-1_2013]**

(A) 2 (B) –1 (C) –2 (D) 1

Q.16 If x, y, z are positive real numbers and a, b, c are rational numbers, then the value of

$$\frac{1}{1+x^{b-a}+x^{c-a}} + \frac{1}{1+x^{a-b}+x^{c-b}} + \frac{1}{1+x^{b-c}+x^{a-c}}$$ **[Raj.NTSE Stage-1_2014]**

(A) –1 (B) 0 (C) 1 (D) None of these

Q.17 If $x^2 - x - 1 = 0$, then the value of $x^3 - 2x + 1$ is **[Harayana NTSE Stage-1_2014]**

(A) 0 (B) 2 (C) $\frac{1+\sqrt{5}}{2}$ (D) $\frac{1-\sqrt{5}}{2}$

Q.18 The graph of $y = p(x)$ is given below. The number of zeroes of polynomial p(x), is **[Raj. NTSE Stage-1_2015]**

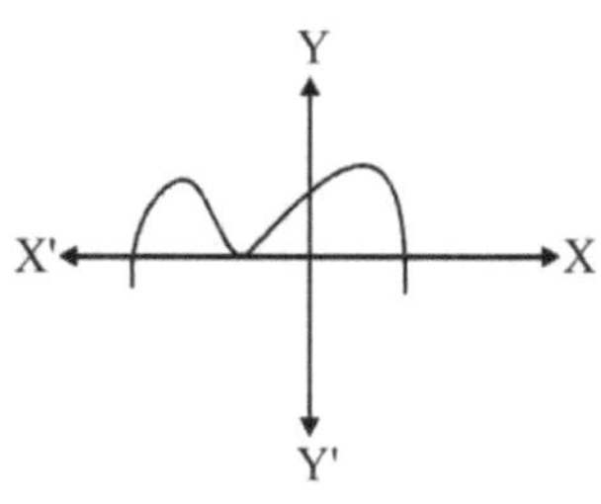

(A) 3 (B) 2 (C) 1 (D) 0

Q.19 On dividing $6x^3 + 8x^2 - 3x + 8$ by a polynomial g(x), the quotient and remainder were $3x + 4$ and $6x + 20$, respectively. Find g(x) **[IMO - 2016]**

(A) $2x - 3$ (B) $2x^2 + 4$ (C) $3x^2 - 4$ (D) $2x^2 - 3$

Q.20 Find the number of zeroes of f(x), in each case **[IMO - 2016]**

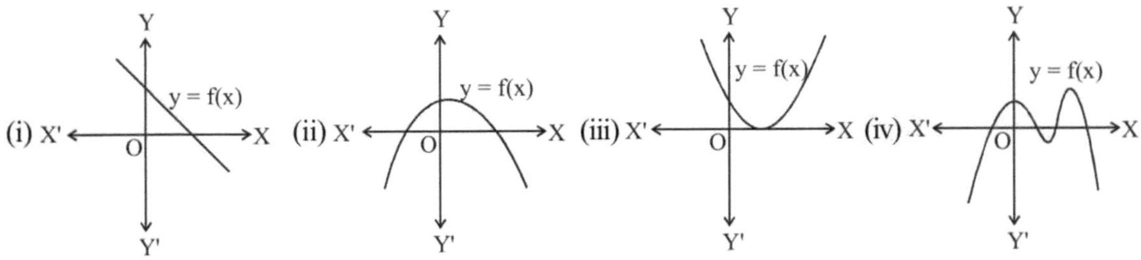

	(i)	(ii)	(iii)	(iv)
(A)	1	2	1	4
(B)	1	2	4	1
(C)	4	2	1	4
(D)	1	2	3	4

Q.21 The cube root of $x + y + 3x^{\frac{1}{3}}y^{\frac{1}{3}}\left(x^{\frac{1}{3}} + y^{\frac{1}{3}}\right)$ is **[NTSE - 2016]**

(A) $x + y$ (B) $x^{\frac{1}{3}} + y^{\frac{1}{3}}$ (C) $(x + y)^{\frac{1}{3}}$ (D) $(x + y)^3$

Q.22 If $\left(x + \sqrt{2}\right)$ is a factor $kx^2 - \sqrt{2}x + 1$, then the value of k is **[NTSE - 2016]**

(A) $\frac{-3}{2}$ (B) $\frac{-2}{3}$ (C) $\frac{3}{2}$ (D) $\frac{2}{3}$

Q.23 If $a = x - y$, $b = y - z$ and $c = z - x$ then the value of $a^3 + b^3 + c^3$ is **[NTSE - 2016]**

(A) $3(x - y)(y - z)(z - x)$ (B) $(x - y)^3 (y - z)^3 (z - x)^3$

(C) $(x + y + z)^3$ (D) $x^3 + y^3 + z^3$

CONCEPT APPLICATION LEVEL - III

SECTION-A

- **Fill in the blanks**

1. A polynomial of degree 1 is called __________.
2. A quadratic polynomial can have __________ zeros.
3. If α, β, γ are the zeroes of the cubic polynomial $ax^3 + bx^2 + cx + d = 0$ then $\alpha\beta + \beta\gamma + \alpha\gamma =$ __________
4. Graph of a quadratic polynomial $p(x) = ax^2 + bx + c$ is a __________ open. If $a < 0$.
5. If discriminant $D < 0$, a quadratic polynomial $ax^2 + bx + c$ has _________ real roots.

SECTION-B

- **Multiple choice questions with one correct answer**

Q.1 Zero of $p(x) = x^2 - 2x - 3$ is :

(A) 0 (B) 1 (C) –1 (D) –3

Q.2 If one root of the polynomial $5x^2 + 13x + K$ is reciprocal of the other, then the value of k is :

(A) 0 (B) 5 (C) 6 (D) 1/6

Q.3 If α, β are the zeroes of the polynomial $f(x) = x^2 - p(x + 1) - c$ then $(\alpha + 1)(\beta + 1)$ is equal to :

(A) $1 + c$ (B) $1 - c$ (C) $c - 1$ (D) c

Q.4 Quadratic polynomial having zeroes 1 and –2 is :

(A) $x^2 - x + 2$ (B) $x^2 - x - 2$ (C) $x^2 + x - 2$ (D) $x^2 + x + 2$

Q.5 If a, b, c are three natural numbers such that c is a factor of ab and c is coprime to a then :

(A) b is a factor of c (B) c is a factor of b (C) a is a factor of b (D) b is a factor of a

Q.6 If deg p(x) = m and deg q(x) = n, then deg [p(x) – q(x)] equal to:

(A) max {m, n} (B) min {m, n} (C) m + n (D) m – n

Q.7 p(x) and q(x) are two reducible (factorisable) unequal polynomial with real coefficient and neither of them is a factor of the other. If ℓ and h are their LCM and HCF respectively, then ℓ and h must satisfy the equality:

(A) $\ell p(x) = hq(x)$ (B) $hp(x) = \ell q(x)$ (C) $p(x)q(x) = \ell h$ (D) $\ell h = 1$

Q.8 The G.C.D. of $(x + a)^2$ and $x^3 + a^3$ is :

(A) $(x + a)^2$ (B) $x^2 - a^2$ (C) $x + a$ (D) $x^2 + a^2$

Q.9 The graph of the polynomial $f(x) = ax^2 + bx + c$ is as shown below, then which of the following is true :

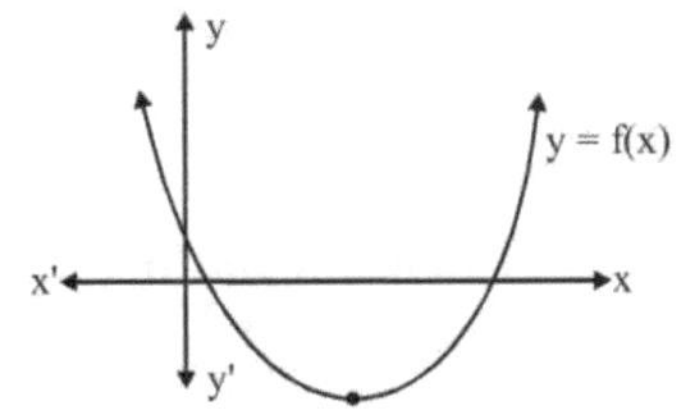

(A) $a > 0, b < 0, c > 0, D > 0$

(B) $a > 0, b > 0, c > 0, D > 0$

(C) $a < 0, b < 0, c > 0, D > 0$

(D) $a < 0, b > 0, c < 0, D < 0$

Q.10 The graph of the polynomial $f(x) = ax^2 + bx + c$ is as shown in fig, then which of the following is true :

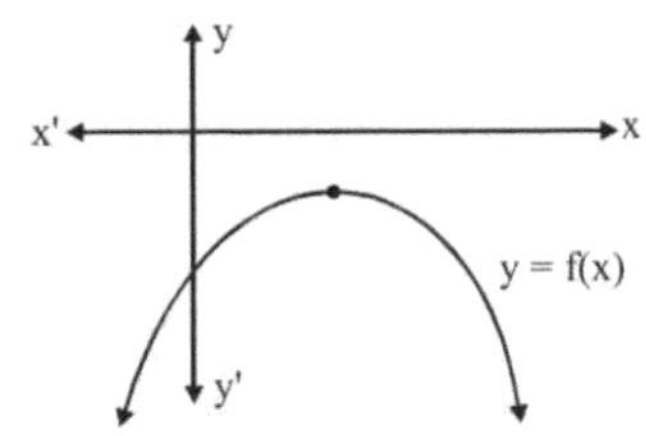

(A) $a > 0, b > 0, c < 0, D < 0$

(B) $a < 0, b > 0, c > 0, D < 0$

(C) $a < 0, b > 0, c < 0, D < 0$

(D) $a < 0, b < 0, c < 0, D > 0$

Q.11 If α and β are the zeroes of the polynomials $f(x) = x^2 - 5x + k$ such that $\alpha - \beta = 1$, then value of k is

(A) 4 (B) –6 (C) 6 (D) 12

Q.12 If zeroes of the polynomial $f(x) = x^3 - 3px^2 + qx - r$ are in A.P, then :

(A) $2p^3 = pq - r$ (B) $2p^3 = pq + r$ (C) $p^3 = pq - r$ (D) None of these

Q.13 If the sum of two roots of the polynomial $f(x) = x^3 - px^2 + qx - r$ is zero, then which of the following condition holds good :

(A) $p^3 = r^3$ (B) $pq = r$ (C) $p^3 - pr + r = 0$ (D) $p^2q^2 = r^3$

Q.14 The coordinates of the vertex of the parabola $4u^2 + 8u$ are :

(A) (–1, 0) (B) (–1, –4) (C) (1, 4) (D) (–1, 4)

Q.15 The product of the zeroes of the polynomial $bx(ax + b) - c(ax + b)$ is :

(A) c/b (B) $\frac{ac - b^2}{ab}$ (C) $-c/a$ (D) $-b/a$

SECTION-C

- **Multiple choice questions with one or more than one correct answers**

Q.1 If the zeroes of a quadratic polynomial $ax^2 + bx + c$ are equal but opposite in sign then :

(A) $a = b - c$ (B) $c = 0$ (C) $b = a$ (D) $b = 0$

Q.2 If the zeroes of a quadratic polynomial $\alpha x^2 + \beta x + \gamma$ are reciprocals of each other then :

(A) $\beta = \alpha$ (B) $\gamma = \alpha$ (C) $\gamma - \alpha = 0$ (D) $\gamma = \alpha + \beta$

Q.3 The polynomials of degree 2 is/are :

(A) $xy + 1$ (B) $x^2 + ax + c$ (C) $x^2 + 5x + y^3$ (D) $xy + yz + xz$

Q.4 If $(x + a)$ is the factor of the polynomials $x^2 + px + q$ and $x^2 + mx + n$, then which of the following is/are true :

(A) $am - pa - n + q = 0$ (B) $am - pm = an + q$

(C) $a = \dfrac{n-q}{m-p}$ (D) $a = \dfrac{m-q}{n-p}$

Q.5 If $(x^2 - 1)$ is a factor of $ax^4 + bx^3 + cx^2 + dx + e$, then which of the following is/are correct :

(A) $a + c + e = b + d$ (B) $a + b + c + d + e = 0$

(C) $a + b + e = c + d$ (D) $a + c + e = 0$

Q.6 What are the value of a for which $3x^5 + 9x^4 - 7x^3 - 5x^2 - 3ax + 3a^2$ is divisible by $x - 1$?

(A) 0 (B) 2 (C) –1 (D) 1

Q.7 What is the remainder when $3x^3 - 2x^2y - 13xy^2 + 10y^3$ is divided by $x - 2y$?

(A) $x + y$ (B) 0 (C) $0x^9$ (D) $x + 2y$

Q.8 If $x - y = 1$ and $x^2 + y^2 = 41$, then the value of $x + y$ will be :

(A) 5 (B) 9 (C) 4 (D) –9

Q.9 If $(x + a)$ is the HCF of $x^2 + px + q$ and $x^2 + \ell x + m$, then the value of 'a' is given by :

(A) $\dfrac{q-m}{p-\ell}$ (B) $\dfrac{p-\ell}{q-m}$ (C) $\dfrac{q+m}{p+\ell}$ (D) $\dfrac{-(m-q)}{p-\ell}$

Q.10 If the polynomial $f(x) = ax^3 + bx - c$ is divisible by the polynomial $g(x) = x^2 + bx + c$, then :

(A) $ab = 1$ (B) $ac - 2b^2 = 0$ (C) $ac = 2b^2$ (D) $ab + 1 = 0$

SECTION-D

- **Assertion & Reason (From Q. 1 to Q. 3)**

Instructions: In the following questions an Assertion (A) is given followed by a Reason (R). Mark your responses from the following options.

(A) Both Assertion and Reason are true and Reason is the correct explanation of 'Assertion'

(B) Both Assertion and Reason are true and Reason is not the correct explanation of 'Assertion'

(C) Assertion is true but Reason is false

(D) Assertion is false but Reason is true

Q.1 **Assertion:** If α, β, γ are the zeroes of $x^3 - 2x^2 + qx - r$ and $\alpha + \beta = 0$, then $2q = r$.

Reason: If α, β, γ are the zeroes of $ax^3 + bx^2 + cx + d$, then $\alpha + \beta + \gamma = \frac{-b}{a}$, $\alpha\beta + \beta\gamma + \gamma\alpha = \frac{c}{a}$,

$\alpha\beta\gamma = \frac{-d}{a}$.

Q.2 **Assertion:** If one zero of polynomial $p(x) = (k^2 + 4)x^2 + 13x + 4k$ is reciprocal of other, then $k = 2$.
Reason: If $x - \alpha$ is a factor of $p(x)$, then $p(\alpha) = 0$, i.e. α is a zero of $p(x)$.

Q.3 **Assertion:** Degree of a zero polynomial is not defined.
Reason: Degree of a non-zero constant polynomial is '0'.

SECTION-E

- **Match the following (one to many)**

Column-I and **column-II** contains **four** entries each. Entries of column-I are to be matched with some entries of column-II. One or more than one entries of column-I may have the matching with the some entries of column-II and one entry of column-II may have one or more than one matching with entries of column-I

Q.1 **Match the polynomials given in column I with their zeros in column II**

	Column I		Column II
(i)	$4 - x^2$	(p)	7
(ii)	$x^3 - 2x^2$	(q)	-2
(iii)	$6x^2 - 3 - 7x$	(r)	2
(iv)	$-x + 7$	(s)	3/2
		(t)	0
		(u)	$-1/3$

ANSWER KEY

CONCEPT APPLICATION LEVEL - II

Q.1	B	Q.2	D	Q.3	B	Q.4	A	Q.5	B	Q.6	D	Q.7	B
Q.8	A	Q.9	A	Q.10	B	Q.11	B	Q.12	B	Q.13	B	Q.15	A
Q.16	C	Q.17	B	Q.18	A	Q.19	D	Q.20	A	Q.21	B	Q.22	A
Q.23	A												

CONCEPT APPLICATION LEVEL - III

SECTION-A

Q.1 Linear polynomial Q.2 At most 2 Q.3 c/a

Q.4 parabola, down wards. Q.5 no

SECTION-B

Q.1	C	Q.2	B	Q.3	B	Q.4	C	Q.5	B	Q.6	A	Q.7	C
Q.8	C	Q.9	A	Q.10	C	Q.11	C	Q.12	A	Q.13	B	Q.14	B
Q.15	C												

SECTION-C

Q.1	D	Q.2	BC	Q.3	ABD	Q.4	AC	Q.5	ABD	Q.6	AD	Q.7	BC
Q.8	BD	Q.9	AD	Q.10	AD								

SECTION-D

Q.1 A Q.2 B Q.3 B

SECTION-E

Q.1 (i) r, q; (ii) r, t; (iii) s, u; (iv) p

3 PAIR OF LINEAR EQUATIONS IN TWO VARIABLES

THEORY

3.1 INTRODUCTION

While solving the problems, in most cases, first we need to frame an equation. In this chapter, we learn how to frame and solve equations. There are given some methods to solve these equations. We will further study about word problems and application of simultaneous equations.

Equation: A statement in which two algebraic expressions are equal is known as equation.

For example: $2x + 3 = 0$, $\frac{2y}{3} + 1 = \frac{y}{3}$

Algebraic expressions: Algebraic expessions are made of numbers, symbols and the basic arithmetical operations. E.g., $x + 3y$, $4x^2 - 2x + 5\sqrt{x}$ are algebraic expressions.

Linear equation: An equation involving linear polynomials is called a linear equation. For example

$\frac{3x}{2} + 4 = 2x - 3$

Remark: A linear equation in one variable has the standard form

$$ax + b = 0, \quad a \neq 0, \text{ a, b} \in R$$

Solution (root) of a linear equation: The value of the variable which makes the two sides of the equation equal and satisfies the equation is called the solution of the equation.

Rules for solving an equation:

(i) The same number is added or subtracted to both sides of an equation, the resulting equation is equivalent to the first.

(ii) If both sides of an equation are multiplied by the same non-zero number the resulting equation is equivalent to the first.

Remark: Every linear equation in one variable has only one (unique) solution.

In this chapter we shall study about system of linear equation in two variables, solution of a system of linear equations in two variables.

3.2 LINEAR EQUATION IN TWO VARIABLES

Definition: $ax + by + c = 0$, is called the standard form of a linear equation in two variables if $a \neq 0$, $b \neq 0$ and $a, b, c \in R$.

Eg.: $3x + 2y = 7$; $2x - \sqrt{3}y = \sqrt{5}$

The equation is linear equation in two variables if

(i) neither x nor y is under a radical sign.

(ii) neither x nor y is in the denominator.

(iii) the exponent (power) of x and y in each term is one.

Simultaneous equation: A pair of linear equations in two variables is said to form a system of simultaneous equation.

Solution of a linear equation in two variables: The pair of values of x and y which satisfies the given equation is called a solution of the equation.

Graphical method of solution of pair (Simultaneous) of line:

Let us consider a linear equation $ax + by + c = 0$ where $a \neq 0$, $b \neq 0$

Step-I: Write down $y = \left(\frac{ax + c}{b}\right)$

Step-II: Substitute any arbitrary value of x in step-I and obtain the corresponding value of y.

Step-III: Plot these points on the graph paper

Step-IV: Join these points. The line thus obtained is the required graph of $ax + by + c = 0$

Consistent system: A system of simultaneous linear equations is said to be consistent, if it has at least one solution.

Inconsistent system: A system of simultaneous linear equations is said to be in-consistent if it has no solution.

Some Important points:

(i) The graph of $x = a$ is a straight line parallel to y-axis.

(ii) The graph of $y = b$ is a straight line parallel to x-axis

(iii) The graph of $y = 0$ is x-axis and graph of $x = 0$ is y-axis.

(iv) If there is no constant term in the equation then the graph of $ax + by = 0$ will pass through the origin.

3.3 ALGEBRAIC METHODS OF SOLVING A PAIR OF LINEAR EQUATIONS

There are four methods for solving a pair of linear equations

(i) Substitution method

(ii) Elimination method

(iii) Cross-multiplication method

(iv) Graphical Method

3.3.1 Substitution method

Step–I: Obtain the two equations: $a_1x + b_1y + c_1 = 0$ and $a_2x + b_2y + c_2 = 0$

Step–II: Find the value of one variable, say y in terms of the other variable.

Step–III: Substitute this value of y in the other equation and reduce it to an equation in one variable.

Illustration 1

Solve the following pair of equations by substitution method:

$2x + 3y = 9;\ \ 3x + 4y = 5$

Solution

Step–I: $2x + 3y = 9$ ....(i) or $y = \left(\frac{9-2x}{3}\right)$ ...(ii)

Step–II: Substituting this value of y in equation $3x + 4y = 5$ from equation (ii)

$$\Rightarrow \quad 3x + 4\left(\frac{9-2x}{3}\right) = 5$$

$$9x + 36 - 8x = 15$$

$$x = 15 - 36$$

$$x = -21$$

Step–III: Putting the value of x in equation (ii),

$$y = \left(\frac{9-2(-21)}{3}\right)$$

$$y = \frac{9+42}{3} \quad \Rightarrow \quad y = \frac{51}{3} \Rightarrow y = 17$$

Therefore the solution of the given system of equations is $x = -21, y = 17$.

3.3.2 Elimination Method

Step–I: Obtain the two equations

Step–II: First multiply both the equations by some suitable non-zero constant to make the coefficient of one variable (either x or y) numerically equal.

Step–III: Add or subtract one equation from the other, then one variable gets eliminated.

Step–IV: Solve the equation in one variable.

Step–V: Substitute the value of x (or y) in any one of the given equations and find the value of another variable.

Illustrations

Illustration 2

Solve the system of linear equations by Elimination method

(i) $4x - y = 5$ (ii) $3x + 2y = 12$

Solution

Equation (i) is multiplied by '2' and adding to the equation (ii) then

$$8x - 2y = 10$$
$$3x + 2y = 12$$

$$11x = 22 \Rightarrow x = 2$$

Putting the value of x in equation (ii)

$$3 \times 2 + 2y = 12 \Rightarrow 6 + 2y = 12$$
$$2y = 6 \Rightarrow y = 3$$

Hence the solution of the given system is $x = 2, y = 3$

3.3.3 Cross Multiplication Method

Step–I: Obtain the two equations : $a_1x + b_1y + c_1 = 0;\ a_2x + b_2y + c_2 = 0$

Step–II:

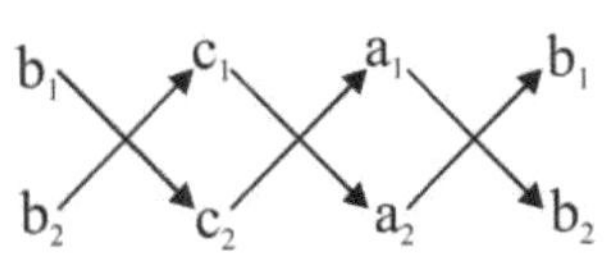

The down arrows (↘) show the term with a plus sign and up arrows (↗) show the term with a negative sign.

Then the solution is given by

$$\frac{x}{b_1c_2 - b_2c_1} = \frac{y}{c_1a_2 - c_2a_1} = \frac{1}{a_1b_2 - a_2b_1}\ ;\ \frac{x}{b_1c_2 - b_2c_1} = \frac{-y}{a_1c_2 - c_1a_2} = \frac{1}{a_1b_2 - a_2b_1}$$

Illustrations

Illustration 3

Solve the system of equation by cross multiplication method

$$\frac{x}{a}+\frac{y}{b}=a+b,\ \frac{x}{a^2}+\frac{y}{b^2}=2$$

Solution

The given equations are

$$\frac{x}{a}+\frac{y}{b}=a+b \quad \Rightarrow \quad bx+ay=ab(a+b);\ \ bx+ay-ab\,(a+b)=0 \qquad .....(i)$$

$$\frac{x}{a^2}+\frac{y}{b^2}=2 \quad \Rightarrow \quad b^2x+a^2y=2a^2b^2;\ \ b^2x+a^2y-2a^2b^2=0 \qquad .....(ii)$$

From equation (i) and (ii),

$bx+ay-ab(a+b)=0;\ \ b^2x+a^2y-2a^2b^2=0$

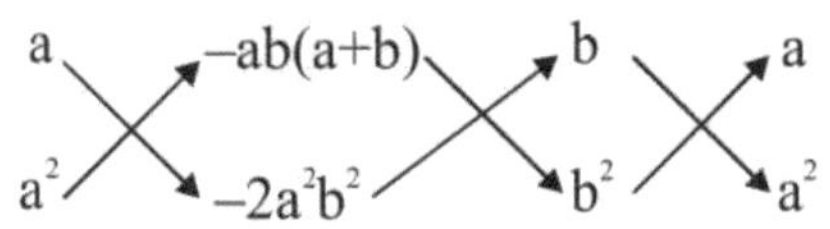

$$\frac{x}{-2a^3b^2+a^3b(a+b)}=\frac{y}{-ab^3(a+b)+2a^2b^3}=\frac{1}{a^2b-ab^2}$$

or $$\frac{x}{-2a^3b^2+a^4b+a^3b^2}=\frac{y}{ab^3\{2a-a-b\}}=\frac{1}{ab\,(a-b)}$$

or $$\frac{x}{a^3b(a-b)}=\frac{y}{ab^3(a-b)}=\frac{1}{ab(a-b)}$$

or $$x=\frac{a^3b\,(a-b)}{ab\,(a-b)}=a^2,\ y=\frac{ab^3\,(a-b)}{ab\,(a-b)}=b^2$$

Hence the solution of the given system of linear equation be $x=a^2$ and $y=b^2$.

3.3.4 Graphical Method:

In graphical method, we draw the graph of both equations using same pair of horizontal and vertical lines called X-axis and Y-axis respectively. Coordinates of the point(s) of intersection of the two lines is/are the solution.

Nature of solutions:

When we try of solve a pair of equations we could arrive at three possible results. They are, having

(a) a unique solution

(b) an infinite number of solutions

(c) no solution

Let the pair of equations be $a_1x + b_1y + c_1 = 0$ and $a_2x + b_2y + c_2 = 0$, where a_1 and a_2 are the coefficients of x; b_1 and b_2 are the coefficients of y; while c_1 and c_2 are the known constant quantities.

(i) If $\frac{a_1}{a_2} \neq \frac{b_1}{b_2}$ then graph will represent two intersecting lines and system has **unique solution** and is known as **consistent pair of linear equations.**

Illustrations

Illustration 4

$4x + 5y = 37$ and $5x + 4y = 35$, for these two equations, $a_1 = 4, a_2 = 5, b_1 = 5, b_2 = 4, c_1 = -37, c_2 = -35$.

Solution

$$\therefore \quad \frac{a_1}{a_2} \neq \frac{b_1}{b_2} \quad \Rightarrow \quad \frac{4}{5} \neq \frac{5}{4}.$$

The above pair of equations has a unique solution.

(ii) If $\frac{a_1}{a_2} = \frac{b_1}{b_2} \neq \frac{c_1}{c_2}$ then graph will represent two parallel lines and system has **no common solution** and is known as **inconsistent pair of linear equations.**

Illustrations

Illustration 5

$6x + 5y = 16$ and $12x + 10y = 50$, for these two equations $a_1 = 6, a_2 = 12, b_1 = 5, b_2 = 10, c_1 = -16, c_2 = -50$.

Solution

$$\text{Therefore, } \frac{a_1}{a_2} = \frac{b_1}{b_2} \neq \frac{c_1}{c_2} \quad \Rightarrow \quad \frac{6}{12} = \frac{5}{10} \neq \frac{-16}{-50}$$

The above pair of equations has no common solution.

(iii) If $\frac{a_1}{a_2} = \frac{b_1}{b_2} = \frac{c_1}{c_2}$ then graph will represent two coinciding lines and system has **infinitely many solutions** and is known as **dependant consistent pair of linear equations.**

Illustration 6

$4x + 7y = 29$ and $12x + 21y = 87$, for these two equations, $a_1 = 4$, $a_2 = 12$, $b_1 = 7$, $b_2 = 21$, $c_1 = -29$, $c_2 = -87$.

Solution

Therefore, $\frac{a_1}{a_2} = \frac{b_1}{b_2} = \frac{c_1}{c_2} \quad \Rightarrow \quad \frac{4}{12} = \frac{7}{21} = \frac{-29}{-87}$

The above pair of equations has infinitely many solutions.

A pair of equations is said to be consistent if equations have a solution (finite or infinite).

Illustration 7

Draw the graph of the equation $x + y = -1$ and $x - y = 5$.

Solution

(i) $x + y = -1$

x	–3	–2	–1	0	1	2	3
y = –1 – x	2	1	0	–1	–2	–3	–4

Some of the ordered pairs which satisfy the equation $x + y = -1$ are

(–3, 2), (–2, 1), (–1, 0), (0, –1), (1, –2), (2, – 3), (3, –4)

(ii) $x - y = 5$

x	–2	–1	0	1	2	3	4
y = x – 5	–7	–6	–5	–4	–3	–2	–1

$\therefore$ Some of the ordered pairs which satisfy the equation $x - y = 5$ are

(–2, –7), (–1, –6), (0, –5), (1, –4), (2, –3), (3, –2), (4, –1)

The ordered pairs which satisfy the equations $x + y = -1$ and $x - y = 5$ are plotted on a graph paper. We find that each equation represents a line.

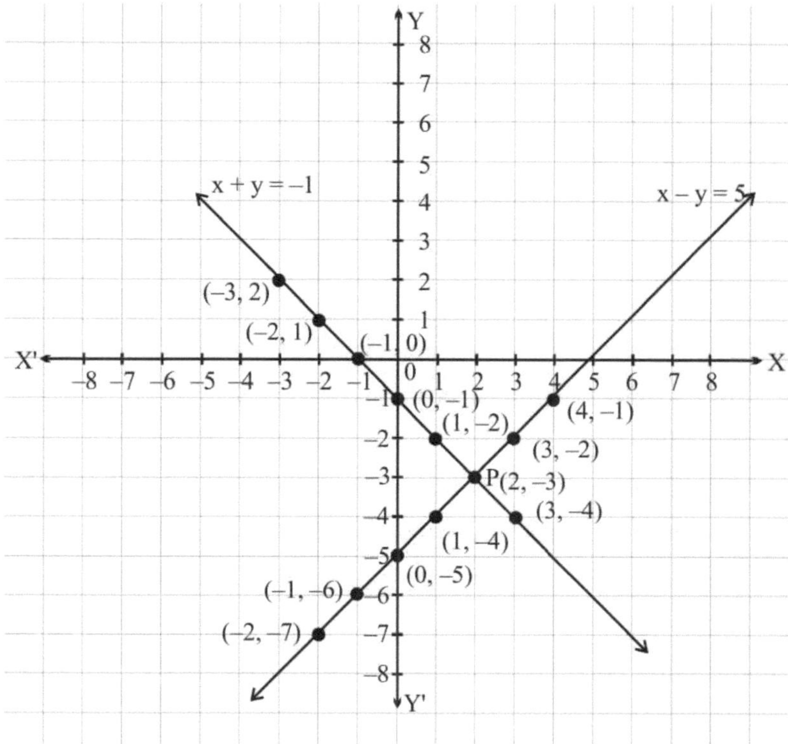

From the graph, we notice that the two given lines intersect at the point (2, –3).

That is, lines $x + y = -1$ and $x - y = 5$ have a common point P(2, –3). Therefore (2, –3) is the solution of the equations $x + y = -1$ and $x - y = 5$.

Verification

$x + y = -1$ .....(1)

$x - y = 5$ .....(2)

Solving (1) and (2), we get,

$x = 2$ and $y = -3$

$\therefore$ (2, –3) is the solution of $x + y = -1$ and $x - y = 5$.

Note : From the above example, we notice that we can find the solution for simultaneous equations by representing them in graph i.e. by using the graphical method.

3.4 DEFINITION OF A STRAIGHT LINE

A straight line is the simplest geometric curve such that every point on the line segment joining any two points on it lies on it.

Slope (Gradient) of a line : The trigonometrical tangent of the angle that a line makes with the positive direction of the x-axis in anticlockwise sense is called the slope or gradient of the line.

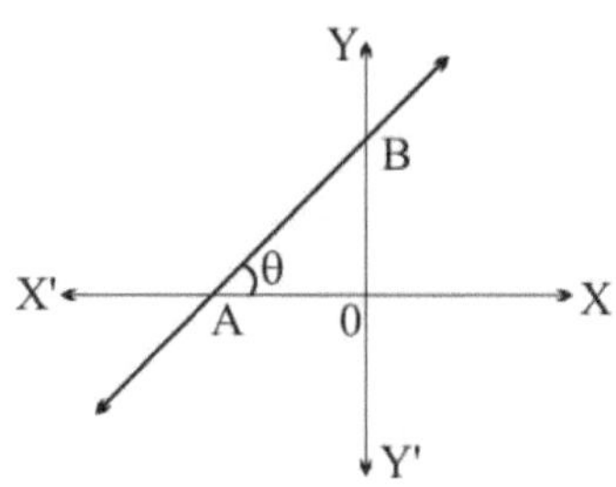

The slope of a line is generally denoted by m. Thus, $m = \tan\theta$.

(i) A straight line parallel to x-axis at a given distance from it.

AB is a straight line parallel to x-axis at a distance b from it. Draw PM perpendicular to the x-axis then OM = x and MP = y

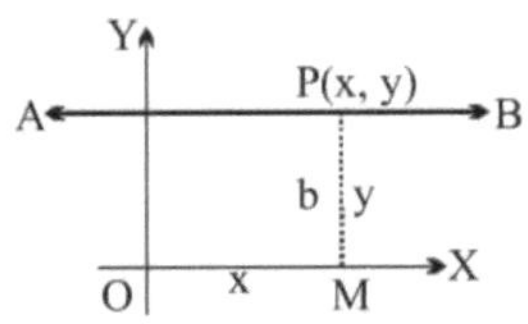

The straight line can be considered as the locus of a moving point P(x, y) whose distance from x-axis is equal to b from all positions of P.

So, MP = b, we get y = b

The equation of the x-axis is y = 0. Since b = 0 in this case.

(ii) A straight line parallel to the y-axis at a given distance from it.

AB is a straight line parallel to y axis at a distance a from it

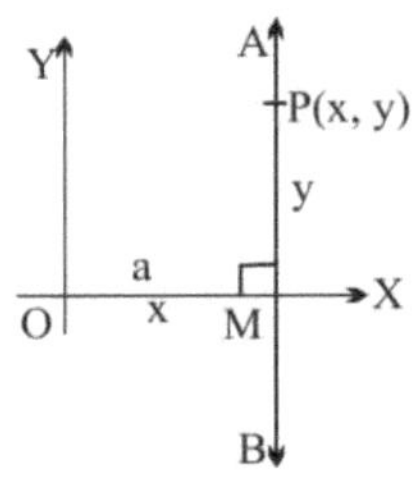

Let PM be the perpendicular from P to the x-axis. Then OM = x and MP = y. Using condition OM = a, we get x = a.

The equation of the y-axis is x = 0 since a = 0 in this case.

Important: The equation of a line parallel to the x-axis does not contain x and the equation of a line parallel to y-axis does not contain y.

3.4.1 Intercept Definition

If a straight line meets the x-axis at A and y axis at B then

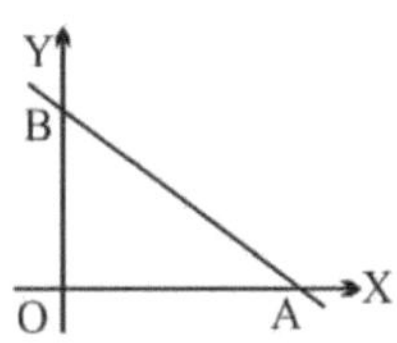

(i) OA (i.e. the distance of A from the origin) is called the intercept made by the line on the x-axis or simply x-intercept.

(ii) OB (i.e. the distance of B from the origin) is called the intercept made by the line on the y-axis or simply y-intercept.

(iii) The two together OA and OB are called the intercepts made by the line on the coordinate axes.

Rules for the signs of the intercepts

(i) The intercept on the x-axis is positive if measured to the right of the origin and negative if measured to the left of the origin.

(ii) The intercept on the y-axis is positive if it is measured above the origin and negative if measured below the origin

(iii) Rule to find intercepts of a line on the axis.

We know that a line cuts the x-axis at a point whose ordinate (y-coordinate) is zero and cuts the y-axis at a point whose abscissa (x-coordinate) is zero. Hence,

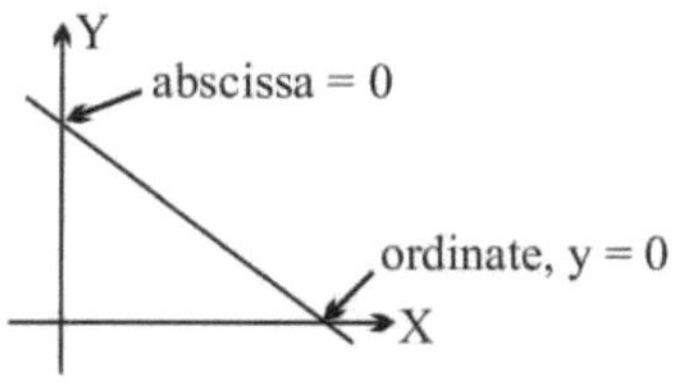

(a) To get the x-intercept we put y = 0 in the equation of the line and find value of x.

(b) To get the y-intercept we put x = 0 in the equation of the line and find the value of y.

3.4.2 Special forms of equation of the straight line

(i) **Slope intercept form:** To find the equation of the straight line whose gradient or slope is m and whose intercept on the y axis is c.

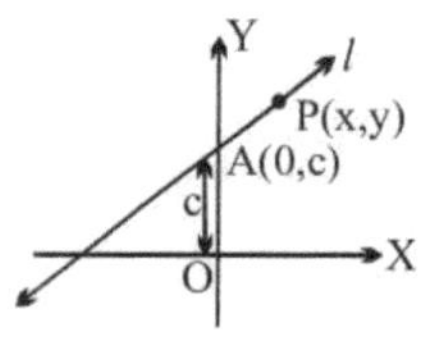

Let l be the line whose intercept OA on the y-axis is c and whose slope is m.

Since, intercept on y-axis = AO = c

Therefore, the coordinates of A are (0,c)

Let P(x, y) be any point on the line

Then, Slope, $AP = \frac{y_2 - y_1}{x_2 - x_1} = \frac{y - c}{x - 0}$

$m = \frac{y - c}{x} \quad \Rightarrow \quad y = mx + c$

which is the required equation

As it invovles slope and y intercept of the straight line. It is some times referred to as slope intercept form.

For example, The equation of the line having slope = –3 and intercept on y axis is = 7 is

$y = mx + c; \; y = -3x + 7$

(ii) **Point Slope form:** The equation of the straight line passing through a given point (x_1, y_1) and having a gradient m is

$$y - y_1 = m(x - x_1)$$

(iii) **Two points form:** The equation of the straight line passing through two given points (x_1, y_1) and (x_2, y_2) is

$$y - y_1 = \frac{y_2 - y_1}{x_2 - x_1}(x - x_1)$$ which is required equation

(iv) **The Intercept form of a line:** A line which cuts off intercept a and b respectively from x-axis and y-axis is

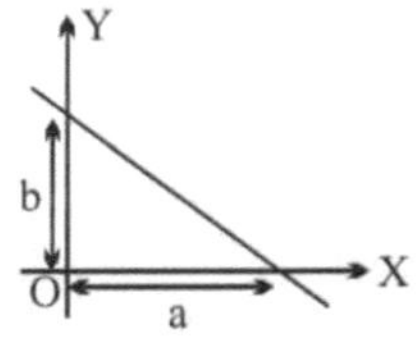

$$\frac{x}{a} + \frac{y}{b} = 1$$

This is the equation of the line in the intercept form.

3.4.3 Angle between two lines:

Angle between two lines : The acute angle θ between the lines having slopes m_1 and m_2 is given by

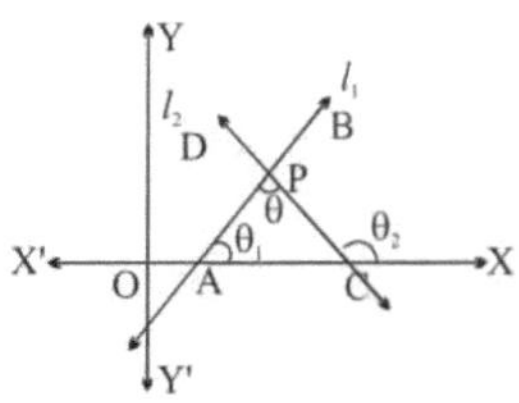

$$\tan\theta = \left|\frac{m_2 - m_1}{1 + m_1 m_2}\right|$$

or $$\tan\theta = \pm\frac{m_2 - m_1}{1 + m_1 m_2}$$

$$m_1 = \tan\theta_1, \; m_2 = \tan\theta_2$$

Condition for two lines to be perpendicular:

If two lines $y = m_1x + c_1$ and $y = m_2x + c_2$ are perpendicular then

i.e. $\theta = 90°$

$\tan\theta = \tan 90°$

or $\tan\theta = \infty$

$$\left|\frac{m_2 - m_1}{1 + m_1 m_2}\right| = \infty$$

$$\mathbf{m_1\, m_2 = -1}$$

When two lines are perpendicular the product of their slopes is –1.

Condition for two lines to be parallel:

If two lines $y_1 = m_1x + c_1$ and $y_2 = m_2x + c_2$ are parallel then their slopes will be equal. In this case angle between these two lines is 0°.

i.e. $\theta = 0°$

$\tan\theta = \tan 0$

or $\left|\frac{m_2 - m_1}{1 + m_1m_2}\right| = 0$

or $m_1 = m_2$

Thus when two lines are parallel their slopes are equal.

Illustration 8

State the equation of the line which has y-intercept –1 and parallel to $y = 5x - 7$.

Solution

Intercept $= -1$, $m = 5$ So equation, $y = 5x - 1$

3.5 SOLVING THE WORD PROBLEMS

Many problems can be solved quickly and easily by converting them into a system of a pair of linear equations in two variables as follows:

(i) Represent the unknown quantities by variable x and y, which are to be determined.

(ii) Find the conditions given in the problem and translate the verbal conditions into a pair of simultaneous linear equations.

(iii) Solve these equations and obtain the required quantities with appropriate units.

Illustration 9

The numerator of a fraction is 4 less than the denominator if the numerator is decreased by 2 and the denominator is increased by 1, then the denominator is eight times the numerator. Find the fraction.

Solution

Let the numerator and denominator of the fraction be x and y respectively.

Then required fraction $= \frac{x}{y}$

$\therefore \quad y - x = 4 \quad .....(1)$

and $\quad y + 1 = 8(x - 2)$

$\Rightarrow \quad y - 8x = -17 \quad .....(2)$

Subtracting (1) and (2),

$y - 8x - (y - x) = -17 - 4$

$-7x = -21 \Rightarrow x = \frac{21}{7} = 3$

$\therefore \quad y = 4 + 3 = 7 \quad \therefore \quad$ Required fraction $= \frac{3}{7}$

3.6 SOLUTION OF A SYSTEM OF A PAIR OF EQUATIONS REDUCIBLE TO THE SYSTEM OF A PAIR OF LINEAR EQUATIONS IN TWO VARIABLES

By using the suitable substitution or simplification first we convert the given system into the system of a pair of linear equations in two variables. Then after using any algebraic or graphical method we solve the system.

Illustrations

Illustration 10

Solve for x and y : $\frac{3}{x}+\frac{4}{y}=1;\ \frac{4}{x}+\frac{2}{y}=\frac{11}{12}$

Solution

$$\frac{3}{x}+\frac{4}{y}=1 \qquad .....(1)$$

$$\frac{4}{x}+\frac{2}{y}=\frac{11}{12} \qquad .....(2)$$

Multiplying (2) by 2

$$\Rightarrow \quad \frac{8}{x}+\frac{4}{y}=\frac{22}{12} \qquad .....(3)$$

Subtracting (1) from (3)

$$\Rightarrow \quad \frac{5}{x}=\frac{10}{12}$$

$$\therefore \quad x=\frac{5\times 12}{10}=6$$

Substituting $x=6$ in (1)

$$\Rightarrow \quad \frac{3}{6}+\frac{4}{y}=1$$

$$\Rightarrow \quad \frac{4}{y}=1-\frac{1}{2}=\frac{1}{2}$$

$\therefore \quad y=8$. Hence, $x=6$ and $y=8$

SOLVED EXAMPLES

Example 1

Solve for x and y : $152x - 378y = -74$ & $-378x + 152y = -604$

Solution

$152x - 378y = -74$ ...(i)

$-378x + 152y = -604$ ...(ii)

Add (i) & (ii)

$-226x - 226y = -678$

$\Rightarrow \quad x + y = 3$ ....(iii)

Subtract (ii) from (i)

$530x - 530y = 530$

$\Rightarrow \quad x - y = 1$ ....(iv)

Solving equation (iii) & (iv)

$x = 2$ and $y = 1$

Example 2

For what value of k, will the following pair of linear equations have no solution? $2x + 3y = 1$ and $(3k - 1)x + (1 - 2k)y = 2k + 3$.

Solution

From the given equations

$a_1 = 2$, $a_2 = 3k - 1$, $b_1 = 3$, $b_2 = 1 - 2k$, $c_1 = -1$ and $c_2 = -(2k + 3)$

The coordination for the given equations to have no solution is

$$\frac{a_1}{a_2} = \frac{b_1}{b_2} \neq \frac{c_1}{c_2}$$

Considering,

$$\frac{a_1}{a_2} = \frac{b_1}{b_2} \quad \Rightarrow \quad \frac{2}{3k-1} = \frac{3}{1-2k}$$

$$\Rightarrow \quad 2(1 - 2k) = 3(3k - 1) \quad \Rightarrow \quad 2 + 3 = 9k + 4k$$

$$\Rightarrow \quad 5 = 13\,k \quad \Rightarrow \quad k = \frac{5}{13}$$

Example 3

For what value of k do the equations $3(k - 1)x + 4y = 24$ and $15x + 20y = 8(k + 13)$ have infinite solutions?

Solution

From the given pair of equations

$a_1 = 3(k - 1)$, $a_2 = 15$, $b_1 = 4$, $b_2 = 20$, $c_1 = -24$ and $c_2 = -8(k + 13)$

The condition for the given equations to have infinite solutions is

$$\frac{a_1}{a_2} = \frac{b_1}{b_2} = \frac{c_1}{c_2} \quad \Rightarrow \quad \frac{3(k-1)}{15} = \frac{4}{20} = \frac{-24}{-8(k+13)}$$

Considering,

$$\frac{3(k-1)}{15} = \frac{4}{20} \quad \text{or} \quad 3k - 3 = \frac{4 \times 15}{20}$$

or $\quad 3k - 3 = 3 \quad$ or $\quad 3k = 6$

or $\quad k = 2$

Example 4

Solve the equations : $\frac{2x+1}{3}+\frac{3y+2}{5}=2$ **and** $\frac{2(2x+1)}{3}-\frac{3(3y+2)}{5}=-1$

Solution

Give equations are : $\frac{2x+1}{3}+\frac{3y+2}{5}=2$ .....(i)

and $\frac{2(2x+1)}{3}-\frac{3(3y+2)}{5}=-1$ .....(ii)

Let $\frac{2x+1}{3}=u$ and $\frac{3y+2}{5}=v$

Then, the equations become

$u+v=2$ .....(iii)

$2u-3v=-1$ .....(iv)

Multiplying (iii) by 3,

$3u+3v=6$ .....(v)

Adding (iv) and (v), $5u=5$

$\Rightarrow$ $u=1$

Substituting this value of u in (iii), $1+v=2 \Rightarrow v=2-1=1$

Then, $\frac{2x+1}{3}=u=1$ and $\frac{3y+2}{5}=v=1$

$\Rightarrow$ $2x+1=3$ and $3y+2=5$

$\Rightarrow$ $2x=3-1=2$ and $3y=5-2=3$

$\Rightarrow$ $x=1$ and $y=1$

Example 5

Solve the following pairs of equations by reducing them to a pair of linear equations

(i) $6x+3y=6xy;\ 2x+4y=5xy$

(ii) $\frac{1}{3x+y}+\frac{1}{3x-y}=\frac{3}{4};\ \frac{1}{2(3x+y)}-\frac{1}{2(3x-y)}=\frac{-1}{8}$

Solution

(i) Given equations are $6x+3y=6xy$ and $2x+4y=5xy$

Dividing both the sides of both the equation by xy, we get $\frac{6}{y}+\frac{3}{x}=6$ and $\frac{2}{y}+\frac{4}{x}=5$

Let $\frac{1}{x}=u$ and $\frac{1}{y}=v$. Equations become $3u+6v=6$ and $4u+2v=5$

or $u+2v=2$ .....(i)

and $4u+2v=5$ .....(ii)

Subtracting (i) from (ii)

we get, $3u=3 \Rightarrow$ $u=1$ and $1+2v=2$ $\Rightarrow v=\frac{1}{2}$

$u=1=\frac{1}{x}$ $\Rightarrow$ $x=1$ and $v=\frac{1}{2}=\frac{1}{y}$ $\Rightarrow y=2$

So, $x=1$ and $y=2$

(ii) Given equation are $\frac{1}{3x+y}+\frac{1}{3x-y}=\frac{3}{4}$ and $\frac{1}{2(3x+y)}-\frac{1}{2(3x-y)}=\frac{-1}{8}$

Let us take $u=\frac{1}{3x+y}$ and $\frac{1}{3x-y}=v$

So, equations become, $u+v=\frac{3}{4}$ and $\frac{u}{2}-\frac{v}{2}=\frac{-1}{8}$

or $4u+4v=3$ and $4u-4v=-1$

Adding both we get $8u=2 \Rightarrow u=\frac{1}{4}$ and $4\times\frac{1}{4}+4v=3 \Rightarrow v=\frac{2}{4}=\frac{1}{2}$

$$u=\frac{1}{3x+y}=\frac{1}{4} \Rightarrow 3x+y=4 \quad .....(i)$$

and $$v=\frac{1}{3x-y}=\frac{1}{2} \Rightarrow 3x-y=2 \quad .....(ii)$$

Adding (1) and (2) we get,

$6x=6 \Rightarrow x=1$

and putting $x=1$ in any equation, say equation (1),

$3\times 1+y=4 \Rightarrow y=1$

So, $x=1, y=1$

Example 6

Solve: $2x-\frac{1}{3}(2y-1)=3\frac{5}{24}+\frac{1}{4}(3x-2y);$

$4y-\frac{1}{4}(5-2x)=6-\frac{1}{5}(3-2y)$

Solution

$$2x-\frac{1}{3}(2y-1)=3\frac{5}{24}+\frac{1}{4}(3x-2y)$$

$$2x-\frac{2y}{3}+\frac{1}{3}=\frac{77}{24}+\frac{3x}{4}-\frac{y}{2} \Rightarrow \frac{5x}{4}-\frac{y}{6}=\frac{69}{24}$$

$$\Rightarrow \frac{5x}{2}-\frac{y}{3}=\frac{69}{24} \Rightarrow 15x-2y=\frac{69}{2} \quad ....(i)$$

$$\Rightarrow 4y-\frac{1}{4}(5-2x)=\frac{6-1}{5}(3-2y) \Rightarrow 4y-\frac{5}{4}+\frac{x}{2}=6-\frac{3}{5}+\frac{2}{5}y$$

$$\Rightarrow \frac{18}{5}y+\frac{x}{2}=\frac{133}{20} \Rightarrow \frac{36y+5x}{10}=\frac{133}{20} \quad ....(ii)$$

By Mlutiplying (ii) by 3 we get, $15x+108y=\frac{399}{2}$. ....(iii)

Ans. $x=2\frac{1}{2}, y=1\frac{1}{2} \Rightarrow -13y=13 \Rightarrow y=\frac{13}{-13} \Rightarrow y=-1$

Example 7

Solve the following system of linear equations for x and y

$a(x + y) + b(x - y) - (a^2 - ab + b^2) = 0$ and $a(x + y) - b(x - y) - (a^2 + ab + b^2) = 0$

Solution

The given system of equations is

$a(x + y) + b(x - y) - (a^2 - ab + b^2) = 0$ and $a(x + y) - b(x - y) - (a^2 + ab + b^2) = 0$

This can be written as

$(a + b)x + (a - b)y - (a^2 - ab + b^2) = 0$ and $(a - b)x + (a + b)y - (a^2 + ab + b^2) = 0$

Here $a_1 = a + b,\ b_1 = a - b$

$a_2 = a - b,\ b_2 = a + b$

and $\frac{a_1}{a_2} \neq \frac{b_1}{b_2}$ i.e. $\frac{a+b}{a-b} \neq \frac{a-b}{a+b}$

Also, $a_1b_2 - a_2b_1 = (a + b)(a + b) - (a - b)(a - b) = (a + b)^2 - (a - b)^2 = 4ab \neq 0$

Therefore, the given system of equations has a unique solution.

Now, we can solve this system of equations by using cross-multiplication method which gives:

$$\Rightarrow \quad \frac{x}{b_1c_2 - b_2c_1} = \frac{y}{c_1a_2 - c_2a_1} = \frac{1}{a_1b_2 - a_2b_1}$$

$$\Rightarrow \quad \frac{x}{-(a-b)(a^2+ab+b^2)+(a+b)(a^2-ab+b^2)}$$

$$= \frac{y}{-(a-b)(a^2-ab+b^2)+(a+b)(a^2+ab+b^2)} = \frac{1}{(a+b)(a+b)-(a-b)(a-b)}$$

$$\Rightarrow \quad \frac{x}{-(a^3-b^3)+(a^3+b^3)} = \frac{y}{2b(2a^2+b^2)} = \frac{1}{4ab}$$

$$\Rightarrow \quad \frac{x}{2b^3} = \frac{y}{2b(2a^2+b^2)} = \frac{1}{4ab}$$

$$\Rightarrow \quad x = \frac{2b^3}{4ab} = \frac{b^2}{2a} \text{ and } y = \frac{2b(2a^2+b^2)}{4ab} = \frac{2a^2+b^2}{2a}$$

Hence, the solution of the system is $x = \frac{b^2}{2a}$ and $y = \frac{2a^2+b^2}{2a}$

Example 8

The difference between two numbers is 2. Their product is 84 greater than the square of the smaller number. What is the sum of numbers.

Solution

smaller = x; larger = y

Let $y - x = 2$ ...(i)

$xy = 84 + x^2$ ...(ii)

From equation (i) & (ii)

$x(x + 2) = 84 + x^2$

$\Rightarrow$ $x = 42$

$\therefore$ from (i) $y = 44$

$\therefore$ $x + y = 86$

Example 9

Astha and Saumya each have certain number of oranges. Astha says to Saumya, "If you give me 10 of your orianges, I will have twice the number of oranges left with you. "Saumya replies, "If you give me 10 of your oranges, I will have the same number of orianges as left with you." Find the number of oranges with Astha and Saumya respectively.

Solution

Let Astha will have x number of oranges and Saumya will have y number of oranges. Then,

$(x + 10) = 2(y - 10) \Rightarrow x - 2y = -30$ ...(i)

and $(x - 10) = (y + 10) \Rightarrow x - y = 20$ ...(ii)

Subtracting equation (ii) from equation (i),

We get, $-y = -50 \quad \Rightarrow y = 50$

$x = 70$

Example 10

A test has 50 questions. A student scores 1 mark for a correct answer, –1/3 for a wrong answer and – 1/6 for not attempting a question. If the net score of a student is 32, find the number of questions answered wrongly by that student cannot be less than.

Solution

Let the number of correct answers be 'x', number of wrong answers by 'y' and number of questions not attempted by 'z'.

Thus, $x + y + z = 50$ ...(i)

And $x - \frac{y}{3} - \frac{z}{6} = 32$

The above equation can be written as,

$6x - 2y - z = 192$ ...(ii)

Adding the two equations we get, $7x - y = 242$ or $x = \frac{242}{7} + \frac{y}{7}$

Since, x and y are both integers, y cannot be 1 or 2.

The minimum value that y can have is 3.

Example 11

At a certain fast food restaurant, Amit can buy 3 burgers, 7 shakes and one order of fries for Rs. 120. At the same place, it would cost Rs. 164.50 for 4 burgers,10 shakes and one order of fries. How much would it cost for an ordinary meal of one burger, one shake and one order of fries ?

Solution

Let the cost of 1 burger, 1 shake and one order of fries be x, y and z. Then

$3x + 7y + z = 120$ ...(i)

$4x + 10y + z = 164.50$ ...(ii)

Subtracting (i) from (ii)

$x + 3y = 44.50$ ...(iii)

Multiplying (iii) by 4 and subtracting (ii) from it,

we find, $2y - z = 13.5$ ...(iv)

Subtracting (iv) from (iii),

we get $x + y + z = 31$.

CONCEPT APPLICATION LEVEL - I [NCERT Questions]

Q.1 On comparing the ratios $\frac{a_1}{a_2}$, $\frac{b_1}{b_2}$ and $\frac{c_1}{c_2}$, find out whether the lines representing the following pairs of linear equations intersect at a point, are parallel or coincident:

(i) $5x - 4y + 8 = 0; 7x + 6y - 9 = 0$

(ii) $9x + 3y + 12 = 0; 18x + 6y + 24 = 0$

(iii) $6x - 3y + 10 = 0; 2x - y + 9 = 0$

Sol. (i)

$$5x - 4y + 8 = 0$$
$$7x + 6y - 9 = 0$$

Here, $a_1 = 5, b_1 = -4, c_1 = 8$

$a_2 = 7, b_2 = 6, c_1 = -9$

We see that $\frac{a_1}{a_2} \neq \frac{b_1}{b_2}$

Hence, the lines representing the given pair of linear equations intersect at a point.

(ii)

$$9x + 3y + 12 = 0$$
$$18x + 6y + 24 = 0$$

Here, $a_1 = 9, b_1 = 3, c_1 = 12$

$a_2 = 18, b_2 = 6, c_2 = 24$

We see that $\frac{a_1}{a_2} = \frac{b_1}{b_2} = \frac{c_1}{c_2}$

Hence, the lines representing the given pair of linear equations are coincident.

(iii)

$$6x - 3y + 10 = 0$$
$$2x - y + 9 = 0$$

Here $a_1 = 6, b_1 = -3, c_1 = 10$

$a_2 = 2, b_2 = -1, c_1 = 9$

We see that $\frac{a_1}{a_2} = \frac{b_1}{b_2} \neq \frac{c_1}{c_2}$

Hence, the lines representing the given pair of linear equations are parallel.

Q.2 On comparing the ratios $\frac{a_1}{a_2}$, $\frac{b_1}{b_2}$ and $\frac{c_1}{c_2}$, find out whether the lines equations are consistent, or inconsistent:

(i) $3x + 2y = 5; 2x - 3y = 7$ (ii) $2x - 3y = 8; 4x - 6y = 9$

Sol. (i) $3x + 2y = 5 ; 2x - 3y = 7$

Here, $a_1 = 3, b_1 = 2, c_1 = -5$

$a_2 = 2, b_2 = -3, c_2 = -7$

$\therefore \quad \frac{a_1}{a_2} = \frac{3}{2}, \frac{b_1}{b_2} = \frac{-2}{3}$ and $\frac{c_1}{c_2} = \frac{-5}{-7}$

We see that $\frac{a_1}{a_2} \neq \frac{b_1}{b_2}$

Hence, the given lines are intersecting.

So, the given pair of linear equations has exactly one solution and therefore it is consistent.

(ii) $2x - 3y = 8; 4x - 6y = 9$

Here, $a_1 = 2, b_1 = -3, c_1 = -8$

$a_2 = 4, b_2 = -6, c_2 = -9$

$\therefore \quad \frac{a_1}{a_2} = \frac{2}{4} = \frac{1}{2}, \frac{b_1}{b_2} = \frac{-3}{-6} = \frac{1}{2}$ and $\frac{c_1}{c_2} = \frac{-8}{-9}$

We see that $\frac{a_1}{a_2} = \frac{b_1}{b_2} \neq \frac{c_1}{c_2}$

Hence, the given lines are parallel. So, the given pair of linear equations has no solution and therefore it is inconsistent.

Q.3 Draw the graphs of the equations $x - y + 1 = 0$ and $3x + 2y - 12 = 0$. Determine the coordinates of the vertices of the triangle formed by these lines and the x-axis, and shade the triangular region.

Sol. The given equations are

$x - y + 1 = 0$ ......(1)

$3x + 2y - 12 = 0$ ......(2)

Let us draw the graphs of equation (1) and (2) by finding two solutions for each of the equation. These two solutions of the equations (1) and (2) are given below in table 1 and table 2 respectively.

For equation (1)

$$x - y + 1 = 0$$

$$\Rightarrow \quad y = x + 1$$

Table 1 of solutions

x	0	–1
y	1	0

For equation (2)

$$3x + 2y - 12 = 0$$

$$\Rightarrow \quad 2y = 12 - 3x$$

$$\Rightarrow \quad y = \frac{12 - 3x}{2}$$

Table 2 of solutions

x	4	0
y	0	6

We plot the points A(0, 1) and B(–1, 0) on a graph paper and join these points to form the line AB representing the equation (1) as shown in the figure. Also, we plot the points C(4, 0) and D(0, 6) on the same graph paper and join these points to form the line CD representing the equation (2) as shown in the same figure.

In the figure we observe that the coordinates of the vertices of the triangle formed by these given lines and the x-axis are E(2, 3), B(–1, 0) and C(4, 0).

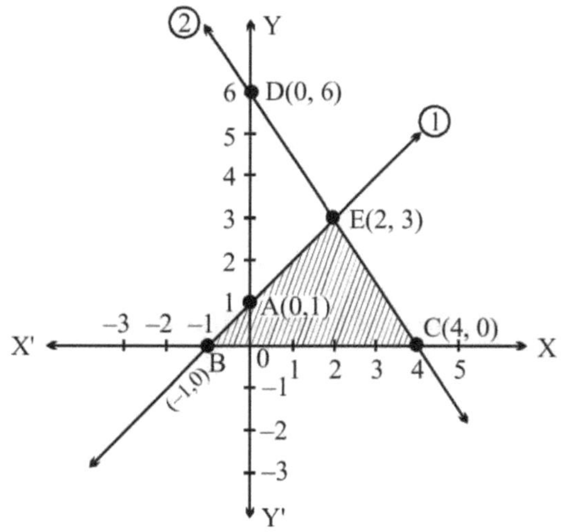

The triangular region EBC has been shaded.

Q.4 Solve the following pair of linear equations by the substitution method

(i) $0.2x + 0.3y = 1.3;\ 0.4x + 0.5y = 2.3$ (ii) $\sqrt{2}x + \sqrt{3}y = 0\ ;\ \sqrt{3}x - \sqrt{8}y = 0$

Sol. (i) The given system of linear equation is

$$0.2x + 0.3y = 1.3 \quad .....(1)$$

$$0.4x + 0.5y = 2.3 \quad .....(2)$$

For equation (1),

$$0.3y = 1.3 - 0.2x$$

$$\Rightarrow \quad y = \frac{1.3 - 0.2x}{0.3} \quad .....(3)$$

Substituting this value of y in equation (2), we get

$$0.4x + 0.5\left(\frac{1.3 - 0.2x}{0.3}\right) = 2.3$$

$$\Rightarrow \quad 0.12x + 0.65 - 0.1x = 0.69$$

$$\Rightarrow \quad 0.12x - 0.1x = 0.69 - 0.65$$

$$\Rightarrow \quad 0.02x = 0.4$$

$$\Rightarrow \quad x = \frac{0.04}{0.02} = 2$$

Substituting this value of x in equation (3), we get

$$y = \frac{1.3 - 0.2(2)}{0.3} = \frac{1.3 - 0.4}{0.3} = \frac{0.9}{0.3} = 3$$

Therefore the solution is $x = 2, y = 3$.

Verification : Substituting $x = 2$ and $y = 3$, we find that both the equations (1) and (2) are satisfied as shown below:

$0.2x + 0.3y = (0.2)\ (2) + (0.3)\ (3) = 0.4 + 0.9 = 1.3$

$0.4x + 0.5y = (0.4)\ (2) + (0.5)\ (3) = 0.8 + 0.15 = 2.23$

This verifies the solution

(ii) The given pair of linear equation is

$$\sqrt{2}x + \sqrt{3}y = 0 \quad .....(1)$$

$$\sqrt{3}x - \sqrt{8}y = 0 \quad .....(2)$$

For equation (2),

$$\sqrt{3}x = \sqrt{8}y \quad \Rightarrow \quad x = \frac{\sqrt{8}}{\sqrt{3}}y \quad .....(3)$$

Substituting this value of x in equation (1), we get

$$\sqrt{2}\cdot\frac{\sqrt{8}}{\sqrt{3}}y+\sqrt{3}y=0 \Rightarrow \frac{4}{\sqrt{3}}y+\sqrt{3}y=0$$

$$\Rightarrow \quad \left(\frac{4}{\sqrt{3}}+\sqrt{3}\right)y=0 \Rightarrow y=0$$

Substituting this value of y in equation (3), we get

$$x=\frac{\sqrt{8}}{\sqrt{3}}(0)=0$$

Therefore the solutions is $x = 0, y = 0$

Verification : Substituting $x = 0$ and $y = 0$, we find that both the equations (1) and (2) are satisfied as shown below:

$$\sqrt{2}x+\sqrt{3}y = \sqrt{2}(0)+\sqrt{3}(0)=0$$

$$\sqrt{3}x-\sqrt{8}y = \sqrt{3}(0)-\sqrt{8}(0)=0$$

This verifies the solution.

Q.5 Form the pair of linear equations for the following problems and find their solution by substitution method.

(i) The larger of two supplementary angles exceeds the smaller by 18 degrees. Find them.

(ii) The coach of a cricket team buys 7 bats and 6 balls for Rs. 3800. Later, she buys 3 bats and 5 balls for Rs.1750. Find the cost of each bat and each ball.

(iii) The taxi charges in a city consist of a fixed charge together with the charge for the distance covered. For a distance of 10 km, the charge paid is Rs. 105 and for a journey of 15 km, the charge paid is Rs.155. What are the fixed charges and the charge per km? How much does a person have to pay for travelling a distance of 25 km?

Sol. (i) Let the larger and the smaller of two supplementary angles be $x°$ and $y°$ respectively.

Then, according to the question.

The pair of linear equations formed is

$$x° = y° + 18° \quad .....(1)$$

$$x° + y° = 180° \quad .....(2)$$ ($\because$ The two angles are supplementary)

Substitute the value of $x°$ from equation (1) in equation (2), we get

$$y° + 18° + y° = 180°$$

$$\Rightarrow \quad 2y° + 18° = 180° \Rightarrow 2y° = 180° - 18°$$

$$\Rightarrow \quad 2y° = 162° \Rightarrow y° = \frac{162°}{2} = 81°$$

Substituting this value of y° in equation (1), we get

$$x^\circ = 81^\circ + 18^\circ = 99^\circ$$

Hence, the larger and the smaller of the two supplementary angles are 99° and 81° respectively.

Verification : Substituting $x^\circ = 99^\circ$ and $y^\circ = 81^\circ$, we find that both the equations (1) and (2) are satisfies as shown below:

$$y^\circ + 18^\circ = 81^\circ + 18^\circ = 99^\circ = x^\circ$$

$$x^\circ + y^\circ = 99^\circ + 81^\circ = 180^\circ$$

This verifies the solution.

(ii) Let the cost of each bat and each ball be Rs. x and Rs. y respectively.

Then, according to the question,

The pair of linear equations formed is

$$7x + 6y = 3800 \quad .....(1)$$

$$3x + 5y = 1750 \quad .....(2)$$

From equation (2),

$$5y = 1750 - 3x$$

$$y = \frac{1750 - 3x}{5} \quad .....(3)$$

Substitute this value of y in equation (1), we get

$$7x + 6\left(\frac{1750 - 3x}{5}\right) = 3800$$

$\Rightarrow$ $35x + 10500 - 18x = 19000$

$\Rightarrow$ $17x + 10500 = 19000$

$\Rightarrow$ $17x = 19000 - 10500$

$\Rightarrow$ $17x = 8500$

$\Rightarrow$ $x = \frac{8500}{17} = 500$

Substituting this value of x in equation (3), we get

$$y = \frac{1750 - 3(500)}{5} = \frac{1750 - 1500}{5} = \frac{250}{5} = 50$$

Hence, the cost of each bat and each ball is Rs. 500 and Rs.50 respectively.

Verification : Substituting x = 500 and y = 50, we find that both the equations (1) and (2) are satisfied as shown below :

$$7x + 6y = 7(500) + 6(50) = 3500 + 300 = 3800$$

$$3x + 5y = 3(500) + 5(50) = 1500 + 250 = 1750$$

This is verifies the solution.

(iii) Let the fixed charges be Rs. x and the charge per kilometer be Rs. y.

Then, according to the question

The pair of linear equations formed is

$x + 10y = 105$ .....(1)

$x + 15y = 155$ .....(2)

From equation (1),

$x = 105 - 10y$ .....(3)

Substitute this value of x in equation (2), we get

$105 - 10y + 15y = 155$

$\Rightarrow \quad 05 + 5y = 155 \quad \Rightarrow \quad 5y = 155 - 105$

$\Rightarrow \quad 5y = 50 \quad \Rightarrow \quad y = \frac{50}{5} = 10$

Substituting this value of y in equation (3), we get

$x = 105 - 10(10) = 105 - 100 = 5$

Hence, the fixed charges are Rs.5 and the charge per kilometer is Rs.10.

Verification: Substituting x = 5 and y = 10, we find that both the equation (1) and (2) are satisfied as shown below:

$x + 10y = 5 + 10(10) = 5 + 100 = 105$

$x + 15y = 5 + 15(10) = 5 + 150 = 155$

This verifies the solution.

Again, for travelling a distance of 25 km, a person will have to pay $= 5 + 10(25)$

$= 5 + 250 = 255$ Rs.

Q.6 Solve the following pair of linear equations by the elimination method and the substitution method:

(i) $3x - 5y - 4 = 0$ and $9x = 2y + 7$ **(ii) $\frac{x}{2} + \frac{2y}{3} = -1$ and $x - \frac{y}{3} = 3$**

Sol. (i) **(I) By Elimination method**

The given system of equations is

$3x - 5y - 4 = 0$ ....(1)

$9x = 2y + 7$

$\Rightarrow \quad 9x - 2y - 7 = 0$ .....(2)

Multiplying equation (1) by 3, we get

$9x - 15y - 12 = 0$ .....(3)

Substracting equation (3) from equation (2), we get

$13y + 5 = 0 \quad \Rightarrow \quad 13y = -5 \quad \Rightarrow \quad y = \frac{-5}{13}$

Substituting this value of y in equation (1), we get

$$3x - 5\left(\frac{-5}{13}\right) - 4 = 0$$

$$\Rightarrow \quad 3x - \frac{27}{13} = 0 \Rightarrow 3x = \frac{27}{13} \Rightarrow x = \frac{9}{13}$$

So, the solution of the given system of equations is $x = \frac{9}{13}, y = \frac{-5}{13}$.

(II) By Substitution method

The given system of equations is

$$3x - 5y - 4 = 0 \quad .....(1)$$

$$9x = 2y + 7 \quad .....(2)$$

From equation (2)

$$x = \frac{2y+7}{9} \quad .....(3)$$

Substitute this value of x in equation (1), we get

$$3\left(\frac{2y+7}{9}\right) - 5y - 4 = 0$$

$$\Rightarrow \quad \frac{2y+7}{9} - 5y - 4 = 0 \quad \Rightarrow \quad 2y + 7 - 15y - 12 = 0$$

$$\Rightarrow \quad -13y - 5 = 0 \quad \Rightarrow \quad 13y = -5 \quad \Rightarrow \quad y = \frac{-5}{13}$$

Substituting this value of y in equation (3), we get

$$x = \frac{2\left(\frac{-5}{13}\right) + 7}{9} = \frac{-\frac{10}{13} + 7}{9} = \frac{-10+91}{117} = \frac{81}{117} = \frac{9}{13}$$

So, the solution of the given system of equations is

$$x = \frac{9}{13}, y = \frac{-5}{13}$$

Verification : Substituting $x = \frac{9}{13}$, $y = \frac{-5}{13}$, we find that both the equation (1) and (2) are satisfied as shown below:

$$3x - 5y - 4 = 3\left(\frac{9}{13}\right) - 5\left(\frac{-5}{13}\right) - 4 = \frac{27}{13} + \frac{25}{13} - 4 = \frac{52}{13} - 4 = 4 - 4 = 0$$

$$2y + 7 = 2\left(\frac{-5}{13}\right) + 7 = \frac{-10}{13} + 7 = \frac{81}{13} = 9\left(\frac{9}{13}\right) = 9x$$

Hence, the solution is correct.

(ii) **(I) By Elimination method**

The given system of equations as

$$\frac{x}{2}+\frac{2y}{3}=-1 \qquad .....(1)$$

$$x-\frac{y}{3}=3 \qquad .....(2)$$

Multiplying equation (2) by 2, we get

$$2x-\frac{2y}{3}=6 \qquad .....(3)$$

Adding equation (1) and equation (3), we get

$$\frac{5}{2}x=5 \quad \Rightarrow \quad x=\frac{5\times 2}{5} \quad \Rightarrow \quad x=2$$

Subtracting this value of x in equation (2), we get

$$2-\frac{y}{3}=3 \quad \Rightarrow \quad \frac{y}{3}=2-3=-1 \quad \Rightarrow \quad y=-3$$

So, the solution of the given system of equations is $x=2, y=-3$.

(II) By Substitution method

The given system of equations is

$$\frac{x}{2}+\frac{2y}{3}=-1 \qquad .....(1)$$

$$x-\frac{y}{3}=3 \qquad .....(2)$$

From equation (2)

$$x=\frac{y}{3}+3 \qquad .....(3)$$

Substitute this value of x in equation (1), we get

$$\frac{1}{2}\left(\frac{y}{3}+3\right)+\frac{2y}{3}=-1$$

$$\Rightarrow \quad \frac{y}{6}+\frac{3}{2}+\frac{2y}{3}=-1 \quad \Rightarrow \quad \frac{5y}{6}=-1-\frac{3}{2}$$

$$\Rightarrow \quad \frac{5y}{6}=\frac{-5}{2} \quad \Rightarrow \quad y=-3$$

Substituting this value of y in equation (3), we get

$$x = \frac{-3}{3} + 3 = -1 + 3 = 2$$

So, the solution of the given system of equations

$x = 2, y = -3$

Verification : Substituting x = 2, y = –3, we find that both the equations (1) and (2) are satisfied as shown below:

$$\frac{x}{2}+\frac{2y}{3} = \frac{2}{2}+\frac{2(-3)}{3} = 1 - 2 = -1$$

$$x - \frac{y}{3} = 2 - \frac{(-3)}{3} = 2 + 1 = 3$$

Hence, the solution is correct.

Q.7 Form the pair of linear equation in the following problems, and find their solutions (if they exist) by the elimination method:

(i) Five years ago, Nuri was thrice as old as Sonu. Ten years later, Nuri will be twice as old as Sonu. How old are Nuri and Sonu?

(ii) The sum of the digits of a two-digit number is 9. Also, nine times this number is twice the number obtained by reversing the order of the digits. Find the number.

Sol. (i) Let Nuri and Sonu be x years and y years old respectively at present.

Then, according to the question,

$x - 5 = 3(y - 5)$

$x + 10 = 2(y + 10)$

$\Rightarrow \quad x - 5 = 3y - 15$

$x + 10 = 2y + 20$

$\Rightarrow \quad x - 3y = -10 \quad .....(1)$

$x - 2y = 10 \quad .....(2)$

Substracting equation (2) from equation (1), we get

$-y = -20 \quad \Rightarrow \quad y = 20$

Substituting this value of y in equation (2), we get

$x - 2(20) = 10 \quad \Rightarrow \quad x - 40 = 10$

$\Rightarrow \quad x = 40 + 10 \quad \Rightarrow \quad x = 50$

Hence, Nuri and Sonu are 50 years and 20 years old respectively at present.

Verification : Substituting the values of x = 50 and y = 20, we find that both the equation (1) and (2) are satisfied as shown below:

$x - 3y = 50 - 3(20) = 50 - 60 = -10$

$x - 2y = 50 - 2(20) = 50 - 40 = 10$

Hence, the solution is correct.

(ii) Let the unit's digit and the ten's digit in the two-digit number be x and y respectively.

Then the number = $10y + x$

Also, the number obtained by reversing the order of the digits = $10x + y$

According to the question,

$$x + y = 9 \quad .....(1)$$

$$9(10y + x) = 2(10x + y)$$

$$\Rightarrow 90y + 9x = 20x + 2y \quad \Rightarrow \quad 11x - 88y = 0 \quad \Rightarrow \quad x - 8y = 0$$

Subtracting equation (2) from equation (1), we get

$$x + 1 = 9 \quad \Rightarrow \quad x = 9 - 1 = 8$$

Hence, the required number is 18.

Verification : Substituting $x = 8$ and $y = 1$, we find that both the equations (1) and (2) are satisfied as shown below.

$$x + y = 8 + 1 = 9$$

$$x - 8y = 8 - 8(1) = 0$$

Hence, the solution is correct.

Q.8 (i) For which values of a and b does the following pair of linear equations have an infinite number of solutions?

$2x + 3y = 7$; $(a - b)x + (a + b)y = 3a + b - 2$

(ii) For which value of k will the following pair of linear equations have no solution?

$3x + y = 1$; $(2k - 1)x + (k - 1)y = 2k + 1$

Sol. (i) The given pair of linear equation is

$$2x + 3y = 7$$

$$(a - b)x + (a + b)y = 3a + b - 2$$

Here $a_1 = 2, b_1 = 3, c_1 = -7$

$a_2 = a - b, b_2 = a + b,$

$c_2 = -(3a + b - 2)$

For having an infinite number of solutions, we must have

$$\frac{a_1}{a_2} = \frac{b_1}{b_2} = \frac{c_1}{c_2} \quad \Rightarrow \quad \frac{2}{a-b} = \frac{3}{a+b}$$

$$\Rightarrow \quad 2(a + b) = 3(a - b) \quad \Rightarrow \quad 2a + 2b = 3a - 3b$$

$$\Rightarrow \quad a - 5b = 0 \quad .....(1)$$

For last two,

$$\frac{3}{a+b} = \frac{7}{3a+b-2} \quad \Rightarrow \quad 3(3a + b - 2) = 7(a + b)$$

$$\Rightarrow \quad 9a + 3b - 6 = 7a + 7b \quad \Rightarrow \quad 2a - 4b - 6 = 0$$

$$\Rightarrow \quad a - 2b - 3 = 0 \quad .....(2) \quad \text{(Dividing throughout by 2)}$$

To solve the equation (1) and (2) by cross-multiplication method, we draw the diagram below:

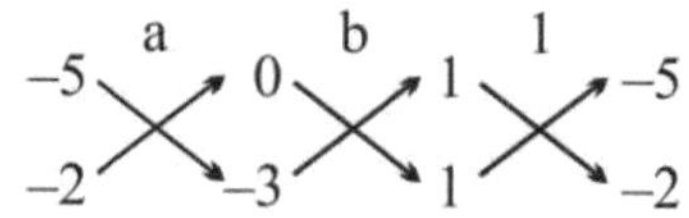

Then, $\dfrac{a}{(-5)(-3)-(-2)(0)} = \dfrac{b}{(0)(1)-(-3)(1)} = \dfrac{1}{(1)(-2)-(1)(-5)}$

$\Rightarrow \quad \dfrac{a}{15} = \dfrac{b}{3} = \dfrac{1}{3}$

$\Rightarrow \quad a = \dfrac{15}{3} = 5$ and $b = \dfrac{3}{3} = 1$

Hence, the required values of a and b are 5 and 1 respectively.

(ii) The given pair of linear equations is

$$3x + y = 1$$

$$(2k-1)x + (k-1)y = 2k+1$$

$\Rightarrow \quad 3x + y - 1 = 0$

Here, $(2k-1)x + (k-1)y - (2k+1) = 0$

$a_1 = 3,\ b_1 = 1,\ c_1 = -1$

$a_2 = 2k-1,\ b_2 = k-1,$

$c_2 = -(2k+1)$

For having no solution, we must have

$$\frac{a_1}{a_2} = \frac{b_1}{b_2} \neq \frac{c_1}{c_2}$$

$\Rightarrow \quad \dfrac{3}{2k-1} = \dfrac{1}{k-1} \neq \dfrac{-1}{-(k+1)}$

From above, we have

$$\frac{3}{2k-1} = \frac{1}{k-1}$$

$\Rightarrow \quad 3(k-1) = 2k-1$

$\Rightarrow \quad 3k - 3 = 3 - 1$

$\Rightarrow \quad k = 2$

Hence , the required value of k is 2.

Q.9 Solve the following pair of linear equations by the substitution and cross-multiplication methods:
$8x + 5y = 9$; $3x + 2y = 4$

Sol. The given pair of linear equations

$$8x + 5y = 9 \quad .....(1)$$

$$3x + 2y = 4 \quad .....(2)$$

(I) By Substitution method

From equation (2),

$$2y = 4 - 3x \Rightarrow y = \frac{4-3x}{2} \quad .....(3)$$

Substitute this value of y in equation (1), we get

$$8x + 5\left(\frac{4-3x}{2}\right) = 9$$

$\Rightarrow$ $16x + 20 - 15x = 18$ $\Rightarrow$ $x + 20 = 18$

$\Rightarrow$ $x = 18 - 20$ $\Rightarrow$ $x = -2$

Substituting this value of x in equation (3), we get

$$y = \frac{4-3(-2)}{2} = \frac{4+6}{2} = \frac{10}{2} = 5$$

So the solution of the given pair of linear equations is $x = -2, y = 5$

(II) By Cross-multiplication method

Let us write the given pair of linear equations is

$$8x + 5y - 9 = 0 \quad .....(1)$$

$$3x + 2y - 4 = 0 \quad .....(2)$$

To solve the equations (1) and (2) by cross multiplication method, we draw the diagram below:

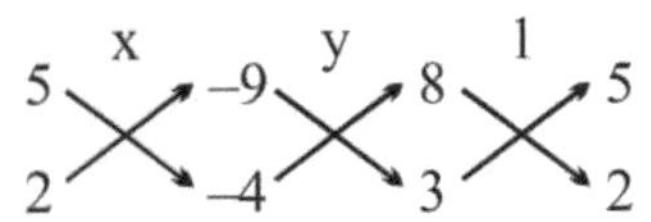

Then, $$\frac{x}{(5)(-4)-(2)(-9)} = \frac{y}{(-9)(3)-(-4)(8)} = \frac{1}{(8)(2)-(3)(5)}$$

$$= \frac{x}{-20+18} = \frac{y}{-27+32} = \frac{1}{16-15} = \frac{x}{-2} = \frac{y}{5} = \frac{1}{1}$$

$\Rightarrow$ $x = -2$ and $y = 5$

Hence, the required solution of the given pair of linear equations is

$x = -2, y = 5$

Verification: Substituting $x = -2, y = 5$, we find that both the equations (1) and (2) are satisfied as shown below:

$$8x + 5y = 8(-2) + 5(5) = -16 + 25 = 9$$

$$3x + 2y = 3(-2) + 2(5) = -6 + 10 = 4$$

Hence, the solution is correct.

Q.10 Form the pair of linear equations in the following problem and find their solution (if they exist) by any algebraic method.

Places A and B are 100 km apart on a highway. One car starts from A and another from B at the same time. If the cars travel in the same direction at different speeds, they meet in 5 hours. If they travel towards each other, they meet in 1 hour. What are the speeds of the two cars?

Sol. Let the speeds of two cars be x km/hour and y km/hour respectively.

Case I: When the cars travel in the same direction

Let they meet at P.

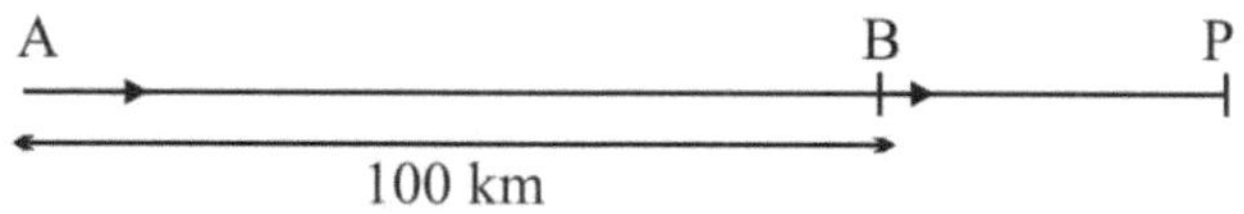

Distance travelled by the car starting from A in 5 hours = AP = 5x km

(Distance = speed × time)

Distance travelled by the car starting from B in 5 hours = BP = 5y km

(Distance = speed × time)

Now, $AP - BP = 100$

$\Rightarrow \quad 5x - 5y = 100$

$\Rightarrow \quad x - y = 20$ .....(1)

(Dividing throughout by 5)

Case II: When the cars travel towards each other

Let they meet at Q.

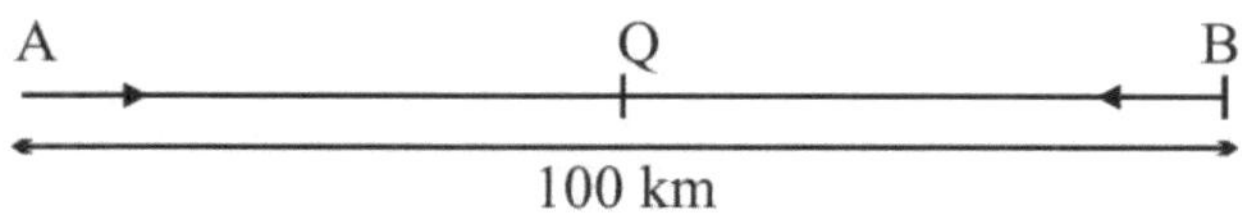

Distance travelled by the car starting from A in 1 hour = AQ = x km

Distance travelled by the car starting from B in 1 hour = BQ = y km

Now, $AQ + BQ = 100$

$\Rightarrow \quad x + y = 100$ .....(2)

Equation (1) and (2) can be re-written as

$x - y - 20 = 0$ .....(3)

$x + y - 100 = 0$ .....(4)

To solve the equations (3) and (4) by cross-multiplication method, we draw the diagram below:

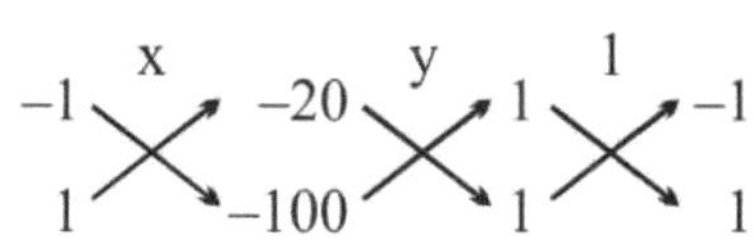

Then, $\dfrac{x}{(-1)(-100)-(1)(-20)} = \dfrac{y}{(-20)(1)-(-100)(1)} = \dfrac{1}{(1)(1)-(1)(-1)}$

$\Rightarrow \quad \dfrac{x}{100+20} = \dfrac{y}{-20+100} = \dfrac{1}{1+1}$

$\Rightarrow \quad \dfrac{x}{120} = \dfrac{y}{80} = \dfrac{1}{2}$

$\Rightarrow \quad x = \dfrac{120}{2} = 60$ and $y = \dfrac{80}{2} = 40$

Hence, the speeds of the two cars are 60 km/hour and 40 km/hour respectively.

Verification: Substituting $x = 60$, $y = 40$, we find that both the equations (1) and (2) are satisfied as shown below:

$x - y = 60 - 40 = 20$

$x + y = 60 + 40 = 100$

Hence, the solution we have got is correct.

Q.11 Solve the following pairs of equations by reducing them to a pair of linear equations:

(i) $\dfrac{1}{2x} + \dfrac{1}{3y} = 2;\ \dfrac{1}{3x} + \dfrac{1}{2y} = \dfrac{13}{6}$ **(ii)** $\dfrac{2}{\sqrt{x}} + \dfrac{3}{\sqrt{y}} = 2;\ \dfrac{4}{\sqrt{x}} - \dfrac{9}{\sqrt{y}} = -1$

(iii) $\dfrac{1}{3x+y} + \dfrac{1}{3x-y} = \dfrac{3}{4};\ \dfrac{1}{2(3x+y)} - \dfrac{1}{2(3x-y)} = \dfrac{-1}{8}$

Sol. (i) The given pair of equations is

$$\frac{1}{2x} + \frac{1}{3y} = 2 \quad .....(1)$$

$$\frac{1}{3x} + \frac{1}{2y} = \frac{13}{6} \quad .....(2)$$

Put $\dfrac{1}{x} = X$ .....(3)

and $\dfrac{1}{y} = Y$ .....(4)

Then the equations (1) and (2) can be rewritten as

$$\frac{1}{2}X + \frac{1}{3}Y = 2 \quad .....(5)$$

$$\frac{1}{3}X + \frac{1}{2}Y = \frac{13}{6} \quad .....(6)$$

$$\Rightarrow \quad 3X + 2Y = 12 \quad .....(7)$$

$$2X + 3Y = 13 \quad .....(8)$$

Multiplying equation (7) by 3 and equation (8) by 2, we get

$$9X + 6Y = 36 \quad .....(9)$$

$$4X + 6Y = 26 \quad .....(10)$$

Subtracting equation (10) from equation (9), we get

$$9(2) + 6Y = 36 \quad .....(11)$$

$$\Rightarrow \quad 18 + 6Y = 36$$

$$\Rightarrow 6Y = 36 - 18 = 18$$

$$\Rightarrow \quad Y = \frac{18}{6} = 3 \quad .....(12)$$

From equation (3) and equation (11), we get

$$\frac{1}{x} = 2 \quad \Rightarrow \quad x = \frac{1}{2}$$

From equation (4) and equation (12), we get

$$\frac{1}{y} = 3 \quad \Rightarrow \quad y = \frac{1}{3}$$

Hence, the solution of the given pair of equations is

$$x = \frac{1}{2}, y = \frac{1}{3}$$

Verification : Substituting $x = \frac{1}{2}, y = \frac{1}{3}$, we find that both the equations (1) and (2) are satisfied as shown below:

$$\frac{1}{2x} + \frac{1}{3y} = \frac{1}{2 \cdot \frac{1}{2}} + \frac{1}{3 \cdot \frac{1}{3}} = 1 + 1 = 2$$

$$\frac{1}{3x} + \frac{1}{2y} = \frac{1}{3 \cdot \frac{1}{2}} + \frac{1}{2 \cdot \frac{1}{3}} = \frac{2}{3} + \frac{3}{2} = \frac{13}{6}$$

Hence, the solution we have got is correct.

(ii) The given pair of equations is

$$\frac{2}{\sqrt{x}}+\frac{3}{\sqrt{y}}=2 \qquad .....(1)$$

$$\frac{4}{\sqrt{x}}-\frac{9}{\sqrt{y}}=-1 \qquad .....(2)$$

Put $\frac{1}{\sqrt{x}}=u$ .....(3)

and $\frac{1}{\sqrt{y}}=v$ .....(4)

Then equations (1) and (2) can be rewritten as

$2u+3v=2$ .....(5)

$4u-9v=-1$ .....(6)

Multiplying equations (5) by 3, we get

$6u+9v=6$ .....(7)

Adding equation (6) and equation (7), we get

$10u=5$

$\Rightarrow \quad u=\frac{5}{10}=\frac{1}{2}$ .....(8)

Substituting the value of x in equation (5), we get

$$2\left(\frac{1}{2}\right)+3v=2$$

$\Rightarrow \quad 1+3v=2$

$\Rightarrow \quad 3v=2-1=1$

$\Rightarrow \quad v=\frac{1}{3}$ .....(9)

From equation (3) and equation (8), we get

$$\frac{1}{\sqrt{x}}=\frac{1}{2} \Rightarrow \sqrt{x}=2 \Rightarrow x=4 \qquad \text{(Squaring)}$$

From equation (4) equation (9), we get

$$\frac{1}{\sqrt{y}}=\frac{1}{3} \Rightarrow \sqrt{y}=3 \Rightarrow x=9 \qquad \text{(Squaring)}$$

Hence, the solution if the given pair of equation is

$x=4,\ y=9$

Verification : Substituting x = 4, y = 9, we find that both the equations (1) and (2) are satisfied as shown below.

$$\frac{2}{\sqrt{x}}+\frac{3}{\sqrt{y}} = \frac{2}{\sqrt{4}}+\frac{3}{\sqrt{9}} = \frac{2}{2}+\frac{3}{3} = 1+1=2$$

$$\frac{4}{\sqrt{x}}-\frac{9}{\sqrt{y}} = \frac{4}{\sqrt{9}}-\frac{9}{\sqrt{9}} = \frac{4}{2}-\frac{9}{3} = 2-3=-1$$

Hence, the solution we have got is correct.

(iii) The given pair of equations is

$$\frac{1}{3x+y}+\frac{1}{3x-y}=\frac{3}{4} \quad .....(1)$$

$$\frac{1}{2(3x+y)}-\frac{1}{2(3x-y)}=\frac{-1}{8} \quad .....(2)$$

Put $$\frac{1}{3x+y}=u \quad .....(3)$$

and $$\frac{1}{3x-y}=u \quad .....(4)$$

Then equations (1) and (2) can be rewritten as

$$u+v=\frac{3}{4} \quad .....(5)$$

$$\frac{1}{2}u-\frac{1}{2}v=\frac{-1}{8} \quad .....(6)$$

(6) gives, $$u-v=\frac{-1}{4} \quad .....(7)$$ (Multiplying both sides by 2)

Adding equation (5) and equation (7), we get

$$2u=\frac{3}{4}-\frac{1}{4}=\frac{1}{2}$$

$$\Rightarrow \quad u=\frac{1}{4} \quad .....(8)$$

Subtracting equation (7) from equation (5), we get

$$2v = \frac{3}{4} + \frac{1}{4} = 1 \qquad .....(9)$$

From equation (3) and equation (8), we get

$$\frac{1}{3x+y} = \frac{1}{4}$$

$$\Rightarrow \qquad 3x + y = 4 \qquad .....(10)$$

From equation (4) and equation (9), we get

$$\frac{1}{3x+y} = \frac{1}{2}$$

$$\Rightarrow \qquad 3x - y = 2 \qquad .....(11)$$

Adding equation (10) and equation (11), we get

$$6x = 6 \quad \Rightarrow \quad x = \frac{6}{6} = 1$$

Substituting this value of x in equation (10), we get

$$3(1) + y = 4 \quad \Rightarrow \quad 3 + y = 4 \quad \Rightarrow \quad y = 4 - 3 = 1$$

Hence, the solution of the given pair of equation is

$$x = 1, y = 1$$

Verification : Substituting $x = 1, y = 1$, we find that both the equations (1) and (2) are satisfied as shown below :

$$\frac{1}{3x+y} + \frac{1}{3x-y} = \frac{1}{3(1)+1} + \frac{1}{3(1)-1} = \frac{1}{4} + \frac{1}{2} = \frac{3}{4}$$

$$\frac{1}{2(3x+y)} + \frac{1}{2(3x-y)} = \frac{1}{2(3\times1+1)} + \frac{1}{2(3\times1-1)} = \frac{1}{8} - \frac{1}{4} = \frac{-1}{8}$$

Q.12 Formulate the following problems as a pair of equations, and hence find their solutions:

(i) Ritu can row downstream 20 km in 2 hours, and upstream 4 km in 2 hours. Find the speed of rowing in still water and the speed of the current.

(ii) 2 women and 5 men can together finish an embroidery work in 4 days, while 3 women and 6 men can finish it in 3 days. Find the time taken by 1 woman alone to finish the work, and also that taken by 1 man alone.

(iii) Roohi travels 300 km to her home partly by train and partly by bus. She takes 4 hours if she travels 60 km by train and the remaining by bus. If she travels 100 km by train and the remaining by bus, she takes 10 minutes longer. Find the speed of the train and the bus separately.

Sol. (i) Let her speed of rowing in still water be x km/hour and the speed of the current by y km/hour.
Then, her speed of rowing downstream = (x + y) km/hour.
and, her speed of rowing upstream = (x – y) km/hour.

Also, $\text{Time} = \frac{\text{Distance}}{\text{Speed}}$

In the first case, when she goes 20 km downstream, then the time taken is 2 hours.

$$\therefore \quad \frac{20}{x+y} = 2 \quad \Rightarrow \quad x + y = 10 \qquad .....(1)$$

In the second case, when she goes 4 km upstream, then the time taken is 2 hours.

$$\therefore \quad \frac{4}{x-y} = 2 \quad \Rightarrow \quad x - y = 2 \qquad .....(2)$$

Adding equation (1) and equation (2), we get

$$2x = 12 \quad \Rightarrow \quad x = \frac{12}{2} = 6$$

Substituting this value of x in equation (1), we get

$$6 + y = 10 \quad \Rightarrow \quad y = 10 - 6 = 4$$

Hence, the speed of her rowing in still water is 6 km/hour and the speed of the current is 4 km/hour.

Verification : Substituting x = 6, y = 4 we find that both the equations (1) and (2) are satisfied as shown below:

$$x + y = 6 + 4 = 10$$
$$x - y = 6 - 4 = 2$$

Hence, the solution we have got is correct.

(ii) Let the time taken by 1 woman alone to finish the embroidery by x days and the time taken by 1 man alone to finish the embroidery be y days. Then

$$1 \text{ woman's } 1 \text{ day's work} = \frac{1}{x}$$

and $$1 \text{ man's } 1 \text{ day's work} = \frac{1}{y}$$

$$\therefore \quad 2 \text{ women's } 1 \text{ day's work} = \frac{2}{x}$$

and $$2 \text{ men's } 1 \text{ day's work} = \frac{5}{y}$$

$\because$ 2 women and 5 men can together finish a piece of embroidery in 4 days.

$$\therefore \quad 4\left(\frac{2}{x}+\frac{5}{y}\right) = 1 \quad \Rightarrow \quad \frac{2}{x}+\frac{5}{y} = \frac{1}{4} \quad .....(1)$$

Again, 3 women's 1 day's work $= \dfrac{3}{x}$

and 6 men's 1 day's work $= \dfrac{6}{y}$

$\because$ 3 women and 6 men can together finish a piece of embroidery in 3 days.

$$\therefore \quad 3\left(\frac{3}{x}+\frac{6}{y}\right) = 1 \quad \Rightarrow \quad \frac{3}{x}+\frac{6}{y} = \frac{1}{3} \quad .....(2)$$

Put $\dfrac{1}{x} = u$ .....(3)

and $\dfrac{1}{y} = v$ .....(4)

Then equations (1) and (2) can be rewritten as

$$2u + 5v = \frac{1}{4} \quad .....(5)$$

$$3u + 6v = \frac{1}{3} \quad .....(6)$$

Multiplying equation (5) by 3 and equation (6) by 2, we get

$$6u + 15v = \frac{3}{4} \quad .....(7)$$

$$6u + 12v = \frac{2}{3} \quad .....(8)$$

Subtracting equation (8) from equation (7), we get

$$3v = \frac{3}{4} - \frac{2}{3} = \frac{1}{12} \quad \Rightarrow \quad v = \frac{1}{36} \quad .....(9)$$

Substituting this value of v in equation (5), we get

$$2u + 5\left(\frac{1}{36}\right) = \frac{1}{4} \quad \Rightarrow \quad 2u + \frac{5}{36} = \frac{1}{4}$$

$\Rightarrow \quad 2u = \frac{1}{4} - \frac{5}{36} \qquad \Rightarrow \quad 2u = \frac{9}{36} - \frac{5}{36}$

$\Rightarrow \quad 2u = \frac{4}{36} = \frac{1}{9} \qquad \Rightarrow \quad u = \frac{1}{18}$ .....(10)

From equation (3) and equation (10), we get

$\frac{1}{x} = \frac{1}{18} \qquad \Rightarrow \quad x = 18$

From equation (4) and equation (9), we get

$\frac{1}{y} = \frac{1}{36} \qquad \Rightarrow \quad y = 36$

Hence, the time taken by 1 woman alone to finish the embroidery is 18 days and the time taken by 1 man alone to finish the embroidery is 36 days.

Verification : Substituting x = 18, y = 36 we find that both the equation (1) and (2) are satisfied as shown below:

$$\frac{2}{x} + \frac{5}{y} = \frac{2}{18} + \frac{5}{36} = \frac{1}{9} + \frac{5}{36} = \frac{1}{4}$$

$$\frac{3}{x} + \frac{6}{y} = \frac{3}{18} + \frac{6}{36} = \frac{1}{6} + \frac{1}{6} = \frac{1}{3}$$

This verifies the solution.

(iii) Let the speed of the train and the bus be x km/hour and y km/hour respectively.

Case I When she travels 60 km by train and the remaining (300 – 60) km, i.e. 240 km by bus, the time taken is 4 hours.

$\therefore \quad \frac{60}{x} + \frac{240}{y} = 4 \qquad \left(\because \text{Time} = \frac{\text{Distance}}{\text{Speed}}\right)$

$\Rightarrow \quad \frac{1}{x} + \frac{4}{y} = \frac{1}{15}$ .....(1) (Dividing by 60)

Case II When she travels 100 km by train and the remaining (300 – 400) km i.e. 200 km by bus, the time taken is 4 hours 10 minutes, i.e. $\frac{25}{6}$ hours.

$\therefore \quad \frac{100}{x} + \frac{200}{y} = \frac{25}{6} \qquad \Rightarrow \quad \frac{4}{x} + \frac{8}{y} = \frac{1}{6}$ .....(2) (Dividing by 25)

Multiplying equation (1) by 2, we get

$$\frac{2}{x}+\frac{8}{y}=\frac{2}{15} \qquad .....(3)$$

Subtracting equation (3) from equation (2), we get

$$\frac{2}{x}=\frac{1}{6}-\frac{2}{15}=\frac{1}{30} \quad \Rightarrow \quad x=60$$

Substituting this value of x in equation (3) we get

$$\frac{2}{60}+\frac{8}{y}=\frac{2}{15} \quad \Rightarrow \quad \frac{1}{30}+\frac{8}{y}=\frac{2}{15}$$

$$\Rightarrow \quad \frac{8}{y}=\frac{2}{15}-\frac{1}{30}=\frac{1}{10} \quad \Rightarrow \quad y=80$$

So, the solution of the equations (1) and (2) is x = 60 and y = 80.

Hence, the speed of the train is 60 km/hour and the speed of the bus is 80 km/hour.

Verification : Substituting x = 60, y = 80, we find that both the equations (1) and (2) and satisfied as shown below :

$$\frac{1}{x}+\frac{1}{y}=\frac{1}{60}+\frac{4}{80}=\frac{1}{60}+\frac{1}{20}=\frac{1}{15}$$

$$\frac{4}{x}+\frac{8}{y}=\frac{4}{60}+\frac{8}{80}=\frac{1}{15}+\frac{1}{10}=\frac{1}{6}$$

This verifies the solution.

Q.13 The ages of two friends Ani and Biju differ by 3 years. Ani's father Dharam is twice as old as Ani and Biju is twice as old as his sister Cathy. The ages of Cathy and Dharam differ by 30 years. Find the ages of Ani and Biju.

Sol. Let the ages of Ani and Biju be x years and y years respectively. Then, according to the question,

$$x-y=\pm 3 \qquad .....(1)$$

Age of Ani's father Dharm = 2x years

Age of Biju's sister = $\frac{y}{2}$ years

According to the question,

$$2x-\frac{y}{2}=30 \quad \Rightarrow \quad 4x-y=60 \qquad .....(2)$$

Case I When $x - y = 3$

Then, we have

$$x - y = 3 \quad .....(1)$$

$$4x - y = 60 \quad .....(2)$$

Subtracting equation (1) from equation (2)

$$3x = 57 \quad .....(3)$$

$$x = \frac{57}{3} = 19 \text{ years}$$

Substituting the value of x is equation (1)

$$19 - y = 3 \quad \Rightarrow \quad y = 19 - 3 = 16$$

Ani's age = 19 years

Biju's age = 16 year

Verification :

$$x - y = 19 - 16 = 3$$

$$4x - \frac{y}{4} = 4 \times 19 - 16 = 76 - 16 = 60$$

This verifies the solution.

Case II When $x - y = -3$

Then, we have

$$x - y = -3 \quad .....(1)$$

$$4x - y = 60 \quad .....(2)$$

Subtracting equation (1) from equation (2)

$$3x = 63$$

$$x = \frac{63}{3} = 21 \text{ years}$$

Substituting the value of x is equation (1), we get

$$21 - y = -3 \quad \Rightarrow \quad y = 24$$

Ani's age = 21 years

Biju's age = 24 year

$$x - y = 21 - 24 = 3$$

$$4x - y = 4(21) - 24 = 84 - 24 = 60$$

This satisfied the solution.

Q.14 A train covered a certain distance at a uniform speed. If the train would have been 10 km/h faster, it would have taken 2 hours less than the scheduled time. And, if the train were slower by 10 km/hr, it would have taken 3 hours more than the scheduled time. Find the distance covered by the train.

Sol. Let the actual speed of the train be x km/hour and the actual time taken by y hours. Then,

$$\text{Distance} = (xy)\text{ km} \quad .....(1) \quad (\text{Distance} = \text{speed} \times \text{time})$$

According to the equation,

$$xy = (x + 10)(y - 2)$$

$\Rightarrow$ $xy = xy - 2x + 10y - 20$

$\Rightarrow$ $2x - 10y + 20 = 0$

$\Rightarrow$ $x - 5y + 10 = 0$ (Dividing throughout by 2)

and $xy = (x - 10)(y + 3)$

$\Rightarrow$ $xy = xy + 3x - 10y - 30$

$\Rightarrow$ $3x - 10y - 30 = 0$ .....(2)

To solve the equations (1) and (2) by the cross-multiplication method, we draw the diagram below:

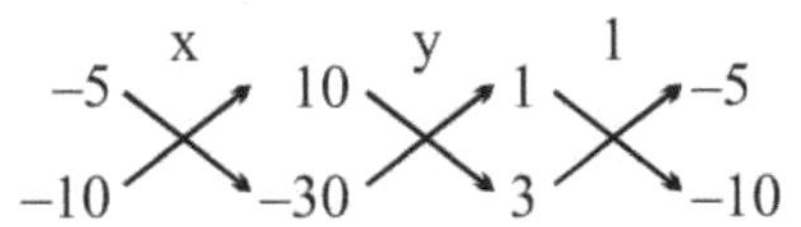

Then, $$\frac{x}{(-5)(-30)-(-10)(10)} = \frac{y}{(10)(3)-(-30)(1)} = \frac{1}{(1)(-10)-(3)(-5)}$$

$\Rightarrow$ $$\frac{x}{150+100} = \frac{y}{30+30} = \frac{1}{-10+15}$$

$\Rightarrow$ $$\frac{x}{250} = \frac{y}{60} = \frac{1}{5}$$

$\Rightarrow$ $$x = \frac{250}{5} = 50$$

and $$y = \frac{60}{5} = 12$$

So, the solution of the equations (1) and (2) is x = 50 and y = 12. Hence, the distance covered by the train is 50 × 12 = 600 km

Verification : Substituting x = 50, y = 12, we find that both the equations (1) and (2) are satisfied as shown below. Hence, the solution we have got is correct.

Q.15 Solve the following pair of linear equations

$(a - b)x + (a + b)y = a^2 - 2ab - b^2$; $(a + b)(x + y) = a^2 + b^2$

Sol. The given pair of linear equations is

$$(a - b)x + (a + b)y = a^2 - 2ab - b^2 \quad .....(1)$$

$$(a + b)(x + y) = a^2 + b^2$$

$$\Rightarrow \quad (a + b)x + (a + b)y = a^2 + b^2 \quad .....(2)$$

Subtracting equation (2) from equation (1), we get

$$-2bx = -2ab - 2b^2$$

$$\Rightarrow \quad x = \frac{-2ab - 2b^2}{-2b} = a\frac{-2b(a+b)}{-2b} = a + b$$

Subtracting this value of x is equation (1), we get

$$(a - b)(a + b) + (a + b)y = a^2 - 2ab - b^2$$

$$\Rightarrow \quad a^2 - b^2 + (a + b)y = a^2 - 2ab - b^2$$

$$\Rightarrow \quad (a + b)y = -2ab$$

$$\Rightarrow \quad y = \frac{-2ab}{a+b}$$

Hence, the solution of the given pair of linear equation is

$$x = a + b,\ y = \frac{-2ab}{a+b}$$

Verification : Substituting $x = a + b, y = \frac{-2ab}{a+b}$, we find that both the equation (1) and (2) are satisfied as shown below:

$$(a - b)x + (a + b)y = (a - b)(a + b) + (a + b)\left(\frac{-2ab}{a+b}\right) = a^2 - b^2 - 2ab$$

$$(a + b)(x + y) = (a + b)\left(a + b - \frac{2ab}{a+b}\right) = (a + b)^2 - 2ab = a^2 + b^2$$

This verifies the solution.

CONCEPT APPLICATION LEVEL - II [Previous Year Questions]

Q.1 If 6 years hence a man's age will be 3 times the age of his son and three years ago he was 9 times as old as his son, then what is the present age of the man? **[NSTSE-2013]**
(A) 25 years (B) 35 years (C) 15 years (D) 30 years

Q.2 If the system of equation $2x + 3y = 7$ and $2ax + (a + b)y = 28$ represents coincident lines, which of the condition holds true? **[NSTSE-2013]**
(A) $b = 2a$ (B) $a = 2b$ (C) $2a + b = 0$ (D) $a + 2b = 0$

Q.3 For which values of 'a' and 'b' does the following pair of linear equations have an infinite number of solutions **[NSTSE-2013]**
$2x + 3y = 7$; $(a - b)x + (a + b)y = 3a + b - 2$
(A) $a = 5, b = 1$ (B) $a = 4, b = 2$ (C) $a = 1, b = 5$ (D) $a = 2, b = 4$

Q.4 Find the equation of the line passing through (3, 7) whose slope is $\frac{-3}{2}$ **[NIMO]**
(A) $3x + 2y = 23$ (B) $3x + 3y = 24$ (C) $3x + 4y = 23$ (D) None of these

Q.5 Two lines with slopes m_1 and m_2 are parallel to each other if **[NIMO]**
(A) $m_1 = m_2$ (B) $m_1 m_2 = 1$ (C) $\frac{m_1}{m_2} = 1$ (D) $m_1 + m_2 = 1$

Q.6 Find the slope of a line whose inclination with the x-axis is 150° **[NIMO]**
(A) $\frac{1}{2}$ (B) $\sqrt{3}$ (C) $\frac{-1}{\sqrt{3}}$ (D) None of these

Q.7 If twice the area of a smaller square is subtracted from the area of a larger square, the result is 14 cm^2. However if twice the area of the large square is added to three times the area of the smaller square, the result is 203 cm^2. Determine the sides of the two squares. **[NIMO]**
(A) 7 cm, 4 cm (B) 6 cm, 3 cm (C) 8 cm, 5 cm (D) None of these

Q.8 The denominator of a rational number is greater than its numerator by 3. If 3 is subtracted from the numerator and 2 is added to the denominator, the new number becomes $\frac{1}{5}$. What was the original number? **[NIMO]**
(A) $\frac{5}{8}$ (B) $\frac{3}{5}$ (C) $\frac{7}{11}$ (D) $\frac{3}{8}$

Q.9 Find the values of x and y in the given rectangle if its length is cube root of 2197 and width is one less than the fourth multiple of first prime number **[5th IMO]**
(A) 6, 1 (B) 3, 2
(C) 4, 1 (D) 13, 7

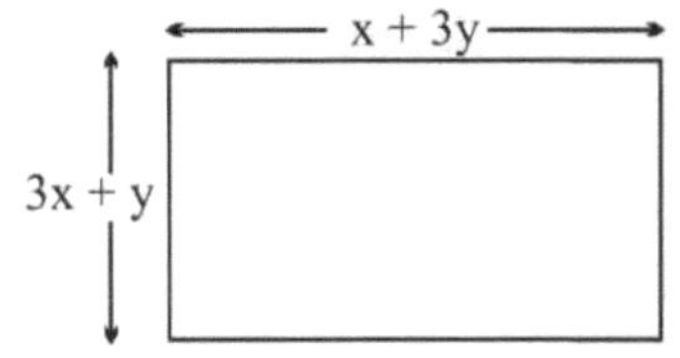

Q.10 The coach of a cricket team buys 7 bats and 6 balls for Rs.3800. Later he buys 3 bats and 5 balls for Rs.1750. Find the cost of each ball **[IOM-2012]**

(A) Rs.75 (B) Rs.50 (C) Rs.30 (D) Rs.80

Q.11 A number consists of two digits whose sum is 5. When the digits are reversed the number becomes greater by 9. Find the given number **[IMO-2012]**

(A) 23 (B) 21 (C) 19 (D) 25

Q.12 Five years age, Rani was thrice as old as Tanvi, ten years later, Rani will be twice as old as Tanvi. How old is Rani? **[IMO-2012]**

(A) 40 years (B) 50 years (C) 45 years (D) 52 years

Q.13 A boat covers 32 km upstream and 36 km downstream in 7 hours. Also, it covers 40 km upstream and 48 km downstream in 9 hours. Find the speed of boat in still water **[IOM-2012]**

(A) 10 km/h (B) 8 km/h (C) 5 km/h (D) 2 km/h

Q.14 Find the nature of solution of the system of linear equations give by $3x + 4y = 5$ and $4x - 6y = 8$

(A) unique solution (B) no solution

(C) infinitely many solutions (D) inadequate data **[IOM-2013]**

Q.15 Which one of the following is the condition for no solution? **[IOM-2013]**

(A) $a_1 a_2 = b_1 b_2$ (B) $\frac{a_1}{a_2} \neq \frac{b_1}{b_2}$ (C) $\frac{a_1}{a_2} = \frac{b_1}{b_2} \neq \frac{c_1}{c_2}$ (D) $\frac{a_1}{a_2} = \frac{b_1}{b_2} = \frac{c_1}{c_2}$

Q.16 For which values of 'a' and 'b' does the following pair of linear equations have an infinite number of solutions ; $2x + 3y = 7$, $(a - b)x + (a + b)y = 3a + b - 2$ **[Raj.NTSE Stage-1_2013]**

(A) $a = 5, b = 1$ (B) $a = 4, b = 2$ (C) $a = 1, b = 5$ (D) $a = 2, b = 4$

Q.17 If the system of equations $kx + 3y - (k - 3) = 0$, $12x + ky - k = 0$ has infinitely many solution, then $k =$ **[Raj. NTSE Stage-1_2014]**

(A) 6 (B) –6 (C) 0 (D) None of these

Q.18 Which of the following system of equations has no solution? **[IMO - 2016]**

(A) $3x - y = 2, 9x - 3y = 6$ (B) $4x - 7y + 28 = 0, 5y - 7x + 9 = 0$

(C) $3x - 5y - 11 = 0, 6x - 10y - 7 = 0$ (D) None of these

Q.19 In the equations $3x + 2y = 13xy$ and $4x - 5y = 2xy$, the values of x and y that satisfy the equations are **[NTSE - 2016]**

(A) (2, 3) (B) (3, 2) (C) $\left(\frac{1}{2}, \frac{1}{3}\right)$ (D) $\left(\frac{1}{3}, \frac{1}{2}\right)$

CONCEPT APPLICATION LEVEL - III

SECTION-A

- **Multiple choice questions with one correct answer**

Q.1 The pair of equations $3^{x+y} = 81, 81^{x-y} = 3$ has
(A) no solution
(B) the solution x = 2½, y = 2½
(C) the solution x = 2, y = 2
(D) the solution $x = 2\frac{1}{8}, y = 1\frac{7}{8}$

Q.2 The points (7,2) and (–1,0) lie on a line
(A) 7y = 3x – 7 (B) 4y = x +1 (C) y = 7x + 7 (D) x = 4y +1

Q.3 The condition for which the system of equations kx – y = 2 and 6x–2y = 3 has a unique solution is
(A) k = 3 (B) $k \neq 3$ (C) $k \neq 0$ (D) k = 0

Q.4 The equations ax +b = 0 and cx + d = 0 are consistent if
(A) ad = bc (B) ad + bc = 0 (C) ab –cd = 0 (D) ab + cd = 0

Q.5 The solution to the system of equation |x+y| = 1 and x–y = 0 is given by
(A) x = y = 1/2
(B) x = y = –1/2
(C) x = 1, y = 0
(D) x = y = 1/2 or x = y = –1/2

Q.6 The value of x + y in the solution of equations $\frac{x}{4}+\frac{y}{3}=\frac{5}{12}$ and $\frac{x}{2}+y=1$ is
(A) 1/2 (B) 3/2 (C) 2 (D) 5/2

Q.7 Simplify $|x-3|+2|x+1|=4$
(A) 1 (B) –1 (C) 3 (D) many solution

Q.8 If $1+\frac{1}{x}=\frac{x+1}{x}$, what does x equal to ?
(A) 1 or 2 only (B) +1 only (C) +1 & -1 only (D) any number except.

Q.9 If $4x+5y=82,\ 3x+2z=54,\ 5y+4z=110$, what is the value of $5x+2y+z$?
(A) 50 (B) 65 (C) 75 (D) 100

Q.10 The total number of integer pairs (x,y) satisfying the equation x + y = xy is
(A) 0 (B) 1 (C) 2 (D) None of these

Q.11 x and y are 2 different digits. If the sum of the two numbers formed by using both digits is a perfect square, then find x + y
(A) 10 (B) 11 (C) 12 (D) 13

Q.12 Two candles of the same length are highted at the same time. the first is consumed in 6 hours and the second in 4 hours. Assuming each candle burns at a constant rate, in how many hours after being lighted was the first candle twice the length of the second.

(A) 1 hour (B) 2 hour (C) 3 hours (D) 5 hours

Q.13 A boat travels with speed of 15 km/hour in still water. In a river flowing at 5 km/hour the boat travels. Some distance downsteam and then returns. The ratio of average speed to the speed in still water is

(A) 8 : 3 (B) 3 : 8 (C) 8 : 9 (D) 9 : 8

Q.14 Evaluate: $|3| + |-2-3| - 3 - |-7|$

(A) –2 (B) 2 (C) 10 (D) –10

Q.15 Find the equation of the line which is parallel to $3x - 2y + 5 = 0$ and passes through point (5 –6)

(A) $3x - 2y + 27 = 0$ (B) $2x - 3y + 27 = 0$ (C) $3x - 2y - 27 = 0$ (D) $3x + y + 27 = 0$

Q.16 State whether the two lines through (5,6) and (2,3) through (9,–2) and (6–5) are

(A) parallel (B) perpendicular

(C) neither parallel nor perpendicular (D) none of these

Q.17 Find the equation of line which cuts off an intercept 4 on the positive direction of x-axis and an intercept 3 cm the negative direction of y-axis.

(A) $3x - 4y = 12$ (B) $3x + 4y = 12$ (C) $4x - 3y = 12$ (D) $4x + 3y = 12$

Q.18 What can be said regarding a line of its slop is ∞.

(A) The line is y-axis. (B) The line is x-axis (C) Parallel to x-axis (D) None of these

Q.19 Find the set of value of z satisfying $\left|\frac{5-x}{3}\right| < 2$:

(A) $1 < x < 11$ (B) $-1 < x < 11$ (C) $x < 11$ (D) None of these

Q.20 If a and b are real no's the equation $3x - 5 + a = bx + 1$ has a unique solution x

(A) For all a and b (B) if $a \neq 2b$ (C) if $a \neq b$ (D) if $b \neq 3$

SECTION-B

- **Multiple choice question with one or more than one correct answers**

Q.1 The equations $2x + y - 5 = 0$ and $6x + 3y - 15 = 0$ shows

(A) Coincident lines (B) Infinite number of solution

(C) Unique solution (D) no solution

Q.2 If $p > q$ and $r < 0$, which of the following is/are true:-

(A) $pr < qr$ (B) $p + r > q + r$ (C) $p - r < q - r$ (D) $2p + r < 2q + r$

Q.3 If u is between 0 and 1, but $u \neq 0$ or 1 which of the following increases as u increases ?

(A) $1 - u^2$ (B) $u - 1$ (C) $1/u^2$ (D) u^2

Q.4 Simplify $x^2 + |x-1| = 1$

(A) 1 (B) –1 (C) 0 (D) 2

Q.5 The simultaneous equations $2x+3y=5,\ 4x+6y=10$ represents.

(A) several solutions (B) only two solutions (C) parallel lines (D) coincident lines

Q.6 Consider the following statements : The system of equations $2x-y=4$, $px-y=q$, which of the following statements is/are true for above system of equations:-

(A) has a unique solution if $p \neq 2$ (B) represents parallel lines if p = 2

(C) has infinitely many solutions if $p=2, q=4$ (D) has no solution if $p \neq 2$

SECTION-C

• **Assertion & Reason**

Instructions: In the following questions as Assertion (A) is given followed by a Reason (R). Mark your responses from the following options.

(A) Both Assertion and Reason are true and Reason is the correct explanation of 'Assertion'

(B) Both Assertion and Reason are true and Reason is not the correct explanation of 'Assertion'

(C) Assertion is true but Reason is false

(D) Assertion is false but Reason is true

Q.1 **A :** The graph of equation y + 8 = x + 8 passes through origin.

B : The graph of a linear equation with its constant term = 0 always passes through origin

Q.2 **A :** The equation 2x +3y = 3(2 + y) has a unique solution.

B : The linear equation in two variables has a unique solution.

SECTION-D

• **Comprehension**

Draw the graph of the linear function whose respective values of x and y are given below

x	–3	–2	–1	0	1
y	5	—	3	–	1

Q.1 Write down the linear relation between x and y

(A) x + y = 2 (B) x – y = 2 (C) 2x – y = 2 (D) x – 2y = 2

Q.2 Find the missing numbers from the graph

(A) (4,2) (B) (3,4) (C) (1,2) (D) None of these

Q.3 Find the slope of the above graph

(A) –2 (B) 1 (C) –1 (D) None of these

ANSWER KEY

CONCEPT APPLICATION LEVEL - II

Q.1	D	Q.2	A	Q.3	A	Q.4	A	Q.5	A	Q.6	C	Q.7	C
Q.8	A	Q.9	C	Q.10	B	Q.11	A	Q.12	B	Q.13	A	Q.14	A
Q.15	C	Q.16	A	Q.17	A	Q.18	C	Q.19	C				

CONCEPT APPLICATION LEVEL - III

SECTION-A

Q.1	D	Q.2	B	Q.3	B	Q.4	A	Q.5	D	Q.6	B	Q.7	C
Q.8	D	Q.9	C	Q.10	C	Q.11	B	Q.12	C	Q.13	C	Q.14	A
Q.15	C	Q.16	A	Q.17	A	Q.18	A	Q.19	B	Q.20	D		

SECTION-B

Q.1	(A,B)	Q.2	(A,B)	Q.3	(B,D)	Q.4	(A,C)	Q.5	(A,D)	Q.6	(A,C)

SECTION-C

Q.1 A Q.2 C

SECTION-D

Q.1 A Q.2 A Q.3 C

4 INTRODUCTION TO TRIGONOMETRY

THEORY

4.1 INTRODUCTION :

The word 'trigonometry' comes from greek word. 'tri' (means three) gon (means side) and metron (means measurment). Trigonometry is the study of relationship between the side and angle of triangle.

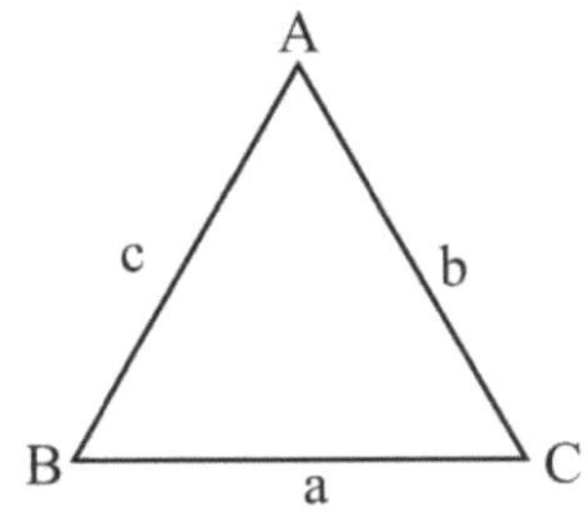

4.2 MEASUREMENT OF ANGLES :

Thus, an angle is considered as the figure obtained by rotating a given ray about its end-point.

Measure of an angle: The measure of an angle is the amount of rotation from the initial side to the terminal side.

Sense of An angle: The sense of an angle is said to be positive or negative according as the initial side rotates in anticlockwise direction or clockwise direction to the terminal side.

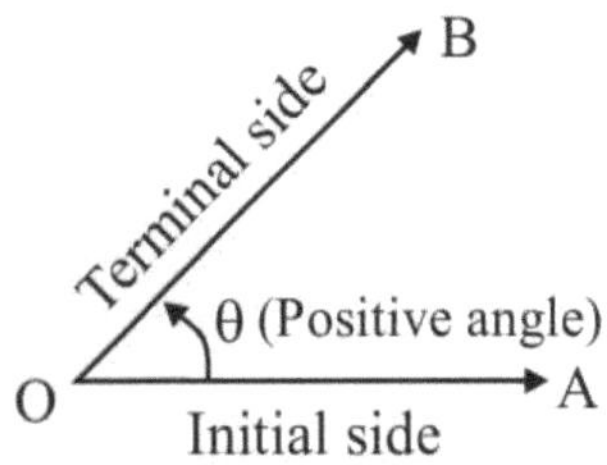

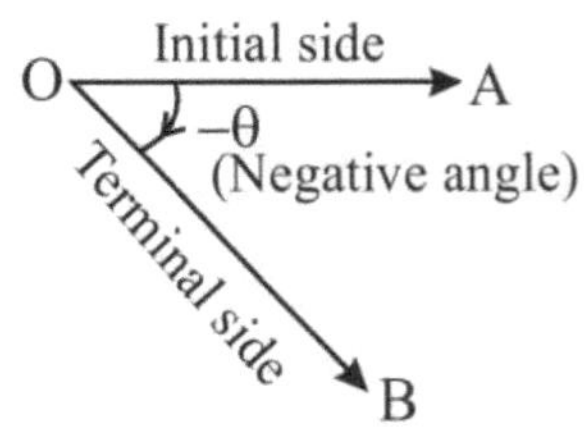

4.3 STANDARD POSITION OF THE ANGLE :

The angle is said to be in standard position if its inital side coincides with the positive X-axis.

Note :

1. Rotation of terminal side in anticlockwise direction we consider the angle formed is positive and rotation in clock wise direction the angle formed is negative.
2. Depending upon the position of terminal side we decide the angle in different quadrants.

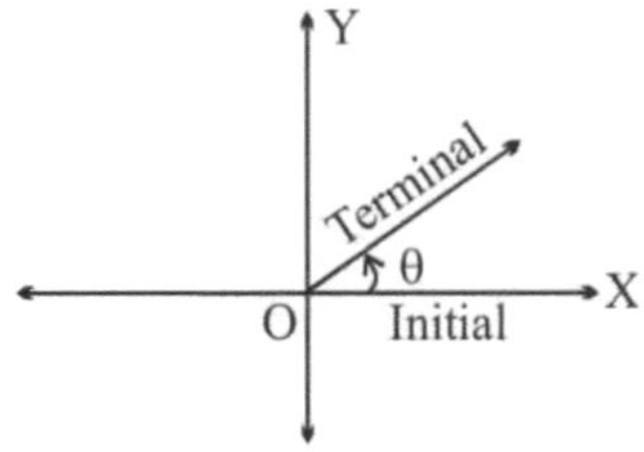

4.4 COTERMINAL ANGLES :

The angles that differ by either 360° or the integral multiples of 360° are called coterminal angles.

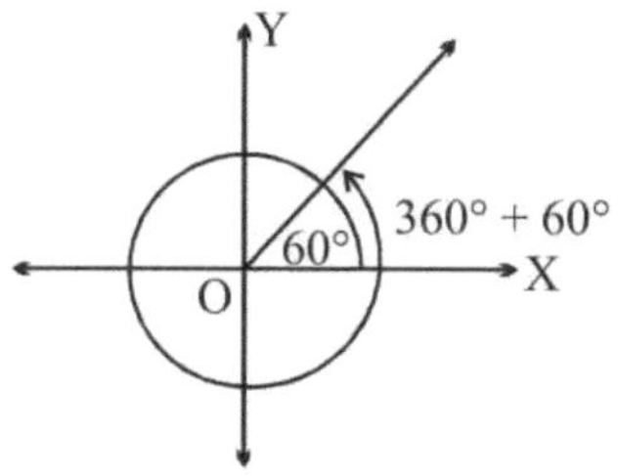

Example :

60°, 360° + 60° = 420°, 2 × 360° + 60° = 780° are coterminal angles.

Note :

1. If θ is an angle then its coterminal angle is in the form of $(n \times 360° + \theta)$.
2. The terminal side of coterminal angles in their standard position coincides.

4.5 SYSTEMS OF MEASUREMENT OF ANGLE :

4.5.1 Sexagesimal system

This system is also called as **British System**.

In this system a right angle is divided into 90 equal parts, called degree. The symbol 1° is used to denote one degree. Thus, one degree is one-ninetieth part of a right angle. Each degree is divided into 60 equal parts, called minutes. The symbol 1' is used to denote one minute. And each minute is divided into 60 equal parts, called second. The symbol 1" is used to denote one second.

Thus, 1 right angle = 90 degrees (= 90°)

1° = 60 mintues (= 60')

1' = 60 seconds (= 60")

4.5.2 Centesimal system

This system is also called as **French System**.

In this system a right angle is divided into 100 equal parts, called grades; each grade is subdivided into 100 minutes, and each minute into 100 seconds.

The symbols 1^g, 1' and 1" are used to denote a grade, a minute, and a second respectively.

Thus, 1 right angle = 100 grades (= 100^g)

1 grade = 100 minutes (=100')

1 minute = 100 seconds (= 100")

4.5.3 Circular System

In this system the unit of measurement is radian as defined below.

One radian, written as 1^c, is the measure of an angle subtended at the centre of a circle an arc of length equal to the radius of the circle.

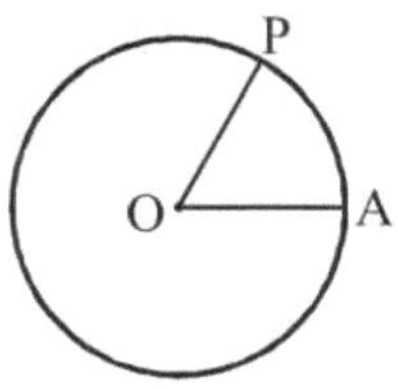

Consider a circle of radius r having centre at O. Let A be a point on the circle. Now cut off an arc AP whose length is equal to the radius r of the circle. Then by the definition of the measure ∠AOP is 1 radian (= 1^c).

4.6 RELATION BETWEEN DEGREES AND RADIANS :

Consider a circle with centre O and radius r. Let A be a point on the circle. Join OA and cut off an arc OP of length equal to the radius of the circle.Then, $\angle AOP = 1$ radian. Produce AO to meet the circle at B.

$\therefore\ \angle AOB =$ a straight angle $= 2$ right angles

We know that the angles at the centre of a circle are proportional to the arcs subtending them.

$$\therefore \quad \frac{\angle AOP}{\angle AOB} = \frac{\text{arc AP}}{\text{arc APB}}$$

$$\Rightarrow \quad \frac{\angle AOP}{2 \text{ right angles}} = \frac{r}{\pi r}$$

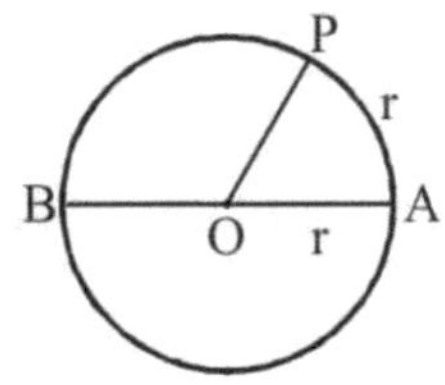

$$\Rightarrow \quad \angle AOP = \frac{2 \text{ right angles}}{\pi}$$

$$\Rightarrow \quad 1^c = \frac{180^\circ}{\pi}$$

Hence, one radian $= \dfrac{180^\circ}{\pi} \Rightarrow \pi$ radians $= 180^\circ$

Remark 1

When an angle is expressed in radians, the word radian is generally omitted.

Remark 2

Since $180^\circ = \pi$ radians. Therefore, $1^\circ = \pi/180$ radian.

Hence, $30^\circ = \dfrac{\pi}{180} \times 30 = \dfrac{\pi}{6}$ radians,

$$45^\circ = \frac{\pi}{180} \times 45 = \frac{\pi}{4} \text{ radians,}$$

$$60^\circ = \frac{\pi}{180} \times 60 = \frac{\pi}{3} \text{ radians,}$$

$$90^\circ = \frac{\pi}{180} \times 90 = \frac{\pi}{2} \text{ radians,}$$

Remark 3

We have,

π radians $= 180^\circ$

$$\therefore \quad 1 \text{ radian} = \frac{180^\circ}{\pi} = \left(\frac{180^\circ}{22} \times 7\right)^\circ = 57^\circ\ 16'\ 22'' \text{ (approx.)}$$

Remark 4

We have,

$180^\circ = \pi$ radians

$$\Rightarrow \quad 1^\circ = \frac{\pi}{180} \text{ radian} = \left(\frac{22}{7 \times 180}\right) \text{ radian} = 0.01746 \text{ radian.}$$

Remember

Note :

(1) The measure of an angle is a real number.

(2) If no unit of measurement is indicated for any angle, it is considered as radian measure.

4.7 RELATION BETWEEN THREE SYSTEMS OF MEASUREMENT OF AN ANGLE

Let D be the number of degrees, R be the number of radians and G be the number of grades in an angle θ. Then the relation between three systems of measurement of an angle is :

$$\frac{\mathbf{D}}{\mathbf{90}} = \frac{\mathbf{G}}{\mathbf{100}} = \frac{\mathbf{R}}{\frac{\pi}{2}}$$

Now, $90° = 1$ right angle

$\Rightarrow \quad 1° = \frac{1}{90}$ right angle

$\Rightarrow \quad D° = \frac{D}{90}$ right angles

$\Rightarrow \quad \theta = \frac{D}{90}$ right angles .....(i)

100 grades = 1 right angle

$\Rightarrow \quad$ 1 grade $= \frac{1}{100}$ right angle

$\Rightarrow \quad$ G grades $= \frac{G}{100}$ right angles

$\Rightarrow \quad \theta = \frac{G}{100}$ right angles .....(ii)

And, Angles, π radians = 2 right angles

$\Rightarrow \quad$ 1 radian $= \frac{2}{\pi}$ right angles

$\Rightarrow \quad$ R radians $= \frac{2R}{\pi}$ right angles

$\Rightarrow \quad \theta = \frac{2R}{\pi}$ right angles .....(iii)

From (i), (ii) and (iii), we get

$$\frac{D}{90} = \frac{G}{100} = \frac{2R}{\pi}$$

This is required relation between the three systems of measurement of an angle. Where D denotes degrees, G grades and R radians.

Illustration 1

Convert 45° into circular measure.

Solution :

Given, $D = 45°$

We have, $\frac{D}{90} = \frac{R}{\frac{\pi}{2}}$,

So, $\frac{45}{90} = \frac{R}{\frac{\pi}{2}}$

$\Rightarrow \quad \frac{1}{2} \times \frac{\pi}{2} = R$

i.e. $R = \frac{\pi}{4}$

Hence, circular measure of 45° is $\frac{\pi^c}{4}$.

Illustration 2

Convert 150^g into sexagesimal measure.

Solution :

Given, $G = 150^g$

We have, $\frac{D}{90} = \frac{G}{100}$,

So, $\frac{D}{90} = \frac{150}{100}$

$\Rightarrow \quad D = \frac{3}{2} \times 90 = 135$

Hence, sexagesimal measure of 150^g is 135°.

Illustration 3

Find the length of an arc of a circle of radius 5 cm subtending a central angle measuring 15°.

Solution

Let s be the length of the arc subtending an angle θ^c at the centre of a circle or radius r. Then, $\theta = \frac{s}{r}$.

Here, $r = 5$ cm and $\theta = 15° = \left(15 \times \frac{\pi}{180}\right)^c = \left(\frac{\pi}{12}\right)^c$

$\therefore \quad \theta = \frac{s}{r} \Rightarrow \frac{\pi}{12} = \frac{s}{5} \Rightarrow s = \frac{5\pi}{12}$ cm.

Illustration 4

Find the degrees the angle subtended at the centre of a circle of diameter 50 cm by an arc of length 11 cm.

Solution

Here, r = 25 cm and s = 11 cm

$$\therefore \quad \theta = \left(\frac{s}{r}\right)^c \Rightarrow \theta = \left(\frac{11}{25}\right)^c = \left(\frac{11}{25} \times \frac{180^\circ}{\pi}\right)^o = \left(\frac{11}{25} \times \frac{180}{22} \times 7\right)^o$$

$$\Rightarrow \quad \theta = \left(\frac{126}{5}\right)^o = \left(25\frac{1}{5}\right)^o = 25^\circ\left(\frac{1}{5} \times 60\right)' = 25^\circ 12'$$

Illustration 5

In a circle of diameter 40 cm the length of a chord is 20 cm. Find the length of minor arc corresponding to the chord.

Solution

Let arc AB = s. It is given that OA = 20 cm and chord AB = 20 cm. Therefore, ΔOAB is an equilateral triangle. Hence,

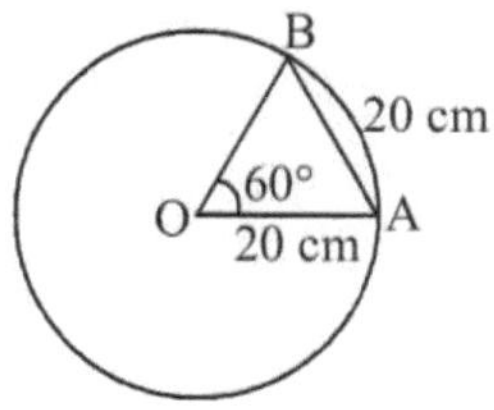

$$\angle AOB = 60^\circ = \left(60 \times \frac{\pi}{180}\right)^c = \left(\frac{\pi}{3}\right)^c$$

Now, $\theta = \frac{\text{arc}}{\text{radius}} \Rightarrow \frac{\pi}{3} = \frac{s}{20} \Rightarrow s = \frac{20\pi}{3}$ cm.

4.8 TRIGONOMETRIC RATIOS :

With reference to angle A in a right angled ΔABC, right angle at C. a is opposite side of angle $\angle A$ (Perpendicular), b is opposite side of angle $\angle B$ and c is opposite side of angle $\angle C$.

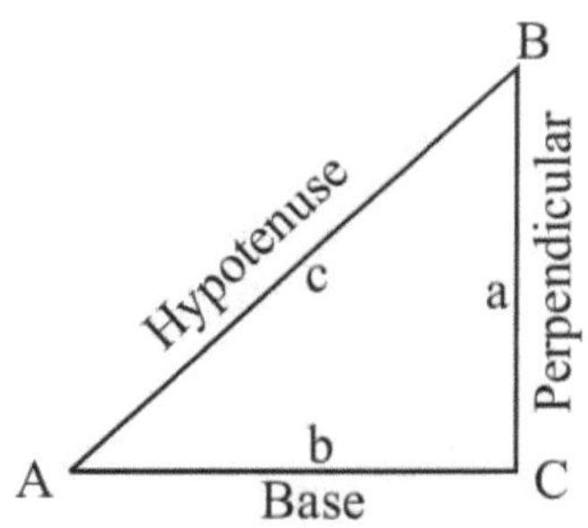

The ratio of sides $\frac{a}{c}, \frac{b}{c}, \frac{a}{b}, \frac{b}{a}, \frac{c}{b}, \frac{c}{a}$ have the following names

$\frac{a}{c}$ is called the sine of A, written as sin A

$\frac{b}{c}$ is called the co-sine of A, written as cos A

$\frac{a}{b}$ is called the tangent of A, written as tan A.

$\frac{b}{a}$ is called the co-tangent of A. written as cot A

$\frac{c}{b}$ is called the secant of A, written as sec A

$\frac{c}{a}$ is called the co-secant of A, written as cosec A.

So there are six trigonometric Ratios :

$$\sin A = \frac{\text{Perpendicular}}{\text{Hypotenuse}} = \frac{a}{c} \qquad \Rightarrow \qquad \cos\ A = \frac{\text{Base}}{\text{Hypotenuse}} = \frac{b}{c}$$

$$\tan A = \frac{\text{Prependicular}}{\text{Base}} = \frac{a}{b} \qquad \Rightarrow \qquad \cot A = \frac{\text{Base}}{\text{Prependicular}} = \frac{b}{a}$$

$$\text{cosec}\, A = \frac{\text{Hypotenuse}}{\text{Prependicular}} = \frac{c}{a} \qquad \Rightarrow \qquad \sec A = \frac{\text{Hypotenuse}}{\text{Base}} = \frac{c}{b}$$

TRICK : **SOME PEOPLE HAVE CURLY BROWN HAIR TO PRODUCE BEAUTY**

Fundamental Relation :

(a) Reciprocal Relation

$$\text{cosec}\, A = \frac{1}{\sin A}, \qquad \sin A = \frac{1}{\text{cosec}\, A}$$

$$\sec A = \frac{1}{\cos A}, \qquad \cos A = \frac{1}{\sec A}$$

$$\cot A = \frac{1}{\tan A}, \qquad \tan A = \frac{1}{\cot A}$$

(b) Quotient Relation

$$\tan A = \frac{\sin A}{\cos A} \qquad \cot A = \frac{\cos A}{\sin A}$$

Illustrations

Illustration 6

Find trigonometric ratio:

In a triangle ABC, right-angled at B, AB = 24 cm, BC = 7 cm. Determine

(i) sin A, cos A (ii) sin C, cos C

Solution

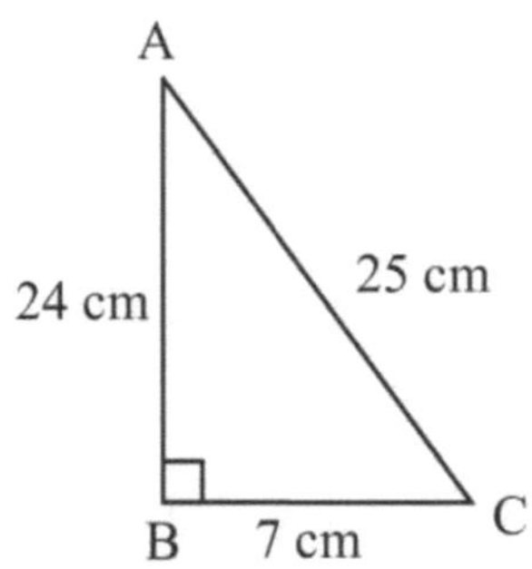

In Δ ABC,

$AB^2 + BC^2 = AC^2$

$\Rightarrow$ $(24)^2 + (7)^2 = AC^2$

$AC^2 = 625$

$\Rightarrow$ $AC = 25$

hypotenuse = 25 cm

(i) For $\angle A$, AB = base
Perpendicular = BC &
hypotenuse = AC

$$\sin A = \frac{\text{Perpendicular}}{\text{hypotenuse}} = \frac{BC}{AC} = \frac{7}{25}$$

$$\cos A = \frac{\text{Base}}{\text{hypotenuse}} = \frac{24}{25}$$

(ii) For $\angle C$, base = BC and
Perpendicular = AB and
hypotenuse = AC

$$\sin C = \frac{\text{Perpendicular}}{\text{hypotenuse}} = \frac{24}{25}$$

$$\cos C = \frac{\text{Base}}{\text{hypotenuse}} = \frac{7}{25}$$

$\therefore$ **(B)**

4.9 TRIGONOMETRIC RATIOS OF SOME SPECIFIC ANGLES 0°, 30°, 45°, 60° AND 90°:

Angle / Ratio	0°	30°	45°	60°	90°
sin	0	$\frac{1}{2}$	$\frac{1}{\sqrt{2}}$	$\frac{\sqrt{3}}{2}$	1
cos	1	$\frac{\sqrt{3}}{2}$	$\frac{1}{\sqrt{2}}$	$\frac{1}{2}$	0
tan	0	$\frac{1}{\sqrt{3}}$	1	$\sqrt{3}$	Not defined
cot	Not defined	$\sqrt{3}$	1	$\frac{1}{\sqrt{3}}$	0
sec	1	$\frac{2}{\sqrt{3}}$	$\sqrt{2}$	2	Not defined
cosec	Not defined	2	$\sqrt{2}$	$\frac{2}{\sqrt{3}}$	1

Trigonometric ratios of 0° and 90° :

Let $\angle XAY = \theta$ be an acute angle and let P be a point on its terminal side AY. Draw perpendicular PM from P on AX.

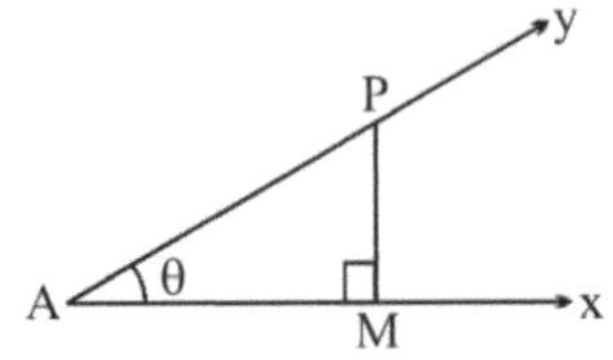

In ΔAMP, we have

$$\sin\theta = \frac{PM}{AP}, \cos\theta = \frac{AM}{AP} \text{ and } \tan\theta = \frac{PM}{AM}$$

It is evident from ΔAMP that as θ becomes smaller and smaller, line segment PM also becomes smaller and smaller; and finally when θ become 0°; the point P will coincide with M. Consequently, we have

$$PM = 0 \text{ and } AP = AM$$

$$\therefore \quad \sin 0° = \frac{PM}{AP} = \frac{0}{AP} = 0; \ \cos 0° = \frac{AM}{AP} = \frac{AP}{AP} = 1 \ \text{ and, } \quad \tan 0° = \frac{PM}{AP} = \frac{0}{AP} = 0$$

Thus, we have, $\sin 0° = 0$, $\cos 0° = 1$ and $\tan 0° = 0$

From ΔAMP, it is evident that as θ increases, line segment AM becomes smaller and smaller and finally when θ become 90°, then point M will coincide with A. Consequently, we have

$$AM = 0, AP = PM$$

$$\therefore \quad \sin 90° = \frac{PM}{AP} = \frac{PM}{PM} = 1 \quad \text{and} \quad \cos 90° = \frac{AM}{AP} = \frac{0}{AP} = 0$$

Thus, we have, $\sin 90° = 1$ and $\cos 90° = 0$

Remark : It is evident from the above discussion that $\tan 90° = \frac{PM}{AM} = \frac{PM}{0}$ is not defined.

Similarly, sec 90°, cosec 0°, cot 0° are not definied.

Trigonometric ratios of 30° and 60° :

Consider an equilateral triangle ABC with each side of length 2a. Since each angle of an equilateral triangle is of 60°. Therefore, each angle of ΔABC is of 60°. Let AD be perpendicular from A on BC. Since the triangle is equilateral. Therefore, AD is the bisector of $\angle$A and D is the mid-point of BC.

$\therefore \quad BD = DC = a$ and $\angle BAD = 30°$

Thus, in ΔABD, $\angle$D is a right angle, hypotenuse AB = 2a and BD = a.

So, by Pythagoras theorem, we have

$$AB^2 = AD^2 + BD^2$$

$$\Rightarrow \quad (2a)^2 = AD^2 + a^2$$

$$\Rightarrow \quad AD^2 = 4a^2 - a^2$$

$$\Rightarrow \quad AD = \sqrt{3}a$$

Trigonometric ratios of 30° :

In right triangle ADB, in reference with the acute angle $\angle A$,

Base = AD = $\sqrt{3}a$, Perpendicular = BD = a, Hypotenuse = AB = 2a and $\angle DAB = 30°$.

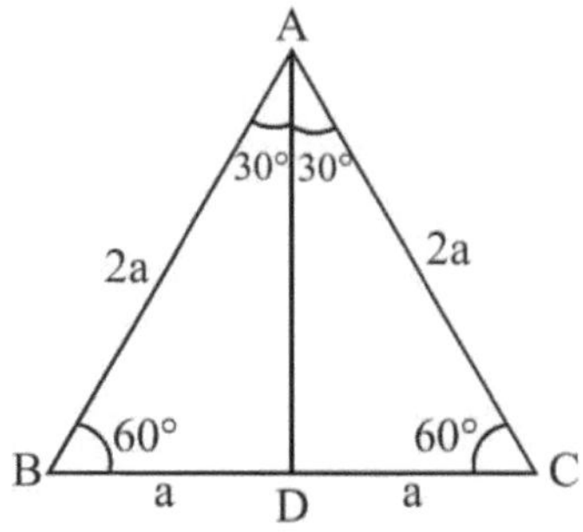

$$\therefore \quad \sin 30° = \frac{BD}{AB} = \frac{a}{2a} = \frac{1}{2}$$

$$\cos 30° = \frac{AD}{AB} = \frac{\sqrt{3}a}{2a} = \frac{\sqrt{3}}{2}$$

$$\tan 30° = \frac{BD}{AD} = \frac{a}{\sqrt{3}a} = \frac{1}{\sqrt{3}};$$

$$\text{cosec } 30° = \frac{1}{\sin 30°} = 2;$$

$$\sec 30° = \frac{1}{\cos 30°} = \frac{2}{\sqrt{3}};$$

$$\cot 30° = \frac{1}{\tan 30°} = \sqrt{3}$$

Trigonometric ratios of 60° :

In right triangle ADB, in reference with the acute angle $\angle A$,

Base =BD = a, Perpendicular = AD = $\sqrt{3}a$, Hypotenuse = AB = 2a and $\angle ABD = 60°$.

$$\therefore \quad \sin 60° = \frac{AD}{AB} = \frac{\sqrt{3}a}{2a} = \frac{\sqrt{3}}{2} \qquad \cos 60° = \frac{BD}{AB} = \frac{a}{2a} = \frac{1}{2}$$

$$\tan 60° = \frac{AD}{BD} = \frac{\sqrt{3}a}{a} = \sqrt{3}; \qquad \text{cosec } 60° = \frac{1}{\sin 60°} = \frac{2}{\sqrt{3}};$$

$$\sec 60° = \frac{1}{\cos 60°} = 2; \qquad \cot 60° = \frac{1}{\tan 60°} = \frac{1}{\sqrt{3}}$$

Trigonometric ratios of 45° :

Consider a right triangle ABC with right angle of B such that

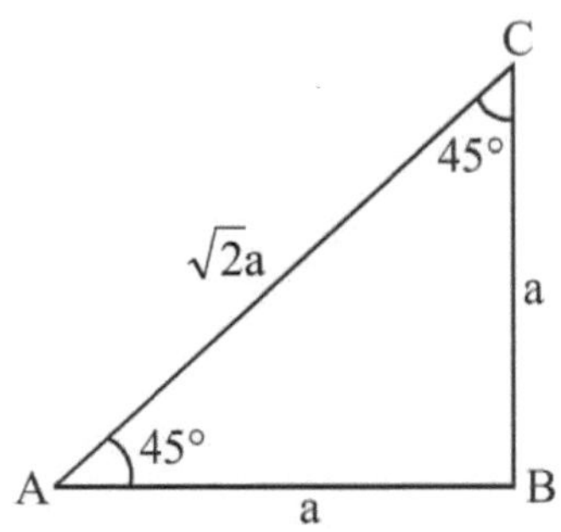

$\angle A = 45°$, Then,

$\angle A + \angle B + \angle C = 180°$

$\Rightarrow \quad 45° + 90° + \angle C = 180°$

$\Rightarrow \quad \angle C = 45°$

$\therefore \quad \angle A = \angle C$

$\Rightarrow \quad AB = BC$

Let AB = BC = a. Then, by Pythagoras theorem, we have

$AC^2 = AB^2 + BC^2$

$\Rightarrow \quad AC^2 = a^2 + a^2 \qquad \Rightarrow \quad AC^2 = 2a^2 \qquad \Rightarrow \quad AC = \sqrt{2}a$

Thus, in ΔABC, we have

$\angle A = 45°$, Base $= AB = a$, Perpendicular $= BC = a$ and Hypotenuse $= AC = \sqrt{2}a$

$\therefore \quad \sin 45° = \dfrac{BC}{AC} = \dfrac{a}{\sqrt{2}a} = \dfrac{1}{\sqrt{2}}, \qquad \cos 45° = \dfrac{AB}{AC} = \dfrac{a}{\sqrt{2}a} = \dfrac{1}{\sqrt{2}}$

$\tan 45° = \dfrac{BC}{AB} = \dfrac{a}{a} = 1, \qquad \text{cosec } 45° = \dfrac{1}{\sin 45°} = \sqrt{2},$

$\sec 45° = \dfrac{1}{\cos 45°} = \sqrt{2}, \qquad \cot 45° = \dfrac{1}{\tan 45°} = \dfrac{1}{1} = 1$

Illustrations

Illustration 7

Find the value of the following:

$4\cos^2 60° + 4\sin^2 45° - \sin^2 30°$

Solution

$4\cos^2 60° + 4\sin^2 45° - \sin^2 30°$

$$4\left(\frac{1}{2}\right)^2 + 4\left(\frac{1}{\sqrt{2}}\right)^2 - \left(\frac{1}{2}\right)^2 = 4\times\frac{1}{4} + 4\times\frac{1}{2} - \frac{1}{4} = \frac{11}{4}$$

4.10 TRIGONOMETRIC RATIOS OF COMPLEMENTARY ANGLES :

Let ΔABC be a right angle triangle at $\angle C = 90°$

so $\quad \angle A + \angle B = 90°$

So $\quad \angle A$ & $\angle B$ are complement angle of each other

$\angle B = 90° - \angle A$

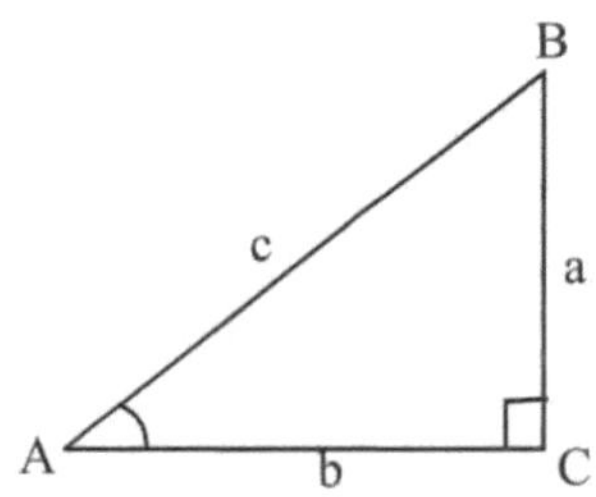

$\sin A = \dfrac{a}{c} = \cos B = \cos(90° - A)$

$\cos A = \dfrac{b}{c} = \sin B = \sin(90° - A)$

$\tan A = \dfrac{a}{b} = \cot B = \cot(90° - A)$

$\cot A = \dfrac{b}{a} = \tan B = \tan(90° - A)$

$\sec A = \dfrac{c}{b} = \text{cosec } B = \text{cosec}(90° - A)$

$\text{cosec } A = \dfrac{c}{a} = \sec B = \sec(90° - A)$

so $\quad \sin(90° - A) = \cos A \qquad \cos(90° - A) = \sin A$

$\tan(90° - A) = \cot A \qquad \cot(90° - A) = \tan A$

$\sec(90° - A) = \text{cosec } A \qquad \text{cosec}(90° - A) = \sec A$

For example :

$$\sin 30^\circ = \sin (90^\circ - 60^\circ) = \cos 60^\circ$$
$$\tan 68^\circ = \tan (90^\circ - 22^\circ) = \cot 22^\circ$$

Illustrations

Illustration 8

Without using trigonometric table, find the value of

(a) $\sin^2 40^\circ - \cos^2 50^\circ$ **(b)** $\dfrac{\cot 54^\circ}{\tan 36^\circ} + \dfrac{\tan 20^\circ}{\cot 70^\circ} - 2$

Solution

(a) $\sin^2 40^\circ - \cos^2 (90^\circ - 40^\circ)$
$= \sin^2 40^\circ - \sin^2 40^\circ = 0$

(b) $\dfrac{\cot 54^\circ}{\tan 36^\circ} + \dfrac{\tan 20^\circ}{\cot 70^\circ} - 2$

$$= \frac{\cot (90^\circ - 36^\circ)}{\tan 36^\circ} + \frac{\tan 20^\circ}{\cot (90^\circ - 20^\circ)} - 2$$

$$= \frac{\tan 36^\circ}{\tan 36^\circ} + \frac{\tan 20^\circ}{\tan 20^\circ} - 2 = 1 + 1 - 2 = 0$$

4.11 TRIGONOMETRIC IDENTITIES

If two expressions are equal for all values of the variables, then the relation is called an identity.

For example, $\dfrac{x+2}{3} + x = \dfrac{4x+1}{3}$ is an identity since L.H.S. = R.H.S for all real value of x.

There are three fundamental trignometric identities

(i) $\cos^2 A + \sin^2 A = 1$
(ii) $1 + \tan^2 A = \sec^2 A$
(iii) $1 + \cot^2 A = \text{cosec}^2 A$

Trigonometric Identities :

An equation involving trigonometric ratios of an angle is called a **trigonometric identity,** if it is true for all values of the angle(s) involved.

In ΔABC, right-angled at B (see Fig.), we have:

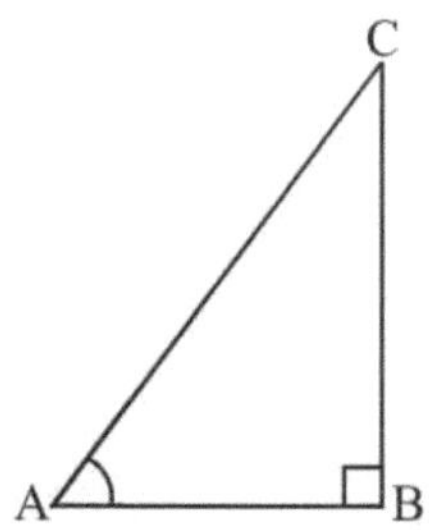

$$AB^2 + BC^2 = AC^2 \quad .....(1)$$

Dividing each term of (1) by AC^2, we get

$$\frac{AB^2}{AC^2} + \frac{BC^2}{AC^2} = \frac{AC^2}{AC^2}$$

i.e., $\left(\dfrac{AB}{AC}\right)^2 + \left(\dfrac{BC}{AC}\right)^2 = \left(\dfrac{AC}{AC}\right)^2$

i.e., $(\cos A)^2 + (\sin A)^2 = 1$

i.e., $\cos^2 A + \sin^2 A = 1 \quad .....(2)$

This is true for all A such that $0^\circ \le A \le 90^\circ$. So, this is a trigonometric identity.

Let us now divide (1) by AB^2. We get

$$\frac{AB^2}{AB^2}+\frac{BC^2}{AB^2}=\frac{AC^2}{AB^2} \quad \text{or,} \quad \left(\frac{AB}{AB}\right)^2+\left(\frac{BC}{AB}\right)^2=\left(\frac{AC}{AB}\right)^2$$

i.e. $\mathbf{1 + tan^2 A = sec^2 A}$ .....(3)

tan A and sec A are not defined for A = 90°. So, (3) is true for all A such that $0° \le A < 90°$.

Let us now divide (1) by BC^2. We get

$$\frac{AB^2}{BC^2}+\frac{BC^2}{BC^2}=\frac{AC^2}{BC^2} \quad \text{i.e.,} \quad \left(\frac{AB}{BC}\right)^2+\left(\frac{BC}{BC}\right)^2=\left(\frac{AC}{BC}\right)^2$$

i.e., $\mathbf{cot^2 A + 1 = cosec^2 A}$ .....(4)

Note that cosec A and cot A are not defined for A = 0°. Therefore (4) is true for all A such that $0° < A \le 90°$.

Using these identities, we can express each trigonometric ratio in terms of other trigonometric ratios, i.e., if any one of the ratios is known, we can also determine the values of other trigonometric ratios.

4.12 RELATION BETWEEN AN ARC, RADIUS AND ANGLE SUBTENDED BY THE ARC AT THE CENTRE OF THE CIRCLE :

Consider a circle with centre 'O', radius 'r',

$\angle AOB = \theta$ and length of arc AB = l as shown in the figure.

Relation between θ, r and l :

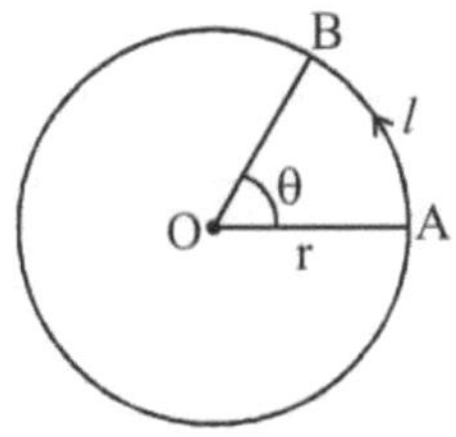

$$\text{angle} = \frac{\text{arc}}{\text{radius}}; \theta = \frac{l}{r}$$

Here θ is always in radian and unit of l and r are always same.

4.13 TRIGONOMETRIC RATIOS OF COMPOUND ANGLES :

1. $\sin(A+B) = \sin A \cos B + \cos A \sin B$
2. $\sin(A-B) = \sin A \cos B - \cos A \sin B$.
3. $\cos(A+B) = \cos A \cos B - \sin A \sin B$
4. $\cos(A-B) = \cos A \cos B + \sin A \sin B$.
5. $\tan(A+B) = \dfrac{\tan A + \tan B}{1 - \tan A \tan B}$
6. $\tan(A-B) = \dfrac{\tan A - \tan B}{1 + \tan A \tan B}$
7. $\sin 2A = 2 \sin A \cos A$ (by taking A = B in the above (1) relation)
8. $\cos 2A = \cos^2 A - \sin^2 A = 2\cos^2 A - 1 = 1 - 2\sin^2 A$ (by taking A = B in the above (3) relation)
9. $\tan 2A = \dfrac{2\tan A}{1 - \tan^2 A}$ (by taking A = B in the above (5) relation)

Illustrations

Illustration 9

Find the value of sin 75°.

Solution:

We have,

$$\sin 75° = \sin(45° + 30°)$$
$$= \sin 45° \cos 30° + \cos 45° \sin 30°$$
$$= \frac{1}{\sqrt{2}} \cdot \frac{\sqrt{3}}{2} + \frac{1}{\sqrt{2}} \cdot \frac{1}{2} = \frac{\sqrt{3}+1}{2\sqrt{2}}$$

$$\therefore \quad \sin 75° = \frac{\sqrt{3}+1}{2\sqrt{2}}.$$

Illustration 10

Find the value of tan 15°.

Solution:

We have,

$$\tan 15° = \tan(45° - 30°) = \frac{\tan 45° - \tan 30°}{1 + \tan 45° \tan 30°}$$

$$= \frac{1 - \frac{1}{\sqrt{3}}}{1 + \frac{1}{\sqrt{3}}} = \frac{\sqrt{3}-1}{\sqrt{3}+1} = \frac{(\sqrt{3}-1)}{(\sqrt{3}+1)} \times \frac{(\sqrt{3}-1)}{(\sqrt{3}-1)}$$

$$= \frac{(\sqrt{3}-1)^2}{3-1} = \frac{3+1-2\sqrt{3}}{2} = \frac{4-2\sqrt{3}}{2} = 2-\sqrt{3}$$

$$\therefore \quad \tan 15° = \frac{\sqrt{3}-1}{\sqrt{3}+1} \text{ or } 2-\sqrt{3}.$$

4.14 SIGNS OF TRIGONOMETRIC RATIOS :

(i) If θ lies in the first quadrant, i.e. $0 < \theta < \frac{\pi}{2}$, then all the trigonometric ratios are taken positive.

(ii) If θ lies in the second quadrant, i.e. $\frac{\pi}{2} < \theta < \pi$, then only $\sin\theta$ and $\operatorname{cosec}\theta$ are taken positive and all the other trigonometric ratios are taken negative.

(iii) If θ lies in the third quadrant, i.e. $\pi < \theta < \frac{3\pi}{2}$, then only $\tan\theta$ and $\cot\theta$ are taken positive and all the other trigonometric ratios are taken negative.

(iv) If θ lies in the fourth quadrant, i.e. $\frac{3\pi}{2} < \theta < 2\pi$, then only $\cos\theta$ and $\sec\theta$ are taken positive and all the other trigonometric ratios are taken negative.

Trigonometric Ratios of $(90° - \theta)$:

$\sin(90° - \theta) = \cos\theta$; $\cos(90° - \theta) = \sin\theta$

$\tan(90° - \theta) = \cot\theta$; $\cot(90° - \theta) = \tan\theta$

$\text{cosec}(90° - \theta) = \sec\theta$; $\sec(90° - \theta) = \text{cosec}\,\theta$

Trigonometric Ratios of $(90° + \theta)$:

$\sin(90° + \theta) = \cos\theta$; $\cos(90° + \theta) = -\sin\theta$

$\tan(90° + \theta) = -\cot\theta$; $\cot(90° + \theta) = -\tan\theta$

$\text{cosec}(90° + \theta) = \sec\theta$; $\sec(90° + \theta) = -\text{cosec}\,\theta$

Trigonometric Ratios of $(180° - \theta)$:

$\sin(180° - \theta) = \sin\theta$; $\cos(180° - \theta) = -\cos\theta$

$\tan(180° - \theta) = -\tan\theta$; $\cot(180° - \theta) = -\cot\theta$

$\text{cosec}(180° - \theta) = \text{cosec}\,\theta$; $\sec(180° - \theta) = -\sec\theta$

Trigonometric Ratios of $(180° + \theta)$:

$\sin(180° + \theta) = -\sin\theta$; $\cos(180° + \theta) = -\cos\theta$

$\tan(180° + \theta) = \tan\theta$; $\cot(180° + \theta) = \cot\theta$

$\text{cosec}(180° + \theta) = -\text{cosec}\,\theta$; $\sec(180° + \theta) = -\sec\theta$

Similarly, the trigonometric ratios of $270° \pm \theta$ and $360° \pm \theta$ can be written.

Note: The trigonometic ratios of $(-\theta)$ are the same the trigonometric ratios of $(360° - \theta)$.
So, $\sin(-\theta) = \sin(360° - \theta) = -\sin\theta$ and as on.

Illustrations

Illustration 11

Find the value of $\sin^2 135° + \sec^2 135°$.

Solution

$$\sin 135° = \sin(180° - 45°) = \sin 45° = \frac{1}{\sqrt{2}}$$

$$\sec 135° = \sec(180° - 45°) = -\sec 45° = -\sqrt{2}$$

$$\therefore \quad \sin^2 135° + \sec^2 135° = \left(\frac{1}{\sqrt{2}}\right)^2 + (-\sqrt{2})^2 = \frac{1}{2} + 2 = \frac{5}{2}$$

SOLVED EXAMPLES

Example 1

If θ is an acute angle and $\tan\theta + \cot\theta = 2$, find the value of $\tan^7\theta + \cot^7\theta$.

Solution

$\tan\theta + \cot\theta = 2$

$\Rightarrow \quad \tan\theta + \dfrac{1}{\tan\theta} = 2 \qquad \Rightarrow \quad \tan^2\theta + 1 = 2\tan\theta$

$\Rightarrow \quad \tan^2\theta - 2\tan\theta + 1 = 0 \qquad \Rightarrow \quad (\tan\theta - 1)^2 = 0$

$\Rightarrow \quad \tan\theta = 1 \qquad \Rightarrow \quad \theta = 45°$

$\tan^7\theta + \cot^7\theta = (\tan 45°)^7 + (\cot 45°)^7$

$= 1 + 1 = 2$

Example 2

If $\dfrac{\cos\theta - \sin\theta}{\cos\theta + \sin\theta} = \dfrac{1-\sqrt{3}}{1+\sqrt{3}}$, then find the acute angle θ.

Solution

$$\frac{\cos\theta - \sin\theta}{\cos\theta + \sin\theta} = \frac{1-\sqrt{3}}{1+\sqrt{3}}$$

Applying componendo and dividendo

$$\Rightarrow \quad \frac{(\cos\theta - \sin\theta) + (\cos\theta + \sin\theta)}{(\cos\theta - \sin\theta) - (\cos\theta + \sin\theta)} = \frac{\left(1-\sqrt{3}\right) + \left(1+\sqrt{3}\right)}{\left(1-\sqrt{3}\right) - \left(1+\sqrt{3}\right)}$$

$\Rightarrow \quad \dfrac{2\cos\theta}{-2\sin\theta} = \dfrac{2}{-2\sqrt{3}} \qquad \Rightarrow \quad \cot\theta = \dfrac{1}{\sqrt{3}}$

$\Rightarrow \quad \tan\theta = \sqrt{3} \qquad \Rightarrow \quad \theta = 60°$

Example 3

In an acute angled triangle ABC if $\tan(A + B - C) = 1$ and $\sec(B + C - A) = 2$, find the value of A, B and C.

Solution

We have

$\Rightarrow \quad \tan(A + B - C) = 1 \quad$ and $\quad \sec(B + C - A) = 2$

$\Rightarrow \quad \tan(A + B - C) = \tan 45° \quad$ and $\quad \sec(B + C - A) = \sec 60°$

$\Rightarrow \quad A + B - C = 45° \quad$ .....(1)

and $\quad B + C - A = 60° \quad$ .....(2)

Adding equations (1) and (2), we get

$2B = 105°$

$\Rightarrow \quad B = 52\frac{1}{2}°$

Putting $52\frac{1}{2}^\circ$ in $B + C - A = 60^\circ$, we get

$$52\frac{1}{2}^\circ + C - A = 60^\circ$$

$\Rightarrow \quad C - A = 7\frac{1}{2}^\circ$ .....(3)

Also, in ΔABC we have

$$A + B + C = 180^\circ$$

$\Rightarrow \quad A + 52\frac{1}{2}^\circ + C = 180^\circ$

$\Rightarrow \quad C + A = 127\frac{1}{2}^\circ$ .....(4)

Adding and substituting (3) and (4), we get

$$2C = 135^\circ \text{ and } 2A = 120^\circ$$

$\Rightarrow \quad C = 67\frac{1}{2}^\circ$ and $A = 60^\circ$

So, $\quad A = 60^\circ,\ B = 52\frac{1}{2}^\circ$ and $C = 67\frac{1}{2}^\circ$

Example 4

Prove that

(a) $\sqrt{\sec^2\theta + \operatorname{cosec}^2\theta} = \tan\theta + \cot\theta$ **(b)** $\dfrac{\cot A + \operatorname{cosec} A - 1}{\cot A - \operatorname{cosec} A + 1} = \dfrac{1 + \cos A}{\sin A}$

Solution

(a) LHS $= \sqrt{\sec^2\theta + \operatorname{cosec}^2\theta} = \sqrt{(1+\tan^2\theta) + (1+\cot^2\theta)}$

$$= \sqrt{2 + \tan^2\theta + \cot^2\theta} = \sqrt{\tan^2\theta + 2\tan\theta.\cot\theta + \cot^2\theta}$$

$$= \sqrt{(\tan\theta + \cot\theta)^2} = \tan\theta + \cot\theta$$

$$= \text{RHS}$$

(b) LHS $= \dfrac{\cot A + \operatorname{cosec} A - 1}{\cot A - \operatorname{cosec} A + 1} = \dfrac{(\cot A + \operatorname{cosec} A) - (\operatorname{cosec}^2 A - \cot^2 A)}{(\cot A - \operatorname{cosec} A) + 1}$

$$= \frac{(\operatorname{cosec} A + \cot A) - (\operatorname{cosec} A - \cot A)(\operatorname{cosec} A + \cot A)}{\cot A - \operatorname{cosec} A + 1}$$

$$= \frac{(\operatorname{cosec} A + \cot A) \times [1 - (\operatorname{cosec} A - \cot A)]}{(\cot A - \operatorname{cosec} A + 1)}$$

$$= \frac{(\operatorname{cosec} A + \cot A)\ (1 - \operatorname{cosec} A + \cot A)}{(1 - \operatorname{cosec} A + \cot A)}$$

$$= \operatorname{cosec} A + \cot A = \text{RHS}$$

Example 5

Prove : $\dfrac{\sin A+\cos A}{\sin A-\cos A}+\dfrac{\sin A-\cos A}{\sin A+\cos A}=\dfrac{2}{\sin^2 A-\cos^2 A}=\dfrac{2}{1-2\cos^2 A}$

Solution

L.H.S. $\dfrac{\sin A+\cos A}{\sin A-\cos A}+\dfrac{\sin A-\cos A}{\sin A+\cos A}$

$$=\frac{\sin^2+\cos^2 A+2\sin A\cos A+\sin^2 A+\cos^2 A-2\sin A\cos A}{(\sin A+\cos A)(\sin A-\cos A)}$$

$$=\frac{2}{\sin^2 A-\cos^2 A}=\frac{2}{1-\cos^2 A-\cos^2 A}=\frac{2}{1-2\cos^2 A} \quad \text{R.H.S.}$$

Example 6

For all values of α, what is the value of the expression $\cot^2\alpha\dfrac{\sec\alpha-1}{1+\sin\alpha}+\sec^2\alpha\dfrac{\sin\alpha-1}{1+\sec\alpha}$.

Solution

$$\cot^2\alpha\,\frac{\sec\alpha-1}{1+\sin\alpha}+\sec^2\alpha\,\frac{\sin\alpha-1}{1+\sec\alpha}$$

$$=\frac{\cot^2\alpha(\sec^2\alpha-1)+\sec^2\alpha(\sin^2\alpha-1)}{(1+\sin\alpha)(1+\sec\alpha)}=\frac{\cot^2\alpha\tan^2\alpha-\sec^2\alpha(1-\sin^2\alpha)}{(1+\sin\alpha)(1+\sec\alpha)}$$

$$=\frac{1-\sec^2\alpha\cos^2\alpha}{(1+\sin\alpha)(1+\sec\alpha)}=\frac{1-1}{(1+\sin\alpha)(1+\sec\alpha)}=0.$$

Example 7

If a sec θ + b tan θ + c = 0 and p sec θ + q tanθ + r = 0. Prove that $(br-qc)^2-(pc-ar)^2=(aq-pb)^2$

Sol. We have

$a\sec\theta+b\tan\theta+c=0$ and $p\sec\theta+q\tan\theta+r=0$

Solving these two equations for secθ and tanθ by the cross multiplication, we get

$$\frac{\sec\theta}{br-qc}=\frac{\tan\theta}{cp-ar}=\frac{1}{aq-bp}$$

$$\sec\theta=\frac{br-cq}{aq-bp}\text{ and }\tan\theta=\frac{cp-ar}{aq-bp}$$

Now, $\sec^2\theta-\tan^2\theta=1$

$$\Rightarrow\quad\left(\frac{br-cq}{aq-bp}\right)^2-\left(\frac{cp-ar}{aq-bp}\right)^2=1$$

$$\Rightarrow\quad(br-cq)^2-(cp-ar)^2=(aq-bp)^2$$

Example 8

If $\sin\theta + \sin^2\theta + \sin^3\theta = 1$, then prove that $\cos^6\theta - 4\cos^4\theta + 8\cos^2\theta = 4$

Solution

We have

$\sin\theta + \sin^2\theta + \sin^3\theta = 1$

$\Rightarrow \sin\theta + \sin^3\theta = 1 - \sin^2\theta$

$\Rightarrow \sin\theta(1 + \sin^2\theta) = \cos^2\theta$

Now squaring both side

$\Rightarrow \sin^2\theta(1 + \sin^2\theta)^2 = \cos^4\theta$

$\Rightarrow (1 - \cos^2\theta)\{1 + (1 - \cos^2\theta\}^2 = \cos^4\theta$

$\Rightarrow (1 - \cos^2\theta)\{2 - \cos^2\theta\}^2 = \cos^4\theta$

$\Rightarrow (1 - \cos^2\theta)(4 - 4\cos^2\theta + \cos^4\theta) = \cos^4\theta$

$\Rightarrow 4 - 4\cos^2\theta + \cos^4\theta - 4\cos^2\theta + 4\cos^4\theta - \cos^6\theta = \cos^4\theta$

$\Rightarrow 4 - 8\cos^2\theta + 4\cos^4\theta - \cos^6\theta = 0$

$\Rightarrow \cos^6\theta - 4\cos^4\theta + 8\cos^2\theta = 4$

Example 9

If $\sec\theta + \tan\theta = p$, obtain the value of $\sec\theta$, $\tan\theta$ and $\sin\theta$ in terms of P

Solution

Its given that

$\because \sec\theta + \tan\theta = P$ .....(1)

$\sec^2\theta - \tan^2\theta = 1$

$\Rightarrow (\sec\theta + \tan\theta)(\sec\theta - \tan\theta) = 1$

$\Rightarrow p(\sec\theta - \tan\theta) = 1$

$\Rightarrow (\sec\theta - \tan\theta) = 1/p$ .....(2)

Adding equations (1) and (2), we get

$$2\sec\theta = p + \frac{1}{p} = \frac{p^2+1}{p}$$

$$\sec\theta = \frac{p^2+1}{2p} \text{ and } \tan\theta = \frac{p^2-1}{2p}$$

$$\sin\theta = \frac{\tan\theta}{\sec\theta} = \frac{p^2-1}{p^2+1}$$

CONCEPT APPLICATION LEVEL - I [NCERT Questions]

Q.1 In ΔABC, right angled at B, AB = 24 cm, BC = 7 cm. Determine:

(i) sin A, cos A (ii) sin C, cos C

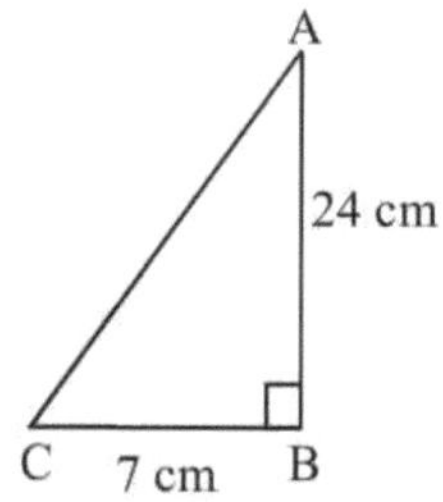

Sol. (i) In ΔABC,

$\because \angle B = 90°$ (Given)

$\therefore AC^2 = AB^2 + BC^2$ (By Pythagoras theorem)

$= (24)^2 + (7)^2 = 576 + 49 = 625$

$\Rightarrow AC = \sqrt{625} = 25$ cm

$\therefore \sin A = \frac{BC}{AC} = \frac{7}{25}$

and $\cos A = \frac{AB}{AC} = \frac{24}{25}$.

(ii) $\sin C = \frac{AB}{AC} = \frac{24}{25}$; $\cos C = \frac{BC}{AC} = \frac{7}{25}$

Q.2 If $\sin A = \frac{3}{4}$, calculate cos A and tan A.

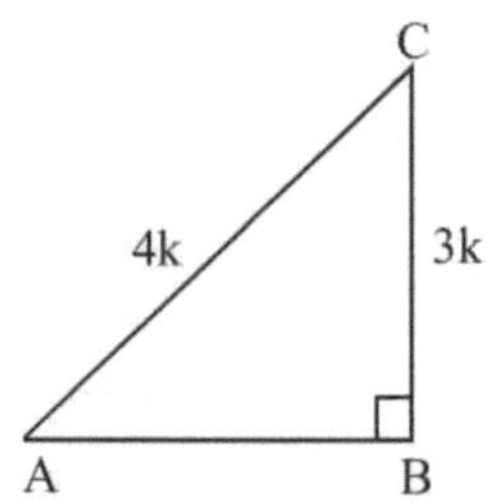

Sol. Let us draw a right triangle ABC.

$\sin A = \frac{3}{4}$ (Given)

$\Rightarrow \frac{BC}{AC} = \frac{3}{4}$ $\Rightarrow \frac{BC}{3} = \frac{AC}{4} = k$ (say)

where k is a positive number

$\Rightarrow BC = 3k;\quad AC = 4k$

By using the Pythagoras theorem, we have

$AC^2 = AB^2 + BC^2$

$\Rightarrow (4k)^2 = AB^2 + (3k)^2$

$\Rightarrow 16k^2 = AB^2 + 9k^2$

$\Rightarrow AB^2 = 16k^2 - 9k^2$

$\Rightarrow AB^2 = 7k^2$

$\Rightarrow AB = \sqrt{7}k$

Now, $\cos A = \frac{AB}{AC} = \frac{\sqrt{7}k}{4k} = \frac{\sqrt{7}}{4}$

and $\tan A = \frac{BC}{AB} = \frac{3k}{\sqrt{7}k} = \frac{3}{\sqrt{7}}$

Q.3 In ΔPQR, right angled at Q, PR + QR = 25 cm and PQ = 5 cm. Determine the values of sin P, cos P and tan P.

Sol. In ΔPQR,

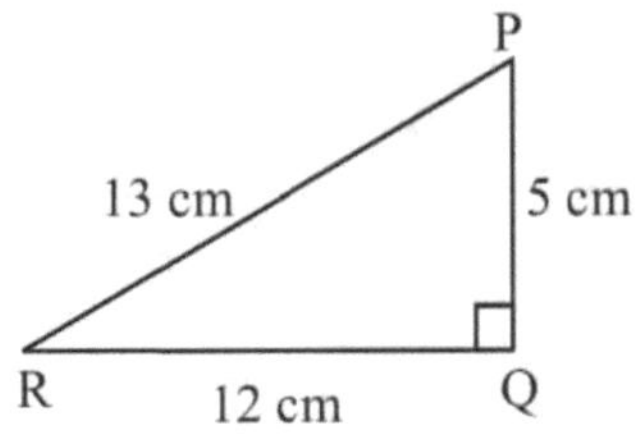

$\because \quad \angle Q = 90°$ (Given)

$\therefore \quad PR^2 = PQ^2 + QR^2$ (By Pythagoras theorem)

$\Rightarrow \quad (25 - QR)^2 = (5)^2 + QR^2$ ($\because$ PR + QR = 25 (given))

$\Rightarrow \quad 625 + QR^2 - 50QR = 25 + QR^2$

$\Rightarrow \quad 50\ QR = 600$

$\Rightarrow \quad QR = \frac{600}{50} = 12 \text{ cm}$

Now, $PR + QR = 25$

$\Rightarrow \quad PR + 12 = 25$

$\Rightarrow \quad PR = 25 - 12$

$\Rightarrow \quad PR = 13 \text{ cm}$

So, $\sin P = \frac{QR}{PR} = \frac{12}{13}$; $\cos P = \frac{PQ}{PR} = \frac{5}{13}$ and $\tan P = \frac{QR}{PQ} = \frac{12}{5}$

Q.4 State whether the following are true or false. Justify your answer.

(i) The value of tan A is always less than 1.

(ii) $\sec A = \frac{12}{5}$ for some value of angle A.

(iii) cos A is the abbreviation used for the cosecant of angle A.

(iv) cot A is the product of cot and A.

(v) $\sin \theta = \frac{4}{3}$ for some angle θ.

Sol. (i) **False** since $\tan A = \frac{\text{Perpendicular}}{\text{Base}}$ and perpendicular may be longer than base.

(ii) **True** since $\sec A = \frac{\text{Hypotenuse}}{\text{Base}}$ and hypotenuse being the longest side may be $\frac{12}{5}$ times the base.

(iii) **False** since cos A is the abbreviation used for the cosine of angle A.

(iv) **False** since cot A is used as an abbreviation for 'the cotangent' of the angle A.

(v) **False** since the hypotenuse is the longest side in a right triangle. As such the value of sin A is always less than 1 (or, in particular equal to 1).

Q.5 Evaluate the following

(i) $\dfrac{\sin 30° + \tan 45° - \text{cosec } 60°}{\sec 30° + \cos 60° + \cot 45°}$ **(ii)** $\dfrac{5\cos^2 60° + 4\sec^2 30° - \tan^2 45°}{\sin^2 30° + \cos^2 30°}$

Sol. (i)

$$\frac{\sin 30° + \tan 45° - \text{cosec } 60°}{\sec 30° + \cos 60° + \cot 45°} = \frac{\frac{1}{2}+1-\frac{2}{\sqrt{3}}}{\frac{2}{\sqrt{3}}+\frac{1}{2}+1} = \frac{\frac{\sqrt{3}+2\sqrt{3}-4}{2\sqrt{3}}}{\frac{4+\sqrt{3}+2\sqrt{3}}{2\sqrt{3}}} = \frac{\frac{3\sqrt{3}-4}{2\sqrt{3}}}{\frac{4+3\sqrt{3}}{2\sqrt{3}}} = \frac{3\sqrt{3}-4}{4+3\sqrt{3}}$$

$$= \frac{(3\sqrt{3}-4)}{(4+3\sqrt{3})} \times \frac{(4-3\sqrt{3})}{(4-3\sqrt{3})} = \frac{12\sqrt{3}-27-16+12\sqrt{3}}{16-27}$$

$$= \frac{24\sqrt{3}-43}{-11} = \frac{43-24\sqrt{3}}{11}$$

(ii)

$$\frac{5\cos^2 60° + 4\sec^2 30° - \tan^2 45°}{\sin^2 30° + \cos^2 30°} = \frac{5\left(\frac{1}{2}\right)^2 + 4\left(\frac{2}{\sqrt{3}}\right)^2 - (1)^2}{\left(\frac{1}{2}\right)^2 + \left(\frac{\sqrt{3}}{2}\right)^2} = \frac{\frac{5}{4}+\frac{16}{3}-1}{\frac{1}{4}+\frac{3}{4}}$$

$$= \frac{\frac{15+64-12}{12}}{1} = \frac{67}{12}$$

Q.6 If $\tan(A+B) = \sqrt{3}$ and $\tan(A-B) = \dfrac{1}{\sqrt{3}}$; $0° < A + B \le 90°$; $A > B$, find A and B.

Sol. $\tan(A+B) = \sqrt{3} = \tan 60° \Rightarrow A + B = 60°$ .....(1)

$\tan(A-B) = \dfrac{1}{\sqrt{3}} = \tan 30° \Rightarrow A - B = 30°$ .....(2)

Solving (1) and (2), we get

$\angle A = 45°$ and $\angle B = 15°$

Q.7 If tan A = cot B, prove that A + B = 90°.

Sol. $\tan A = \cot B$

$\Rightarrow \tan A = \tan(90° - B)$ $(\because \tan(90° - \theta) = \cot\theta)$

$\Rightarrow A = 90° - B$ $(\because$ A and $90° - B$ are both acute angles$)$

$\Rightarrow A + B = 90°$

Q.8 Evaluate :

(i) $\dfrac{\tan 26^\circ}{\cot 64^\circ}$ (ii) $\text{cosec } 31^\circ - \sec 59^\circ$

Sol. (i) $\dfrac{\tan 26^\circ}{\cot 64^\circ} = \dfrac{\tan 26^\circ}{\cot(90^\circ - 26^\circ)} = \dfrac{\tan 26^\circ}{\tan 26^\circ}$ $(\because \cot(90^\circ - \theta) = \tan\theta)$

$= 1$

(ii) $\text{cosec } 31^\circ - \sec 59^\circ = \text{cosec } 31^\circ - \sec(90^\circ - 31^\circ)$

$= \text{cosec } 31^\circ - \text{cosec } 31^\circ$ $(\because \sec(90^\circ - \theta) = \text{cosec }\theta)$

$= 0$

Q.9 If sec 4A = cosec (A – 20°), where 4A is an acute angle, find the value of A.

Sol. $\sec 4A = \text{cosec }(A - 20^\circ)$

$\Rightarrow$ $\text{cosec }(90^\circ - 4A) = \text{cosec }(A - 20^\circ)$ $(\because \text{cosec }(90^\circ - \theta) = \sec\theta)$

$\Rightarrow$ $90^\circ - 4A = A - 20^\circ$ $(\because 90^\circ - 4A$ and $A - 20^\circ$ are both acute angles)

$\Rightarrow$ $5A = 110^\circ$

$\Rightarrow$ $A = \dfrac{110^\circ}{5} = 22^\circ$

Q.10 If A, B and C are interior angles of a triangle ABC, then show that $\sin\left(\dfrac{B+C}{2}\right) = \cos\dfrac{A}{2}$.

Sol. L.H.S. $= \sin\left(\dfrac{B+C}{2}\right) = \sin\left(\dfrac{180^\circ - A}{2}\right)$

$[\because A + B + C = 180^\circ$ (the sum of the interior angles of a triangle is 180°)]

$= \sin\left(90^\circ - \dfrac{A}{2}\right) = \cos\dfrac{A}{2}$ $(\because \sin(90^\circ - \theta) = \cos\theta)$

= R.H.S.

Q.11 Expresss the trigonometric ratios sin A, sec A and tan A in terms of cot A.

Sol. (i) $\sin A = \dfrac{1}{\text{cosec } A} = \dfrac{1}{\sqrt{\text{cosec}^2 A}} = \dfrac{1}{\sqrt{1 + \cot^2 A}}$

(ii) $\sec A = \sqrt{\sec^2 A} = \sqrt{1 + \tan^2 A} = \sqrt{1 + \dfrac{1}{\cot^2 A}} = \dfrac{\sqrt{1 + \cot^2 A}}{\cot A}$

(iii) $\tan A = \dfrac{1}{\cot A}$

Q.12 Write all the other trigonometric ratios of $\angle A$ in terms of sec A.

Sol. $$\sin A = \frac{1}{\text{cosec } A} = \frac{1}{\sqrt{\text{cosec}^2 A}} = \frac{1}{\sqrt{1+\cot^2 A}} = \frac{1}{\sqrt{1+\frac{1}{\tan^2 A}}} = \frac{1}{\sqrt{\frac{\tan^2 A+1}{\tan^2 A}}} = \frac{1}{\sqrt{\frac{\tan^2 A+1}{\tan A}}}$$

$$= \frac{\tan A}{\sqrt{\tan^2 A+1}} = \frac{\tan A}{\sec A} = \frac{\sqrt{\tan^2 A}}{\sec A} = \frac{\sqrt{\sec^2 A-1}}{\sec A}$$

Aliter.

$$\sin A = \frac{\sin A}{1} = \frac{\frac{\sin A}{\cos A}}{\frac{1}{\cos A}} = \frac{\tan A}{\sec A} = \frac{\sqrt{\tan^2 A}}{\sec A} = \frac{\sqrt{\sec^2 A-1}}{\sec A};$$

$$\cos A = \frac{1}{\sec A}; \qquad \tan A = \sqrt{\tan^2 A} = \sqrt{\sec^2 A-1};$$

$$\text{cosec } A = \frac{1}{\sin A} = \frac{\sec A}{\sqrt{\sec^2 A-1}}; \qquad \cot A = \frac{1}{\tan A} = \frac{1}{\sqrt{\sec^2 A-1}}$$

Q.13 Prove the following identies, where the angles involved are acute angles for which the expressions are defined.

(i) $$\frac{\tan\theta}{1-\cot\theta} + \frac{\cot\theta}{1-\tan\theta} = 1 + \sec\theta + \text{cosec }\theta$$

[Hint : Write the expression in terms of sin θ and cos θ]

(ii) $$\frac{1+\sec A}{\sec A} = \frac{\sin^2 A}{1-\cos A}$$

[Hint : Simplify LHS and RHS separately]

(iii) $$\frac{\cos A-\sin A+1}{\cos A+\sin A-1} = \text{cosec } A + \cot A$$

using the identity $\text{cosec}^2 A = 1 + \cot^2 A$

(iv) $$\frac{\sin\theta - 2\sin^3\theta}{2\cos^3\theta - \cos\theta} = \tan\theta$$

(v) $$(\text{cosec } A - \sin A)(\sec A - \cos A) = \frac{1}{\tan A + \cot A}$$

Sol. **(i)** L.H.S. $= \dfrac{\tan\theta}{1-\cot\theta} + \dfrac{\cot\theta}{1-\tan\theta}$

$$= \frac{\frac{\sin\theta}{\cos\theta}}{1-\frac{\cos\theta}{\sin\theta}} + \frac{\frac{\cos\theta}{\sin\theta}}{1-\frac{\sin\theta}{\cos\theta}}$$

$$= \frac{\sin^2\theta}{\cos\theta(\sin\theta-\cos\theta)} + \frac{\cos^2\theta}{\sin\theta(\cos\theta-\sin\theta)}$$

$$= \frac{\sin^3\theta-\cos^3\theta}{\sin\theta\cos\theta\,(\sin\theta-\cos\theta)}$$

$$= \frac{(\sin\theta-\cos\theta)\,(\sin^2\theta+\cos^2\theta+\sin\theta\cos\theta)}{\sin\theta\cos\theta\,(\sin\theta-\cos\theta)}$$

$$= \frac{1+\sin\theta\cos\theta}{\sin\theta\cos\theta} \qquad (\because\ \sin^2\theta+\cos^2\theta=1)$$

$$= \frac{1}{\sin\theta\cos\theta} + \frac{\sin\theta\cos\theta}{\sin\theta\cos\theta}$$

$$= \frac{1}{\sin\theta}\,\frac{1}{\cos\theta} + 1 = \text{cosec}\,\theta\,\sec\theta + 1$$

$= 1 + \sec\theta \cdot \text{cosec}\,\theta$

$=$ R.H.S.

(ii) L.H.S. $= \dfrac{1+\sec A}{\sec A} = \dfrac{1+\frac{1}{\cos A}}{\frac{1}{\cos A}}$

$$= \frac{\frac{\cos A+1}{\cos A}}{\frac{1}{\cos A}} = \cos A + 1 = 1 + \cos A$$

$$= \frac{(1+\cos A)\,(1-\cos A)}{1-\cos A}$$

$$= \frac{1-\cos^2 A}{1-\cos A} = \frac{\sin^2 A}{1-\cos A} \qquad (\because\ \sin^2 A+\cos^2 A=1)$$

$=$ R.H.S.

(iii) L.H.S. $= \dfrac{\cos A - \sin A + 1}{\cos A + \sin A - 1} = \dfrac{\dfrac{\cos A}{\sin A} - \dfrac{\sin A}{\sin A} + \dfrac{1}{\sin A}}{\dfrac{\cos A}{\sin A} + \dfrac{\sin A}{\sin A} - \dfrac{1}{\sin A}}$

[Dividing the numerator and denominator by sin A]

$= \dfrac{\cot A - 1 + \operatorname{cosec} A}{\cot A + 1 - \operatorname{cosec} A} = \dfrac{\cot A + \operatorname{cosec} A - 1}{\cot A - \operatorname{cosec} A + 1}$

$= \dfrac{\{(\cot A + \operatorname{cosec} A) - 1\}(\cot A + \operatorname{cosec} A)}{\{(\cot A - \operatorname{cosec} A) + 1\}(\cot A + \operatorname{cosec} A)}$

[Multiplying both numerator and denominator by $(\cot A + \operatorname{cosec} A)$]

$= \dfrac{\{(\cot A + \operatorname{cosec} A) - 1\}(\cot A + \operatorname{cosec} A)}{\{(\cot^2 A - \operatorname{cosec}^2 A) + (\cot A + \operatorname{cosec} A)\}}$

$= \dfrac{\{(\cot A + \operatorname{cosec} A) - 1\}(\cot A + \operatorname{cosec} A)}{\{-1 + (\cot A + \operatorname{cosec} A)\}}$ $(\because 1 + \cot^2 A = \operatorname{cosec}^2 A)$

$= \operatorname{cosec} A + \cot A =$ R.H.S.

(iv) L.H.S. $= \dfrac{\sin\theta - 2\sin^3\theta}{2\cos^3\theta - \cos\theta} = \dfrac{\sin\theta(1 - 2\sin^2\theta)}{\cos\theta(2\cos^2\theta - 1)}$

$= \dfrac{\sin\theta(\cos^2\theta + \sin^2\theta - 2\sin^2\theta)}{\cos\theta(2\cos^2\theta - \cos^2\theta - \sin^2\theta)}$ $(\because \cos^2\theta + \sin^2\theta = 1)$

$= \dfrac{\sin\theta(\cos^2\theta - \sin^2\theta)}{\cos\theta(\cos^2\theta - \sin^2\theta)} = \tan\theta =$ R.H.S.

(v) L.H.S. $= (\operatorname{cosec} A - \sin A)(\sec A - \cos A)$

$= \left(\dfrac{1}{\sin A} - \sin A\right)\left(\dfrac{1}{\cos A} - \cos A\right)$

$= \dfrac{1 - \sin^2 A}{\sin A} \cdot \dfrac{1 - \cos^2 A}{\cos A} = \dfrac{\cos^2 A}{\sin A} \cdot \dfrac{\sin^2 A}{\cos A}$ $(\because \sin^2 A + \cos^2 A = 1)$

$= \dfrac{\sin A \cos A}{1} = \dfrac{\sin A \cos A}{\sin^2 A + \cos^2 A}$ $(\because \sin^2 A + \cos^2 A = 1)$

$= \dfrac{\dfrac{\sin A \cos A}{\sin A \cos A}}{\dfrac{\sin^2 A}{\sin A \cos A} + \dfrac{\cos^2 A}{\sin A \cos A}}$ (Dividing the numerator and denominator by sin A cos A)

$= \dfrac{1}{\tan A + \cot A}$

= R.H.S.

CONCEPT APPLICATION LEVEL - II [Previous Year Questions]

Q.1 Find the value of the given expression $3(\sin x - \cos x)^4 + 6(\sin x + \cos x)^2 + 4(\sin^6 x + \cos^6 x)$

[NSTSE-2013]

(A) $1 - 3\sin^2 x\cos^2 x$ (B) 11 (C) 13 (D) $2\cos x \sin x - 1$

Q.2 Find the value of the trigonometric expression $\cot\left(\frac{\pi}{20}\right)\cot\left(\frac{3\pi}{20}\right)\cot\left(\frac{5\pi}{20}\right)\cot\left(\frac{7\pi}{20}\right)\cot\left(\frac{9\pi}{20}\right)$

[NSTSE-2013]

(A) 0 (B) $3\sqrt{3}$ (C) $\frac{1}{3\sqrt{3}}$ (D) 1

Q.3 Evaluate $\sin^2\left(\frac{\pi}{4}\right) + \sin^2\left(\frac{3\pi}{4}\right) + \sin^2\left(\frac{5\pi}{4}\right) + \sin^2\left(\frac{7\pi}{4}\right)$ [NSTSE-2013]

(A) 0 (B) 1 (C) 2 (D) $2\sqrt{2}$

Q.4 If $\sin(A+B) = \frac{\sqrt{3}}{2}$, $\cos(A-B) = \frac{\sqrt{3}}{2}$ and $0 < A + B \le 90^\circ$, if $A > B$, then the value of A and B are

[NTSE-2013]

(A) $A = 45^\circ, B = 15^\circ$ (B) $A = 60^\circ, B = 30^\circ$ (C) $A = 0^\circ, B = 30^\circ$ (D) $A = 30^\circ, B = 0^\circ$

Q.5 In a right triangle, perpendicular is 1 and hypotenuse is 2. Find the value of $\frac{2\tan\theta}{1-\tan^2\theta}$.

[IOM-2011]

(A) $\sqrt{3}$ (B) $\frac{1}{\sqrt{3}}$ (C) $\frac{1}{2}$ (D) $\frac{1}{\sqrt{2}}$

Q.6 If $\sec\theta = \frac{5}{4}$, then find the value of $\frac{1-\tan^2\theta}{1+\tan^2\theta}$. [IOM-2011]

(A) $\frac{9}{25}$ (B) $\frac{9}{16}$ (C) $\frac{7}{25}$ (D) $\frac{7}{16}$

Q.7 Find the value of $\frac{\cos 60^\circ + \sin 45^\circ - \cot 30^\circ}{\tan 60^\circ + \sec 45^\circ - \operatorname{cosec} 30^\circ} \div \frac{\sin 30^\circ + \sin 45^\circ - \tan 60^\circ}{\cot 30^\circ + \operatorname{cosec} 45^\circ - \sec 60^\circ}$ [IOM-2011]

(A) $\frac{2+\sqrt{2}-2\sqrt{6}}{2\sqrt{6}+4-4\sqrt{2}}$ (B) 1 (C) $\frac{2-\sqrt{2}-2\sqrt{6}}{2\sqrt{6}+4+4\sqrt{2}}$ (D) 0

Q.8 Find the value of $\frac{\tan A + \tan B}{1 - \tan A \tan B}$, if $A = 60°$ and $B = 30°$. **[IOM-2011]**

(A) ∞ (B) $\sqrt{3}$ (C) $\frac{-1}{\sqrt{3}}$ (D) $\frac{1}{\sqrt{3}}$

Q.9 Which one is correct? **[NIMO]**

(A) $\sin^2\theta + \cos^2\theta = 1$ (B) $1 + \tan^2\theta = \text{cosec}^2\theta$

(C) $1 + \cot^2\theta = \sec^2\theta$ (D) None of these

Q.10 Evaluate : $\sec 40° \sin 50° + \cos 50° \text{ cosec } 40°$ **[NIMO]**

(A) 1 (B) 3 (C) 2 (D) None of these

Q.11 Evaluate : $\frac{\sin 23°}{\cos 67°}$ **[NIMO]**

(A) 2 (B) 0 (C) 1 (D) None of these

Q.12 If θ is an acute angle and $\tan\theta = \frac{8}{15}$, find the value of $\sin\theta$. **[NIMO]**

(A) $\frac{17}{8}$ (B) $\frac{8}{17}$ (C) $\frac{17}{15}$ (D) None of these

Q.13 If $\tan 2\theta = \cot(\theta + 6°)$, where 2θ and $\theta + 6°$ are acute angles, find the value of θ. **[NIMO]**

(A) 26° (B) 27° (C) 28° (D) None of these

Q.14 Evaluate : **[NIMO]**

$$\frac{\cos^2 20° + \cos^2 70°}{\sec^2 50° - \cot^2 40°} + 2\,\text{cosec}^2 58° - 2\cot 58° \tan 32° - 4\tan 13° \tan 37° \tan 45° \tan 53° \tan 77°$$

(A) 1 (B) 2 (C) –1 (D) –2

Q.15 The value of $\frac{\sin\theta}{1+\cos\theta} + \frac{1+\cos\theta}{\sin\theta}$ is **[5th IMO]**

(A) $2\sin\theta$ (B) $2\,\text{cosec}\,\theta$ (C) $2\tan\theta$ (D) $2\cot\theta$

Q.16 If $\sin(A+B) = \frac{\sqrt{3}}{2}$, $\cos(A-B) = \frac{\sqrt{3}}{2}$ and $0 < A + B \le 90°$. If $A > B$ then the value of A and B are

[Raj. NTSE Stage-1_2013]

(A) $A = 45°, B = 15°$ (B) $A = 60°, B = 30°$ (C) $A = 0°, B = 30°$ (D) $A = 30°, B = 0°$

Q.17 If $\cos A + \cos^2 A = 1$, then the value of $\sin^2 A + \sin^4 A$ is **[Delhi NTSE Stage-1_2013]**

(A) 1 (B) $\frac{1}{2}$ (C) 2 (D) 3

Q.18 If $\sin\phi$ and $\cos\phi$ are the roots of the equation $ax^2 + bx + c = 0$, then **[Harayana NTSE Stage-1_2013]**
(A) $(a-c)^2 + c^2 = b^2$ (B) $(a-c)^2 - c^2 = b^2$ (C) $(a+c)^2 + c^2 = b^2$ (D) $(a+c)^2 - c^2 = b^2$

Q.19 If $\tan A + \sec A = 2$, $0° < A < 90°$, then value of $\cos A$ lies between **[Harayana NTSE Stage-1_2013]**
(A) 0.7 and 0.9 (B) 0.7 and 0.8 (C) 0.8 and 0.9 (D) 0.5 and 0.7

Q.20 If $\sin\theta + \cos\theta = 1$, then $\sin\theta\cos\theta$ is equal to **[MP NTSE Stage-1_2013]**
(A) 0 (B) $\frac{1}{\sqrt{3}-1}$ (C) 1 (D) $\frac{1+\sqrt{2}}{1+\sqrt{3}}$

Q.21 If $\sin\theta - \cos\theta = \sqrt{2}\,\sin(90° - \theta)$, then $\tan\theta =$ **[Raj. NTSE Stage-1_2014]**
(A) $\sqrt{2}-1$ (B) $\sqrt{2}$ (C) $1-\sqrt{2}$ (D) $\sqrt{2}+1$

Q.22 If $\tan\theta + 4\cot\theta = 4$, the value of $\tan^3\theta + \cot^3\theta$ is **[West Bengal NTSE Stage-1_2014]**
(A) $8\frac{1}{8}$ (B) 16 (C) $7\frac{9}{8}$ (D) $27\frac{1}{27}$

Q.23 The maximum value of $\cos^6\theta + \sin^6\theta$ is **[West Bengal NTSE Stage-1_2014]**
(A) 1 (B) 0 (C) 4 (D) 2

Q.24 If $\sin\theta + \cos\theta = a$, then find the value of $\sin^6\theta + \cos^6\theta$. **[IMO - 2016]**
(A) $\frac{3-4(a^2+1)^2}{4}$ (B) $\frac{4-3(a^2-1)^2}{4}$ (C) $\frac{4-3(a^2+1)^2}{4}$ (D) $\frac{3-4(a^2-1)^2}{4}$

Q.25 Select the INCORRECT match **[IMO - 2016]**
(A) $\cos^2\theta + \frac{1}{1+\cot^2\theta} = 1$ (B) $(1+\tan^2\theta)(1+\sin\theta)(1-\sin\theta) = 1$
(C) $\frac{\tan\theta+\sin\theta}{\tan\theta-\sin\theta} = \frac{\sec\theta-1}{\sec\theta+1}$ (D) $\frac{\sin^3\theta+\cos^3\theta}{\sin\theta+\cos\theta} + \sin\theta\cos\theta = 1$

Q.26 If $\sin\theta = p$ and $\cos\theta = q$, then the value of $\frac{p-2p^3}{2q^3-q}$ is **[NTSE-2016]**
(A) $\sec\theta$ (B) $\operatorname{cosec}\theta$ (C) $\cot\theta$ (D) $\tan\theta$

Q.27 Value of $\tan 25° \tan 35° \tan 45° \tan 55° \tan 65°$ is **[NTSE-2016]**
(A) 0 (B) 1 (C) $\sqrt{2}$ (D) $\sqrt{3}$

CONCEPT APPLICATION LEVEL - III

SECTION-A

- **Multiple choice questions with one correct answer**

Q.1 If $\sin\theta + \cos\theta = \sqrt{2}\cos(90^\circ - \theta)$ then $\cot\theta$ is equal to

(A) $\frac{1}{\sqrt{2}}$ (B) $\frac{\sqrt{3}}{2}$ (C) $\frac{1}{\sqrt{2}-1}$ (D) $\sqrt{2}-1$

Q.2 If $\sec\theta + \tan\theta = x$ then the value of $\sec\theta - \tan\theta$ is equal to

(A) $-x$ (B) $\frac{1}{x}$ (C) $-\frac{1}{x}$ (D) $\sqrt{x}$

Q.3 If $x = a\sin\theta$ and $y = b\cos\theta$, then the value of $b^2x^2 + a^2y^2$ is

(A) a^2b^2 (B) ab (C) $\frac{1}{a^2b^2}$ (D) $\frac{1}{ab}$

Q.4 An equation is called an identity if
(A) If is true for all values of variable
(B) Not for all values of variabls but some values of variables
(C) Exactly one value of variables
(D) Exactly two value of variables

Q.5 If $x = (\sec A + \tan A)(\sec B + \tan B)(\sec C + \tan C)$ & $y = (\sec A - \tan A)(\sec B - \tan B)(\sec C - \tan C)$ and $x = y$ then x & y is equal to
(A) ± 1 (B) 0 (C) ± 2 (D) None of these

Q.6 If $x = \cot^2\theta - \frac{1}{\sin^2\theta}$, then the value of x is

(A) 1 (B) -1 (C) ± 1 (D) zero

Q.7 $2(\sin^6\theta + \cos^6\theta) - 3(\sin^4\theta + \cos^4\theta)$ is equal
(A) zero (B) 1 (C) -1 (D) None of these

Q.8 $\sqrt{\frac{1+\sin\theta}{1-\sin\theta}}$ is equal to

(A) $\sec\theta + \tan\theta$ (B) $\sec\theta - \tan\theta$ (C) $\sec^2\theta + \tan^2\theta$ (D) $\sec^2\theta - \tan^2\theta$

Q.9 $\sec^4 A - \sec^2 A$ is equal to
(A) $\tan^2 A - \tan^4 A$ (B) $\tan^4 A - \tan^2 A$ (C) $\tan^4 A + \tan^2 A$ (D) $\sec^2 A + \tan^4 A$

Q.10 $\cos^4 A - \sin^4 A$ is equal to

(A) $2\cos^2 A + 1$ (B) $2\cos^2 A - 1$ (C) $2\sin^2 - 1$ (D) $2\sin^2 A + 1$

Q.11 $P = (1 + \cot\theta - \operatorname{cosec}\theta)(1 + \tan\theta + \sec\theta)$, the value of P is equal to

(A) 1 (B) 2 (C) 4 (D) zero

Q.12 $(\operatorname{cosec}\theta - \sin\theta)(\sec\theta - \cos\theta)(\tan\theta + \cot\theta)$ is equal to

(A) zero (B) 1 (C) – 1 (D) none of these

Q.13 If $\operatorname{cosec}\theta - \sin\theta = m$ and $\sec\theta - \cos\theta = n$, then

(A) $(m^2n)^{2/3} + (mn^2)^{2/3} = 1$ (B) $(m^2n^2)^{2/3} + (m^2n^2)^{2/3} = 1$

(C) $(mn)^{2/3} + (mn)^{1/3} = 1$ (D) None of these

Q.14 The expression $\sqrt{\sin^4(37.5)° + 4\cos^2(37.5)°} + \sqrt{\cos^4(37.5)° + 4\sin^2(37.5)°}$ simplifies to:

(A) an irrational number (B) a prime number

(C) a natural number which is not composite (D) a real number of the form $a + \sqrt{b}$

Q.15 If $15\sin^4\alpha + 10\cos^4\alpha = 6$, then the value of $8\operatorname{cosec}^4\alpha + 27\sec^6\alpha$ is

(A) 200 (B) 250 (C) 220 (D) None of these

Q.16 If $\sin\theta$ and $\cos\theta$ are the roots of the equation $ax^2 - bx + c = 0$, then

(A) $a^2 - b^2 = 2ac$ (B) $a^2 + b^2 = 2ac$ (C) $a^2 + b^2 + 2ac = 0$ (D) $b^2 - a^2 = 2ac$

Q.17 If $0 < \theta < \pi$, $2\sin^2\theta + 5\sin\theta - 3 = 0$, then θ, in radians must be

(A) $\frac{\pi}{12}$ (B) $\frac{\pi}{6}$ (C) $\frac{\pi}{3}$ (D) $\frac{5\pi}{6}$

Q.18 Exact value of $\cos^2 73° + \cos^2 47° - \sin^2 43° + \sin^2 107°$ is equal to:

(A) $\frac{1}{2}$ (B) $\frac{3}{4}$ (C) 1 (D) None of these

Q.19 If $\sin\theta$ and $\sec\theta$ $(0 < \theta < \pi/2)$ are the roots of the equation $2x^2 + kx + 1 = 0$, then the value of 'k' is equal to

(A) $-\frac{7\sqrt{2}}{5}$ (B) $\frac{7\sqrt{5}}{5}$ (C) $\frac{7\sqrt{5}}{2}$ (D) $-\frac{7\sqrt{5}}{5}$

Q.20 If $a = \frac{\cot\theta}{\cot\theta - \cot 3\theta}$ and $b = \frac{\tan\theta}{\tan\theta - \tan 3\theta}$, then $\sqrt{a+b}$ is equal to

(A) ± 2 (B) -2 (C) $+1$ (D) -1

Q.21 If $a\cos\theta - b\sin\theta = C$ then $a\sin\theta + b\cos\theta =$

(A) $\pm\sqrt{a^2+b^2+c^2}$ (B) $\pm\sqrt{a^2+b^2-c^2}$ (C) $\pm\sqrt{c^2-a^2-b^2}$ (D) None of these

Q.22 If $a\cos\theta + b\sin\theta = 4$ and $a\sin\theta - b\cos\theta = 3$ then $(a^2 + b^2)$ is equal to

(A) 7 (B) 12 (C) 25 (D) None of these

Q.23 If $\sin\theta + \sin^2\theta + \sin^3\theta = 1$ the value of $\cos^6\theta - 4\cos^4\theta + 8\cos^2\theta = p$ the value of p is

(A) 1 (B) 2 (C) 3 (D) 4

Q.24 If $\cos(\theta + \phi) = m\cos(\theta - \phi)$ then $\tan\theta$ is equal to

(A) $\left(\frac{1+m}{1-m}\right)\tan\phi$ (B) $\left(\frac{1-m}{1+m}\right)\tan\phi$ (C) $\left(\frac{1-m}{1+m}\right)\cot\phi$ (D) $\left(\frac{1+m}{1-m}\right)\cot\phi$

Q.25 If $\sin\theta - \cos\theta = 1$ then the value of $\sin^3\theta - \cos^3\theta$ is if (θ □ $\in$ R)

(A) zero (B) 1 (C) 2/3 (D) 3/2

Q.26 If $0° \le \theta \le 90°$ and $\sqrt{3}\tan\theta - \sec\theta = 1$ then θ has the value

(A) 30° (B) 45° (C) 60° (D) 90°

Q.27 If $a\cot\theta + b\,\text{cosec}\,\theta = p$ and $b\cot\theta + a\,\text{cosec}\,\theta = q$, then $p^2 - q^2$ is equal to:

(A) $a^2 - b^2$ (B) $b^2 - a^2$ (C) $a^2 + b^2$ (D) $b - a$

Q.28 If $\sin^4\theta - \cos^4\theta = x$ then the value of x is

(A) $2\sin^2\theta - 1$ (B) $1 - 2\sin^2\theta$ (C) $\cos^2\theta - \sin^2\theta$ (D) $\sin^2\theta + \cos^2\theta$

Q.29 If $\tan^2\theta + \cot^2\theta = 17/4$ then $(\tan\theta + \cot\theta)$ is equal to

(A) $\frac{\sqrt{17}}{2}$ (B) 5/2 (C) $\frac{\sqrt{17}}{2} + \sqrt{2}$ (D) $\frac{\sqrt{17}}{2} - \sqrt{2}$

SECTION-B

- **Multiple choice questions with one or more than one correct answers**

Q.1 Given that θ lies in the first quadrant and $\cos\theta = \tan\theta$ then $\sin\theta$ is equal to

(A) $\frac{-1+\sqrt{5}}{2}$ (B) $\frac{1+\sqrt{5}}{2}$ (C) $\frac{-1-\sqrt{5}}{2}$ (D) $-\left(\frac{1+\sqrt{5}}{2}\right)$

Q.2 If $y = \tan\alpha\sqrt{1-\sin^2\alpha}$ the y is equal to

(A) $\sin\alpha$ (B) $\cos\alpha$ (C) $\sqrt{1-\cos^2\alpha}$ (D) $\sqrt{1-\sin^2\alpha}$

Q.3 Value of $\dfrac{\sin 60^\circ + \cos 60^\circ}{\tan 60^\circ}$ is

(A) $\dfrac{2\sqrt{3}}{\sqrt{3}+1}$ (B) $\dfrac{\sqrt{3}+1}{2\sqrt{3}}$ (C) $\dfrac{1}{\sqrt{3}(\sqrt{3}-1)}$ (D) $\sqrt{3}(\sqrt{3}-1)$

SECTION-C

- **Comprehension**

If $p = (\sec A + \tan A)(1 - \sin A)$, $q = \dfrac{1+\tan^2 A}{1+\cot^2 A}$ then

Q.1 The value of p^2q is
(A) $\sec^2 A$ (B) $\sin^2 A$ (C) $1 - \cos^2 A$ (D) $\cos^2 A$

Q.2 The value of pq is

(A) $\dfrac{\tan^2 A}{\cos A}$ (B) $\dfrac{\sin^2 A}{\cos A}$ (C) $\dfrac{\sin^2 A}{\sqrt{1-\sin^2 A}}$ (D) $\dfrac{\cos^2 A}{\sqrt{1-\cos^2 A}}$

Q.3 Then the value of $p - \sqrt{q}$
(A) $\cos A$ (B) $\cos A - \tan A$ (C) $\tan A - \cos A$ (D) $\tan A - \sec A$

SECTION-D

- **Match the following (one to many)**

Column-I and **column-II** contains **four** entries each. Entries of column-I are to be matched with some entries of column-II. One or more than one entries of column-I may have the matching with the same entries of column-II and one entry of column-II may have one or more than one matching with entries of column-I

Q.1

Column I	**Column II**
(A) The solution of equation $-\cos^2\theta - \frac{1}{2}\sin\theta + 1 = 0$ lies in the interval	(P) $0^\circ \le \theta < 45^\circ$
(B) If $\sin\theta + \cos\theta > 1$ then θ lies in the interval	(Q) $45^\circ < \theta \le 90^\circ$
(C) If $\sin\theta - \cos\theta < 0$ then θ lies in the interval	(R) $\theta = 0^\circ$ or $\theta = 30^\circ$
(D) If $\cos\theta - \sin\theta < 0$ then θ lies in the interval	(S) $0 < \theta < 90^\circ$

Q.2

Column I	**Column II**
(A) If $\tan^2\theta + \cot^2\theta = x$, then the value of x is	(P) $0 \le x \le 1/16$
(B) If $\sin^4\theta - \cos^4\theta = x$, then the value of x is	(Q) $1/2 \le x \le 1$
(C) If $\sin^4\theta.\cos^4\theta = x$, then the value of x is	(R) $-1 \le x \le 1$
(D) If $\cos^4\theta + \sin^4\theta = x$, then the value of x is	(S) $x \ge 2$

ANSWER KEY

CONCEPT APPLICATION LEVEL - II

Q.1	C	Q.2	D	Q.3	C	Q.4	A	Q.5	A	Q.6	C	Q.7	B
Q.8	A	Q.9	A	Q.10	C	Q.11	C	Q.12	B	Q.13	C	Q.14	C
Q.15	B	Q.16	A	Q.17	A	Q.18	D	Q.19	A	Q.20	A	Q.21	D
Q.22	A	Q.23	A	Q.24	B	Q.25	C	Q.26	D	Q.27	B		

CONCEPT APPLICATION LEVEL - III

SECTION-A

Q.1	D	Q.2	B	Q.3	A	Q.4	A	Q.5	A	Q.6	B	Q.7	C
Q.8	A	Q.9	C	Q.10	B	Q.11	B	Q.12	B	Q.13	A	Q.14	C
Q.15	B	Q.16	D	Q.17	B	Q.18	C	Q.19	D	Q.20	C	Q.21	B
Q.22	C	Q.23	D	Q.24	C	Q.25	B	Q.26	C	Q.27	B	Q.28	A
Q.29	B												

SECTION-B

Q.1 A, D Q.2 A, C Q.3 B, C

SECTION-C

Q.1 B, C Q.2 B,C Q.3 B

SECTION-D

Q.1 (A)-(R), (B)-(S), (C)-(P), (D)-(Q)

Q.2 (A)-(S), (B)-(R), (C)-(P), (D)-(R)

5 SIMILAR TRIANGLES

THEORY

5.1 INTRODUCTION

In previous classes, we have learnt about the congruency of two geometric figures. In this chapter we shall learn about these geometric figures. Which have the same shape but not necessary have the same size. These kind of geometric figures are known as similar figures. So the congruent figures are always similar figures but similar figures need not be congruent figures.

(i) Two line segments are similar

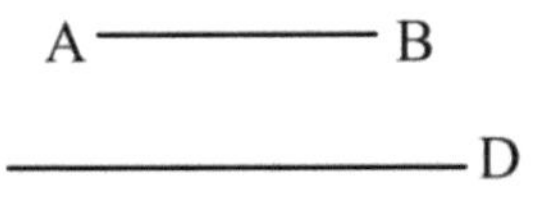

(The two line segments are congruent if they have the same length)

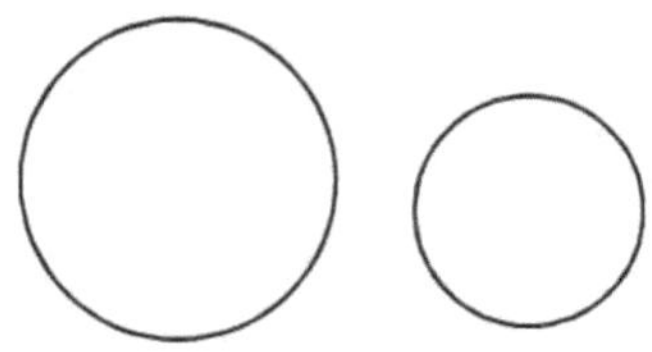

(ii) Two circles are similar.
(The two circles are congruent. If they have the same radius)

5.2 SIMILAR POLYGONS

Two polygons of the same number of sides are said to be similar. If

(i) Their corresponding angles are equal

(ii) Their corresponding sides are in the same ratio

Illustrations

Illustration 1

If two polygons ABCD and PQRS are similar then

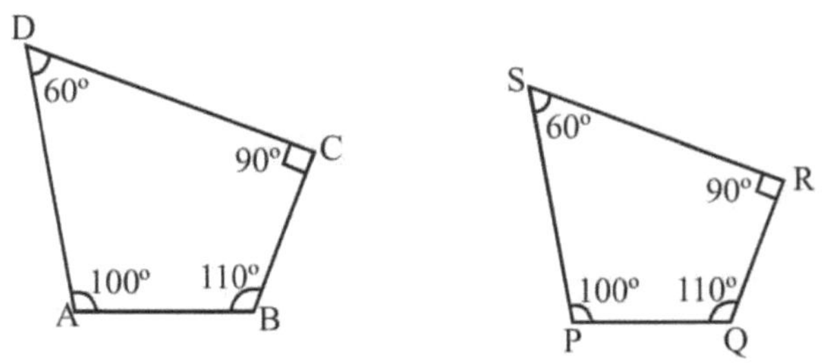

Solution

By the definition

$$\frac{AB}{PQ} = \frac{BC}{QR} = \frac{CD}{RS} = \frac{DA}{SP}$$

So corresponding sides are proportional.

Therefore quadrilateral ABCD and PQRS are similar

Illustration 2

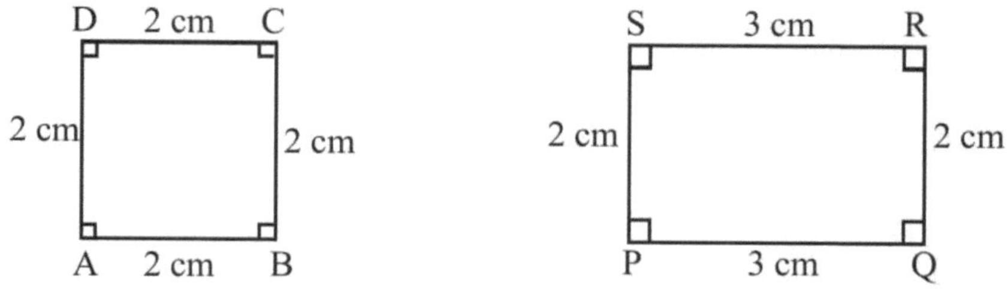

Solution

Clearly A square ABCD and rectangle PQRS are equiangular.
But corresponding sides of square ABCD and rectangle PQRS are not proportional.
Therefore square ABCD and rectangle PQRS are not similar.

Note : If one polygon is similar to a second polygon and the second polygon is similar to a third polygon, then the first polygon is similar to the third polygon.

5.3 SIMILARITY OF TRIANGLES

Two triangles are said to be similar if

(i) Their corresponding angles are equal (or triangles are equiangular)

(ii) Their corresponding sides are in the same ratio (or proportional)

The sign '~' is used to represent the similarity of two triangles. $\Delta ABC \sim \Delta DEF$ means ΔABC is similar to ΔDEF.

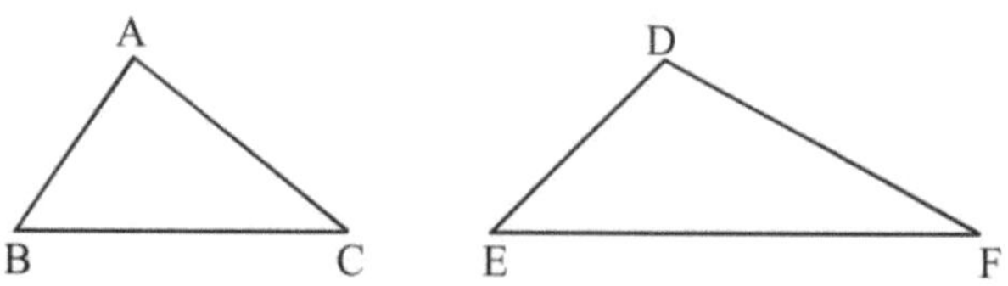

Hence by definition of similarity of two triangles,

$$\angle A = \angle D, \angle B = \angle E, \angle C = \angle F \text{ and } \frac{AB}{DE} = \frac{BC}{EF} = \frac{CA}{FD}$$

(i) Any two congruent figures are always similar but two similar figures are not necessarily congruent.

(ii) Equiangular triangles means that the corresponding angles of the triangles are equal.

5.4 BASIC PROPORTIONALITY THEOREM (THALES THEOREM) :

Statement : In a triangle, a line drawn parallel to one side, to intersect the other sides in distinct points, divides the two sides in the same ratio.

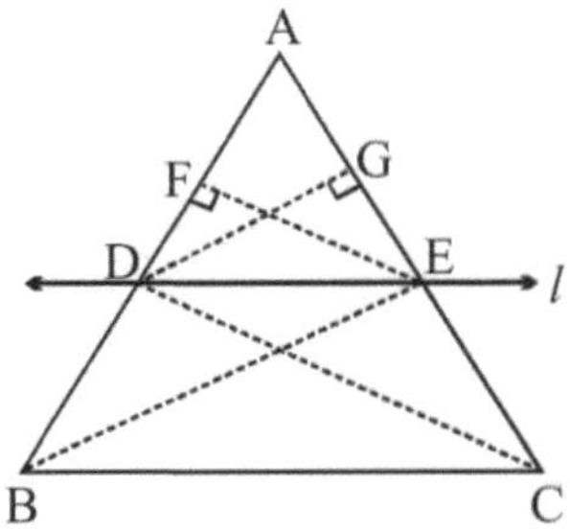

Given : In ΔABC, l is drawn parallel to BC which intersects AB and AC at D and E respectively.

To prove : $\frac{AD}{DB} = \frac{AE}{EC}$

Construction : Join BE and CD and draw $EF \perp AB$ and $DG \perp AC$.

Proof : ΔDBE and ΔCDE are on the same base DE and between the same parallel lines DE and BC.

$\therefore$ Area (ΔBDE) = Area (ΔCDE) .....(1)

Now ΔADE and ΔBDE have the bases AD and DB are on the same straight line AB and their opposite vertices are also same i.e. point E, hence the height of both triangles is EF.

$$\therefore \quad \frac{\text{Area }(\Delta ADE)}{\text{Area }(\Delta BDE)} = \frac{\frac{1}{2} \times AD \times EF}{\frac{1}{2} \times BD \times EF} = \frac{AD}{BD} \quad .....(2)$$

Similarly,

$$\frac{\text{Area }(\Delta ADE)}{\text{Area }(\Delta CDE)} = \frac{\frac{1}{2} \times AE \times DG}{\frac{1}{2} \times EC \times DG} = \frac{AE}{EC} \quad .....(3)$$

Hence from (1), (2) and (3), we get

$$\frac{AD}{DB} = \frac{AE}{EC}$$

In ΔABC, DE is parallel to BC and intersects AB and AC at D and E respectively, then

(i) $\frac{AB}{DB} = \frac{AC}{EC}$ and (ii) $\frac{AB}{AD} = \frac{AC}{AE}$

Proof : (i) By proportionality Theorem $\frac{AD}{DB} = \frac{AE}{EC}$

On adding 1 to both sides

$$\frac{AD}{DB} + 1 = \frac{AE}{EC} + 1$$

$$\Rightarrow \quad \frac{AD + DB}{DB} = \frac{AE + EC}{EC} \quad \Rightarrow \quad \frac{AB}{DB} = \frac{AC}{EC}$$

(ii) $\frac{AD}{DB} = \frac{AE}{EC}$ (By basic proportionality Theorem)

Taking inverse and then adding 1 to both sides

$$1 + \frac{DB}{AD} = 1 + \frac{EC}{AE}$$

$$\Rightarrow \quad \frac{AD + DB}{AD} = \frac{AE + EC}{AE} \qquad \Rightarrow \quad \frac{AB}{AD} = \frac{AC}{AE}$$

5.5 CONVERSE OF BASIC PROPORTIONALITY THEOREM :

Statement : If a line divides any two sides of a triangle in the same ratio, the line must be parallel to the third line.

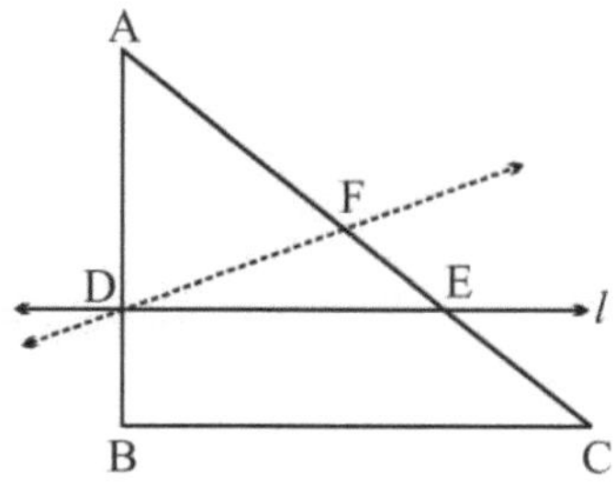

Given : A triangle ABC and line l intersecting AB at D and AC at E such that $\frac{AD}{DB} = \frac{AE}{EC}$.

To Prove : DE || BC

Proof : Let us suppose that DE is not parallel to BC. Then, through D there must be some other line DF (let) parallel to BC. since DF || BC, by basic proportionality theorem, we get

$$\frac{AD}{DB} = \frac{AF}{FC} \qquad .....(1)$$

But $\frac{AD}{DB} = \frac{AE}{EC}$ (given) .....(2)

From (1) and (2), $\frac{AF}{FC} = \frac{AE}{EC}$

On adding 1 to both sides

$$\frac{AF}{FC} + 1 = \frac{AE}{EC} + 1$$

$$\Rightarrow \quad \frac{AF + FC}{FC} = \frac{AE + EC}{EC}$$

$$\Rightarrow \quad \frac{AC}{FC} = \frac{AC}{EC}$$

Hence, FC = EC

But this is impossible unless the points F and E coincide, i.e. DF and DE are coincident lines.

Hence, DE || BC.

Illustration 3

LM || AB. If AL = x – 3, AC = 2x, BM = x – 2, BC = 2x + 3. find the value of x?

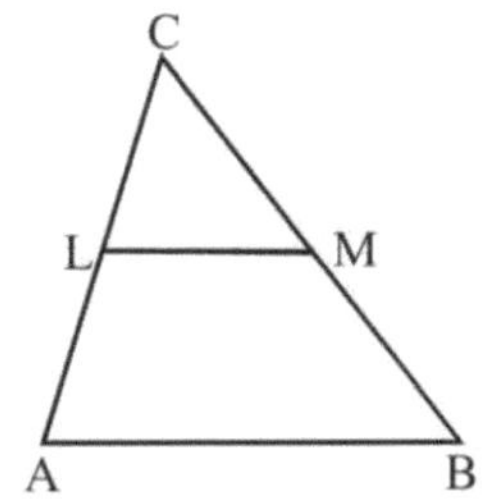

Solution

In Δ ABC we have

LM || AB

$$\frac{AL}{LC} = \frac{BM}{MC} \quad \Rightarrow \quad \frac{AL}{AC - AL} = \frac{BM}{BC - BM}$$

$$\Rightarrow \quad \frac{x-3}{2x-(x-3)} = \frac{x-2}{(2x+3)-(x-2)}$$

$$\Rightarrow \quad \frac{x-3}{x+3} = \frac{x-2}{x+5} \quad \Rightarrow \quad (x-3)(x+5) = (x-2)(x+3)$$

$$\Rightarrow \quad x^2 + 2x - 15 = x^2 + x - 6 \quad \Rightarrow \quad x = 9$$

Illustration 4

In the given figure PA, QB and RC each is perpendicular to AC such that PA = x, RC = y, QB = z, AB = a and BC = b. Prove that $\frac{1}{x} + \frac{1}{y} = \frac{1}{z}$.

Solution

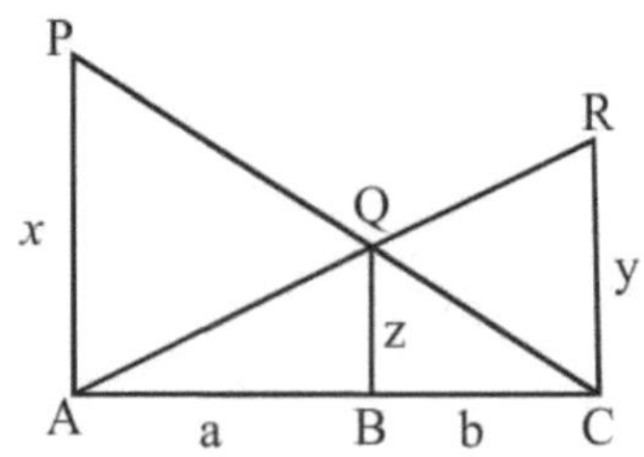

PA ⊥ AC and QB ⊥ AC ⇒ QB || PA

Thus in Δ PAC, QB || PA

so Δ QBC ~ Δ PAC

$$\therefore \quad \frac{QB}{PA} = \frac{BC}{AC}$$

$$\Rightarrow \quad \frac{z}{x} = \frac{b}{a+b} \quad \text{..... (i) (by the property of similar triangle)}$$

In Δ RAC, QB || RC, so Δ QAB ~ Δ RAC

$$\therefore \quad \frac{QB}{RC} = \frac{AB}{AC}$$

$$\Rightarrow \quad \frac{z}{y} = \frac{a}{a+b} \quad \text{..... (ii) (by the property of similar triangle)}$$

Now from (i) and (ii) we get

$$\frac{z}{x} + \frac{z}{y} = \left(\frac{b}{a+b} + \frac{a}{a+b}\right) = 1$$

$$\Rightarrow \quad \frac{z}{x} + \frac{z}{y} = 1 \quad \Rightarrow \quad \left(\frac{1}{x} + \frac{1}{y} = \frac{1}{z}\right)$$

5.6 ANGLE-ANGLE-ANGLE SIMILARITY (AAA-SIMILARITY) (THEOREM) :

Statement : In two triangles, if the corresponding angles are equal then their corresponding sides are in the same ratio (or proportion) and hence two triangles are similar.

OR, Two equiangular triangles are similar.

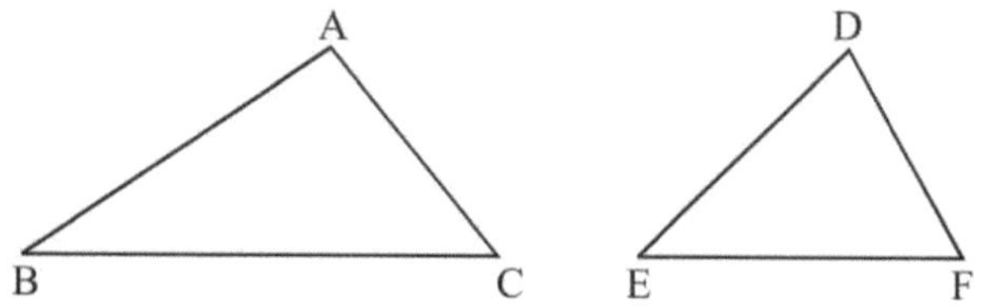

Given : ΔABC and ΔDEF are equiangular.

Hence, $\angle A = \angle D$, $\angle B = \angle E$ and $\angle C = \angle F$

To prove : $\Delta ABC \sim \Delta DEF$

Proof : Here, ΔABC and ΔDEF are equiangular,

i.e., $\angle A = \angle D$, $\angle B = \angle E$ and $\angle C = \angle F$ .....(1)

Three cases arises for sides AB of ΔABC and DE of ΔDEF

(i) $AB = DE$ (ii) $AB > DE$ (iii) $AB < DE$

Case (1) : When $AB = DE$

Proof : In ΔABC and ΔDEF

$\angle A$ and $\angle D$ (Given)

$AB = DE$ (Given)

$\angle B$ and $\angle E$ (Given)

Then by ASA rule of congruence, $\Delta ABC \cong \Delta DEF$

Therefore $BC = EF$, $AC = DE$, $AB = DE$

$$\Rightarrow \quad \frac{AB}{DE} = \frac{BC}{EF} = \frac{AC}{DF} \quad \Rightarrow \quad \Delta ABC \sim \Delta DEF$$

Case (2) : When $AB > DE$

Construction : As in figure taking the point P and Q on side AB and AC such that $AP = DE$ and $AQ = DF$.

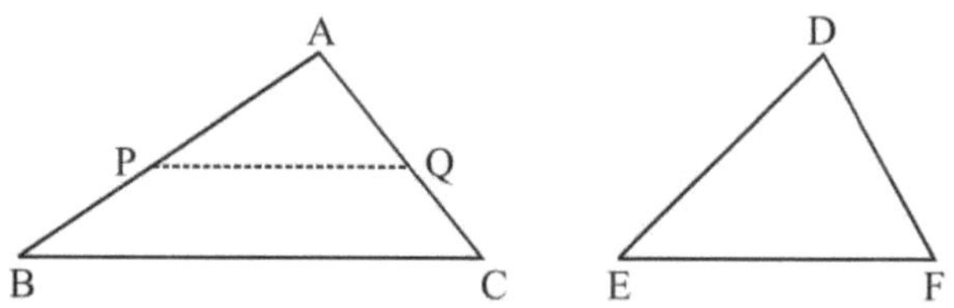

Proof : In ΔAPQ and ΔDEF

$AP = DE$ (By Construction)

$AQ = DF$ (By Construction)

$\angle A = \angle D$ (Given)

Therefore by Side-Angle-Side Rule for congruency

$\Delta APQ \cong \Delta DEF$

So, $\angle APQ = \angle E$ .....(1)

But $\angle B$ and $\angle E$ (Given) .....(2)

$\Rightarrow$ $\angle APQ = \angle B$, which is corresponding angle

Consequently, PQ || BC

Hence $\frac{AP}{AB} = \frac{AQ}{AC}$ (By Basic Proportionality Theorem)

$\Rightarrow$ $\frac{AP}{AQ} = \frac{AB}{AC}$ .....(3)

Also, $\frac{AP}{DE} = \frac{AQ}{DF}$ (By Construction)

$\Rightarrow$ $\frac{AP}{AQ} = \frac{DE}{DF}$ .....(4)

From (3) and (4),

$\Rightarrow$ $\frac{AB}{AC} = \frac{DE}{DF}$ .....(5)

$\Rightarrow$ $\frac{AB}{DE} = \frac{AC}{DF}$

Similarly, $\frac{AB}{DE} = \frac{BC}{EF}$ .....(6)

From (5) and (6), we get

$$\frac{AB}{DE} = \frac{AC}{DF} = \frac{BC}{EF}$$

Hence $\Delta ABC \sim \Delta DEF$

Case (3) : When AB < DE, proof is the same as for case (2).

Corollary : Angle-Angle Similarity (AA similarity)

If two angles of one triangle are respectively equal to two angles of another triangle than the two triangles are similar.

5.7 SIDE-SIDE-SIDE SIMILARITY (SSS-SIMILARITY) (THEOREM) :

Statement : If the corresponding sides of two triangles are proportional (i.e. in the same ratio), their corresponding angles are equal and hence the two triangles are similar.

Given : ΔABC and ΔDEF

$$\frac{AB}{DE}=\frac{BC}{EF}=\frac{AC}{DF}<1$$

To prove : $\Delta ABC \sim \Delta DEF$

Construction : Taking points P on DE and Q on DF such that DP = AB and DQ = AC, then join PQ.

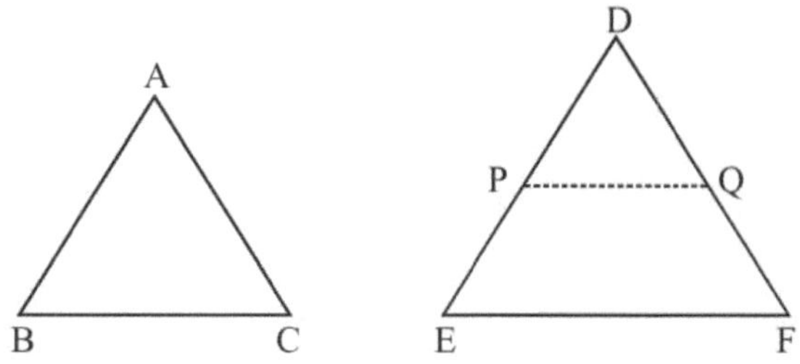

Proof : In $\Delta ABC \sim \Delta DEF$

$$\frac{AB}{DE}=\frac{AC}{DF}=\frac{BC}{EF} \quad .....(1)$$

$$\Rightarrow \quad \frac{AB}{AC}=\frac{DE}{DF} \quad .....(2)$$

and $$\frac{AB}{DP}=\frac{AC}{DQ} \quad \text{(By Construction)}$$

$$\Rightarrow \quad \frac{AB}{AC}=\frac{DP}{DQ} \quad .....(3)$$

From (2) and (3),

$$\frac{DE}{DF}=\frac{DP}{DQ} \quad \Rightarrow \quad \frac{DP}{DE}=\frac{DQ}{DF}$$

Therefore, by basic proportionality theorem, $PQ \parallel EF$

So, $\angle DPQ = \angle DEF$ and $\angle DQP = \angle DFE$ (Corresponding angles)

Hence by AA similarity, $\Delta DPQ \sim \angle DEF$ .....(4)

Hence the corresponding sides of similar triangles ΔDPQ and ΔDEF are proportional.

i.e. $$\frac{DP}{DE}=\frac{PQ}{EF} \quad \Rightarrow \quad \frac{AB}{DE}=\frac{PQ}{EF} \quad .....(5)$$

From (1) and (5),

$$\frac{PQ}{EF}=\frac{BC}{EF} \quad \Rightarrow \quad PQ = BC \quad ......(6)$$

Now, in ΔABC and ΔDPQ

$AB = DP$ (By Construction)

$AC = DQ$ (By Construction)

$BC = PQ$ [From (6)]

So by SSS congruence rule

$\Delta ABC \cong \Delta DPQ$ .....(7)

From (4) and (7)

$\Delta ABC \sim \Delta DPQ \sim \Delta DEF$

$\Rightarrow \quad \Delta ABC \sim \Delta DEF$

5.8 SIDE-ANGLE-SIDE SIMILARITY (SAS-SIMILARITY) (THEOREM) :

Statement : If one angle of one triangle is equal to an angle of other triangle and if the side including the angles are proportional, then the two triangles are similar.

Given : ΔABC and ΔDEF, such that

$$\angle A = \angle D$$

and $$\frac{AB}{DE} = \frac{AC}{DF} < 1$$

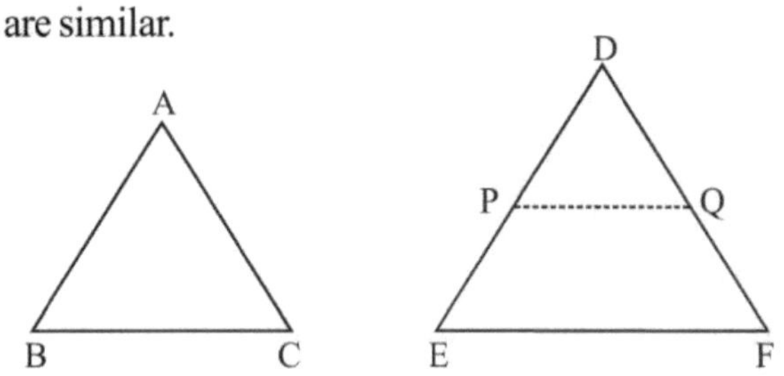

To prove : $\Delta ABC \sim \Delta DEF$

Construction : Taking points P and Q on sides DE and DF respectively such that AB = DP and AC = DQ, join PQ.

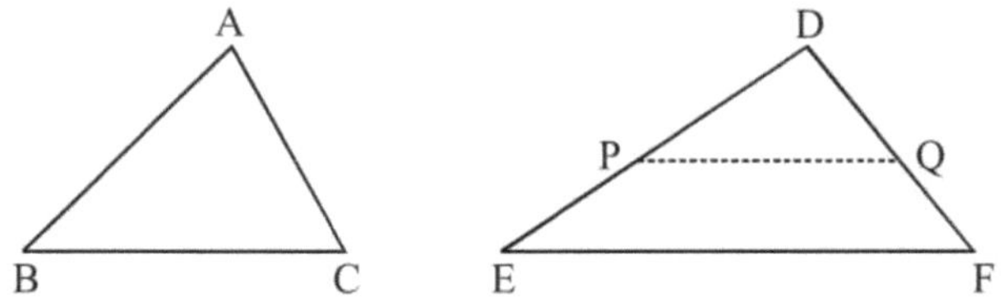

Proof : In ΔABC and ΔDPQ

$AB = DP$ (By Construction)

$AC = DQ$ (By Construction)

$\angle A = \angle D$ (Given)

By SAS rule of congruence

$\Delta ABC \cong \Delta DPQ$ .....(1)

$\frac{AB}{DP} = \frac{AC}{DQ}$ (Given) .....(2)

and $\frac{AB}{DE} = \frac{AC}{DF}$ (By Construction) .....(3)

From (2) and (3),

$$\frac{DP}{DQ} = \frac{DE}{DF} \Rightarrow \frac{DP}{DE} = \frac{DQ}{DF}$$

By converse of basic Proportionality theorem

$PQ \parallel EF$

So, $\angle DPQ = \angle E$ and $\angle DQP = \angle F$ (Corresponding angles)

Consequently, by AA similarity,

$\Delta DPQ \sim \Delta DEF$ .....(4)

From (1) and (4), we

$\Delta ABC \sim \angle DPQ \sim \angle DEF$

$\Rightarrow$ $\Delta ABC \sim \Delta DEF$

Illustrations

Illustration 5

Prove that the ratio of the perimeters of two similar triangles is the same as the ratio of their corresponding sides.

Solution

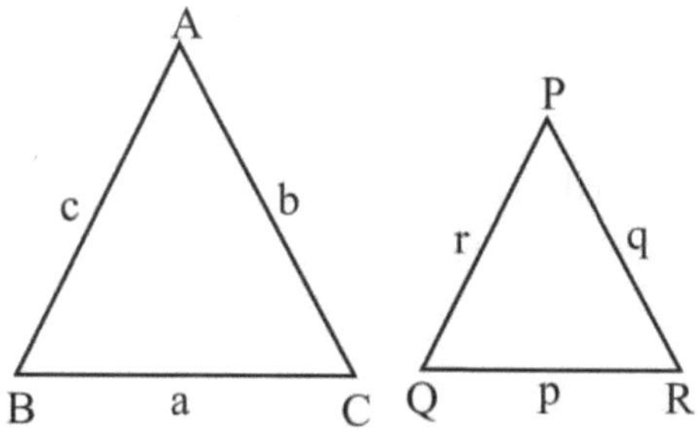

Given: Δ ABC and Δ PQR

BC = a, CA = b, AB = c

and QR = p, RP = q, PQ = r

Also $\Delta ABC \sim \Delta PQR$

To prove: $\frac{a}{p} = \frac{b}{q} = \frac{c}{r} = \frac{a+b+c}{p+q+r}$

Proof: Since Δ ABC and Δ PQR are similar, there for their corresponding sides are proportional

$$\therefore \quad \frac{a}{p} = \frac{b}{q} = \frac{c}{r} = k \text{ (say)} \qquad .....(i)$$

a = kp, b = kq, c = kr

$$\therefore \quad \frac{\text{perimeter of } \Delta ABC}{\text{perimeter of } \Delta PQR} = \frac{a+b+c}{p+q+r} = \frac{kp+kq+kr}{p+q+r}$$

$$= \frac{k(p+q+r)}{(p+q+r)} = k \qquad ..... (ii)$$

From (i) and (ii) we get

$$\frac{a}{p} = \frac{b}{q} = \frac{c}{r} = \frac{a+b+c}{p+q+r} = \frac{\text{perimeter of } \Delta ABC}{\text{perimeter of } \Delta PQR}$$

5.9 RELATION BETWEEN AREAS OF TWO SIMILAR TRIANGLES (THEOREM):

Statement : The ratio of the areas of two similar triangles is equal to the ratio of the square of their corresponding sides.

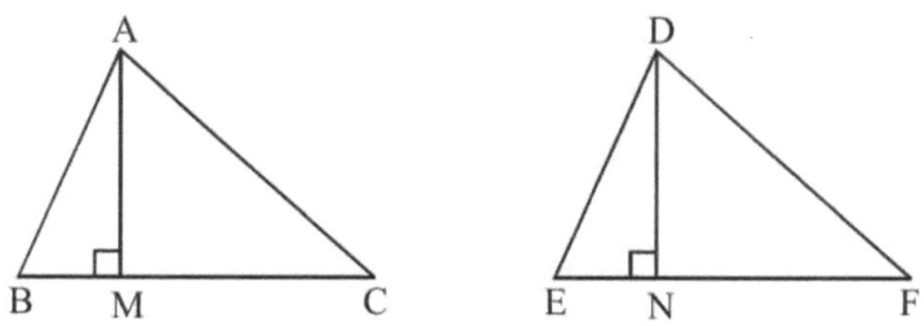

Given : $\Delta ABC \sim \Delta DEF$

$$\therefore \quad \frac{AB}{DE} = \frac{BC}{EF} = \frac{CA}{FD} \qquad .....(1)$$

To prove : $\dfrac{\text{Area } \Delta ABC}{\text{Area } \Delta DEF} = \dfrac{AB^2}{DE^2} = \dfrac{BC^2}{EF^2} = \dfrac{CA^2}{FD^2}$

Construction : Draw $AM \perp BC$ and $DN \perp EF$

Proof : In ΔAMB and ΔDNE,

$\angle B = \angle E$ [$\because$ $\Delta ABC \sim \angle DEF$]

$\angle M = \angle N = 90°$ [By construction]

$\Rightarrow$ $\Delta AMB \sim \Delta DNE$ [By AA similarity]

$$\therefore \quad \frac{AM}{DN} = \frac{AB}{DE} \qquad .....(2)$$

(Ratio of corresponding sides of two similar triangles)

But $\dfrac{AB}{DE} = \dfrac{BC}{EF} = \dfrac{CA}{FD}$ .....(3) [$\because$ $\Delta ABC \sim \angle DEF$]

From equations (2) and (3), we get

$$\therefore \quad \frac{AM}{DN} = \frac{BC}{EF} \qquad .....(4)$$

$$\therefore \quad \frac{\text{Area } \Delta ABC}{\text{Area } \Delta DEF} = \frac{\frac{1}{2} \cdot BC \cdot AM}{\frac{1}{2} \cdot EF \cdot DN}$$

$$= \left(\frac{BC}{EF}\right) \times \left(\frac{AM}{DN}\right) = \frac{BC}{EF} \times \frac{BC}{EF} \qquad \text{[From Equation (4)]}$$

$$= \left(\frac{BC}{EF}\right)^2$$

$$\therefore \quad \frac{\text{Area } \Delta ABC}{\text{Area } \Delta DEF} = \frac{BC^2}{EF^2} = \frac{AB^2}{DE^2} = \frac{CA^2}{FD^2} \quad \left[\because \frac{BC}{EF} = \frac{AB}{DE} = \frac{CA}{FD} \text{ (From equation (1)}\right]$$

Thus, in the above similar triangles ABC and DEF :

Therefore, $\dfrac{\text{Area } \Delta ABC}{\text{Area } \Delta DEF} = \dfrac{AB^2}{DE^2} = \dfrac{BC^2}{EF^2} = \dfrac{AC^2}{DF^2}$

5.10 RESULT ON AREA OF SIMILAR TRIANGLES :

The ratio of areas of the two similar triangles is equal to the ratio of the squares of any two corresponding sides of the triangles.

$$\Delta ABC \sim \Delta DEF \quad \Rightarrow \quad \frac{\text{Area of } \Delta ABC}{\text{Area of } \Delta DEF} = \frac{AB^2}{DE^2} = \frac{BC^2}{EF^2} = \frac{CA^2}{FD^2}$$

(a) The ratio of area of two similar triangles is equal to the ratio of the squares of their corresponding altitudes.

In the following figures, $\Delta ABC \sim \Delta DEF$ and AX, DY are the altitudes.

Then, $$\frac{\text{Area of } \Delta ABC}{\text{Area of } \Delta DEF} = \frac{AX^2}{DY^2}$$

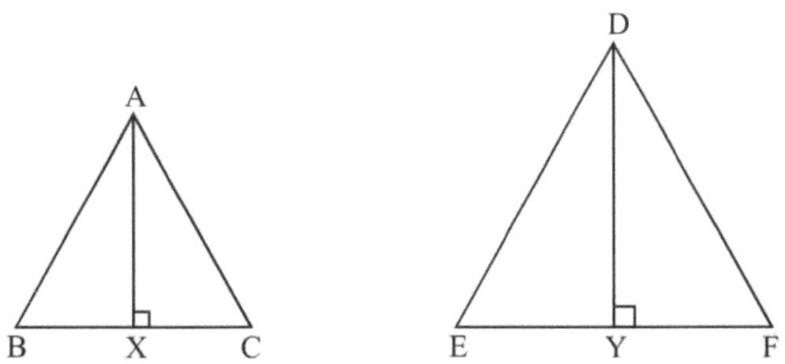

(b) The ratio of area of two similar triangles is equal to the ratio of the squares on their corresponding medians.

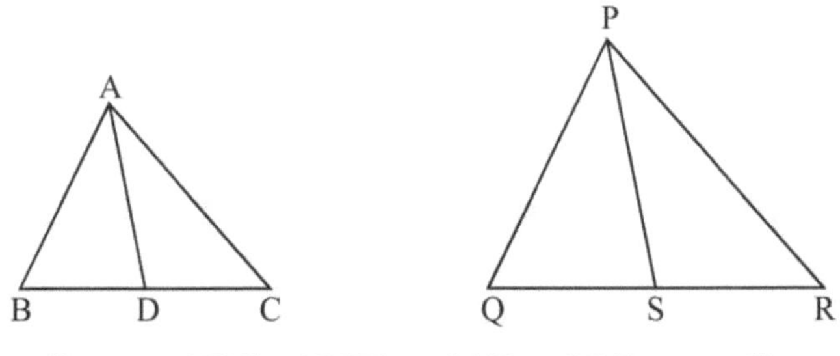

In the above figure, $\Delta ABC \sim \Delta PQR$ and AD and PS are medians.

Then, $$\frac{\text{Area of } \Delta ABC}{\text{Area of } \Delta PQR} = \frac{AD^2}{PS^2}$$

(c) The ratio of area of two similar triangles is equal to the ratio of the squares of their corresponding angle bisector segments.

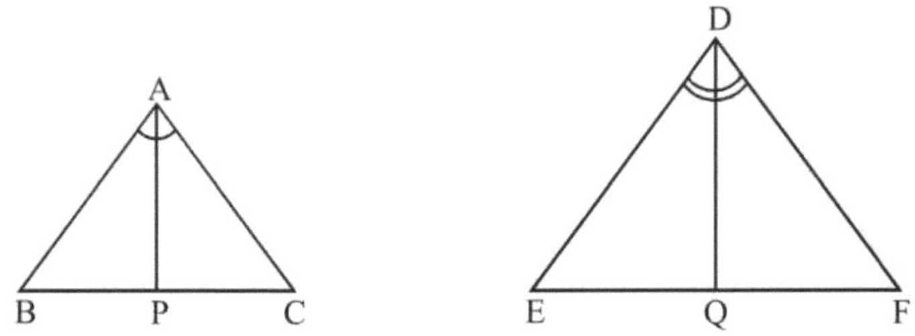

In the figure, $\Delta ABC \sim \Delta DEF$ and AP, DQ are bisectors of $\angle A$ and $\angle D$ respectively, then

$$\frac{\text{Area of } \Delta ABC}{\text{Area of } \Delta DEF} = \frac{AP^2}{DQ^2}$$

5.11 PYTHAGORAS THEOREM :

Statement : In a right triangle, the square of the hypotenuse is equal to the sum of the square of the other two sides.

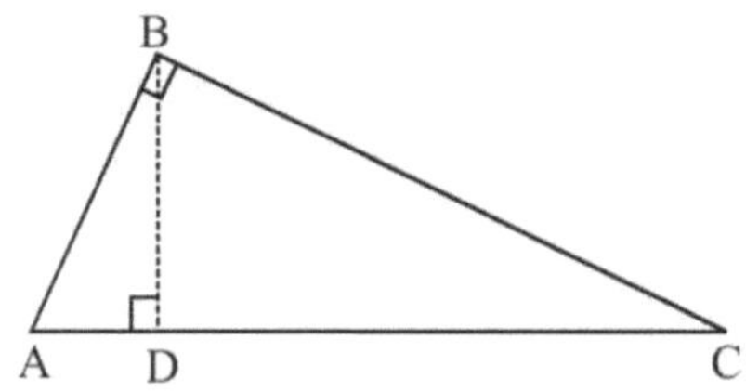

Given : A triangle ABC right angled at B.

Prove that : $AC^2 = AB^2 + BC^2$

$(\text{Hypotenuse})^2 = (\text{Base})^2 + (\text{Perpendicular})^2$

Construction : From B, draw $BD \perp AC$.

Proof : Since $BD \perp AC$

$\therefore \quad \Delta ADB \sim \Delta ABC$ (By the above)

$\therefore \quad \frac{AD}{AB} = \frac{AB}{AC}$

$\therefore \quad AB^2 = AC \times AD$ ......(1)

Also, $\Delta BDC \sim \Delta ABC$ (By the above)

$\therefore \quad \frac{BC}{AC} = \frac{DC}{BC} \Rightarrow BC^2 = AC \times DC$ ......(2)

Adding (1) and (2) we get,

$$AB^2 + BC^2 = AC \times CD + AC \times AD = AC(CD + AD) = AC \times AC$$

$(\because CD + AD = AC)$

$$AB^2 + BC^2 = AC^2$$

5.12 CONVERSE OF PYTHAGORAS THEOREM (THEOREM) :

In a triangle , if the square of one side is equal to the sum of the square of the other two sides then the angle opposite to the first side is right angle.

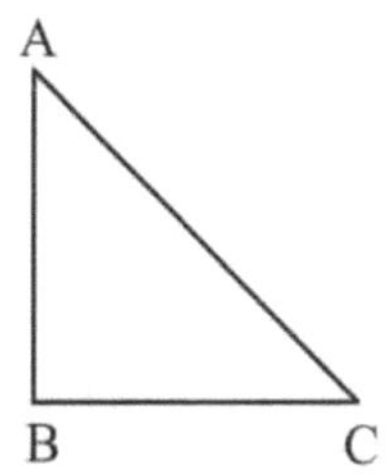

In Δ ABC

$AC^2 = AB^2 + BC^2$

$\angle B = 90^\circ$

5.13 SOME IMPORTANT RESULTS DEDUCED FROM PYTHAGORAS THEOREM :

(a) In the given ΔABC, obtuse angled at B. If $AD \perp CB$ produced, then $AC^2 = AB^2 + BC^2 + 2BC \cdot BD$

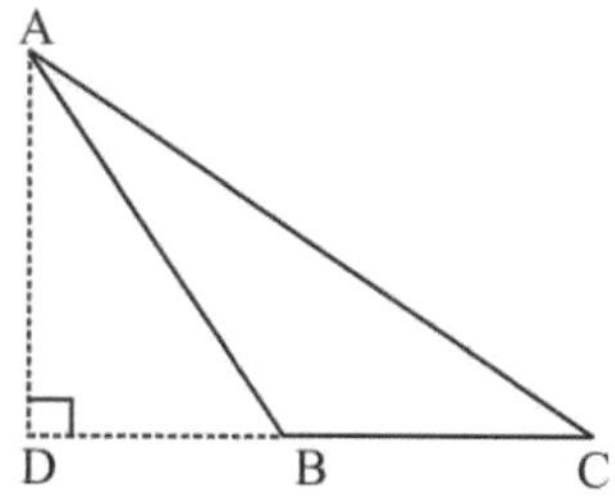

Given : In figure, ABC is a triangle in which $\angle ABC > 90°$ and $AD \perp CB$ produced.

To Prove : $AC^2 = AB^2 + BC^2 + 2BC \cdot BD$

Proof : In right triangle ABC,

$\because \quad \angle D = 90°$

$\therefore \quad AC^2 = AD^2 + DC^2$ (By Pythagoras theorem)

$= AD^2 + (DB + BC)^2$

$= AD^2 + DB^2 + BC^2 + 2\,DB \cdot BC$

$= AB^2 + BC^2 + 2BC \cdot BD$

[$\because$ In right triangle ADB with $\angle D = 90°$, $AB^2 = AD^2 + DB^2$ (By Pythagoras theorem)]

(b) In the given figure, if $\angle B$ of ΔABC is an acute angle and $AD \perp BC$, then $AC^2 = AB^2 + BC^2 - 2BC \cdot BD$

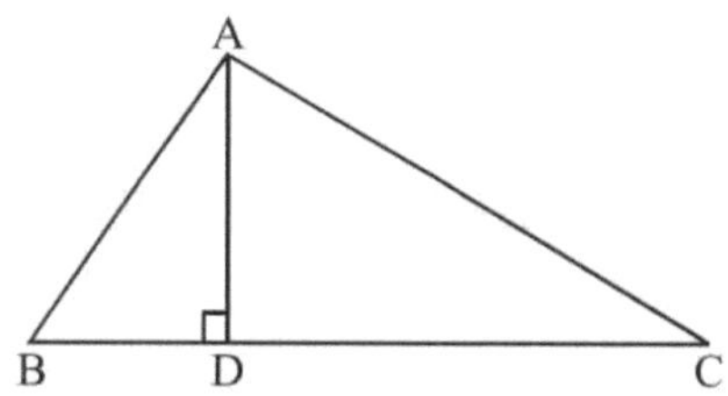

Given : In figure, ABC is a triangle in which $\angle ABC < 90°$ and $AD \perp BC$.

To Prove : $AC^2 = AB^3 + BC^2 - 2BC \cdot BD$

Proof : In the right ΔADC

$\therefore \quad \angle D = 90°$

$\therefore \quad AC^2 = AD^2 + DC^2$ (By Pythagoras theorem)

$= AD^2 + (BC - BD)^2$

$= AD^2 + BC^2 + BD^2 - 2BC \cdot BD$

$= AD^2 + BD^2 + BC^2 - 2BC \cdot BD$

$= AB^2 + BC^2 - 2BC \cdot BD$

[$\because$ In right triangle ADB with $\angle D = 90°$, $AB^2 = AD^2 + BD^2$ (By Pythagoras theorem)]

5.14 VERTICAL ANGLE BISECTOR THEOREM :

Statement : The bisector of the vertical angle of a triangle divides the base in the ratio of the other two sides.

Given : In ΔABC, AD is the bisector of $\angle A$.

To Prove : $\frac{BD}{DC} = \frac{AB}{AC}$

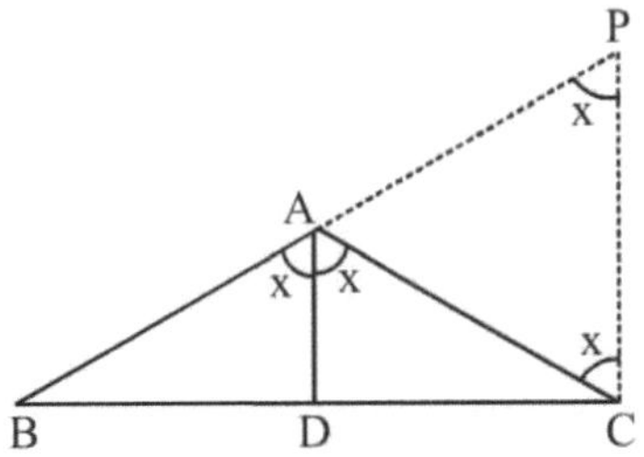

Construction : Draw CP parallel to AD to meet BA produced at P.

Proof : Let $\angle BAD = \angle DAC = x$

$\angle DAC = \angle ACP$ (alternate angles and $\overline{AB} \parallel \overline{CP}$)

$\angle BAD = \angle APC$ (corresponding angles)

But $\angle BAD = \angle DAC$ (given)

$\therefore \quad \angle ACP = \angle APC$

In triangle APC,

$AC = AP$ (sides opposite to equal angles are equal)

In triangle BCP,

$$\frac{BD}{DC} = \frac{BA}{AP} \quad \text{(by basic proportionality theorem)}$$

$$\Rightarrow \quad \frac{BD}{DC} = \frac{BA}{AC}$$

Hence proved.

5.15 CONVERSE OF VERTICAL ANGLE BISECTOR THEOREM :

If a line that passes through a vertex of a triangle, divides the base in the ratio of the other two sides, then it bisects the angle.

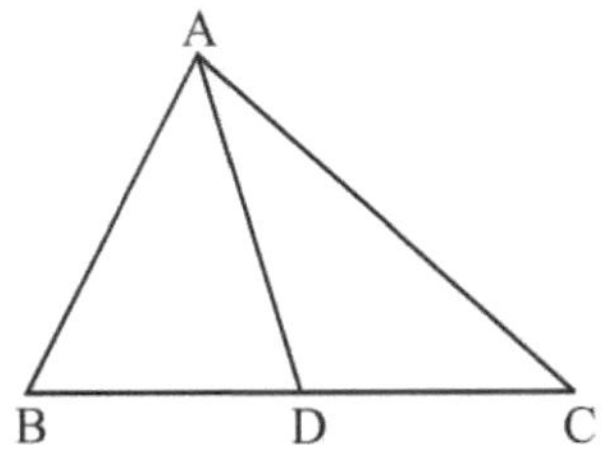

In the adjacent figure, AD divides BC in the ratio $\frac{BD}{DC}$ and if $\frac{BD}{DC} = \frac{AB}{AC}$, then AD is the bisector of $\angle A$.

5.16 CONCURRENCY-GEOMETRIC CENTRES OF A TRIANGLE :

Let us recall that if three or more lines pass through a fixed point, then those lines are said to be concurrent and that fixed point is called the point of concurrence. In this context, we recall different concurrent lines and their points of concurrence associated with a triangle, also called geometric centres of a triangle.

1. **Circumcentre :**

The locus of the point equidistant from the end points of the line segment is the perpendicular bisector of the line segment. The three perpendicular bisectors of the three sides of a triangle are concurrent and the point of their concurrence is called the circumcentre of the triangle and is usually denoted by S. The circumcentre is equidistant from all the vertices of the triangle. The circumcentre of the triangle is the locus of the point in the plane of the triangle, equidistant from the vertices of the triangle.

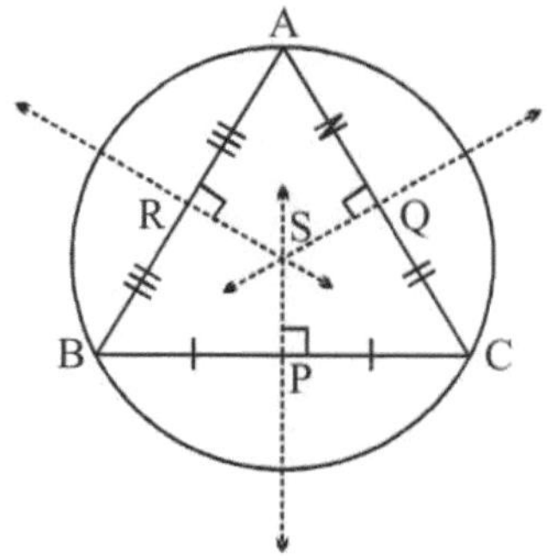

2. **Incentre :**

The angle bisectors of the triangle are concurrent and the point of concurrence is called the incentre and is usually denoted by I. Incentre is equidistant from the sides of the triangle. The incentre of the triangle is the locus of the point, in the plane of the triangle, equidistant from the sides of the triangle.

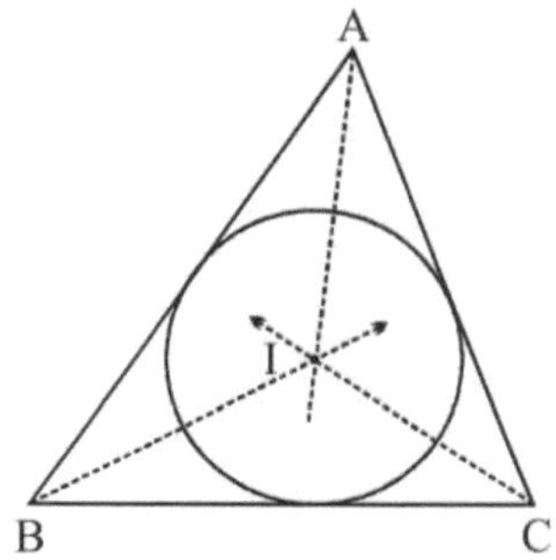

3. **Orthocentre :**

The altitudes of the triangle are concurrent and the point of concurrence of the altitudes of a triangle is called orthocentre and is usually denoted by O.

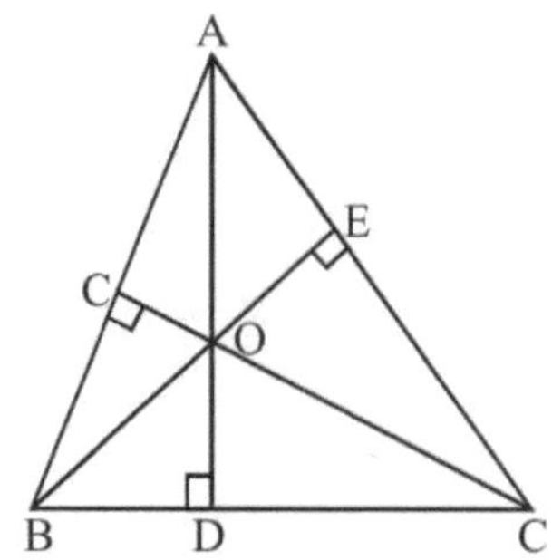

4. **Centroid :**

The medians of a triangle are concurrent and the point of concurrence of the medians of a triangle is called the centroid and it is usually denoted by G. The centroid divides each of the median in the ratio 2 : 1, starting from vertex, i.e. in the figure given,

$$AG : GD = BG : GE = CG : GF = 2 : 1.$$

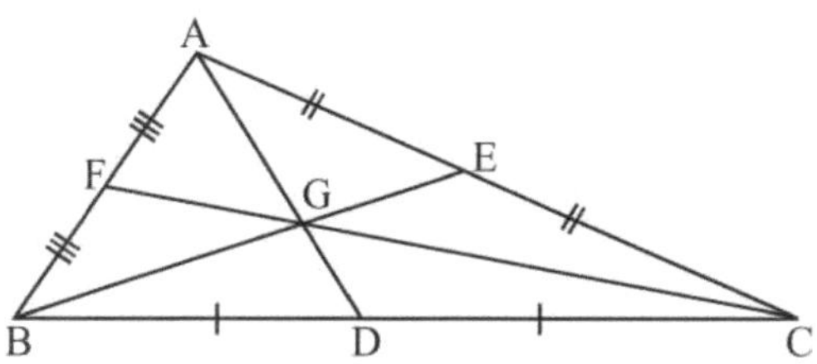

Remember

SOME IMPORTANT POINTS

1. In an equilateral triangle, the centroid, the orthocentre, the circumcentre and the incentre all coincide.
2. In an isosceles triangle, the centroid, the orthocentre, the circumcentre and the incentre all lie on the median to the base.
3. In a right-angled triangle the length of the median drawn to the hypotenuse is equal to half of the hypotenuse. The median is also equal to the circumradius. The midpoint of the hypotenuse is the circumcentre.
4. In an obtuse-angled triangle, the circumcentre and orthocentre lie outside the triangle and for an acute-angled triangle the circumcentre and the orthocentre lie inside the triangle.
5. For all triangles, the centroid and the incentre lie inside the triangle.

SOLVED EXAMPLES

Example 1

In the given figure, if $\angle A = \angle CED$, find the value of x is :

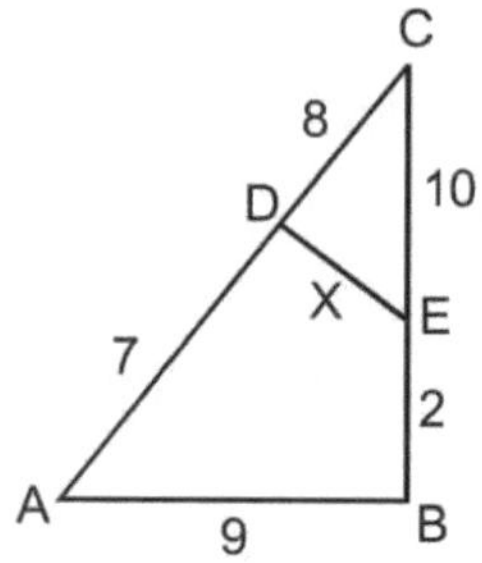

Solution

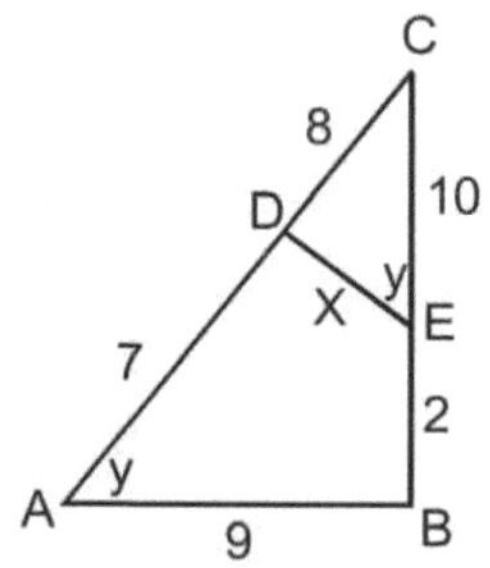

In ΔCAB and ΔCED

$\angle A = \angle CED$ (Given)

$\angle C = \angle C$ (Common to both Δs)

$\therefore$ $\Delta CAB \sim \Delta CED$ (AA critertion of similar Δs)

$\therefore \quad \frac{CA}{CE} = \frac{AB}{DE} = \frac{CB}{CD}$

Consider $\frac{AB}{DE} = \frac{CB}{CD} \therefore \frac{9}{x} = \frac{10+2}{8}$

Or $\quad \frac{9}{x} = \frac{12}{8} \therefore \frac{8 \times 9}{12} = 2 \times 3 = 6.$ Hence $x = 6$

Example 2

In the adjoining figure. ABCD is a quadrilateral and P, Q, R, S are the points of trisection of the sides AB, BC, CD and DA respectively. Prove that PQRS is a parallelogram.

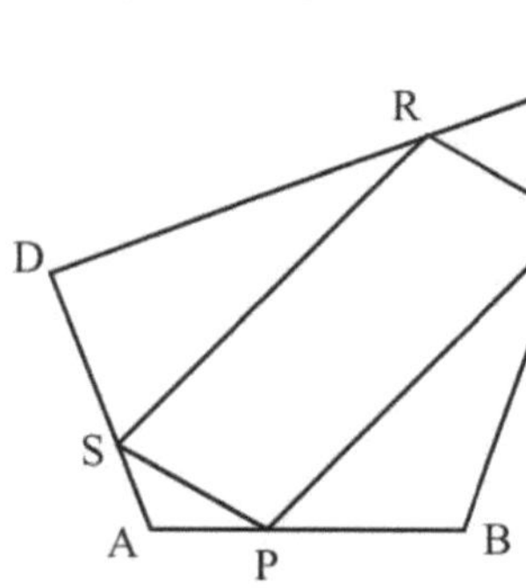

Solution

Here, ABCD is a quadrilateral. Since R and S are points of trisection of sides CD and DA respectively.

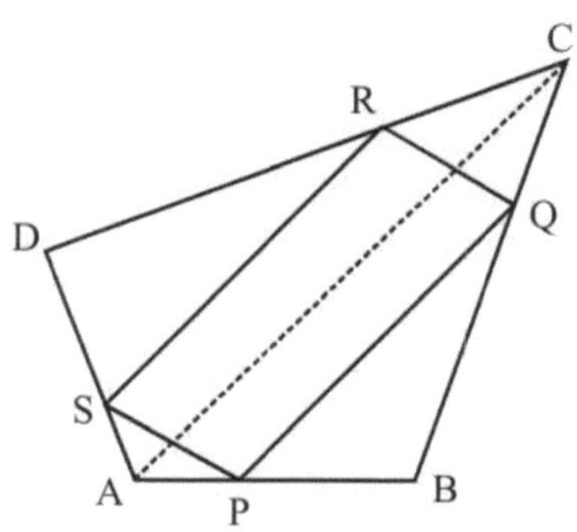

$\therefore \quad CD = 3CR \quad$ or $\quad CR + DR = 3CR$

or $\quad DR = 2CR \quad$ or $\quad \frac{DR}{RC} = \frac{2}{1}$ and

$AD = 3AS \quad$ or $\quad AS + SD = 2AS$

or $\quad DS = 2AS \quad$ or $\quad \frac{DS}{SA} = \frac{2}{1}$

$\Rightarrow \quad \frac{DS}{SA} = \frac{DR}{RC}$

$\therefore$ By converse of basic proportionality theorem,

In Δ DAC, $\frac{DS}{SA} = \frac{DR}{RC}$ $\Rightarrow$ SR || AC

Similarly, PQ || AC

$\therefore$ SR || AC and PQ || AC $\Rightarrow$ SR || PQ

$\Rightarrow$ Similarly one can prove that PS || QR

Hence, PQRS is a parallelogram.

Example 3

Prove that the line segments joining the mid-points of the adjacent sides of a quadrilateral form a parallelogram.

Solution

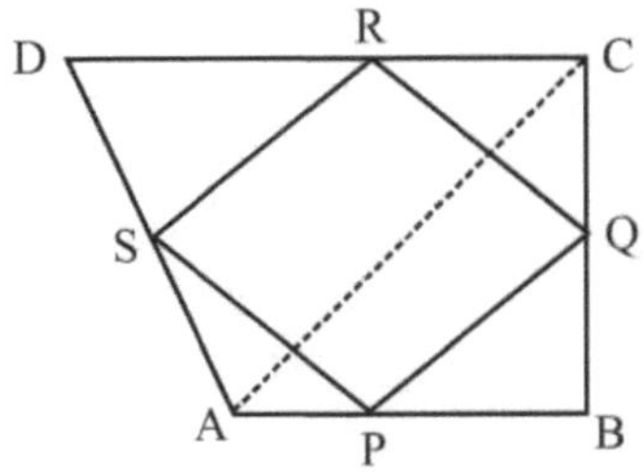

Let P, Q, R and S respectively be the mid-points of the sides AB, BC, CD and DA of the quadrilateral ABCD.

Join PQ, QR, RS and SP.

Also, join AC,

Since S and R are the mid-points of DA and DC respectively

$\therefore$ DS = SA and DR = RC

$\Rightarrow$ $\frac{DS}{SA} = 1$ and $\frac{DR}{RC} = 1 \Rightarrow$ $\frac{DS}{SA} = \frac{DR}{RC}$

$\therefore$ In Δ DAC, $\frac{DS}{SA} = \frac{DR}{RC}$ $\Rightarrow$ SR || AC ..... (i) (By converse of basic proportionality theorem)

Since Q and P are the mid-points of BC and BA respectively.

$\therefore$ BQ = QC and BP = PA

$\Rightarrow$ $\frac{BQ}{QC} = 1$ and $\frac{BP}{PA} = 1 \Rightarrow$ $\frac{BQ}{QC} = \frac{BP}{PA}$

$\therefore$ In Δ BCA, $\frac{BQ}{QC} = \frac{BP}{PA}$

$\Rightarrow$ QP || CA or PQ || AC ..... (ii) (By converse of basic proportionality theorem)

From (i) and (ii), we have

PQ || SR

Similarly, PS || QR

Hence, PQRS is a parallelogram.

Example 4

Sides AB and AC and median AD of a triangle ABC are respectively proportional to sides PQ and PR and median PM of another triangle PQR. Show that Δ ABC ~ ΔPQR.

Solution

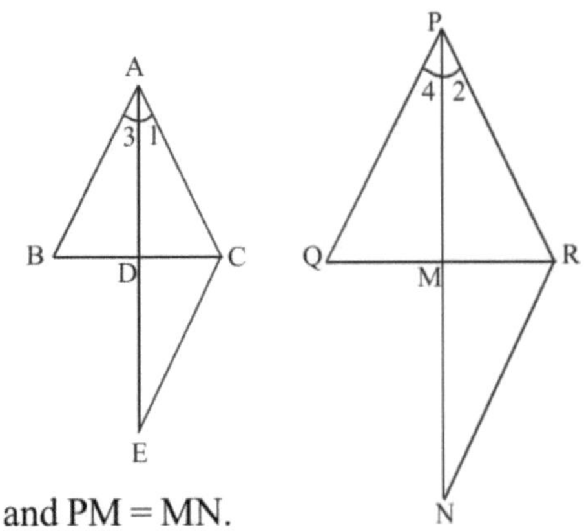

Since sides AB and AC and median AD of a t riangle ABC are respectively proportinal to sides PQ and PR and median PM of another triangle PQR.

$\therefore$ $\frac{AB}{PQ} = \frac{AC}{PR} = \frac{AD}{PM}$

Now, produce AD to E and PM to N such that AD = DE and PM = MN.

Join EC and NR

In triangles ADB and EDC,

$AD = DE$ (construction)

$BD = CD$ ($\because$ AD is median)

$\angle ADB = \angle EDC$ (Vertically opposite angles)

$\therefore$ By S.A.S. congruency criteria,

$\Delta ADB \cong \Delta EDC$

$\Rightarrow$ $AB = EC$ ($\because$ corresponding parts of congruent triangles are equal)

Now, in triangles PMQ and NMR,

$PM = MN$ (construction)

$QM = RM$ ($\because$ PM is median)

$\angle PMQ = \angle NMR$ (vertically opposite angles)

$\therefore$ By S.A.S. congruency criteria,

$\Delta PMQ \cong \Delta NMR$

$\Rightarrow$ $PQ = NR$ ($\because$ corresponding parts of congruent triangles are equal)

Now, $\frac{AB}{PQ} = \frac{AC}{PR} = \frac{AD}{PM}$

$\Rightarrow$ $\frac{EC}{NR} = \frac{AC}{PR} = \frac{AD}{PM}$ [$\because$ AB = EC and PQ = NR (proved above)]

$\Rightarrow$ $\frac{EC}{NR} = \frac{AC}{PR} = \frac{2AD}{2PM}$

$\Rightarrow$ $\frac{EC}{NR} = \frac{AC}{PR} = \frac{AE}{PN}$

$\Rightarrow$ $\Delta AEC \sim \Delta PNR$ (By using S.S.S. similarity criteria)

$\Rightarrow$ $\angle 1 = \angle 2$ ($\because$ Similar triangles are equiangular)

Similarly, we can prove that $\angle 3 = \angle 4$

$\therefore$ $\angle 1 + \angle 3 = \angle 2 + \angle 4$

$\Rightarrow$ $\angle BAC = \angle QPR$

Now, in triangles ABC and PQR,

$\angle BAC = \angle QPR$ (proved above)

$\frac{AB}{PQ} = \frac{AC}{PR}$ (given)

$\therefore$ By S.A.S. similarity criteria,

$\Delta ABC \sim \Delta PQR$

Hence proved.

Example 5

A man, 5ft. high standing at a certain distance from a lamp post, finds that the length of his shadow is 8 ft. On moving in the direction of the shadow through 3 ft, he finds the length of is shadow in now 11 ft. Find the differnce of the height of the post and distance of the man from the post originally.

Solution

Let 'x' be the height of the post and y the distance of the man from the post originally

Let AB be the post, ab the original position of the man, a'b' the position to which he moves.

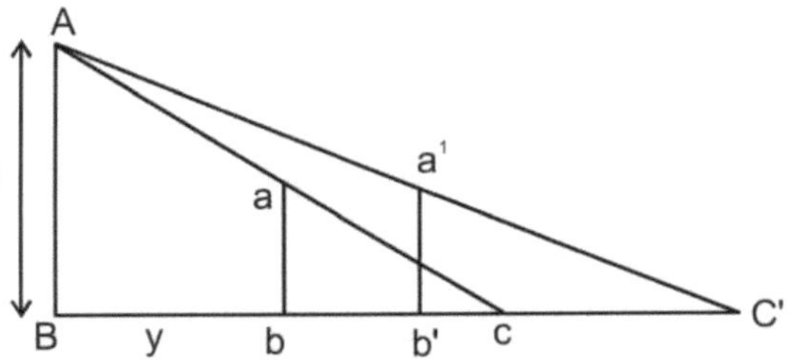

Let bc the length of the shadow initially b'c' the length of the shadow latter.
Then, ab = 5ft. bc = 8 ft.; a'b' = 5ft, bb' = 3ft, b'c' = 11 ft.
Then AB = x ft, Bb = y ft and Bc = Bb + bc = y + 8ft and Bb' = y + 3 ft.

Now, $\frac{AB}{Bc} = \frac{ab}{bc}$ and $\frac{AB}{Bc'} = \frac{a'b'}{b'c'}$

$\therefore \quad \frac{x}{y+8} = \frac{5}{8}$ and $\frac{x}{y+3+11} = \frac{5}{11}$

Or $\quad 8x - 5y = 40 \quad$ ...(i)
and $\quad 11x - 5y = 70 \quad$ ...(ii)
Solving, we have $3x = 30$;
$\therefore \quad x = 10$ft and $y = 8$ft
So the difference = 10 – 8 = 2ft.

Example 6

In a triangle PQR, L and M are two points on the base QR, such that ∠LPQ = ∠QRP and ∠RPM = ∠RQP. Prove that :

(i) $\Delta PQL \sim \Delta RPM$
(ii) $QL \times RM = PL \times PM$
(iii) $PQ^2 = QR \times QL$

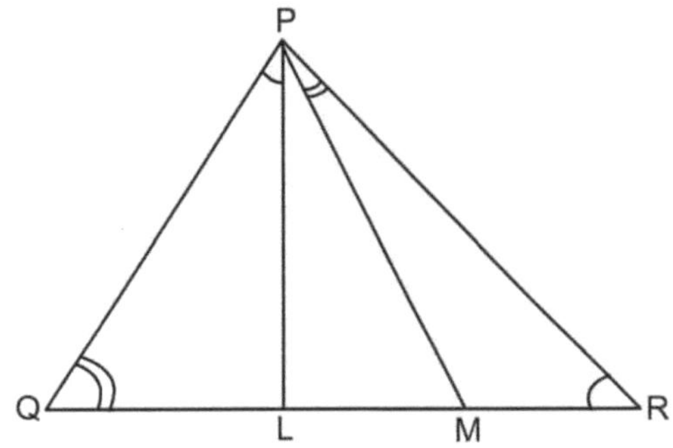

Solution

(i) To prove : $\Delta PQL \sim \Delta RPM$
In ΔPQL and ΔRPM
$\angle PQL = \angle RPM$ (Given)
$\angle QPL = \angle MRP$ (Given)
So, by AA similarity criteria
$\Delta PQL \sim \Delta RPM$

(ii) To prove : $QL \times RM = PL \times PM$
$\because \quad \Delta PQL \sim \Delta RPM$

$$\frac{PL}{RM} = \frac{QL}{PM}$$

$PL \times PM = QL \times RM$

(iii) To prove : $PQ^2 = QR \times QL$
In ΔPQR and PQL
$\angle Q = \angle Q$ (Common)
$\angle QRP = \angle LPQ$ (Given)
So, by AA similarity
$\Delta PQR \sim \Delta LQP$

$\therefore \quad \frac{PQ}{QL} = \frac{QR}{PQ} \Rightarrow PQ^2 = QR \times QL.$

Example 7

Two poles of heights a metres and b metres are p metres apart. Prove that the height of the point of intersection of the lines joining the top of each pole to the foot of the opposite pole is given by $\frac{ab}{a+b}$ metres.

Solution

Let AL and BM represent the two poles of heights a metres and b metres respectively.

Since the poles are p metres apart.

$\therefore$ LM = p metres

Let O be the point of intersection of the lines AM and BL

From O, draw a perpendicular on LM

Let ON = h metres and LN = x metres

$\therefore$ NM = LM – LN = (p – x) metres

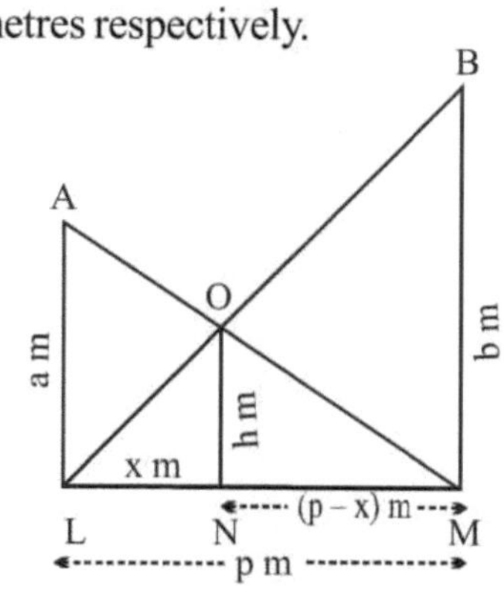

In triangles LMB and LNO,

$\angle LMB = \angle LNO$ (Each = 90°)

$\angle L = \angle L$ (common)

$\therefore$ By A.A. similarity criteria

$\Delta LMB \sim \Delta LNO$

$$\Rightarrow \frac{LM}{LN} = \frac{MB}{NO} \quad \Rightarrow \frac{p}{x} = \frac{b}{h}$$

$$\Rightarrow x = \frac{ph}{b} \quad ..... (i)$$

In triangles MLA and MNO,

$\angle MLA = \angle MNO$ (each 90°)

$\angle LMA = \angle NMO$ (common)

$\therefore$ By A.A. similarity criteria,

$\Delta MLA \sim \Delta MNO$

$$\Rightarrow \frac{ML}{MN} = \frac{LA}{NO} \quad \Rightarrow \frac{p}{p-x} = \frac{a}{h}$$

$$\Rightarrow p - x = \frac{ph}{a} \quad \Rightarrow x = p - \frac{ph}{a} \quad ..... (ii)$$

From (i) and (ii), we have

$$\frac{ph}{b} = p - \frac{ph}{a}$$

$$\Rightarrow \frac{ph}{a} + \frac{ph}{b} = p \quad \Rightarrow ph\left(\frac{1}{a} + \frac{1}{b}\right) = p$$

$$\Rightarrow h\left(\frac{b+a}{ab}\right) = 1 \quad \Rightarrow h = \frac{ab}{a+b}$$

Hence, the required height is $\frac{ab}{a+b}$ metres.

Example 8

In an equilateral triangle ABC, D is a point on side BC such that BD = 1/3 BC. Prove that $9AD^2 = 7AB^2$.

Solution

In equilateral ΔABC, D is a point on side BC such that $BD = \frac{1}{3}BC$.

From A, draw $AE \perp BC$.

Also, join AD

Now, in right angled triangles AEB and AEC,

$\angle B = \angle C$ (each 60°)

$\angle AEB = \angle AEC$ (each 90°)

$\therefore$ By A.A. similarity criteria,

$\Delta AEB \sim \Delta AEC$

$\Rightarrow \frac{AB}{AC} = \frac{AE}{AE} = \frac{BE}{CE}$ ($\because$ corresponding sides of similar triangles are proportional)

$\Rightarrow \frac{AB}{AC} = 1 = \frac{BE}{CE} \quad \Rightarrow \frac{BE}{CE} = 1$

$\Rightarrow BE = CE \quad \Rightarrow BE = EC$

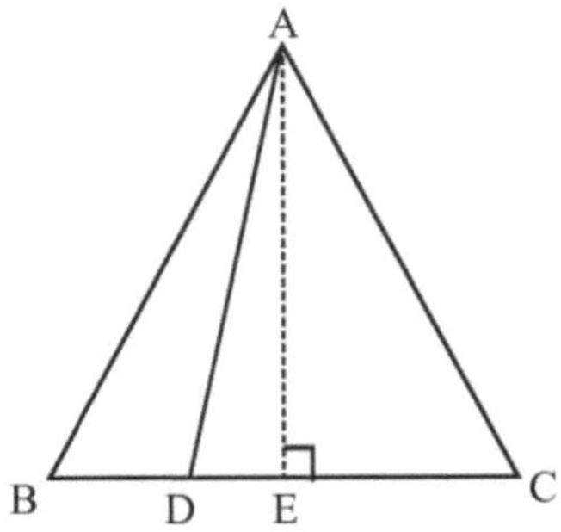

Now, $BD = \frac{1}{3}BC$

$\Rightarrow BC - DC = \frac{1}{3}BC \quad \Rightarrow BC - \frac{1}{3}BC = DC$

$\Rightarrow DC = \frac{2}{3}BC$

Using Pythagoras theorem in right angled triangles AED and AEC, we get

$AD^2 = AE^2 + DE^2$ ..... (i)

$AC^2 = AE^2 + EC^2$ ..... (ii)

From (i) $AD^2 = AE^2 + DE^2 = AE^2 + (DC - EC)^2$

$= AE^2 + DC^2 + EC^2 - 2DC \times EC$

$\Rightarrow AD^2 = (AE^2 + EC^2) + DC^2 - 2DC \times EC$

$\Rightarrow AD^2 = AC^2 + DC^2 - 2DC \times EC$ [By using (ii)]

$\Rightarrow AD^2 = AC^2 + \left(\frac{2}{3}BC\right)^2 - 2\left(\frac{2}{3}BC\right) \times \left(\frac{1}{2}BC\right)$

$\Rightarrow AD^2 = AC^2 + \frac{4}{9}BC^2 - \frac{2}{3}BC^2$

$\Rightarrow AD^2 = AB^2 + \frac{4}{9}AB^2 - \frac{2}{3}AB^2$ ($\because \Delta ABC$ is an equilateral triangle, so $AB = AC = BC$)

$\Rightarrow AD^2 = \frac{9AB^2 + 4AB^2 - 6AB^2}{9}$

$\Rightarrow AD^2 = \frac{7}{9}AB^2$

$\Rightarrow 9AD^2 = 7AB^2$ Hence proved.

CONCEPT APPLICATION LEVEL - I [NCERT Questions]

Q.1 In figure (i) and (ii) DE || BC. Find EC in (i) and AD in (ii).

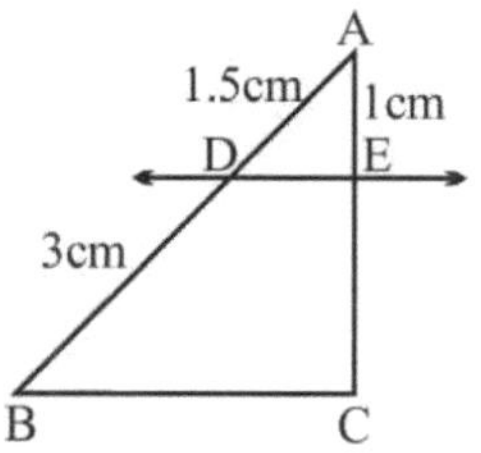

(i)

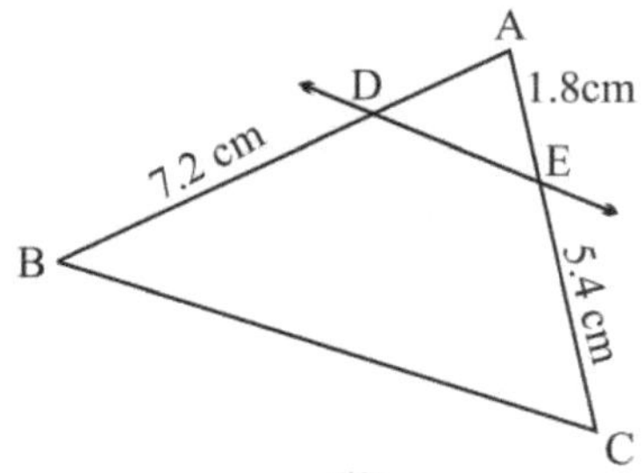

(ii)

Sol. (i) In Δ ABC,

$\therefore$ DE || BC

$\therefore \quad \frac{AD}{DB} = \frac{AE}{EC}$ (By Basic Proportionality Theorem)

$\Rightarrow \quad \frac{1.5}{3} = \frac{1}{EC} \quad \Rightarrow \quad EC = \frac{3}{1.5} \quad \Rightarrow \quad EC = 2$ cm.

(ii) In ΔABC,

$\because$ DE || BC

$\therefore \quad \frac{AD}{DB} = \frac{AE}{EC}$ (By Basic Proportionality Theorem)

$\Rightarrow \quad \frac{AD}{7.2} = \frac{1.8}{5.4} \quad \Rightarrow \quad AD = \frac{7.2 \times 1.8}{5.4} \quad \Rightarrow \quad AD = 2.4$ cm

Q.2 In figure, DE || AC and DF || AE, prove that $\frac{BF}{FE} = \frac{BE}{EC}$.

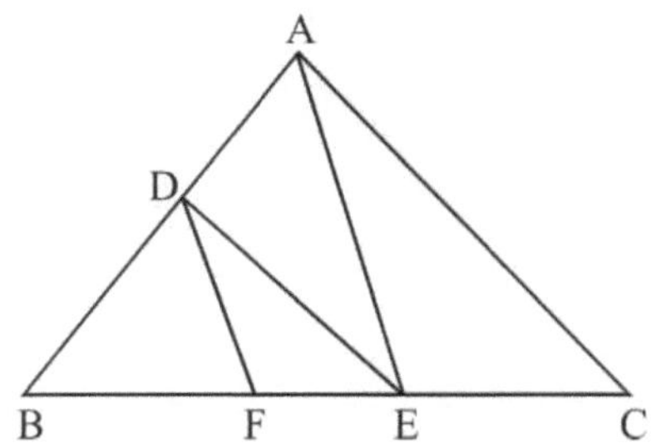

Sol. In ΔABE,

$\because$ DF || AE

$\therefore \quad \frac{AD}{DB} = \frac{FE}{BF}$ .....(1) (By Basic Proportionality theorem)

In ΔABC,

$\because$ DE || AC

$\therefore \quad \frac{AD}{DB} = \frac{EC}{BE}$ .....(2) (By Basic Proportionality theorem)

From (1) and (2),

$\frac{FE}{BF} = \frac{EC}{BE} \quad \Rightarrow \quad \frac{BF}{FE} = \frac{BE}{EC}$ (Taking reciprocals)

Q.3 In figure, A,B and C are points on OP, OQ and OR respectively such that AB || PQ and AC || PR. Show that BC || QR.

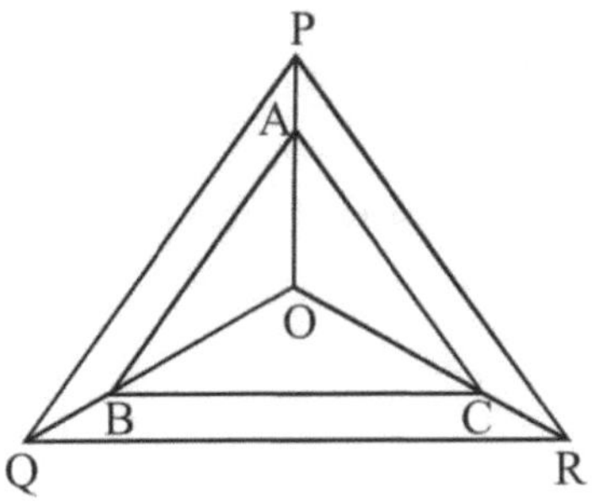

Sol. In Δ OPQ,

∵ AB || PQ

∴ $\frac{OA}{AP}=\frac{OB}{BQ}$ .....(1) (By Basic Proportionality theorem)

In ΔOPR,

∵ AC || PR

∴ $\frac{OA}{AP}=\frac{OC}{CR}$ .....(2) (By Basic Proportionality theorem)

From (1) and (2)

$\frac{OB}{BQ}=\frac{OC}{OR}$

∴ BC || QR (By Converse of basic Proportionality theorem)

Q.4 ABCD is a trapezium in which AB || DC . Its diagonals intersect each other at the point O. Show that $\frac{AO}{BO}=\frac{CO}{DO}$.

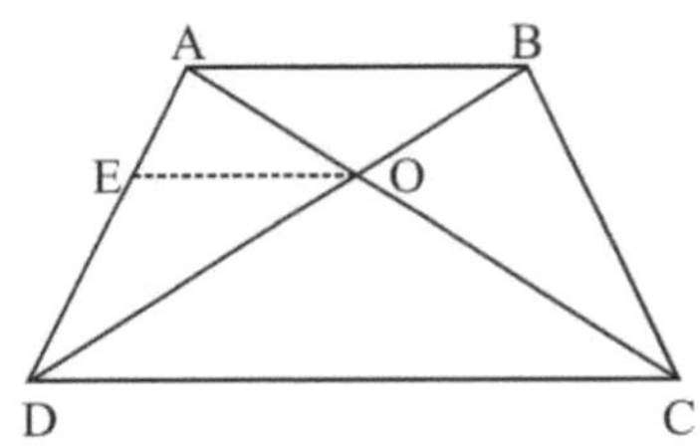

Sol. Given : ABCD is a trapezium in which AB || DC .
Its diagonals intersect each other at the point O.

To Prove : $\frac{AO}{BO}=\frac{CO}{DO}$

Construction : Through O, draw a line OE parallel to AB or DC intersecting AD at E.

Proof : In ΔADC,

∵ OE || DC

∴ $\frac{AO}{CO}=\frac{AE}{DE}$ .....(1) (By Basic Proportionality theorem)

In ΔDBA,

∵ OE || AB

∴ $\frac{DE}{AE}=\frac{DO}{BO}$ (By Basic Proportionality theorem)

⇒ $\frac{AE}{DE}=\frac{BO}{DO}$ .....(2) (By Invertendo)

From (1) and (2),

$\frac{AO}{CO}=\frac{BO}{DO}$ ⇒ $\frac{AO}{BO}=\frac{CO}{DO}$

Q.5 In figure, $\Delta ODC \sim \Delta OBA$, $\angle BOC = 125°$ and $\angle CDO = 70°$. Find $\angle DOC$, $\angle DCO$ and $\angle OAB$.

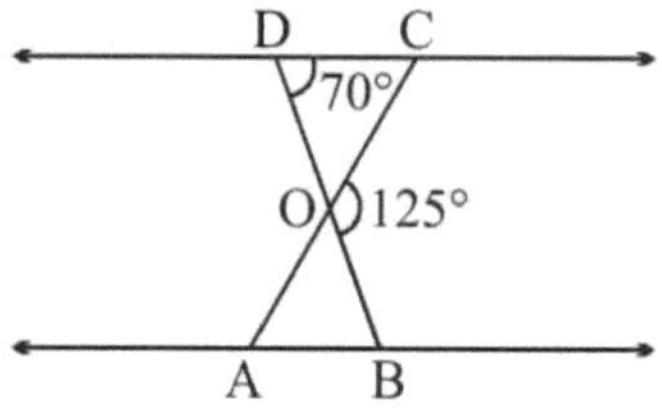

Sol. $\angle DOC + \angle BOC = 180°$ (Linear pair)

$\Rightarrow \angle DOC + 125° = 180°$

$\Rightarrow \angle DOC = 180° - 125°$

$\Rightarrow \angle DOC = 55°$ .....(1)

In ΔDOC,

$\angle DOC + \angle ODC + \angle DCO = 180°$ ($\because$ The sum of the three angles of a triangle in 180°)

$\Rightarrow 55° + 70° + \angle DCO = 180°$

$\Rightarrow 125° + \angle DCO = 180°$

$\Rightarrow \angle DCO = 180° - 125°$

$\Rightarrow \angle DCO = 55°$ .....(2)

$\because \Delta ODC \sim \Delta OBA$ (Given)

$\therefore \angle OCD = \angle OAB$ (Corresponding angles of two similar triangles are equal)

$\Rightarrow \angle DCO = \angle OAB$

$\Rightarrow \angle OAB = \angle DCO$

$\Rightarrow \angle OAB = 55°$ .....(3)

Q.6 In figure, $\frac{QR}{QS} = \frac{QT}{PR}$ and $\angle 1 = \angle 2$. Show that $\Delta PQS \sim \angle TQR$.

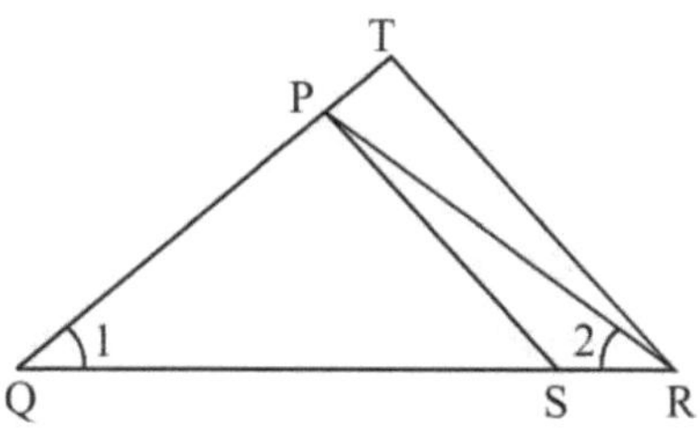

Sol. Given : In figure, $\frac{QR}{QS} = \frac{QT}{PR}$ and $\angle 1 = \angle 2$

To prove : $\Delta PQS \sim \Delta TQR$

Proof : In ΔPQR,

$\because \angle 1 = \angle 2$

$\therefore PR = QP$ .....(1)

($\because$ Sides opposite to equal angles of a triangle are equal)

Now, $\frac{QR}{QS} = \frac{QT}{PR}$ (Given)

$\Rightarrow \frac{QR}{QS} = \frac{QT}{QP}$ .....(2) [Using (1)]

Again, in ΔPQS and ΔTQR,

$\because \frac{QR}{QS} = \frac{QT}{QP}$ [From (2)]

$\therefore \frac{QS}{QR} = \frac{QP}{QT}$

and $\angle SQP = \angle RQT$

$\therefore$ $\Delta PQS \sim \angle TQR$ (SAS similarity criterion)

Q.7 In figure, altitudes AD and CE of ΔABC intersect each other at the point P. Show that

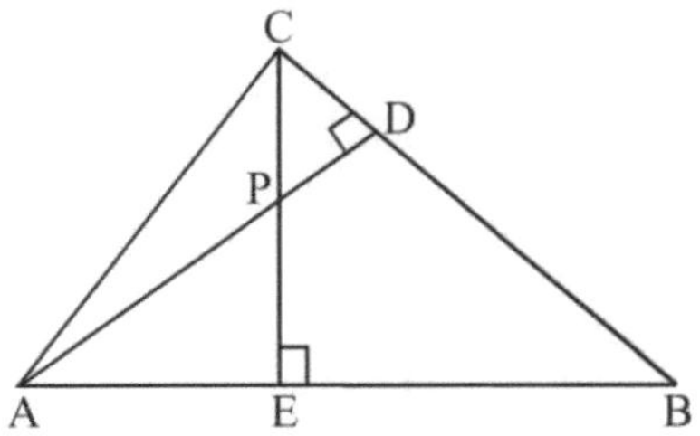

(i) $\Delta AEP \sim \Delta CDP$

(ii) $\Delta ABD \sim \Delta CBE$

(iii) $\Delta AEP \sim \Delta ADB$

(iv) $\Delta PDC \sim \Delta BEC$

Sol. Given : In figure, altitudes AD and CE of ΔABC intersect each other at the point P.

To Prove: (i) $\Delta AEP \sim \Delta CDP$ (ii) $\Delta ABD \sim \Delta CBE$

(iii) $\Delta AEP \sim \Delta ADB$ (iv) $\Delta PDC \sim \Delta BEC$

Proof : (i) In ΔAEP and ΔCDP,

$\angle AEP = \angle CDP$ .....(1) (Each equal to 90°)

$\angle EPA = \angle DPC$ .....(2) (Vert. opp. $\angle$s)

From (1) and (2)

$\Delta AEP \sim \Delta CDP$ (AA similarity criterion)

(ii) In ΔABD and ΔCBE

$\angle ADB = \angle CEB$ .....(1) (Each equal to 90°)

$\angle ABD = \angle CBE$ .....(2) (Common angle)

From (1) and (2)

$\Delta ABD \sim \Delta CBE$ (AA similarity criterion)

(iii) In ΔAEP and ΔADB

$\angle AEP = \angle ADB$ .....(1) (Each equal to 90°)

$\angle EAP = \angle DAB$ .....(2) (Common angle)

From (1) and (2)

$\Delta AEP \sim \Delta ADB$ (AA similarity criterion)

(iv) In ΔPDC and ΔBEC

$\angle PDC = \angle BEC$ .....(1) (Each equal to 90°)

$\angle DCP = \angle ECB$ .....(2) (Common angle)

From (1) and (2)

$\Delta PDC \sim \Delta BEC$ (AA similarity criterion)

Q.8 E is a point on the side AD produced of a parallelogram ABCD and BE intersects CD at F. Show that $\Delta ABE \sim \Delta CFB$.

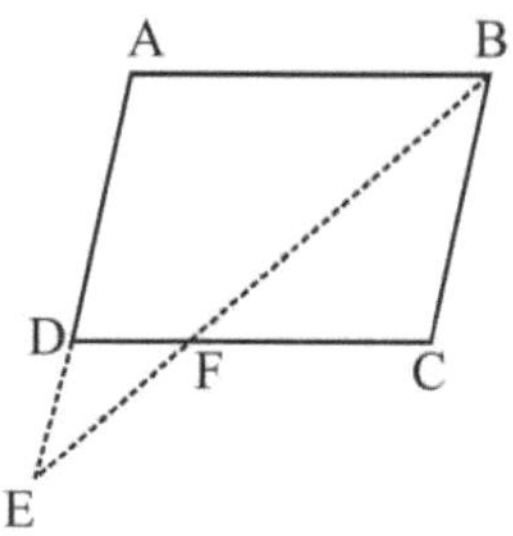

Sol. Given : E is a point on the side AD produced of a parallelogram ABCD and BE intersects CD at F.

To prove : $\Delta ABE \sim \Delta CFB$

Proof : In ΔABE and ΔCFB

$\angle BAE = \Delta FCB$ .....(1) (Opposite $\angle$s of a $\|$ gram)

$\angle AEB = \angle CBF$ .....(2) [($\because$ AE $\|$ BC) and BE intersects them]

From (1) and (2)

$\Delta ABE \sim \Delta CFB$

Q.9 Sides AB and BC and median AD of a triangle ABC are respectively proportional to sides PQ and QR and median PM of ΔPQR (see figure). Show that $\Delta ABC \sim \Delta PQR$.

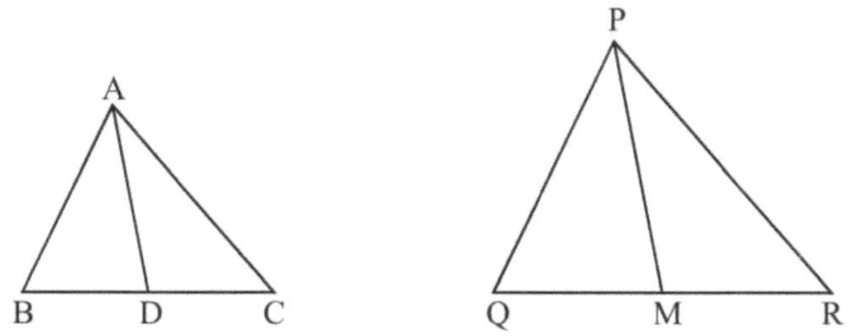

Sol. Given : Sides AB and BC and median AD of a triangle ABC are respectively proportional to sides PQ and QR and median PM of ΔPQR, i.e.

$$\frac{AB}{PQ} = \frac{BC}{QR} = \frac{AD}{PM}$$

To Prove : $\Delta ABC \sim \Delta PQR$

Proof : $\frac{AB}{PQ} = \frac{BC}{QR} = \frac{AD}{PM}$ (Given)

$\Rightarrow \quad \frac{AB}{PQ} = \frac{\frac{1}{2}BC}{\frac{1}{2}QR} = \frac{AD}{PM}$

$\Rightarrow \quad \frac{AB}{PQ} = \frac{BD}{QM} = \frac{AD}{PM}$

$\Rightarrow \quad \Delta ABD \sim \Delta PQM$ (SSS similarity criterion)

$\therefore \quad \angle ABD = \angle PQM$

($\because$ Corresponding angles of two similar triangles are equal)

$\therefore \quad \angle ABC = \angle PQR$

Now, in ΔABC and ΔPQR,

$\frac{AB}{PQ} = \frac{BC}{QR}$ .....(1) (Given)

$\therefore \quad \angle ABC = \angle PQR$ .....(2) (Proved above)

From (1) and (2)

$\Delta ABC \sim \Delta PQR$ (SAS similarity criterion)

Q.10 Sides AB and AC and median AD of a triangle ABC are respectively proportional to sides PQ and PR and median PM of another triangle PQR. Show that $\Delta ABC \sim \Delta PQR$.

Sol. Given : Sides AB and AC and median AD of a ΔABC are respectively proportional to sides PQ and PR and median PM of another ΔPQR, in ΔABC and ΔPQR.

$\Rightarrow \quad \frac{AB}{PQ} = \frac{AC}{PR} = \frac{AD}{PM}$

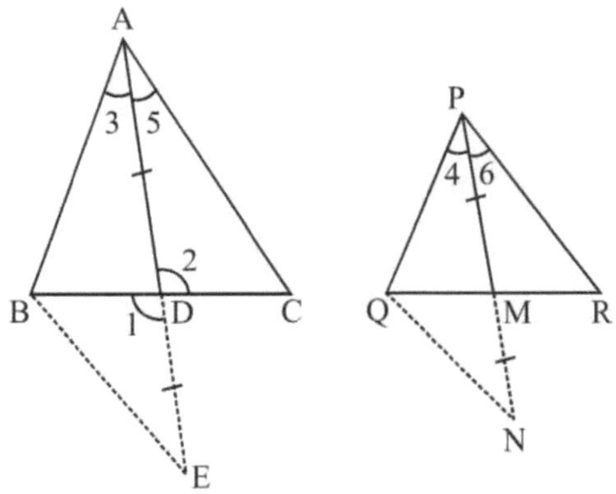

To Prove : $\Delta ABC \sim \Delta PQR$

Construction : Produce AD to a point E such that AD = DE and produce PM to a point N such that PM = MN. Join BE and QN.

Proof : In ΔABC and ΔEDB,

$DC = DB$ ($\because$ AD is a median)

$AD = ED$ (By construction)

$\angle ADC = \angle EDB$ (vert. opp. $\angle$s)

$\therefore \quad \Delta ADC \cong \Delta EDB$ (SAS congruence criterion)

$\therefore \quad AC = EB$ .....(1) (CPCT)

Similarly, we can show that

$\Delta PMR = \Delta NMQ$

$\therefore$ $PR = NQ$ .....(2) (CPCT)

Now, $\frac{AB}{PQ} = \frac{AC}{PR} = \frac{AD}{PM}$ (Given)

$\Rightarrow$ $\frac{AB}{PQ} = \frac{EB}{NQ} = \frac{AD}{PM}$ [From (1) and (2)]

$\Rightarrow$ $\frac{AB}{PQ} = \frac{EB}{NQ} = \frac{AD}{PM} = \frac{2AD}{2PM} = \frac{AE}{PN}$

$\therefore$ $\Delta ABE \sim \Delta PQN$ (SSS similarity criterion)

$\therefore$ $\angle ABE = \angle PQN$

($\because$ Corresponding angles of two similar triangles are equal)

$\therefore$ $\angle 3 = \angle 4$ .....(3)

Similarly, we can prove that

$\angle 5 = \angle 6$ .....(4)

Adding (3) and (4), we get

$\angle 3 + \angle 5 = \angle 4 + \angle 6$

$\Rightarrow$ $\angle A = \angle P$

Now, in ΔABC and ΔPQR,

$\frac{AB}{PQ} = \frac{AC}{PR}$ and $\angle A = \angle P$

$\therefore$ $\Delta ABC \sim \Delta PQR$ (SAS similarity criterion)

Q.11 A vertical pole of length 6 m casts a shadow 4 m long on the ground and at the same time a tower casts a shadow 28 m. Find the height of the tower.

Sol. Let AB denote the vertical pole of length 6 m. BC is the shadow of the pole on the ground BC = 4 m. Let DE denote the Tower. EF is the shadow of the tower on the ground.

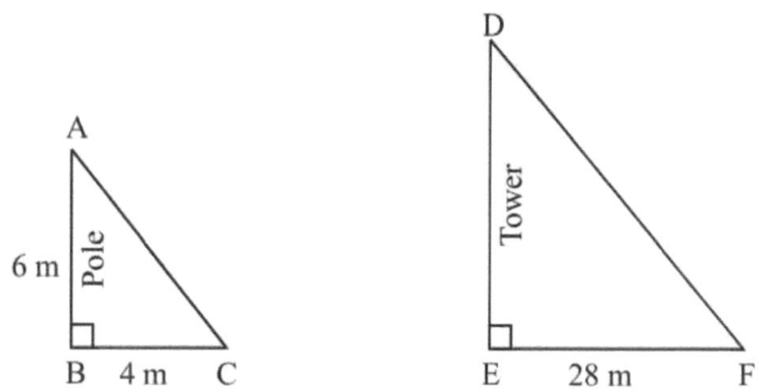

EF = 28 m

Let the height of the tower be h m.

In ΔABC and ΔDEF,

$\angle B = \angle E$ (Each equal to 90° because pole and tower are standing vertical to the ground)

$\angle A = \angle D$ ($\because$ Shadows are cast at the same time)

$\therefore$ $\Delta ABC \sim \Delta DEF$ (AA similarly criterion)

$\therefore$ $\frac{AB}{DE} = \frac{BC}{EF}$ ($\because$ Corresponding sides of two similar triangles are proportional)

$\Rightarrow$ $\frac{6}{h} = \frac{4}{28}$

$\Rightarrow$ $h = \frac{6 \times 28}{4}$

$\Rightarrow$ $h = 42$

Hence, the height of the tower is 42 m.

Q.12 Diagonals of a trapezium ABCD with AB || DC intersect each other at the point O. If AB = 2CD, find the ratio of the areas of triangles AOB and COD.

Sol. In ΔAOB and ΔCOD

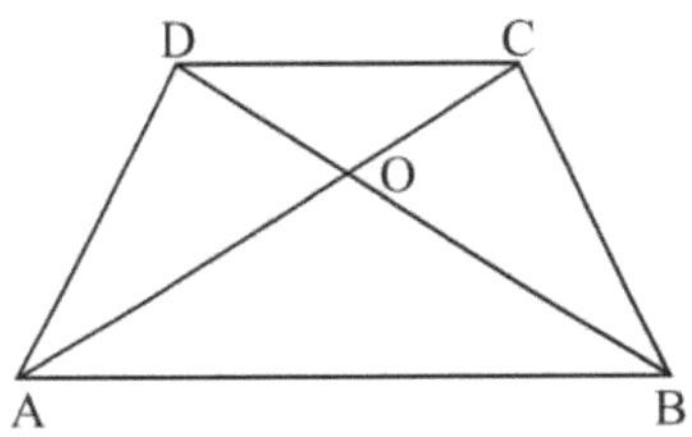

$\angle AOB = \angle COD$ (Vert. opp.$\angle$s)

$\angle OAB = \angle OCD$ (Alt. int. $\angle$s)

$\therefore$ $\Delta AOB \sim \angle COD$ (AA similarity criterion)

$\therefore$ $\frac{ar\,(\Delta AOB)}{ar\,(\Delta COD)} = \left(\frac{AB}{CD}\right)^2$

($\because$ The ratio of the areas of two similar triangles is equal to the square of the ratio of their corresponding sides)

$= \left(\frac{2CD}{CD}\right)^2$ ($\because$ AB = 2CD)

$= \frac{4}{1} = 4 : 1$

Q.13 In figure, ABC and DBC are two triangles on the same base BC. If AD intersects BC at O, show that $\dfrac{ar(\Delta ABC)}{ar(\Delta DBC)} = \dfrac{AO}{DO}$**.**

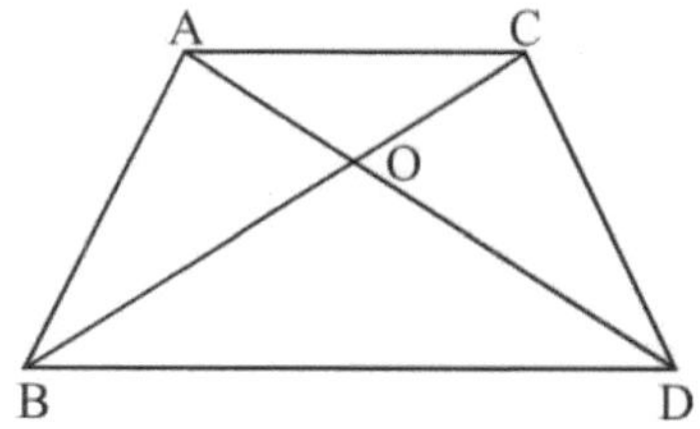

Sol. Given : In figure, ABC and DBC are two triangles on the same base BC. AD intersects BC at O.

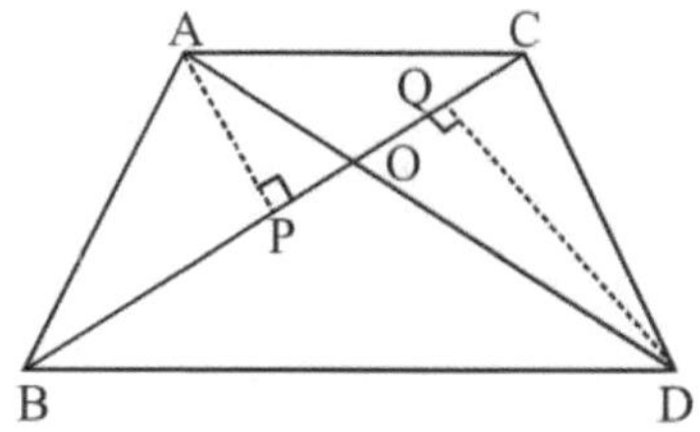

To Prove : $\dfrac{ar(\Delta ABC)}{ar(\Delta DBC)} = \dfrac{AO}{DO}$

Construction : Draw $AP \perp BC$ and $DQ \perp BC$.

Proof : In ΔAOP and ΔDOQ

$\angle APO = \angle DQO$ (Each equal to 90°)

$\angle AOP = \angle DOQ$ (Vert. opp. $\angle$s)

$\therefore$ $\Delta AOP \sim \Delta DOQ$ (AA similarity criterion)

$\therefore$ $\dfrac{AP}{DQ} = \dfrac{AO}{DO}$ .....(1)

($\because$ Corresponding sides of two similar triangles are proportional)

Now, $\dfrac{ar(\Delta ABC)}{ar(\Delta DBC)} = \dfrac{\frac{1}{2}(BC)(AP)}{\frac{1}{2}(BC)(DQ)}$

$= \dfrac{AP}{DQ}$

$= \dfrac{AO}{DO}$ [From (1)]

Q.14 D, E and F are respectively the mid-points of sides AB, BC and CA of ΔABC. Find the ratio of the areas of ΔDEF and ΔABC.

Sol. Given : D, E and F are respectively the mid-points of sides AB, BC and CA of ΔABC.

To Determine : Ratio of the areas of ΔDEF and ΔABC.

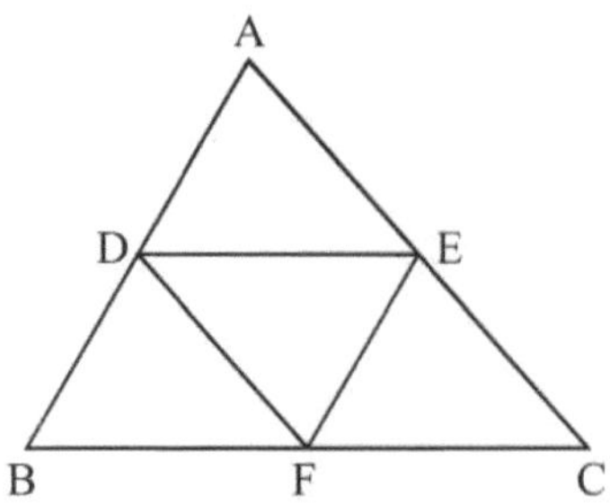

Determination : We have $\dfrac{AD}{AB} = \dfrac{1}{2}$ .....(1)

($\because$ D is the mid-point of AB)

And $\dfrac{AE}{AC} = \dfrac{1}{2}$ .....(2)

($\because$ E is the mid-point of AC)

From (1) and (2)

$$\frac{AD}{AB} = \frac{AE}{AC}$$

$\therefore$ DE || BC (By converse of the basic Proportionality theorem)

$\therefore$ $\angle ADE = \angle ABC$ .....(3) (Corresponding angles)

and $\angle AED = \angle ACB$ (Corresponding angles)

From (3) and (4)

$\Delta ABC \sim \Delta DEF$ (AA similarity criterion)

$\therefore$ $\dfrac{ar\,(\Delta DEF)}{ar\,(\Delta ABC)} = \left(\dfrac{DE}{BC}\right)^2$ ($\because$ The ratio of the areas of two similar triangles is equal to the square of the ratio of their corresponding sides)

$= \left(\dfrac{\frac{1}{2}BC}{BC}\right)^2$ ($\because$ D and E are the mid-points of AB and AC respectively

$\therefore$ DE || BC and DE = $\frac{1}{2}$BC)

$= \dfrac{1}{4}$

$\therefore$ ar (ΔDEF) : ar (ΔABC) = 1 : 4

Q.15 PQR is a triangle right angled at P and M is a point on QR such that PM $\perp$ QR. Show that $PM^2 = QM \cdot MR$.

Sol. Given : PQR is a triangle right angled at P and M is a point on QR such that PM $\perp$ QR.

To Prove : $PM^2 = QM \cdot MR$

Proof : In right triangle PQR,

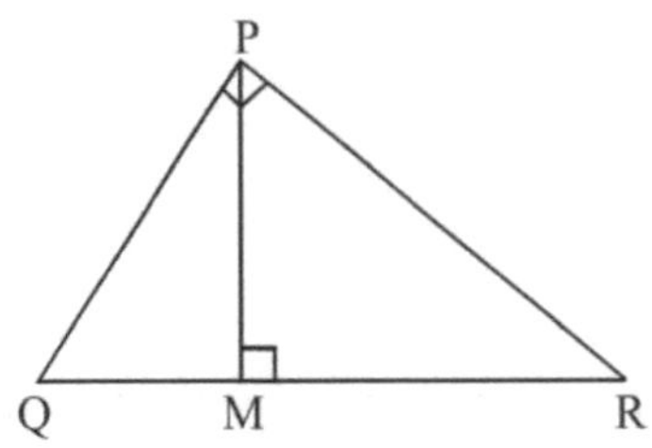

$QR^2 = PQ^2 + PR^2$ .....(1)

(By Pythagoras theorem)

In right triangle PMQ,

$PQ^2 = PM^2 + MQ^2$ .....(2)

(By Pythagoras theorem)

In right triangle PMR,

$PR^2 = PM^2 + MR^2$ .....(3) (By Pythagoras theorem)

Using (2) and (3), (1) gives

$QR^2 = (PM^2 + MQ^2) + (PM^2 + MR^2)$

$\Rightarrow$ $QR^2 = 2PM^2 + MQ^2 + MR^2$

$\Rightarrow$ $(MQ + MR)^2 = 2PM^2 + MQ^2 + MR^2$

$\Rightarrow$ $MQ^2 + MR^2 + 2MQ \cdot MR = 2PM^2 + MQ^2 + MR^2$

$\Rightarrow$ $PM^2 = QM \cdot MR$

Another Method :

In ΔQMP and ΔPMR

$\angle QMP = \angle PMR$ (Each equal to 90°)

$\angle MQP = 90° - \angle MPQ = \angle MPR$

$\therefore$ $\Delta QMP \sim \angle PMR$ (AA similarity criterion)

$\therefore$ $\frac{QM}{PM} = \frac{PM}{RM}$ ($\because$ Corresponding sides of two similar triangles are proportional)

$\Rightarrow$ $PM^2 = QM \cdot RM$

$\Rightarrow$ $PM^2 = QM \cdot MR$

Q.16 In figure, O is a point in the interior of a triangle ABC, OD $\perp$ BC, OE $\perp$ AC and OF $\perp$ AB. Show that

(i) $OA^2 + OB^2 + OC^2 - OD^2 - OE^2 - OF^2 = AF^2 + BD^2 + CE^2$

(ii) $AF^2 + BD^2 + CE^2 = AE^2 + CD^2 + BF^2$

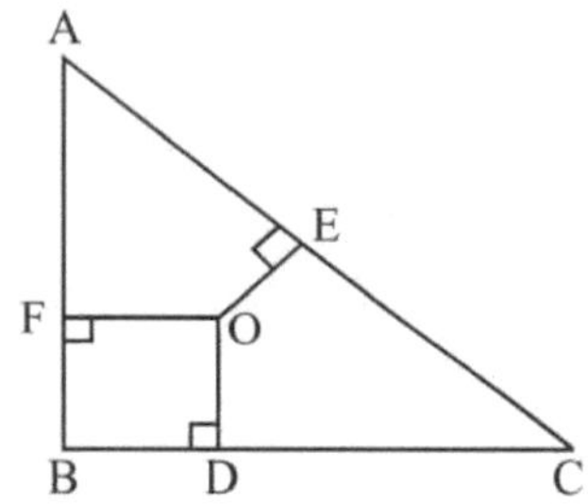

Sol. Given : In figure, O is a point in the interior of a triangle ABC, OD $\perp$ BC, OE $\perp$ AC and OF $\perp$ AB.

To Prove : (i) $OA^2 + OB^2 + OC^2 - OD^2 - OE^2 - OF^2 = AF^2 + BD^2 + CE^2$

(ii) $AF^2 + BD^2 + CE^2 = AE^2 + CD^2 + BF^2$

Construction : Join OA, OB and OC.

Proof : (i) In right triangle OAF,

$OA^2 = OF^2 + AF^2$

(By Pythagoras theorem)

$\Rightarrow$ $AF^2 = OA^2 - OF^2$ .....(1)

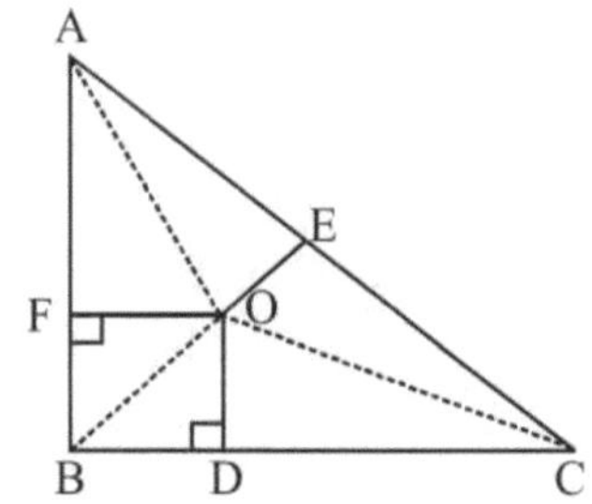

In right triangle OBD,

$OB^2 = OD^2 + BD^2$

(By Pythagoras theorem)

$\Rightarrow$ $BD^2 = OB^2 - OD^2$ .....(2)

In right triangle OCE,

$OC^2 = OE^2 + CE^2$ (By Pythagoras theorem)

$\Rightarrow$ $CE^2 = OC^2 - OE^2$ .....(3)

Adding (1), (2) and (3), we get

$AF^2 + BD^2 + CE^2 = OA^2 + OB^2 + OC^2 - OA^2 - OE^2 - OF^2$

(ii) In right triangle OBD,

$OB^2 = OD^2 + BD^2$ (By Pythagoras theorem)

In right triangle OCD,

$OC^2 = OD^2 + CD^2$ (By Pythagoras theorem)

$\therefore$ $OB^2 - OC^2 = BD^2 - OE^2$ .....(4)

Similarly, by considering right triangles OCE and OAE, we get

$OC^2 - OA^2 = CE^2 - AE^2$ .....(5)

and by considering right triangles OAF and OBF, we get

$OA^2 - OB^2 = AF^2 - BF^2$ .....(6)

Adding (4), (5) and (6), we get

$0 = BD^2 + CE^2 + AF^2 - CD^2 - AE^2 - BF^2$

$\Rightarrow$ $AF^2 + BD^2 + CE^2 = AE^2 + CD^2 + BF^2$

Q.17 An aeroplane leaves an airport and flies due north at a speed of 1000 km per hour. At the same time, another aeroplane leaves the same airport and flies due west at a speed of 1200 km per hour. How far apart will be the two planes after $1\frac{1}{2}$ hours?

Sol. Distance of the aeroplane leaving the airport and flying due north at a speed of 1000 km per hour after $1\frac{1}{2}$ hours = OA.

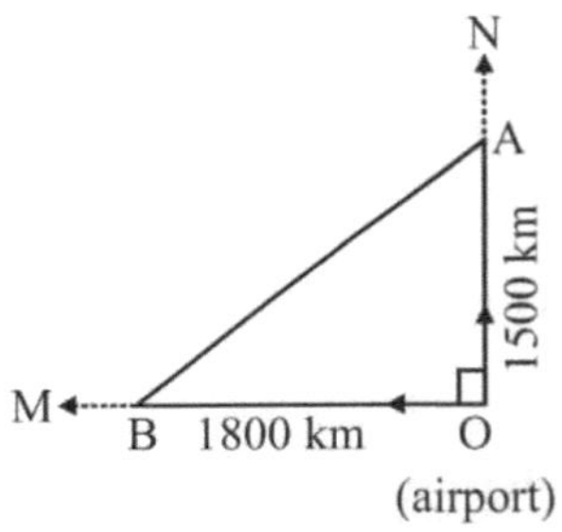

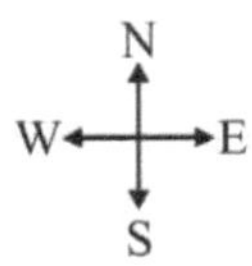

$= 1000 \times 1\frac{1}{2}$ km = 1500 km

Distance of the aeroplane leaving the airport and flying due west at a speed of 1200 km per hour after $1\frac{1}{2}$ hours.

$= OB = 1200 \times 1\frac{1}{2}$ km= 1800 km

In right triangle AOB,

$AB^2 = OA^2 + OB^2$

$= (1500)^2 + (1800)^2 = 2250000 + 3240000 = 5490000$

$\Rightarrow$ $AB = \sqrt{5490000}$

$\Rightarrow$ $AB = \sqrt{61 \times 90000}$

$\Rightarrow$ $AB = 300\sqrt{61}$ km

Hence, the two planes will be $300\sqrt{61}$ km apart after $1\frac{1}{2}$ hours.

Q.18 D and E are points on the sides CA and CB respectively of a triangle ABC right angled at C. Prove that $AE^2 + BD^2 = AB^2 + DE^2$.

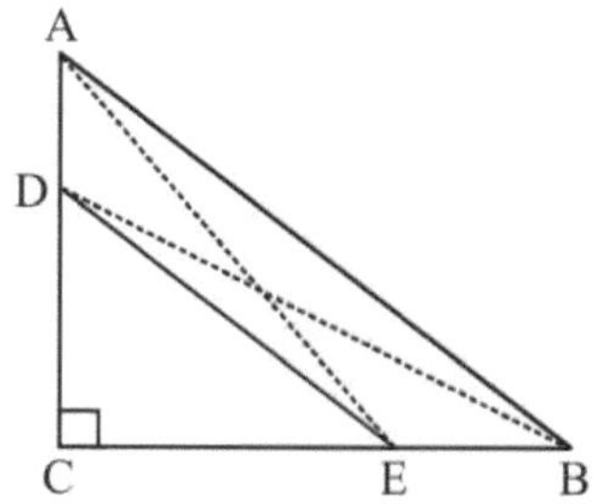

Sol. Given : D and E are points on the sides CA and CB respectively of a triangle ABC right angled at C.

To Prove : $AE^2 + BD^2 = AB^2 + DE^2$

Proof : In right triangle ACB,

$$AB^2 = AC^2 + BC^2 \quad .....(1)$$

(By Pythagoras theorem)

In right triangle DCE,

$$DE^2 = CD^2 + CE^2 \quad .....(2) \quad \text{(By Pythagoras theorem)}$$

Adding (1) and (2), we get

$$AB^2 + DE^2 = (AC^2 + BC^2) + (CD^2 + CE^2)$$
$$= (AC^2 + CE^2) + (BC^2 + CD^2) = AE^2 + BD^2$$

$\because$ In right triangle ACE,

$$AC^2 + CE^2 = AE^2 \quad \text{(By Pythagoras theorem)}$$

and in right triangle BCD,

$$BC^2 + CD^2 = BD^2 \quad \text{(By Pythagoras theorem)}$$

Q.19 The perpendicular from A on side BC of a ΔABC intersects BC at D such that DB = 3CD (see figure). Prove that $2AB^2 = 2AC^2 + BC^2$.

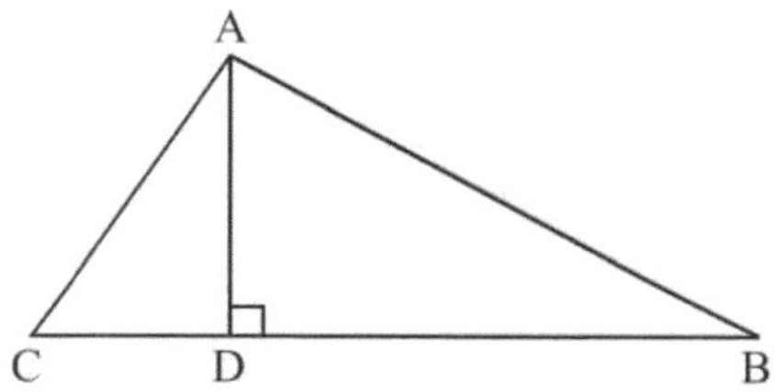

Sol. Given : The perpendicular from A on side BC of a ΔABC intersects BC at D such that DB = 3CD.

To Prove : $2AB^2 = 2AC^2 + BC^2$

Proof : In right triangle ADB,

$$AB^2 = AD^2 + BD^2 \quad .....(1) \quad \text{(By Pythagoras theorem)}$$
$$AC^2 = AD^2 + CD^2 \quad .....(2) \quad \text{(By Pythagoras theorem)}$$

In right triangle ADC,

Subtracting (2) from (1), we get

$$AB^2 - AC^2 = BD^2 - CD^2$$
$$= (BD + CD)(BD - CD)$$
$$= (BC)(3CD - CD) \quad [\because BD = 3\,CD \text{ (given)}]$$
$$= (BC)(2CD)$$
$$AB^2 - AC^2 = 2(BC)(CD) \quad .....(3)$$
$$= 2(BC)\left(\frac{1}{4}BC\right)$$

Now, $DB = 3\,CD$ (Given)

$$\Rightarrow \quad \frac{DB}{CD} = 3$$

Adding 1 on both sides,

$$\Rightarrow \quad \frac{DB}{CD} + 1 = 3 + 1 \quad \Rightarrow \quad \frac{DB + CD}{CD} = 3 + 1$$

$$\Rightarrow \quad \frac{BC}{CD} = 4 \quad \Rightarrow \quad CD = \frac{1}{4}BC \quad .....(4)$$

From equations (3) and (4)

$$AB^2 - AC^2 = 2(BC)\left(\frac{1}{4}BC\right)$$

$$\Rightarrow \quad AB^2 - AC^2 = \frac{1}{2}BC^2$$

$$\Rightarrow \quad 2(AB^2 - AC^2) = BC^2$$

$$\Rightarrow \quad 2AB^2 - 2AC^2) = BC^2$$

$$\Rightarrow \quad 2AB^2 = 2AC^2 + BC^2$$

Q.20 In an equilateral triangle ABC, D is a point on side BC such that $BD = \frac{1}{3}BC$. Prove that $9AD^2 = 7AB^2$.

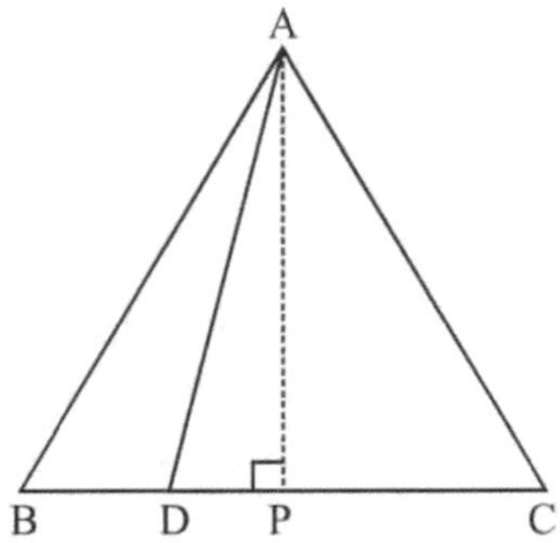

Sol. Given : In an equilateral triangle ABC,

D is a point on side BC such that $BD = \frac{1}{3}BC$.

To Prove: $9AD^2 = 7AB^2$

Construction : Draw $AP \perp BC$

Proof: In right triangle APB,

$AB^2 = AP^2 + BP^2$ .....(1) (By Pythagoras theorem)

In right triangle APD,

$AD^2 = AP^2 + DP^2$ .....(2) (By Pythagoras theorem)

From (2),

$AP^2 = AD^2 - DP^2$ .....(3)

From (3), putting the value of AP^2 in (1), we get

$AB^2 = AD^2 - DP^2 + BP^2$

$$= AD^2 - DP^2 + \left(\frac{BC}{2}\right)^2$$

$[\because \Delta APB \cong \Delta ABC$ (By RHS rule); $\therefore BP = CP = \frac{BC}{2}$ (CPCT)]

$$= AD^2 - DP^2 + \frac{BC^2}{4}$$

$$= AD^2 - (BP - BD)^2 + \frac{BC^2}{4}$$

$$= AD^2 - (BP^2 + BD^2 - 2BP \cdot BD) + \frac{BC^2}{4}$$

$$= AD^2 - BP^2 - BD^2 + 2BP \cdot BD + \frac{BC^2}{4}$$

$$= AD^2 - \left(\frac{BC}{2}\right)^2 - \left(\frac{BC}{3}\right)^2 + 2\left(\frac{BC}{2}\right)\left(\frac{BC}{3}\right) + \frac{BC^2}{4}$$

$$(\because BP = \frac{BC}{2} \text{ and } BD = \frac{BC}{3})$$

$$= AD^2 - \frac{BC^2}{4} - \frac{BC^2}{9} + \frac{BC^2}{3} + \frac{BC^2}{4} = AD^2 + \frac{2}{9}BC^2$$

or $$AB^2 = AD^2 + \frac{2}{9}AB^2 \qquad (\because AB = BC)$$

$$\Rightarrow \quad AB^2\left(1 - \frac{2}{9}\right) = AD^2$$

$$\Rightarrow \quad \frac{7}{9}AB^2 = AD^2$$

$$\Rightarrow \quad 7AB^2 = 9\,AD^2$$

Q.21 In an equilateral triangle prove that three times the square of one side is equal to four times the square of one of its altitudes.

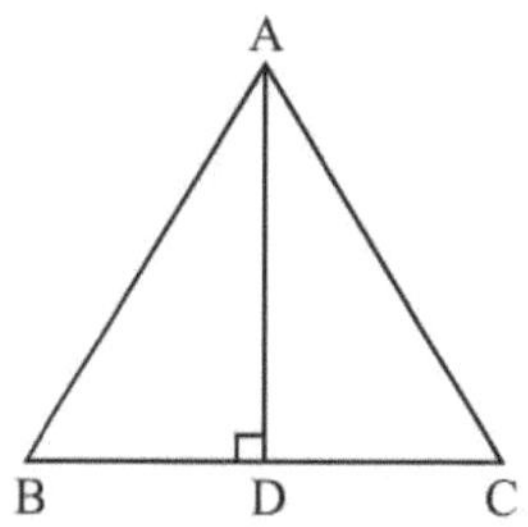

Sol. Given : In ΔABC, $AB = BC = CA$ and $AD \perp BC$

To Prove: $3AB^2 = 4AD^2$

Proof: In right triangle ADB and ADC,

Hyp. AB = Hyp. AC (Given)

$AD = AD$ (Common side)

$\therefore \Delta ADB \cong \Delta ADC$ (RHS congruence criterion)

$\therefore BD = CD$ (CPCT)

$= \frac{1}{2}BC$ ($\because$ D is the mid point of BC)

$= \frac{1}{2}AB$ [$\because BC = AB$ (given)]

Now, in right triangle ADB

$\because \angle ADB = 90°$

$\therefore AB^2 = AD^2 + BD^2$ (By Pythagoras theorem)

$$= AD^2 + \left(\frac{1}{2}AB\right)^2$$

$$AB^2 = AD^2 + \frac{1}{4}AB^2$$

$$\Rightarrow \quad \left(1 - \frac{1}{4}\right)AB^2 = AD^2 \qquad \Rightarrow \quad \frac{3}{4}AB^2 = AD^2$$

$$\Rightarrow \quad 3AB^2 = 4AD^2$$

Q.22 In figure, PS is the bisector of $\angle QPR$ of ΔPQR. Prove that $\frac{QS}{SR} = \frac{PQ}{PR}$.

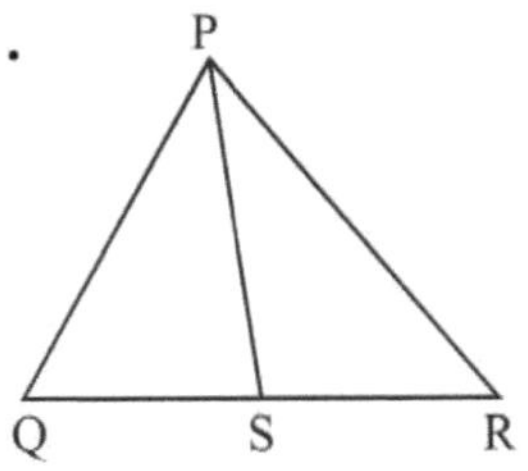

Sol. Given : In figure, PS is the bisector of $\angle QPR$ of ΔPQR.

To Prove : $\frac{QS}{SR} = \frac{PQ}{PR}$

Construction : Draw RT || SP to meet QP produced in T.

Proof : $\because$ RT || SP and transversal PR intersects them

$\angle 1 = \angle 2$ (Alternate interior angles)

$\therefore$ RT || SP and transversal QT intersect is them

$\therefore$ $\angle 3 = \angle 4$ .....(2) (Corresponding angles)

But $\angle 1 = \angle 3$ (Given)

$\therefore$ $\angle 2 = \angle 4$ [From (1) and (2)]

$\therefore$ PT = PR .....(3)

($\because$ sides opposite to equal angles of a triangle are equal)

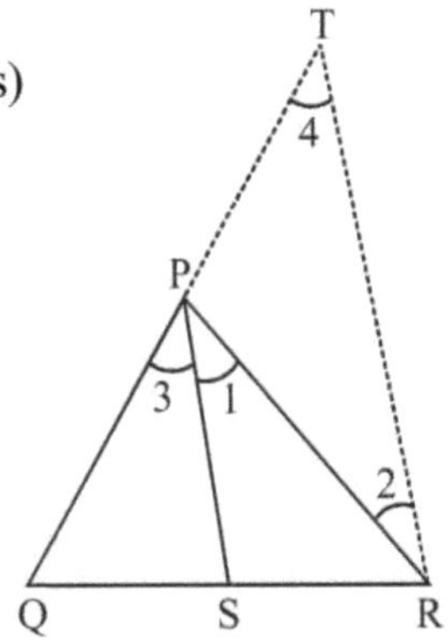

Now, in ΔQRT,

PS = RT (By construction)

$\therefore$ $\frac{QS}{SR} = \frac{PQ}{PT}$ (By basic proportionally theorem)

$\Rightarrow$ $\frac{QS}{SR} = \frac{PQ}{PR}$ [From (3)]

Q.23 In figure, AD is a median of a triangle ABC and AM $\perp$ BC. Prove that

(i) $AC^2 = AD^2 + BC \cdot DM + \left(\frac{BC}{2}\right)^2$

(ii) $AB^2 = AD^2 - BC \cdot DM + \left(\frac{BC}{2}\right)^2$

(iii) $AC^2 + AB^2 = 2AD^2 + \frac{1}{2}BC^2$

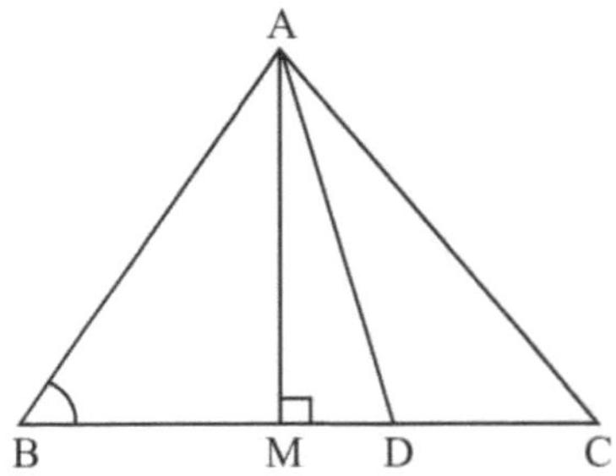

Sol. Given : In figure, AD is a median of a triangle ABC and AM $\perp$ BC.

To Prove : (i) $AC^2 = AD^2 + BC \cdot DM + \left(\frac{BC}{2}\right)^2$ (ii) $AB^2 = AD^2 - BC \cdot DM + \left(\frac{BC}{2}\right)^2$

(iii) $AC^2 + AB^2 = 2AD^2 + \frac{1}{2}BC^2$

Proof : (i) In right triangle AMC,

$\because$ $\angle M = 90°$

$\therefore$ $AC^2 = AM^2 + MC^2$ (By Pythagoras theorem)

$= AM^2 + (MD^2 + DC^2)$
$= AM^2 + MD^2 + DC^2 + 2MD \cdot DC$

$$= AD^2 + \left(\frac{BC}{2}\right)^2 + 2DC \cdot DM$$

[In right triangle AMD with $\angle M = 90°$,
$AM^2 + MD^2 = AD^2$ (By Pythagoras theorem)]
[$\because$ 2DC = BC ($\because$ AD is a median of ΔABC)]

$$= AD^2 + \left(\frac{BC}{2}\right)^2 + BC \cdot DM$$

(ii) In right triangle AMB,

$\because$ $\angle M = 90°$

$\therefore$ $AB^2 = AM^2 + MB^2$
$= AM^2 + (BD - MD)^2$
$= AM^2 + BD^2 + MD^2 - 2BD \cdot MD$
$= AM^2 + MD^2 + BD^2 - (2BD)(MD)$

$$= AD^2 + \left(\frac{BC}{2}\right)^2 - BC \cdot DM$$

[In right triangle AMD with $\angle M = 90°$,
$AM^2 + MD^2 = AD^2$ (By Pythagoras theorem)]
[2BD = BC($\because$ AD is a median of ΔABC)]

$$= AD^2 - BC \cdot DM + \left(\frac{BC}{2}\right)^2$$

(iii) From (i) and (ii), on adding we get

$$AC^2 + AB^2 = 2AD^2 + \frac{1}{2}BC^2$$

Q.24 In figure, two chords AB and CD intersect each other at the point P. Prove that (i) $\Delta APC \sim \Delta DPB$ (ii) $AP \cdot PB = CP \cdot DP$

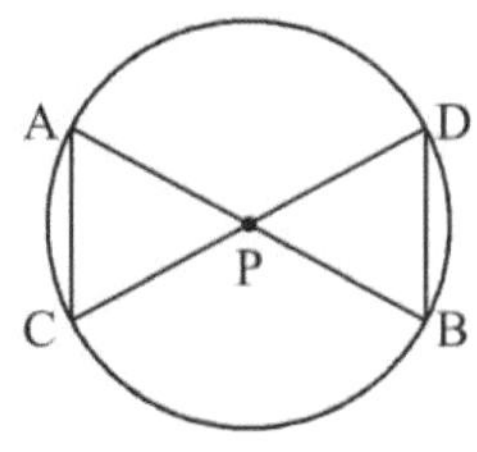

Sol. Given : In figure, two chords AB and CD intersect each other at the point P.

To Prove : (i) $\Delta APC \sim \Delta DPB$
(ii) $AP \cdot PB = CP \cdot DP$

Proof : (i) ΔAPC and ΔDPB

$\angle APC = \angle DPB$ (Vert. Opp. $\angle$s)
$\angle CAP = \angle BDP$ (Angles in the same segment)
$\therefore$ $\Delta APC \sim \Delta DPB$ (AA similarity criterion)

(ii) $\because$ $\Delta APC \sim \Delta DPB$ [Proved above in (1)]

$\therefore$ $\frac{AP}{DP} = \frac{CP}{BP}$ ($\because$ Corresponding sides of two similar triangles are proportional)

$\Rightarrow$ $AP \cdot BP = CP \cdot DP$
$\Rightarrow$ $AP \cdot PB = CP \cdot DP$

Q.25 In figure, two chords AB and CD of a circle intersect each other at the point P (when produced) outside the circle. Prove that

(i) $\Delta PAC \sim \Delta PDB$ (ii) $PA \cdot PB = PC \cdot PD$

Sol. Given : In figure, two chords AB and CD of a circle intersect each other at the point P (when produced) outside the circle.

To Prove : (i) $\Delta PAC \sim \Delta PDB$

(ii) $PA \cdot PB = PC \cdot PD$

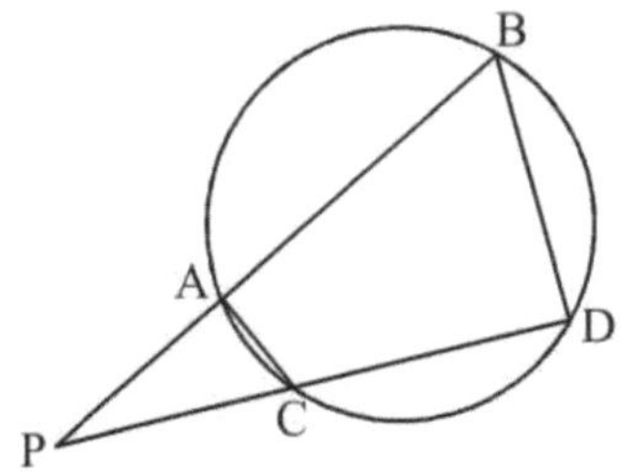

Proof : (i) We know that in a cyclic quadrilateral the exterior angle is equal to the interior opposite angle.

Therefore,

$\angle PAC = \angle PDB$ .....(1)

and $\angle PCA = \angle PBD$ .....(2)

From (1) and (2)

$\Delta PAC \sim \Delta PDB$ [Proved above in (1)]

$\therefore \quad \frac{PA}{PD} = \frac{PC}{PB}$

($\because$ Corresponding sides of two similar triangles are proportional)

$\Rightarrow \quad PA \cdot PB = PC \cdot PD$

CONCEPT APPLICATION LEVEL - II [Previous Year Questions]

Q.1 In the given figure, KL || AC || YZ. B and D are equidistant from AC. If 5KL = YZ, find the ratio of areas of ΔBKL and ΔDYZ **[NSTSE - 2013]**

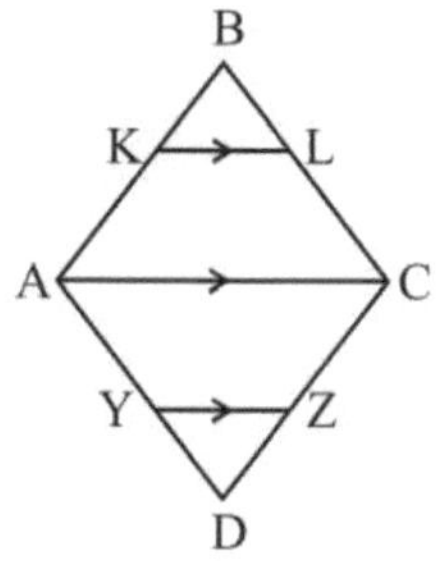

(A) 1 : 25
(B) 5 : 1
(C) 1 : 5
(D) 25 : 1

Q.2 In ΔABC, E is a point on AB, G and D are two points on BC such that EG || AD and ED || AC. Find the value of BC if BG = 4 cm, GD = 6 cm and BE = 8 cm. **[NSTSE - 2013]**
(A) 15 cm (B) 12 cm (C) 25 cm (D) 19 cm

Q.3 In the given figure, if AD is the bisector of ∠BAC. If AB = 10 cm, AC = 14 cm and BC = 6 cm, then find BD and DC. **[IMO]**

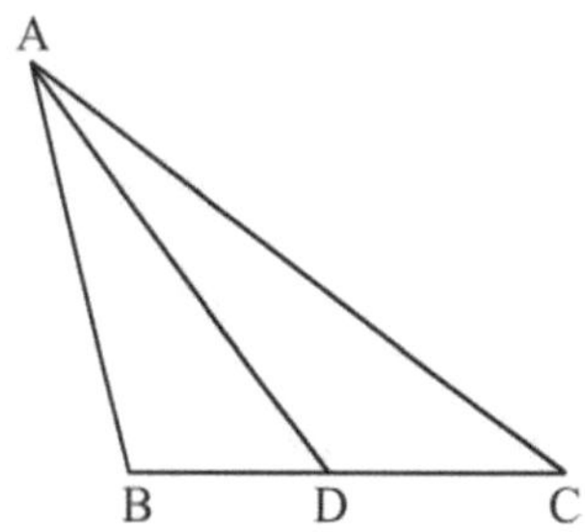

(A) 3 cm, 3 cm (B) 2.5 cm, 3.5 cm (C) 3.5 cm, 4.5 cm (D) 4 cm, 2 cm

Q.4 In a given figure in trapezium ABCD if AB || CD, then the value of x is **[NTSE - 2013]**

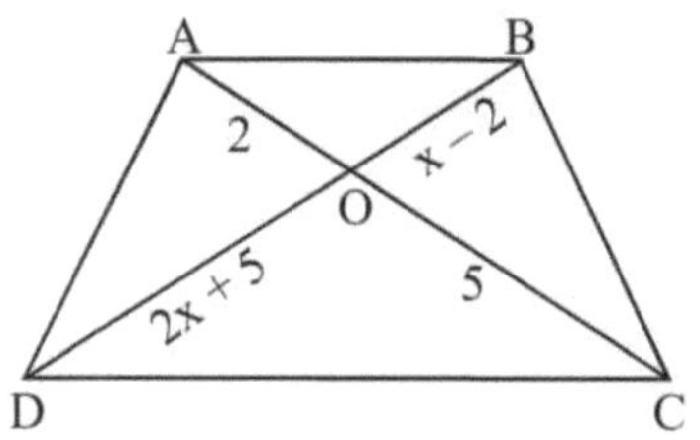

(A) $\frac{29}{8}$ (B) $\frac{8}{29}$
(C) 20 (D) $\frac{1}{20}$

Q.5 In the given figure, ABCD and AEFG are squares. Then which of the following holds true: **[5th IMO]**

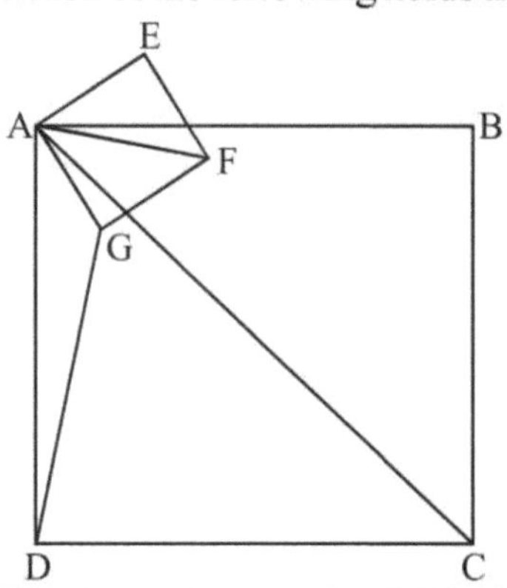

(A) $\frac{GF}{AG} = \frac{AC}{AD}$

(B) $\frac{CF}{AG} = \frac{AF}{DG}$

(C) $\frac{AF}{AC} = \frac{AG}{AD}$

(D) None of these

Q.6 In the right triangle shown here, AB + AD = BC + CD, if AB = x, BC = h and CD = d, then x is equal to **[5th IMO]**

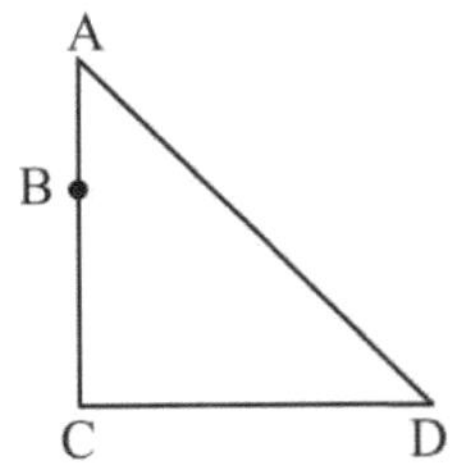

(A) $\frac{hd}{2h+d}$ (B) $d-h$

(C) $h+d$ (D) $\frac{1}{2}h$

Q.7 If the ratio of area of two similar triangle is 64 : 121, then find the ratio of their median **[IOM-11]**

(A) 4 : 11 (B) 8 : 11 (C) 12 : 11 (D) 16 : 11

Q.8 In a ΔABC, $\angle C = 3\angle B = 2(\angle A + \angle B)$. Find the three angles. **[IOM-12]**

(A) 20°, 40°, 120° (B) 60°, 20°, 100° (C) 120°, 20°, 40° (D) 10°, 40°, 130°

Q.9 The hypotenuse of a right angled triangle is $3\sqrt{5}$ cm. If smallest side is tripled and larger side is doubled, the new hypotenuse will be 15 cm. Find the length of larger side. **[IOM-12]**

(A) 6 cm (B) 9 cm (C) 5 cm (D) 10 cm

Q.10 In ΔABC, XY || BC and line XY cuts AB at X and AC at Y. If BY bisects $\angle XYC$, then **[IOM-12]**

(A) BC = BY (B) BC = CY (C) BC ≠ CY (D) BC ≠ BY

Q.11 In the figure given, $\Delta ACB \sim \Delta APQ$. If BC = 8 cm, PQ = 4 cm, BA = 6.5 cm and AP = 2.8 cm, then find CA. **[IOM-12]**

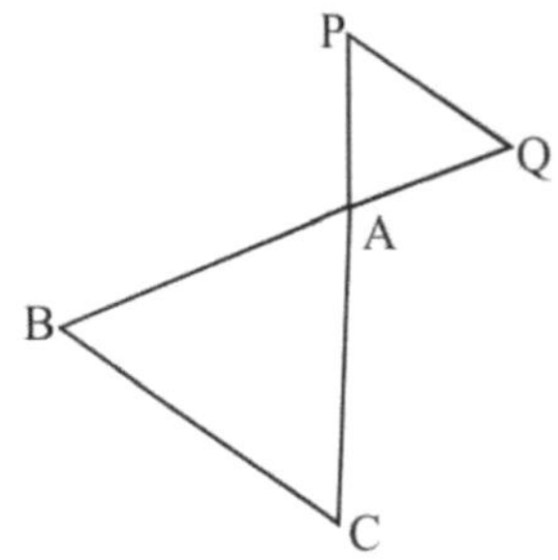

(A) 4.5 cm

(B) 5.6 cm

(C) 5.2 cm

(D) 6.2 cm

Q.12 The value of 'x' in the following figure is **[IOM-12]**

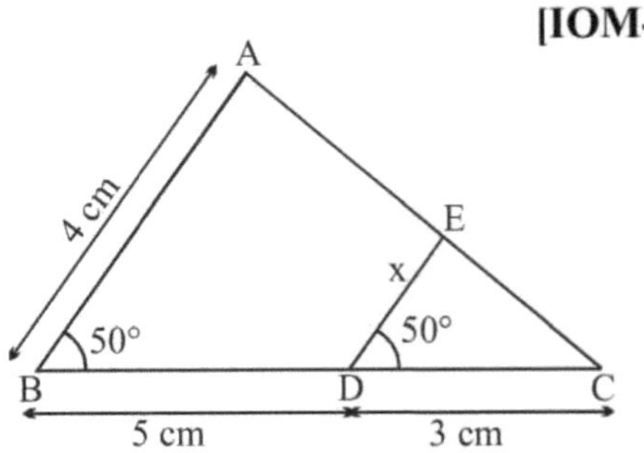

(A) $\frac{5}{2}$cm (B) $\frac{3}{2}$cm

(C) $\frac{5}{3}$cm (D) $\frac{5}{4}$cm

Q.13 In the figure given below, ABC is an equilateral triangle. D, E, F, G, H and I are the trisector points of the side as shown. If the side of the triangle ABC is 6 cm, then the area of the regular hexagon DEFGHI is **[Raj. NTSE Stage-1_2014]**

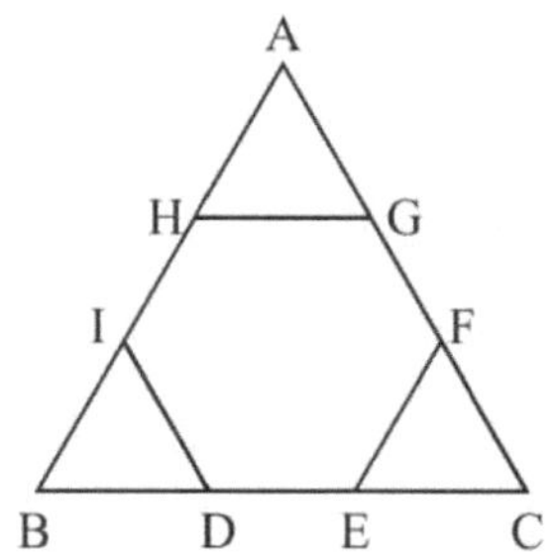

(A) $3\sqrt{3}\ cm^2$ (B) $4\sqrt{3}\ cm^2$ (C) $5\sqrt{3}\ cm^2$ (D) $6\sqrt{3}\ cm^2$

Q.14 $\Delta ABC \sim \Delta PQR$ and $\frac{\text{area } \Delta ABC}{\text{area } \Delta PQR} = \frac{16}{9}$. If PQ = 18 cm and BC = 12 cm, then AB and QR are respectively **[Delhi NTSE Stage-1_2013]**

(A) 9 cm, 24 cm (B) 24 cm, 9 cm (C) 32 cm, 675 cm (D) 135 cm, 16 cm

Q.15 E and F are respectively, the mid points of the sides AD and AC of ΔABC and the area of the quadrilateral BEFC is k times the area of ΔABC. The value of k is **[Delhi NTSE Stage-1_2013]**

(A) $\frac{1}{2}$ (B) 3 (C) $\frac{3}{4}$ (D) 4

Q.16 The ratio of the areas of two similar triangles is equal to **[M.P. NTSE Stage-1_2013]**

(A) The ratio of corresponding medians

(B) The ratio of corresponding sides

(C) The ratio of the squares of corresponding sides

(D) None of these

Q.17 In the figure, ΔABC is similar to ΔEDC. If we have AB = 4 cm, ED = 3 cm, CE = 4.2 m and CD = 4.8 cm, then the values of CA and CB respectively are **[MP NTSE Stage-1_2013]**

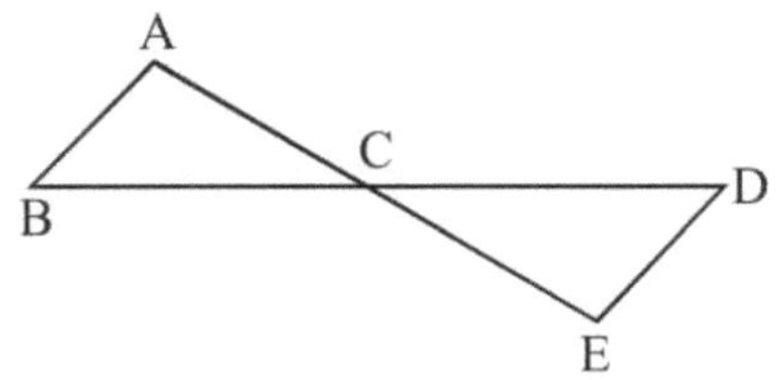

(A) 6 cm, 6.6 cm (B) 4.8 cm, 6.6 cm (C) 5.4 cm, 6.4 cm (D) 5.6 cm, 6.4 cm

Q.18 In the following figure $\angle ACB = 90°$ and $CD \perp AB$. If $AD = 4$ cm and $BD = 9$ cm then the ratio $BC : AC$ is **[NTSE-2016]**

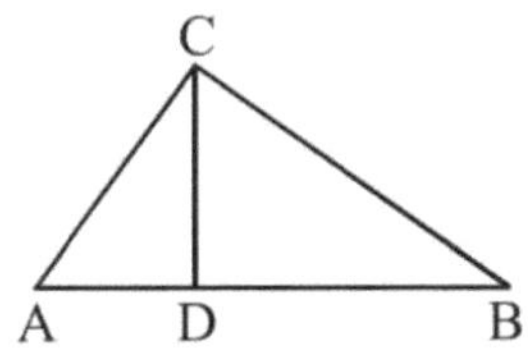

(A) 3 : 2 (B) 2 : 3 (C) 16 : 81 (D) 81 : 16

Q.19 In the following figure of triangle ABC, E is the midpoint of median AD. The ratio of areas of the triangles ABC and BED is **[NTSE-2016]**

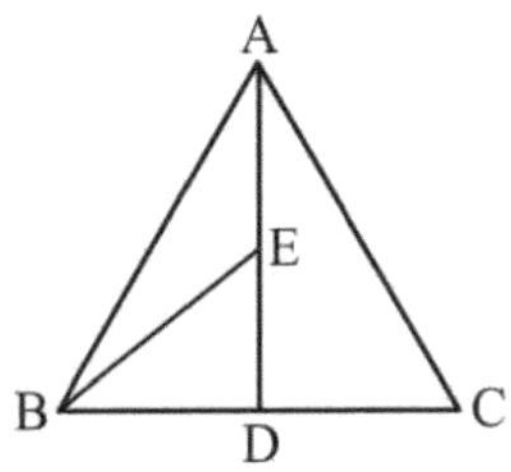

(A) 1 : 4 (B) 3 : 4 (C) 4 : 1 (D) 4 : 3

CONCEPT APPLICATION LEVEL - III

SECTION-A

- **Multiple choice questions with one correct answer**

Q.1 In the given figure $\angle A = 80^\circ$, $B = 60^\circ$, $C = 2x^\circ$ and $\angle BDC = y^\circ$, BD and CD bisect angles B and C respectively. The values of x and y, respectively, are

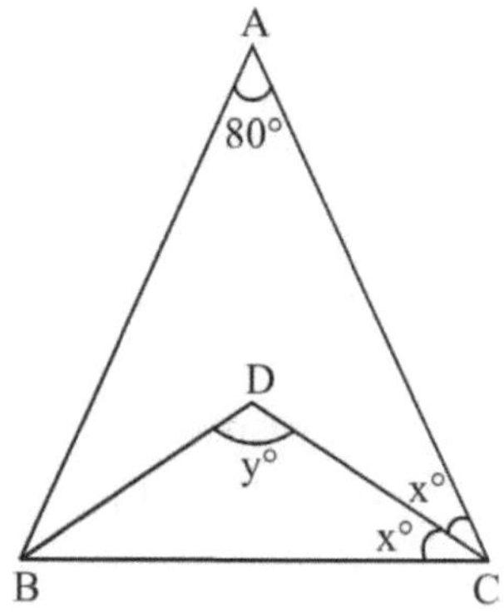

(A) 15°, 70°
(B) 10°, 160°
(C) 20°, 130°
(D) 20°, 125°

Q.2 If D is a point on the side BC = 12 cm of a ΔABC such that BD = 9 cm and $\angle ADC = \angle BAC$, then the length of AC is equal to:

(A) 9 cm (B) 6cm (C) $6\sqrt{3}$ (D) 3 cm

Q.3 In ΔABC medians BE and CF intersect at G. If the straight line AGD meets BC at D in such a way that GD = 1.5 cm, then the length of AD is :

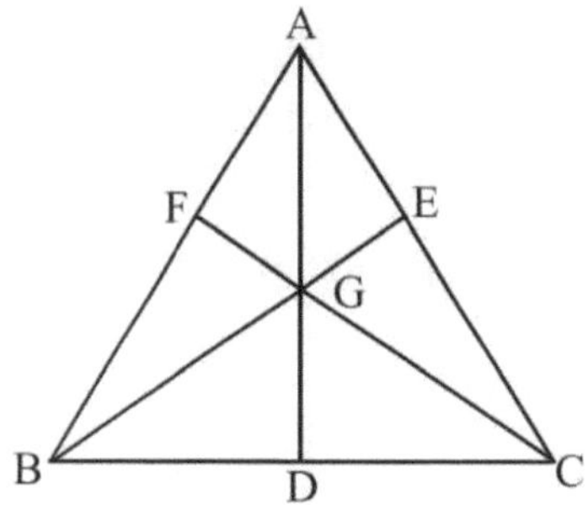

(A) 2.5 cm
(B) 3.0 cm
(C) 4.0 cm
(D) 4.5 cm

Q.4 The side of an equilateral triangle is $20\sqrt{3}$ cm. The numerical value of the radius of the circle circumscribing the triangle is :

(A) 20 cm (B) $20\sqrt{3}$ cm (C) $20\ \pi$ cm (D) $\frac{20}{\pi}$

Q.5 If ΔABC is a right angled triangle with $\angle A = 90^\circ$, AN is perpendicular to BC, BC = 12 cm and AC = 6 cm, then the ratio of $\frac{\text{area } \Delta ANC}{\text{area } \Delta ABC}$:

(A) 1 : 3 (B) 1 : 2 (C) 1 : 4 (D) 1 : 8

Q.6 In a triangle ABC, the sum of the exterior angles at B and C is equal to :
(A) $180^\circ - \angle BAC$ (B) $180^\circ + \angle BAC$ (C) $180^\circ - 2\angle BAC$ (D) $180^\circ + 2\angle BAC$

Q.7 In ΔABC, $\angle B = 3x$, $\angle A = x$, $\angle C = y$ and $3y - 5x = 30$, then the triangle is ;

(A) isosceles (B) equlateral (C) right angled (D) scalene

Q.8 The internal bisectors of $\angle B$ and $\angle C$ of ΔABC meet at O. If $\angle A = 80°$, then $\angle BOC$ is:

(A) 50° (B) 100° (C) 130° (D) 160°

Q.9 The areas of two similar triangles are 12 cm^2 and 48 cm^2. If the height of the samller one is 2.1 cm, then the corresponding height of the bigger triangle is:

(A) 12.6 cm (B) 8.4 cm (C) 4.2 cm (D) 1.05 cm

Q.10 In a triangle DEF shown in given figure, points A, B and C are taken on DE, DF and EF respectively, such that EC = AC and CF = BC. If angle D = 40°, then what is angle ACB in degrees?

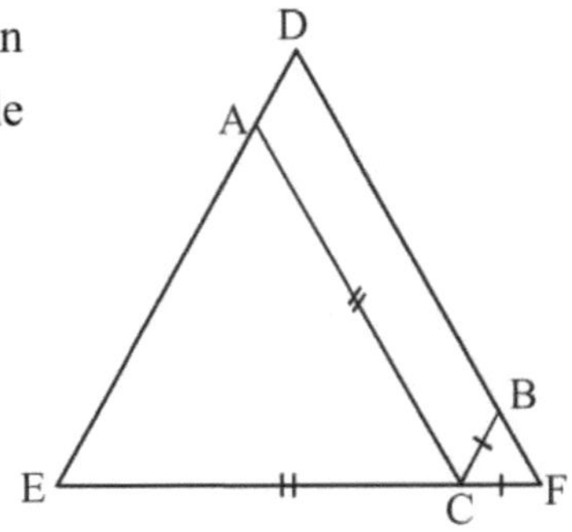

(A) 140

(B) 70

(C) 100

(D) None of these

Q.11 AB ⊥ BC, BD ⊥ AC and CE bisects $\angle C$. If A = 30°. Then, what is $\angle CED$?

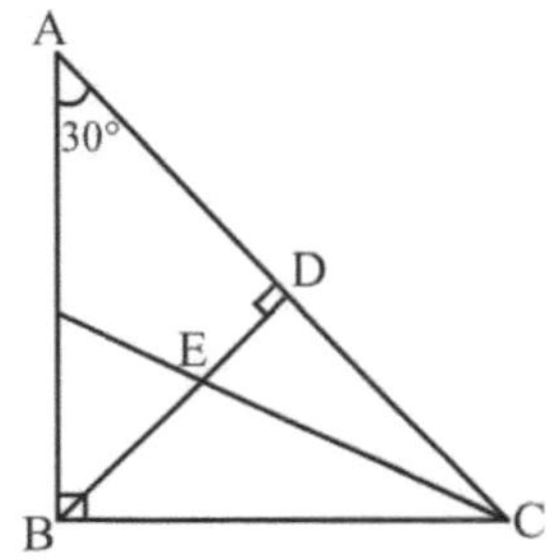

(A) 30°

(B) 60°

(C) 45°

(D) 65°

Q.12 In ΔABC, $\angle A = 90°$, AD ⊥ BC and $\angle B = 45°$. If AB = x, then the value of AD in terms of x is :

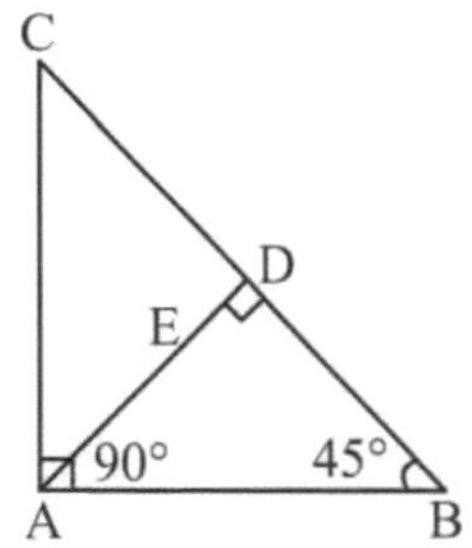

(A) $\frac{x}{2}$ (B) $\frac{\sqrt{x}}{2}$

(C) $\frac{x}{\sqrt{2}}$ (D) $\sqrt{\frac{x}{2}}$

Q.13 Express x in terms of a, b, and c.

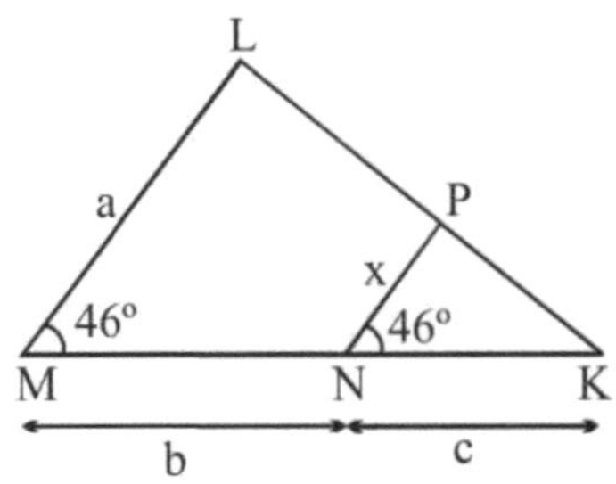

(A) $x = \frac{ac}{b+c}$ (B) $x = \frac{bc}{a+c}$

(C) $x = \frac{b+c}{ac}$ (D) $x = \frac{ab}{a+c}$

Q.14 In ΔABC, if $AD \perp BC$ and $AD^2 = BD \times DC$.

Then find the angle $\angle BAC = ?$

(A) 60°

(B) 90°

(C) 30°

(D) None of these

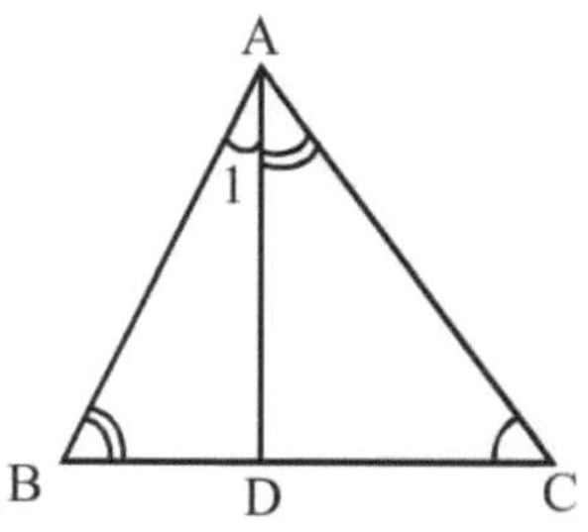

Q.15 PB and QA are perpendiculars to segment AB. If PO = 5 cm, QO = 7 cm and area Δ POB = 150 cm^2, find the area of Δ QOA.

(A) 294 cm^2 (B) 150 cm^2 (C) 250 cm^2 (D) 210 cm^2

Q.16 The corresponding altitude of two similar triangles are 6 cm and 9 cm respectively. Find the ratio of their areas.

(A) 9 : 4 (B) 3 : 2 (C) 4 : 9 (D) 8 : 16

SECTION-B

- **Multiple choice question with one or more than one correct answers**

Q.1 ABC is a triangle right-angled at C with BC = a and AC = b. If p is the length of the prependicular from C on AB then.

(A) $\frac{1}{p^2} = \frac{1}{a^2} + \frac{1}{b^2}$ (B) $p^2 = \frac{a^2b^2}{a^2+b^2}$ (C) $\frac{2}{p^2} = \frac{a^2b^2}{a^2+b^2}$ (D) $p^2 = \frac{a^2b^2}{a^2-b^2}$

Q.2 ABC is a right triangle, right angled at C, let BC = a, CA = b, AB = c and let p be the length of perpendicular from C on AB. Then which of the following is correct?

(A) CP = ab (B) $\frac{a}{c} = \frac{p}{b}$ (C) cb = ap (D) None of these

Q.3 Through the mid-point M of the side CD of a parallelogram ABCD, the line BM is produced intersecting AD at E. Then which of the following is correct?

(A) BM = 2EM (B) AB = 2DM (C) BE = $\frac{1}{2}$ EM (D) BE = 3EM

SECTION-C

- **Comprehension**

$\Delta ACB \sim \Delta APQ$. If BC = 10 cm, PQ = 5 cm, BA = 6.5 cm and AP = 2.8 cm.

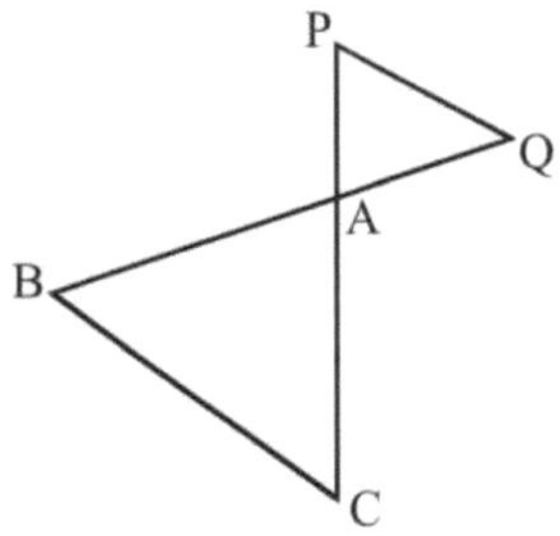

Q.1 Find the length of CA?

(A) 5.6 cm (B) 6 cm (C) 6.5 cm (D) 5 cm

Q.2 Find the the area of ΔACB is

(A) 16.96 (B) 17 (C) 16 (D) None of these

Q.3 Find the ratio of the area of triangle ACB and APQ.

(A) 1 : 4 (B) 4 : 1 (C) 2 : 1 (D) 3 : 1

SECTION-D

- **Match the following (one to one)**

Column-I and **column-II** contains **four** entries each. Entries of column-I are to be matched with some entries of column-II. Only One entries of column-I may have the matching with the some entries of column-II and one entry of column-II Only one matching with entries of column-I

Direction : In the figure, the line segment xy is parallel to the side AC of ΔABC and it divides the triangle into two parts of equal areas, then match the column

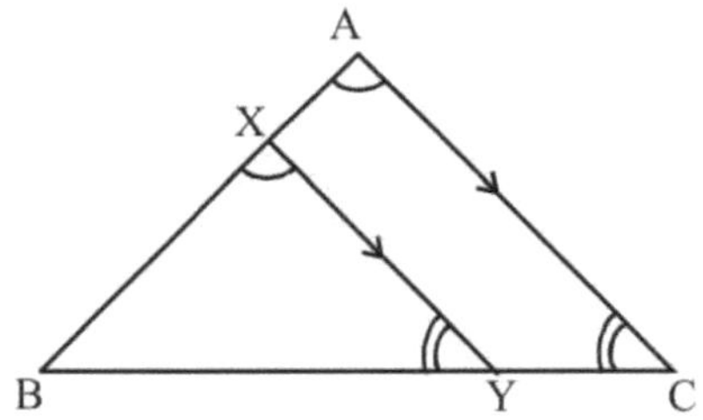

Q.1

Column I	Column II
(A) AB : XB	(P) $\sqrt{2} : 1$
(B) ar (ΔABC) : ar (ΔXBY)	(Q) 2 : 1
(C) AX : AB	(R) $(\sqrt{2}-1)^2 : \sqrt{2}$
(D) $\angle X : \angle A$	(S) 1 : 1

ANSWER KEY

CONCEPT APPLICATION LEVEL - II

Q.1 A	Q.2 C	Q.3 B	Q.4 C	Q.5 C	Q.6 A	Q.7 B
Q.8 A	Q.9 A	Q.10 B	Q.11 B	Q.12 B	Q.13 D	Q.14 B
Q.15 C	Q.16 C	Q.17 D	Q.18 A	Q.19 C		

CONCEPT APPLICATION LEVEL - III

SECTION-A

Q.1 C	Q.2 B	Q.3 B	Q.4 A	Q.5 C	Q.6 B	Q.7 C
Q.8 C	Q.9 C	Q.10 C	Q.11 B	Q.12 C	Q.13 A	Q.14 B
Q.15 A	Q.16 C					

SECTION-B

Q.1 AB Q.2 AB Q.3 BC

SECTION-C

Q.1 A Q.2 A Q.3 B

SECTION-D

Q.1 (A) – P; (B) – Q; (C) – R, (D) – S

6 STATISTICS

THEORY

6.1 INTRODUCTION :

The word 'statistics' is derived from the latin word 'status' meaning 'a (political) state'. In its origin, statistics was simply the collection of data on different aspects of the life of people, useful to the state.

Statistics deals with collection, organisation, analysis and interpretation of data. The word 'statistics' has different meanings in different contexts.

In the second sentence, the word 'statistics' is used as a singular noun, meaning the subject analysis of data as well as drawing of meaningful conclusions from the data.

In this chapter we shall extend the study of these three measures, i.e. mean, median and mode from ungrouped data to that of grouped data and also we shall discuss the concept of cumulative frequency and cumulative frequency distribution ; mean, mode and median of discrete and continuous frequency distribution to draw cumulative frequency curve, called ogive and to find the median by using the ogive

Statistics is basically the study of numerical data. The word statistics is used in two different senses,

(i) In plural sense statistics means data.

(ii) In singular sense, statistics is the science which deals with the collection, analysis and interpretation numberical data .

6.2 SOME BASIC DEFINITIONS :

Data :

The word **data** means information in the form of numerical figures or a set of given facts. It is the collection of facts & figures. For example, the percentage of marks scored by 10 students of a class in a test are : 36, 80, 65, 75, 94, 48, 12, 64, 88 and 98.

The set of these figures is the data related to the marks obtained by 10 students in a class test.

Primary Data :

Fresh or first hand data is called primary data. Investigator collect data himself eg. notes, lists, census study data etc.

Secondary Data :

When investigator does not collect the data himself rather collects the data from other published or unpublished sources. eg. Published reports, official statistics collected by the Government on various facts.

Raw Data :

Data obtained from direct observation is called raw data.

The marks obtained by 10 students in a monthly test is an example of raw data or ungrouped date. So, to make this data clearer and more meaningful, we group it into ordered intervals.

Grouped Data :

To present the data in a more meaningful way, we condense the data into convenient number of classes or groups, generally not exceeding 10 and not less than 5.

Observation :

Each numerical figure in a data is called an observation.

Frequency :

The number of times a particular observation occurs is called its frequency.

Discrete Frequency Distribution :

If each data is given with their frequency, then this type of frequency distribution is called discrete frequency distribution.

Continuous Frequency Distribution :

If the data is given in the form of class interval with frequency, then this type of frequency distribution is called continuous frequency distribution for example

Marks	35-45	45-55	55-65	65-75	75-85	85-95
Frequency	3	4	8	4	5	1

Frequency :

The number of observations in each class is called frequency of that class. In Table the frequency of class 55-65 is 8 and that of the class 85-95 is 1.

Class-Intervals and Class Limits :

In the frequency Table 35-45 is called "class-interval" and the end numbers, 35 and 45 are called "class limits", the smaller number 35 is the lower class limit and the larger number 45 is the upper class limit.

Range :

The difference between the maximum and the minimum value of the given observations is called the range of the data.

Given $x_1, x_2 \ldots\ldots x_n$ (n individual observations)

Range = (Maximum Value) – (Minimum Value)

Note : The range of the class interval is the difference of the actual limits of the class.

Illustration 1

Find the range of $\{2, 7, 6, 4, 3, 8, 5, 12\}$.

Solution

Arranging the given data in the ascending order

We have ; $\{2, 3, 4, 5, 6, 7, 8, 12\}$

$\therefore$ Range = (Maximum value) – (Minimum value) = 12 – 2 = 10

Class Boundaries :

In an **exclusive form**, the lower and upper limits are known as class boundaries or true lower limit and true upper limit of the class respectively.

Thus, the boundaries of 35–45 in exclusive form 35 and 45.

The boundaries in an **inclusive form** are obtained by substracting 0.5 to the lower limit and adding 0.5 to the upper limit.

Thus, the boundaries of 35–45 in the **inclusive form** are 34.5 – 45.5.

The size or width of a Class Interval :

The size or width of a class-interval is the difference between the lower and upper class boundaries.

e.g., size = 44.5 – 34.5 = 10

Class Mark :

Now, for each class-interval, we require a point which would serve as the representative of the whole class. It is assumed that the frequency of each class interval is centred around its mid-point. So the mid-point (or class mark) of each class can be chosen to represent the observations falling in the class. we find the mid-point of a class (or its class mark) by finding the average of its upper and lower limits. That is,

$$\textbf{Class mark} = \frac{\textbf{Upper class limit} + \textbf{Lower class limit}}{\textbf{2}}$$

For example, class mark of class 35 – 45 = $\frac{35+45}{2} = \frac{80}{2} = 40.$

Cumulative Frequency Table : The total of frequencies of all the previous and the given class is called the cumulative frequency of the class e.g.

Class-intervals	Frequency	Cumulative frequency
35-45	3	3
45-55	4	7
55-65	8	15
65-75	4	19
75-85	5	24
85-95	1	25
Total	25	

6.3 TABULATION OR PRESENTATION OF DATA :

A systematical arrangement of the data in a tabular form is called tabulation or presentation of the data. This grouping results in a table called the frequency table which indicates the number of scores within each group.

The quantitative data that is to be analysed statistically can be divided into three categories :

(1) Individual series (2) Discrete series and (3) Continuous series

(1) Individual series :

Any raw data that is not grouped.

Example :

(i) The weights of 5 students :
32, 40, 65, 48 and 54 (in kg)

(ii) Percentage marks obtained by 10 students in a test :
48, 59, 63, 72, 48, 72, 84, 98, 90 and 60

(2) Discrete series :

A discrete series is formulated from raw data by taking the frequency of the observation into consideration.

Example :

Given below is the data showing the number of computers in 12 families of a locality :

1, 1, 2, 3, 2, 1, 4, 3, 2, 2, 1, 1

Arranging the data in the ascending order :

1, 1, 1, 1, 1, 2, 2, 2, 2, 3, 3, 4

We may prepare a frequency table as below :

Number of computers	Number of families (frequency)
1	5
2	4
3	2
4	1

(3) Continuous series :

When the data contains large number of observations, we put them into different groups called class intervals such as 1–10, 11–20, 21–30, etc.

Here, 1 – 10 means data whose values lie between 1 and 10 including both 1 and 10. This form is known as **inclusive form**. Also, 1 is called the **lower limit** and 10 is called the **upper limit**.

Example :

Given below are the marks (out of 50) obtained by 30 students in an examination.

43	19	25	32	48
17	29	9	15	50
7	24	20	37	44
22	2	50	27	25
18	42	16	1	33
25	35	45	35	28

Taking class intervals 1–10, 11–20, 21–30, 31–40, and 41–50, we construct a frequency distribution table for the above data.

First, we write the marks in the ascending order as :

1	2	7	9	15	16	17	18	19	20
22	24	25	25	25	27	28	29	32	33
35	35	37	42	43	44	45	48	50	50

Now, we can prepare the frequency distribution table as below.

Class interval	Frequency
1–10	4
11–20	6
21–30	8
31–40	5
41–50	7

6.4 CENTRAL TENDENCY :

A no. or quantity which is typical or representative of a set of data is called central tendency. The measure of this kind is known as averages.

Measures of central tendancy or average are usually of the following types

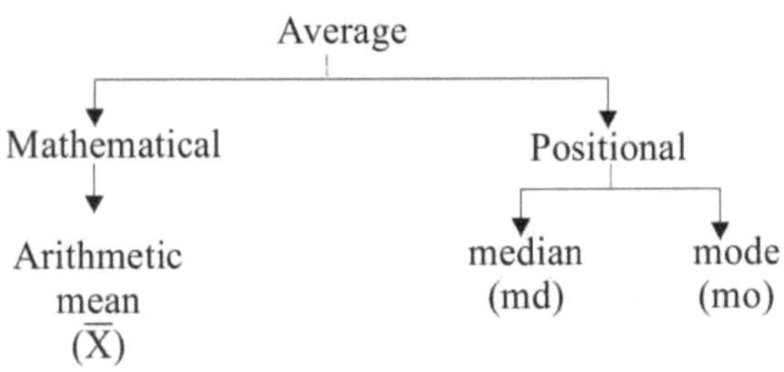

6.5 MEAN (ARITHMETIC MEAN OF INDIVIDUAL OBSERVATIONS) OR UNGROUPED DATA

Mean of 'n' numbers $x_1, x_2, x_3, \ldots\ldots\ldots\ldots x_n = \dfrac{\text{sum of observations}}{\text{number of observations}}$

$$\overline{X} = \frac{x_1 + x_2 + x_3 + \ldots\ldots + x_n}{n}$$

$$= \frac{\sum_{i=1}^{n} x_i}{n}$$

Illustration 2

If the heights of 5 persons are 144 cm, 152 cm, 151 cm, 158 cm and 155 cm respectivly find the mean height.

Solution

$$\text{Mean height} = \frac{144+152+151+158+155}{5} = \frac{760}{5}\text{cm} = 152\text{cm}$$

(I) MEAN OF UNGROUPED DATA OR DISCRETE FREQUENCY DISTRIBUTION

(i) Direct method

(ii) Assumed mean method

(iii) Step deviation method or shortcut method

6.5.1 Direct method (For the discrete frequency distribution)

x_i	x_1	x_2	x_3	....	x_n
f_i	f_1	f_2	f_3	....	f_n

Mean of 'n' observations $x_1, x_2, x_3, x_4 \ldots\ldots\ldots x_n$ with frequencies $f_1, f_2, f_3 \ldots\ldots f_n$ is given by

$$\text{Mean } (\overline{X}) = \frac{f_1x_1 + f_2x_2 + f_3x_3 + \ldots\ldots\ldots + f_nx_n}{f_1 + f_2 + f_3 + \ldots\ldots + f_n} = \frac{\sum_{i=1}^{n} f_ix_i}{\sum_{i=1}^{n} f_i}$$

Illustration : 3

Find the mean of the following distribution:

X :	4	6	9	10	15
f :	5	10	10	7	8

Solution

x_i	f_i	$f_i x_i$
4	5	20
6	10	60
9	10	90
10	7	70
15	8	120
	$N = \sum f_i = 40$	$\sum f_i x_i = 360$

Mean

$$\overline{X} = \frac{\sum f_i x_i}{\sum f_i}$$

$$= \frac{360}{40} = 9$$

$$\overline{X} = 9$$

Illustration : 4

Find the value of K if mean of the following data is 14.

x_i	5	10	15	20	25
f_i	7	k	8	4	5

Solution :

x_i	f_i	$f_i x_i$
5	7	35
10	k	10k
15	8	120
20	4	80
25	5	125
Total	$\sum_{i=1}^{n} f_i = 24 + k$	$\sum_{i=1}^{n} f_i x_i = 360 + 10k$

Now, $\overline{x} = \dfrac{\sum_{i=1}^{n} f_i x_i}{\sum_{i=1}^{n} f_i} \quad \Rightarrow \quad 14 = \dfrac{360 + 10k}{24 + k}$

$\Rightarrow \quad 336 + 14\,k = 360 + 10\,k$

$\Rightarrow \quad 14\,k - 10\,k = 360 - 336$

$\Rightarrow \quad 4\,k = 24$

$\Rightarrow \quad k = 6$

6.5.2 Assumed mean method

Sometimes when the numerical values of x_i and f_i are large, finding the product of x_i and f_i becomes tedious and time consuming. So, for such situations, we use a method of reducing these calculations. We can do nothing with the f_i's, but we can change each x_i to a smaller number so that our calculations become easy. we can do this by subtracting a fixed number from each of these x_i's.

The first step is to choose one among the x_i's as the assumed mean, and denote it by 'a'. Also, to further reduce our calculation work, we may take 'a' to be that x_i which lies in the centre of $x_1, x_2, ..., x_n$.

The second step is to find the difference d_i between 'a' and each of the x_i's, that is, the **deviation** of 'a' from each of the x_i's.

i.e., $d_i = x_i - a$

The third step is to find the product of d_i with the corresponding f_i, and take the sum of all the $f_i d_i$'s.

The mean of the deviations. $= \bar{d} = \dfrac{\sum f_i d_i}{\sum f_i}$.

So, $$\bar{d} = \frac{\sum f_i (x_i - a)}{\sum f_i} = \frac{\sum f_i x_i}{\sum f_i} - \frac{\sum f_i a}{\sum f_i}$$

$$= \bar{x} - a\frac{\sum f_i}{\sum f_i} = \bar{x} - a$$

So, $$\bar{x} = a + \bar{d}$$

i.e. $$\bar{x} = a + \frac{\sum f_i d_i}{\sum f_i}$$

Note : (i) The value of the mean obtained by using "assumed mean method" does not depend on the choice of 'a'. Generally the middle data is considered as assumed mean.

(ii) If there are two middle data, then we can take those middle data as assumed mean, whose frequency is greater.

Let $x_1, x_2, x_3, ...x_n$ be values of a variables 'x' with corresponding frequencies $f_1, f_2, f_3...........f_n$ respectively taking deviations about on arbitrary point 'a'

$$\bar{X} = a + \frac{1}{N}\left(\sum_{i=1}^{n} f_i d_i\right)$$

Where $N = \sum_{i=1}^{n} f_i$

The number 'a' is generally known as the assumed mean and the method is also called assumed mean method:

Illustrations

Illustration 5

The following table shows the weights of 12 students:

Weight (kg)	67	70	72	73	75
Number of students	4	3	2	2	1

Find the mean weight

Solution

Let the assumed mean be $a = 72$

Weight (in kg) x_i	Number of students f_i	$d_i = x_i - a$ $= x_i - 72$	$f_i d_i$
67	4	-5	-20
70	3	-2	-6
72	2	0	0
73	2	1	2
75	1	3	3
	$N = \Sigma_{f_i} = 12$		$\sum f_i d_i = -21$

We have $N = 12$ $\sum f_i d_i = -21$ and $a = 72$

$$\therefore \text{ Mean} = a + \frac{1}{N}\sum f_i d_i$$

$$72 + \left(\frac{-21}{12}\right) = 72 - \frac{7}{4} = \frac{288-7}{4} = \frac{281}{4}$$

$$= 70.25 \text{ kg}$$

6.5.3 Step deviation method

If we divide the values in the entire column of d_i by the class size of each class interval we would get smallest numbers to multiply with f_i.

Let, $u_i = \dfrac{x_i - a}{h}$, where a is the assumed mean and h is the class size.

Now, we calculate u_i in this way and continue as before (i.e. find $f_i u_i$ and then $\sum f_i u_i$).

Let $\bar{u} = \dfrac{\sum f_i u_i}{\sum f_i}$

We have, $u_i = \dfrac{x_i - a}{h}$

Therefore, $$\bar{u} = \frac{\sum f_i u_i}{\sum f_i} = \frac{\sum f_i \frac{(x_i - a)}{h}}{\sum f_i} = \frac{1}{h}\left[\frac{\sum f_i x_i - a\sum f_i}{\sum f_i}\right]$$

$$= \frac{1}{h}\left[\frac{\sum f_i x_i}{\sum f_i} - a\frac{\sum f_i}{\sum f_i}\right] = \frac{1}{h}[\bar{x} - a]$$

So, $h\bar{u} = \bar{x} - a$

i.e. $\bar{x} = a + h\bar{u}$

So, $\bar{x} = a + h\left(\frac{\sum f_i u_i}{\sum f_i}\right)$

$$\left[\overline{X} = a + h\left(\frac{1}{N}\sum_{i=1}^{n} f_i u_i\right)\right]$$

Where h = common number

a = Assumed mean

Note :

(i) The result obtained by all the three methods is the same. So the choice of method to be used depends on the numerical values of x_i and f_i. If x_i and f_i are sufficiently small, then the direct method is an appropriate choice. If x_i and f_i are numerically large numbers, then we can go for the assumed mean method or step-deviation method. If the class sizes are unequal, and x_i are large numerically, we can still apply the step-deviation method by taking h to be a suitable divisor of all the d_i's.

(ii) The assumed mean method and step-deviation method are just simplified forms of the direct method.

Illustration 6

Apply step- deviation method to find the AM of the distribution.

Variate (x) :	5	10	15	20	25	30	35	40	45	50
Frequency (f) :	20	43	75	67	72	45	39	9	8	6

Solution

Let the assumed mean be $a = 25$ & $h = 5$

Variate x_i	Frequency f_i	Deviations $d_i = x_i - 25$	$u_i = \frac{x_i - 25}{5}$	f_iu_i
5	20	-20	-4	-80
10	43	-15	-3	-129
15	75	-10	-2	-150
20	67	-5	-1	-67
25	72	0	0	0
30	45	5	1	45
35	39	10	2	78
40	9	15	3	27
45	8	20	4	32
50	6	25	5	30
	$N = f_i = 384$			$f_iu_i = -214$

We have $N = 384$, $a = 25$, $h = 5$, and $\sum f_i u_i = 214$

$$\therefore \text{ Mean} = \overline{X} = a + h\left(\frac{1}{N}\sum f_i u_i\right)$$

$$\text{Mean} = 25 + 5 \times \left(\frac{-214}{384}\right)$$

$25 - 2 : 786$

$[\overline{X} \quad = 22 : 214]$

(II) MEAN OF CONTINUOUS FREQUENCY DISTRIBUTION (FREQUENCY DISTRIBUTION WITH CLASS INTERVAL) (MEAN OF GROUPED DATA)

(i) The frequency of each class- interval is centred around its mid-point (or class mark)

$$\text{Class mark} = \frac{\text{upper class lim it} + \text{lower class lim it}}{2}$$

Illustration 7

Find the mean of the following frequency distribution.

Class Interval	0-10	10-20	20-30	30-40	40-50
Frequency	7	10	15	8	10

Solution

Class – Interval	Mid – Values (x_i)	Frequency f_i	$d_i = x_i - 25$	$u_i = \frac{x_i - 25}{10}$	$f_i u_i$
0-10	5	7	-20	-2	-14
10-20	15	10	-10	-1	-10
20-30	25	15	0	0	0
30-40	35	8	10	1	8
40-50	45	10	20	2	20
		$N = \sum f_i = 50$			$\sum f_i u_i = 4$

We have $a = 25$, $h = 10$, $N = 50$ and $\sum f_i u_i = 4$

$$\text{Mean} = a + h\left(\frac{1}{n}\sum f_i u_i\right)$$

$$= 25 + 10 \times \frac{4}{50}$$

$$= 25.8$$

Note: We can solve this question by assumed mean method.

6.6 SOME IMPORTANT RESULTS ABOUT MEAN :

1. The algebraic sum of deviations taken about the mean is zero i.e., $\sum_{i=1}^{n}(x_i - \bar{x}) = 0$
2. The value of the mean depends on all the observations.
3. The A.M. of two numbers a and b is $\frac{a+b}{2}$
4. **Combined mean :** If $\bar{x}_1$ and $\bar{x}_2$ are the arithmetic means of two series with n_1 and n_2 observations respectively, then the combined mean is :

   $$\bar{x}_c = \frac{n_1\bar{x}_1 + n_2\bar{x}_2}{n_1 + n_2}$$

   Note: The above result can be extended to any number of groups of data.

5. If $\bar{x}$ is the mean of $x_1, x_2, ...x_n$, then the mean of $x_1 + a, x_2 + a, x_3 + a, ...x_n + a$ is $\bar{x} + a$, for all values of a.
6. If $\bar{x}$ is the mean of $x_1, x_2, ...x_n$, then the mean of $ax_1, ax_2, ... ax_n$ is $a\bar{x}$ and that of $\frac{x_1}{a}, \frac{x_2}{a}, ... \frac{x_n}{a}$ is $\frac{\bar{x}}{a}$.
7. The mean of the first n natural numbers is $\left(\frac{n+1}{2}\right)$
8. The mean of the square of the first n natural numbers $= \frac{(n+1)(2n+1)}{6}$
9. The mean of the cubes of the first n natural numbers $= \frac{n(n+1)^2}{4}$
10. The mean cannot be calculated graphically.

6.7 MEDIAN :

Median is the value of middle item of a series arranged in ascending or descending order of magnitudes.

6.7.1 Median for ungrouped data :

(a) If n is odd the median $= \left(\frac{n+1}{2}\right)^{th}$ term

(b) If n is even, there are two middle terms.

i.e. $\left(\frac{n}{2}\right)^{th}$ term & $\left(\frac{n}{2}+1\right)^{th}$ term

$$\text{median} = \frac{\left(\frac{n}{2}\right)^{th} \text{term} + \left(\frac{n}{2}+1\right)^{th} \text{term}}{2}.$$

6.7.2 Median for Grouped Data :

In a grouped data, we may not be able to find the middle observation by looking at the cumulative frequencies as the middle observation will be some value in a class interval. It is, therefore, necessary to find the value inside a class that divides the whole distribution into two halves.

To find this class, we find the cumulative frequencies of all the classes and $\frac{n}{2}$. We now locate the class whose cumulative frequency is greater than (and nearest to) $\frac{n}{2}$. This is called the median class.

After finding the median class, we use the following formula for calculating the median.

$$\text{Median} = l + \left(\frac{\frac{n}{2} - cf}{f}\right) \times h$$

where, l = lower limit of median class,

n = number of observations,

cf = cumulative frequency of class preceding the median class,

f = frequency of median class,

h = class size (assuming class size to be equal).

In a continuous frequency distribution the value of the median would be in class-interval

$$\text{Median} = l + \frac{\frac{n}{2} - C.f}{f} \times h$$

l = lower limit of median class

n = no. of observations

c.f = cumulative frequency of class preceding the median class.

h = class size (assuming class size to be equal)

Median for Grouped data

Method for finding the median for grouped data

Step–1: For the given frequency distribution, prepare the cumulative frequency table and obtain $N = \Sigma fi$

Step–2: Find (n/2)

Step–3: Look at the cumulative frequency just greater than (n/2) and find the corresponding class, known as median class.

Step–4: Use the formula

$$\text{Median, (Me)} = l + \left\{\frac{(n/2 - C.f.)}{f}\right\} \times h$$

l = Lower limit of median class

h= Width of median class

f = Frequency of median class

C.f. = Cumulative frequency of the class procceding the median class

$n = \sum f_i$

Illustration 8

Calculate the median for the following data.

Marks obtained	Number of students
Below 10	6
Below 20	15
Below 30	29
Below 40	41
Below 50	60
Below 60	70

Solution

Class – Interval	Frequency (f_i)	Cumulative frequency
0-10	6	6
10-20	9	15
20-30	14	29
30-40	12	41
40-50	19	60
50-60	10	70
	$n = \sum f_i = 70$	

$n = 70 \Rightarrow (n/2) = 35$

The cumulative frequency just greater than 35 is 41. and the corresponding class is 30-40.

Thus the median class is 30-40

$\therefore$ l = 30, h = 10, f = 12, C.f.= Cummulative frequency of preceding class = 29

$$\text{Median} = l + \left\{\frac{(n/2 - C.f)}{F}\right\} \times h$$

$$= 30 + \left\{10 \times \frac{(35-29)}{12}\right\}$$

Ans. = 35

6.8 SOME IMPORTANT FACTS ABOUT MEDIAN :

1. The median does not take into consideration all the items.
2. The sum of absolute deviations taken about the median is the least.
3. The median can be calculated graphically while the mean cannot be.
4. The median is not affected by extreme values.
5. The sum of deviation taken about median is less than the sum of absolute deviation taken from any other observation in the data.

Note :

1. For a given data, the mode may or may not exist. In a series of observations, if no item occurs more than once, then the mode is said to be ill-defined.
2. If the mode exists for a given data, it may or may not be unique.
3. Data having unique mode is uni-model while data having two modes is bi-modal.

Illustrations

Illustration 9

The median of the following data is 525. Find the values of x and y, if the total frequency is 100.

Class interval	Frequency
0 - 100	2
100 - 200	5
200 - 300	x
300 - 400	12
400 - 500	17
500 - 600	20
600 - 700	y
700 - 800	9
800 - 900	7
900 - 1000	4

Solution

Class interval	Frequency	Cumulative Frequency
0 - 100	2	2
100 - 200	5	7
200 - 300	x	$7 + x$
300 - 400	12	$19 + x$
400 - 500	17	$36 + x$
500 - 600	20	$56 + x$
600 - 700	y	$56 + x + y$
700 - 800	9	$65 + x + y$
800 - 900	7	$72 + x + y$
900 - 1000	4	$76 + x + y$

It is given that n = 100

So, $76 + x + y = 100$,

i.e., $x + y = 24$ .....(1)

The median is 525, which lies in the class 500 – 600

So, $l = 500, f = 20, cf = 36 + x, h = 100$

Using the formula :

$$\text{Median} = l + \left(\frac{\frac{n}{2} - cf}{f}\right) \times h,$$

We get, $$525 = 500 + \left(\frac{50 - 36 - x}{20}\right) \times 100$$

i.e. $525 - 500 = (14 - x) \times 5$

i.e. $25 = 70 - 5x$

i.e. $5x = 70 - 25 = 45$

So, $x = 9$

Therefore, from (1), we get

$9 + y = 24$

i.e. $y = 15$

6.9 MODE :

It is value of variate which occurs most often.

More precisely mode is that value of variable in the data which has maximum frequency.

It is not necessary that in a series there must be only one mode. A distribution having only one mode is called unimodal, having two, bimodal and more than two multimodal.

Modal class: In a frequency distribution the class having maximum frequency is called modal class.

Example :

(i) The set of numbers 2, 3, 4, 7, 4, 5, 4, 9, 4 has mode 4 as it occurs the maximum number of times.

(ii) The set of numbers 5, 7, 6, 9, 1, 2 has no mode, as no number occurs more number of times than the other numbers.

Mode for grouped Data :

$$Mode = l + \left[\frac{f_1 - f_0}{2f_1 - f_0 - f_2}\right] \times h$$

l = Lower limit of the modal class interval

f_1 = Frequency of the modal class

f_0 = Frequency of the class preceding the modal class

f_2 = Frequency of the class succeeding the modal class

h = Width of the class Interval

Illustration 10

Height (In Cm)	160-162	163-165	166-168	169-171	172-174
No. of Students	15	118	142	127	18

Find the average height of maximum number of students.

Solution

We have to find the mode of the data. The given data is an inclusive series. So we convert it to an exclusive form.

Class	Frequency
159.5 - 162.5	15
162.5 - 165.5	118
165.5 - 168.5	142
168.5 - 171.5	127
171.5 - 174.5	18

The class 165.5 - 168.5 has maximum frequency. So it is the modal class.

$\therefore$ l = 165.5, $f_1 = 142$, $f_0 = 118$ $f_2 = 127$, & $h = 3$

$$\Rightarrow \quad \text{Mode} = l + \left\{\frac{f_1 - f_0}{2f_1 - f_0 - f_2}\right\} \times h$$

$$= 165.5 + \left\{3 \times \frac{(142 - 118)}{(2 \times 142 - 181 - 127)}\right\}$$

$$= 165.5 + 1.85 = 167.35$$

Mode = 67.35 Cm.

Hence the average height of maximum number of students is 167.35 Cm.

6.10 SOME IMPORTANT FACTS ABOUT MODE :

1. Mode can be calculated graphically.
2. Mode is not affected by extereme values.
3. Mode can be used for open-ended distribution and qualitative data.

Remember

(i) We have studied about all the three measures of central tendency, let us discuss **which measure would be best suited for a particular requirement**.

The mean is the most frequently used measure of central tendency because it takes into account all the observations, and lies between the extremes, i.e., the largest and the smallest observations of the entire data. It also enables us to compare two or more distributions. For example, by comparing the average (mean) results of students of different schools of a particular examination, we can conclude which school has a better performance.

In problems where individual observations are not important, and we wish to find out a 'typical' observation, the median is more appropriate, e.g., finding the typical productivity rate of workers, average wage in a country, etc. These are situations where extreme values may be there. So, rather than the mean, we take the median as a better measure of central tendency.

In situations which require establishing the most frequent value or most popular item, the mode is the best choice, e.g., to find the most popular T.V. programme being watched, the consumer item in greatest demand, the colour of the vehicle used by most of the people, etc.

(ii) Mode may be equal or more than the mean also.

(iii) It depends upon the demand of the situation whether we are interested in finding the average marks obtained by the students or the average of the marks obtained by most of the students. In the first situation, the mean is required and in the second situation, the mode is required.

6.11 EMPIRICAL RELATIONSHIP AMONG MEAN, MEDIAN AND MODE :

For moderately symmetric data, the above three measures of central tendency can be related by the formula,

Mode = 3 Median – 2 Mean

Note :

1. For a symmetric distribution, Mean = Median = Mode
2. Given any two of the mean, median and mode the third can be calculated.
3. This formula is to be applied in the absence of sufficient data.

Illustrations

Illustration 11

Find the mode when median is 12 and mean is 16 of a data.

Solution :

Mode = 3 Median – 2 Mean

$= (3 \times 12) - (2 \times 16) = 36 - 32 = 4$

6.12 GRAPHICAL REPRESENTATION :

Graphical Representation : Many types of graphs are employed in statistics, depending upon the nauture of the data involved. Among these are

(i) Bar chart (or Bar graph)

(ii) Histograms

(iii) Frequency Polygon

(iv) Cumulative Frequency Curve (Ogive)

(v) Pie chart (or Pie graph or Pie Diagrams)

Cumulative frequency Curve (Ogive) :

The term 'ogive' is pronounced as 'ojeev' and is derived from the word **ogee**. An ogee is a shape consisting of a concave arc flowing into a convex arc, so forming an S-shaped curve with vertical ends.

Note : For drawing ogives, it should be ensured that the class intervals are continuous. An ogive is the graphical representation of cumulative frequency distribution. We can construct two types of ogives. The first form is "less than ogive" and the second is "more than ogive".

In the "less than" method we start with the upper limit of the classes and go on adding the frequencies. When these are plotted, we get a rising curve.

In the "more than" method we start with the lower limit of the classes and from the total frequencies we subtract the frequency of each class. When these are plotted, we get declining curve, e.g.

6.12.1 The less than method

In this method the Ogive is cumulated upward. Scale the cumulative frequencies along the y-axis, and exact upper limits along the x-axis. The scale along the y-axis should be such as may accommodate the total frequency.

Procedure:

Step–1: Form the cumulative frequency table.

Step–2: Mark the actual upper class limits along the x-axis.

Step–3: Mark the cumulative frequencies of respective classes along the y-axis.

Step–4: Plot the points (upper limits, corresponding cumulative frequency).

To complete the ogive we also plot the point (lower limit of the lowest class, 0).

Step–5: Join these points by a smooth curve.

The curve so obtained is the required ogive.

Illustration 12

Draw a cumulative frequency curve (Ogive) for the following data.

Age (in years)	0-10	10-20	20-30	30-40
Number of patients	15	12	8	20

Solution

When nothing is mentioned then we will draw the 'less than curve'. The cumulative frequency table is as given below.

Age (in years)	Number of patients	Cumulative frequency
0-10	15	15
10-20	12	27
20-30	8	35
30-40	20	55

Upper class limits: 10 20 30 40

Cumulative frequency: 15 27 35 55

Plotting the points (10, 15), (20, 27), (30, 35), (40, 55) and joining them by a free hand curve we get the ogive as shown in figure. To complete it, we join the curve to the point (lower limit of the lowest class, 0), i.e (0,0).

Marks	Number of students (Cumulative frequency)	Plotting points
Less than 10	15	(10,15)
Less than 20	15+12=27	(20,27)
Less than 30	27+8=35	(30,35)
Less than 40	35+20=55	(40,55)

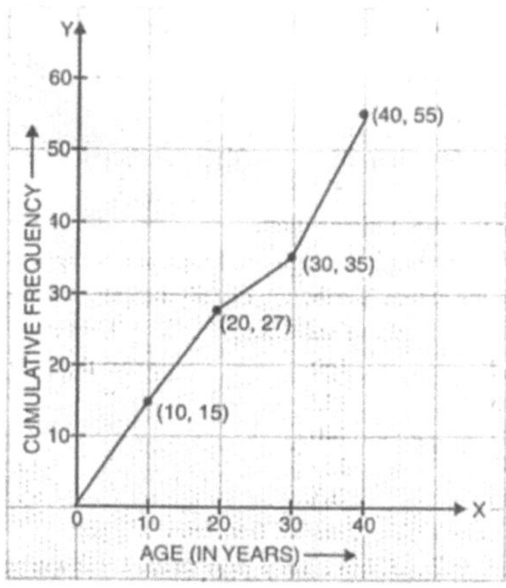

Note: If we join the points by straight lines instead of by means of a free-hand, we get what is called a cumulative Frequency polygon.

6.12.2 "The more than" method :

In this method the ogive is cumulated downward. Scale the cumulative frequencies along the y-axis and the exact lower limits along the x-axis.

Procedure:

Step–1: Scale the cumulative frequencies along the Y-axis and the actual lower limits along the X-axis.

Step-2: Plot the ordered pairs (lower limit, corresponding cumulative frequency).

To complete the ogive we also plot the ordered pair (upper limit of the highest class, 0)

Step–3: Join these plotted points by a smooth curve.

The curve so obtained is the required ogive.

Illustration 13

Draw a 'more than ogive' from the following distribution.

Marks obtained	0-9	10-19	20-29	30-39	40-49	50-59
No. of candidates	4	6	7	5	10	3

Solution

We write the given distribution using actual limits as under:

Marks obtained	-0.5-9.5	9.5-19.5	19.5-29.5	29.5-39.5	39.5-49.5	49.5-59.5
No. of candidates	4	6	7	5	10	3

For "more than ogive" we convert it to cumulative frequency distribution as under

Marks	Number of students (cumulative frequency)	Plotting Points
– 0.5 or more	35	(– 0.5, 35)
9.5 or more	35 – 4 = 31	(9.5, 31)
19.5 or more	31– 6= 25	(19.5, 25)
29.5 or more	25 – 7 = 18	(29.5, 18)
39.5 or more	18 – 5 = 13	(39.5, 13)
49.5 or more	13 – 10 = 3	(49.5, 3)
more than 59.5	3 – 3 = 0	(59.5, 0)

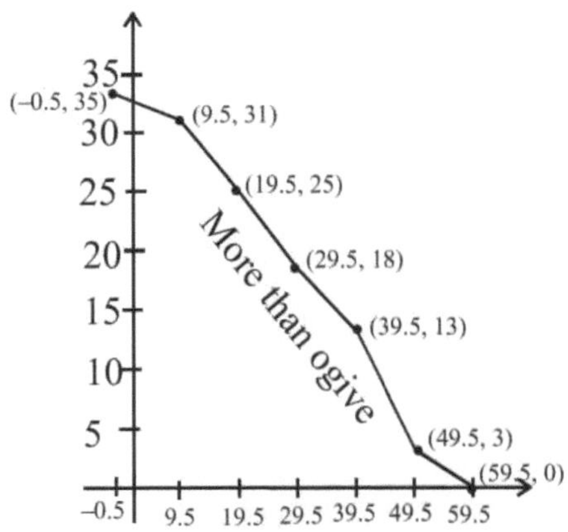

Illustration 14

The annual profits earned by 30 shops of a shopping complex in a locality give rise to the following distribution

Profit (in lakhs Rs.)	No. of shops (frequency)
More than or equal to 5	30
More than or equal to 10	28
More than or equal to 15	16
More than or equal to 20	14
More than or equal to 25	10
More than or equal to 30	7
More than or equal to 35	3

Draw both ogives for the data above. Hence, obtain the median profit.

Solution

We have a more than type cumulative frequency distribution table. We may also prepare a less than type cumulative frequency distribution table from the given data, as given below:

'More than' type

Profit more than (Rs. in lakhs)	No. of shops
5	30
10	28
15	16
20	14
25	10
30	7
35	3

'Less than' type

Profit less than (Rs. in lakhs)	No. of shops
10	2
15	14
20	11
25	20
30	23
35	27
40	30

Now, plot the points A(5,30), B(10,28), C(15,16), D(20,14), E(25,10), F(30,7) and G(35,3) for the more than type cumulative frequency and the points P(10,2), Q(15,14), R(20,16), S(25,20), T(30,23), U(35,27) and V(40,30) for the less than type cumulative frequency table. Join these points by a freehand to get ogives for 'more than' type and 'less than' type.

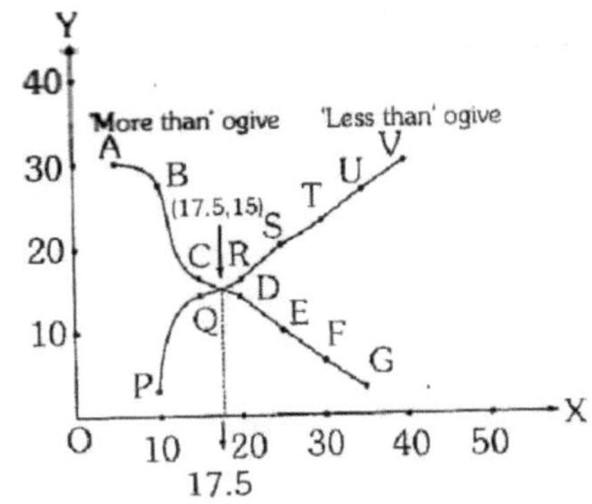

The two ogives intersect each other at point (17.5, 15).
Hence, the median profit is Rs. 17.5 lakhs.

6.13 MEDIAN BY GRAPH :

We can find the median graphically in two ways :

(a) By drawing more than and less than Ogives.

(b) By drawing only less than Ogive.

6.13.1 Median by Drawing Both More Than and Less Than Ogives :

If we draw the two types of curves i.e. Less Than type Ogive and More Than type Ogive on same pair of axes, then these two curves intersect each other at a point. From this point of intersection, if we draw a perpendicular to X-axis, it will intersect the X-axis at some point. The X-coordinate of this point is the **median**.

6.13.2 Median by Drawing Only Less Than Ogive :

Generally, we use only Less Than type Ogive to calculate the median. Steps are as follows:

(i) First prepare a less than type cumulative frequency distribution table.

(ii) Draw less than cumulative frequency curve (ogive).

(iii) If total number of observations is N, then locate $\frac{N}{2}$ on cumulative frequency axis i.e. Y-axis.

(iv) From this point on Y-axis, draw a horizontal line parallel to X-axis which meet the ogive at some point.

(v) Through this point on the curve, draw a perpendicular to X-axis.

(vi) The perpendicular meets the X-axis at some point. X-coordinate of this point is the required median.

Illustration 15

For the following frequency distribution, determine the median by drawing ogives.

Marks Obtained	50 – 60	60 – 70	70 – 80	80 – 90	90 – 100
No. of Students	4	8	12	6	6

Solution :

Marks Obtained	**No. of Students (Cumulative Frequency)**
More than or equal to 50	36
More than or equal to 60	$36-4=32$
More than or equal to 70	$32-8=24$
More than or equal to 80	$24-12=12$
More than or equal to 90	$12-6=6$

Marks Obtained	**No. of Students (Cumulative Frequency)**
Less than 60	4
Less than 70	$4+8=12$
Less than 80	$12+12=24$
Less than 90	$24+6=30$
Less than 100	$30+6=36$

Median by drawing both the Ogives :

On same pair of axes plot (60, 4), (70, 12), (80, 24), (90, 30) and (100, 36) for less than type ogive and plot (50, 36), (60, 32), (70, 24), (80, 12) and (90, 6) for more than type ogive.

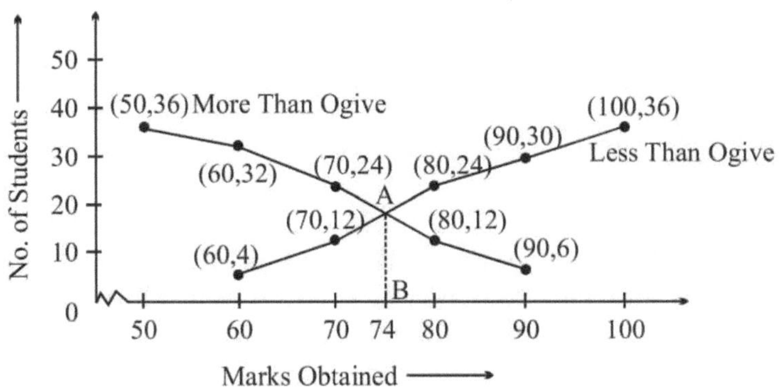

Perpendicular from point of intersection A of two curves intersect X-axis at point B, which corresponds to 74 marks. Hence median = 74.

Median by drawing Less than Ogive only :

Plot the points (60, 4), (70, 12), (80, 24), (90, 30) and (100, 36) for less than ogive.

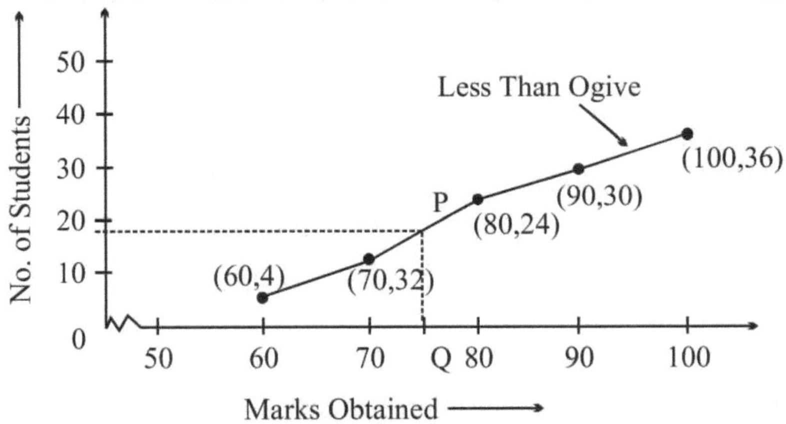

Locate $\frac{N}{2} = \frac{36}{2} = 18$ on Y-axis and draw horizontal line through 18 on Y-axis which intersects curve at point P. Draw perpendicular from P on X-axis which intersects X-axis at Q. Value corresponding to point Q is the median. A value of point Q = 74. Hence Median = 74.

SOLVED EXAMPLES

Example 1

Find the mean of 50 observations. It is given that the mean of first 32 of them is 28 and the mean of remaining 18 observations is 30.

Solution

The total of first 32 observation = $32 \times 28 = 896$

Similarly the total of remaining 18 observations = 540

Hence total of 50 observations $= 896 + 540 = 1436$

Now, req. mean $= \frac{1436}{50} = 28.72$

Example 2

Mean temperature of last week of September was 24° C. If mean temperature of Monday, Tuesday , Wednesday and Thursday was 22 C and that of Thursday, Friday. Saturday and Sunday was 25° then find the temperature on thursday.

Solution

Temperature on thursday

$= 22 \times 4 + 25 \times 4 - 24 \times 7 = 88 + 100 - 168$

$= 188 - 168 = 20$

Example 3

Find the value of p, if the median of following observations is 48.

14, 17, 33, 35, p – 5, p + 7, 57, 63, 69, 80. The above observation are in ascending order.

Solution

n = even

$$\text{Median} = \frac{\left[\left(\frac{n}{2}\right)^{th} \text{observation} + \left(\frac{n}{2}+1\right)^{th} \text{Obsevation}\right]}{2}$$

$48 \times 2 = (5^{th}$ Observation + 6th Observation)

$\Rightarrow \quad 96 = p - 5 + p + 7 \qquad \Rightarrow \quad 96 = 2p + 2$

$\Rightarrow \quad 94 = 2p \qquad \Rightarrow \quad p = \frac{94}{2} = 47$

Example 4

Find the value of p, if the mean of the following distribution is 7.5

x:	3	5	7	9	11	13
f:	6	8	15	p	8	4

Solution

Calculation of Mean

x_i	f_i	f_ix_i
3	6	18
5	8	40
7	15	105
9	p	9p
11	8	88
13	4	52
	$N = \Sigma f_i = 41 + p$	$\Sigma f_ix_i = 303 + 9p$

We have $\Sigma f_i = 41 + p$, $\Sigma f_i x_i = 303 + 9p$

$\therefore \quad \text{Mean} = \dfrac{\Sigma f_i x_i}{\Sigma f_i}$

$\Rightarrow \quad 7.5 = \dfrac{303 + 9p}{41 + p}$

$\Rightarrow \quad 7.5 \times (41 + p) = 303 + 9p$

$\Rightarrow \quad 307.5 + 7.5p = 303 + 9p$

$\Rightarrow \quad 9p - 7.5p = 307.5 - 303$

$\Rightarrow \quad 1.5p = 4.5$

$\Rightarrow \quad p = 3$

Example 5

The following table gives weekly wages in rupees of workers in a ceratin commerical organization. The frequency of class 49–52 is missing. It is known that the mean of the frequency distribution is 47.2. Find the missing frequency

Weekly wages (Rs.)	40-43	43-46	46-49	49-52	52-55
Number of workers	31	58	60	?	27

Solution

Let the missing frequency be f, the assumed mean be a = 47 and h = 3.

Calculation of Mean

Class-intervals	Mid-values (x_i)	(f_i)	$d_i = x_i - 47.5$	$u_i = \dfrac{x_i - 47.5}{3}$	$f_i u_i$
40-43	41.5	31	−6	−2	−62
43-46	44.5	58	−3	−1	−58
46-49	47.5	60	0	0	0
49-52	50.5	f	3	1	f
52-55	53.5	27	6	2	54
	$N = \Sigma f_i = 176 + f$				$\Sigma f_i u_i = f - 66$

We have,

$\overline{X} = 47.2$ a = 47.5 and h = 3

$\therefore \quad \overline{X} = a + h\left\{\dfrac{1}{N}\Sigma f_i u_i\right\}$

$\Rightarrow \quad 47.2 = 47.5 + 3 \times \left\{\dfrac{f - 66}{176 + f}\right\} \quad \Rightarrow \quad -0.3 = 3 \times \left\{\dfrac{f - 66}{176 + f}\right\}$

$\Rightarrow \quad -0.3 = 3 \times \left\{\dfrac{f - 66}{176 + f}\right\} \quad \Rightarrow \quad \dfrac{-1}{10} = \dfrac{f - 66}{176 + f}$

$\Rightarrow \quad -176 - f = 10f - 660 \quad \Rightarrow \quad 11f = 484$

$\Rightarrow \quad f = 44$

Hence, the missing frequency is 44.

Example 6

The median of the following data is 525. Find the values of x and y, if the total frequency is 100.

Class intervals	Frequency(f)
0-100	2
100-200	5
200-300	x
300-400	12
400-500	17
500-600	20
600-700	y
700-800	9
800-900	7
900-1000	4

Solution

Computation of Median

Class intervals	Frequency(f)	Cumulative frequency (f)
0-100	2	0
100-200	5	7
200-300	x	$7 + x$
300-400	12	$19 + x$
400-500	17	$36 + x$
500-600	20	$56 + x$
600-700	y	$56 + x + y$
700-800	9	$65 + x + y$
800-900	7	$72 + x + y$
900-1000	4	$76 + x + y$
		Total = 100

We have

$N = \Sigma f_i = 100$

$\Rightarrow \quad 76 + x + y = 100 \Rightarrow x + y = 24$

It is given that the median is 525. Clearly, it lies in the class 500 – 600.

$\therefore \quad l = 500,\ h = 100,\ f = 20,\ F = 36 + x$ and $N = 100$

Now,

$$\text{Median} = l + \frac{N/2 - F}{f} \times h \quad \Rightarrow \quad 525 = 500 + \frac{50 - (36 + x)}{20} \times 100$$

Example 7

The following table contains the marks obtained by a student of class XI and the approved weightage for every subject prescribed by the selection committee of a professional college.

S.No.	Subject	Weightage (w_i)	Marks Obtained (x_i)
1.	English	1	60
2.	Maths	3	85
3.	Physics	3	79
4.	Chemistry	2	75

Compare the arithmetic mean and weighted mean of the marks obtained.

Solution

Calculation of mean and weighted mean.

S.No.	Subject	w_i	x_i	$w_i x_i$
1.	English	1	60	$1 \times 60 = 60$
2.	Maths	3	85	$3 \times 85 = 255$
3.	Physics	3	79	$3 \times 79 = 237$
4.	Chemistry	2	75	$2 \times 75 = 150$
	Total	$\sum w_i = 9$	$\sum x_i = 299$	$\sum w_i x_i = 702$

Thus, Mean $= \frac{\sum x_i}{n} = \frac{299}{4} = 74.75$ Marks,

and Weighted mean $= \frac{\sum w_i x_i}{\sum w_i} = \frac{702}{9} = 78$ marks

Example 8

The mean of the following frequency distribution is 62.8 and the sum of all the frequencies is 50. Compute the missing frequency f_1 and f_2.

Class	0 - 20	20 - 40	40 - 60	60 - 80	80 - 100	100 - 120
Frequency	5	f_1	10	f_2	7	8

Solution

Let A = 70, h = 20, $u_i = \frac{x_i - A}{h}$

C.I.	x_i	f_i	u_i	$f_i u_i$
0 – 20	10	5	– 3	– 15
20 – 40	30	f_1	– 2	$-2f_1$
40 – 60	50	10	– 1	– 10
60 – 80	70	f_2	0	0
80 – 100	90	7	1	7
100 – 120	110	8	2	16
		$\sum f_i = 30 + f_1 + f_2$		$\sum f_i u_i = -2 - 2f_1$

Given $\overline{x} = 62.8$,

So, $\overline{x} = A + \frac{\sum f_i u_i}{\sum f_i} \times h$ $\Rightarrow$ $62.8 = 70 + \frac{(-2 - 2f_1)}{50} \times 20$

$\Rightarrow$ $-7.2 = (-2 - 2f_1) \times \frac{2}{5}$ $\Rightarrow$ $-36 = -4 - 4f_1$

$\Rightarrow$ $4f_1 = 32$ $\Rightarrow$ $f_1 = 8.$

Also, $30 + f_1 + f_2 = 50$
$f_1 + f_2 = 20$
$f_2 = 20 - f_1$
$f_2 = 20 - 8$
$f_2 = 12$
Hence, $f_1 = 8$ and $f_2 = 12$.

Example 9

If the median of the following frequency distribution is 46, find the missing frequenc

Variable	10-20	20-30	30 - 40	40 - 50	50 -60	60 -70	70 -80	Total
Frequency	12	30	?	65	?	25	18	**229**

Solution

Class Interval	Frequency	C.F.
10 - 20	12	12
20 - 30	30	42
30 - 40	f_1	$42 + f_1$
40 - 50	65	$107 + f_1$
50 - 60	f_2	$107 + f_1+f_2$
60 - 70	25	$132 + f_1+f_2$
70 - 80	18	$150+ f_1+f_2$

(Median Class)

Let the frequency of the class 30 – 40 be f_1 and that of the class 50 – 60 be f_2. The total frequency is 229
$12 + 30 + f_1 + 65 + f_2 + 25 + 18 = 229$
$\Rightarrow \quad f_1 + f_2 = 79$
It is given that median is 46., clearly, 46 lies in the class 40 – 50. So, 40 – 50 is the median class
$\therefore \quad \ell = 40, h = 10, f = 65$ and $C = 42 + f_1$, $N = 229$

$$\text{Median} = \ell + \frac{\frac{N}{2} - C}{f} \times h$$

$$46 = 40 + \frac{\frac{229}{2} - (42 + f_1)}{65} \times 10 \Rightarrow \quad 46 = 40 + \frac{145 - 2f_1}{13}$$

$$\Rightarrow \quad 6 = \frac{145 - 2f_1}{13} \qquad \Rightarrow \quad 2f_1 = 67$$

$\Rightarrow \quad f_1 = 33.5$ or 34
Since, $f_1 + f_2 = 79$
$\therefore \quad f_2 = 45$
Hence, $f_1 = 34$, and $f_2 = 45$.

Example 10

Find the mode of the following distribution :

Daily Wages	31 - 36	37 - 42	43 - 48	49 - 54	55 - 60	61 - 66
No. of workers	6	12	20	15	9	4

Solution

Daily Wages	No. of workers	Daily wages	No of workers
31 - 36	6	30.5 - 36.5	6
37 - 42	12	36.5 - 42.5	12
43 - 48	20	42.5 - 48.5	20
49 - 54	15	48.5 - 54.5	15
55 - 60	9	54.5 - 60.6	9
61 - 66	4	60.5 - 66.5	4

Modal class frequency is 42.5 – 48.5.

$\ell = 42.5$

$f_1 = 20$, $f_0 = 12$, $f_2 = 15$, $h = 6$

$$\therefore \quad \text{Mode} = 42.5 + \frac{20-12}{2(20)-12-15} \times 6$$

$$\therefore \quad \text{Mode} = 46.2$$

CONCEPT APPLICATION LEVEL - I [NCERT Questions]

Q.1 A survey was conducted by a group of students as a part of thier environment awareness programme, in which they collected the following data regarding the number of plants in 20 houses in a locality. Find the mean number of plants per house.

Number of plants	0—2	2—4	4—6	6—8	8—10	10—12	12—14
Number of houses	1	2	1	5	6	2	3

Which method did you use for finding the mean, and why ?

Sol.

Number of plants	Number of houses (f_i)	Class mark (x_i)	$f_i x_i$
0 – 2	1	1	1
2 – 4	2	3	6
4 – 6	1	5	5
6 – 8	5	7	35
8 – 10	6	9	54
10 – 12	2	11	22
12 – 14	3	13	39
Total	$\Sigma f_i = 20$		$\Sigma f_i x_i = 162$

$$\therefore \ \bar{x} = \frac{\Sigma f_i x_i}{\Sigma f_i} = \frac{162}{20} = 8.1 \text{ plants}$$

We have used the direct method for finding the mean becuase numerical values of x_i and f_i are small.

Q.2 Consider the following distrubition of daily wages of 50 workers of a factory.

Daily wages (in Rs.)	100–120	120–140	140–160	160–180	180–200
Number of workers	12	14	8	6	10

Find the mean daily wages of the workers of the factory by using an appropriate method.

Sol. Take a = 150, h = 20

Daily wages (in Rs.)	Number of workers (f_i)	Class mark (x_i)	$d_i = x_i - 150$	$u_i = \frac{x_i - 150}{20}$	$f_i u_i$
100 – 120	12	110	– 40	– 2	– 24
120 – 140	14	130	– 20	– 1	– 14
140 – 160	8	150	0	0	0
160 – 180	6	170	20	1	6
180 – 200	10	190	40	2	20
Total	$\Sigma f_i = 50$				$\Sigma f_i u_i = -12$

Using the step-deviation method,

$$\bar{x} = a + \left(\frac{\Sigma f_i u_i}{\Sigma f_i}\right) \times h = 150 + \left(\frac{-12}{50}\right) \times 20$$

$$= 150 - 4.8 = 145.20$$

Q.3 The following distribution shows the daily pocket allowance of children of a locality. The mean pocket allowance is Rs. 18. Find the missing frequency f.

Daily pocket allowance (in Rs.)	11–13	13–15	15–17	17–19	19–21	21–23	23–25
Number of children	7	6	9	13	f	5	4

Sol.

Daily pocket allowance(in Rs.)	Number of children (f_i)	Class mark (x_i)	f_ix_i
11 – 13	7	12	84
13 – 15	6	14	84
15 – 17	9	16	144
17 – 19	13	18	234
19 – 21	f	20	20f
21 – 23	5	22	110
23 – 25	4	24	96
Total	$\Sigma f_i = f + 44$		$\Sigma f_ix_i = 20f + 752$

Using the direct method,

$$\overline{x} = \frac{\Sigma f_ix_i}{\Sigma f_i}$$

$$\Rightarrow \quad 18 = \frac{20f + 752}{f + 44}$$

$$\Rightarrow \quad 20f + 752 = 18\,(f + 44)$$

$$\Rightarrow \quad 20f + 752 = 18f + 792$$

$$\Rightarrow \quad 20f - 18f = 792 - 752$$

$$\Rightarrow \quad 2f = 40$$

$$\Rightarrow \quad f = \frac{40}{2} = 20$$

Hence, the missing frequency is 20.

Q.4 The following table shows the ages of the patients admitted in a hospital during a year.

Age (in years)	5—15	15—25	25—35	35—45	45—55	55—65
Number of patients	6	11	21	23	14	5

Find the mode and the mean of data given above. Compare and interpert the two measures of central tendency.

Sol. Here, the maximum frequency is 23 and the class corresponding to this frequency is 35–45. So, the modal class is 35–45.

Now, size (h) = 10, lower limit (l) of modal class = 35, frequency (f_1) of the modal class = 23, frequency (f_0) of class preceding the modal class = 21, frequency (f_2) of class succeeding the modal class = 14.

$$\therefore \text{Mode} = l + \frac{f_1 - f_0}{2f_1 - f_0 - f_2} \times h = 35 + \frac{23-21}{2\times 23 - 21 - 14}\times 10$$

$$= 35 + \frac{2}{11}\times 10 = 35 + \frac{20}{11}$$

$= 35 + 1.8$ (approx.)

$= 36.8$ year's (approx.)

Now finding mean : Take a = 40, h = 10

Age (in years)	Number of patients (f_i)	Class mark (x_i)	$d_i = x_i - 40$	$u_i = \frac{x_i - 40}{10}$	f_iu_i
5 – 15	6	10	– 30	– 3	– 18
15 – 25	11	20	– 20	– 2	– 22
25 – 35	21	30	– 10	– 1	– 21
35 – 45	23	40	0	0	0
45 – 55	14	50	10	1	14
55 – 65	5	60	20	2	10
Total	$\Sigma f_i = 80$				$\Sigma f_iu_i = -37$

Using the step-deviation method,

$$\overline{x} = a + \left(\frac{\Sigma f_iu_i}{\Sigma f_i}\right)\times h = 40 + \left(\frac{-37}{80}\right)\times 10$$

$$= 40 - \frac{37}{8} = 40 - 4.63$$

$= 35.37$ years.

Maximum number of patients admitted in the hospital are of the age 36.8 years (approx.), while on an average the age of a patient admittted to the hospital is 35.37 years.

Q.5 The following distribution gives the state-wise teacher-student ratio in higher secondary of India. Find the mode and mean of this data. Interpret, the two measures.

Number of students per teacher	Number of State / U.T.
15 – 20	3
20 – 25	8
25 – 30	9
30 – 35	10
35 – 40	3
40 – 45	0
45 – 50	0
50 – 55	2

Sol. Since the maximum number of states/U.T. have the number of students per teacher in interval 30–35, the modal class in 30–35.

Therefore, $l = 30$; $h = 5$; $f_1 = 10$

$f_0 = 9$; $f_2 = 3$

$$\therefore \quad \text{Mode} = l + \left(\frac{f_1 - f_0}{2f_1 - f_0 - f_2}\right) \times h$$

$$= 30 + \left(\frac{10-9}{2\times10-9-3}\right)\times 5 = 30 + \frac{5}{8} = 30 + 0.6 = 30.6$$

Hence, the mode of the given data is 30.6.

Let us claculated mean now, Take a = 37.5, h = 5.

Number of students per teacher	Number of states / U.T. (f_i)	Class mark (x_i)	$d_i = x_i - 37.5$	$u_i = \frac{x_i - 37.5}{5}$	f_iu_i
15 – 20	3	17.5	– 20	– 4	– 12
20 – 25	8	22.5	– 15	– 3	– 24
25 – 30	9	27.5	– 10	– 2	– 18
30 – 35	10	32.5	– 5	– 1	– 10
35 – 40	3	37.5	0	0	0
40 – 45	0	42.5	5	1	0
45 – 50	0	47.5	10	2	0
50 – 55	2	52.5	15	3	6
Total	$\Sigma f_i = 35$				$\Sigma f_iu_i = -58$

Using the step-deviation method,

$$\bar{x} = a + \left(\frac{\Sigma f_iu_i}{\Sigma f_i}\right) \times h$$

$$= 37.5 + \left(\frac{-58}{35}\right)\times 5 = 37.5 - 8.3 = 29.2$$

Interpretation. Most states/U.T. have a student teacher ratio of 30.6 and on an average, this ratio is 29.2.

Q.6 The following frequency distribution gives the monthly consumption of electricity of 68 consumers of a locality. Find the median, mean and mode of the data and compare them.

Monthly consumption (in units)	Number of consumers
65 – 85	4
85 – 105	5
105 – 125	13
125 – 145	20
145 – 165	14
165 – 185	8
185 – 205	4

Sol. Median :

Monthly consumption (in units)	Number of consumers (f_i)	Cumulative frequency (C.F.)
65 – 85	4	4
85 – 105	5	9
105 – 125	13	22
125 – 145	20	42
145 – 165	14	56
165 – 185	8	64
185 – 205	4	68

Now, $n = 68$ So, $\frac{n}{2} = \frac{68}{2} = 34$

This observation lies is the class 125 – 145. Therefore, 125–145 is the median class.

So, $l = 125$, $cf = 22$, $f = 20$, $h = 20$

$$\therefore \quad \text{Median} = l + \left(\frac{\frac{n}{2} - cf}{f}\right) \times h = 125 + \left(\frac{34 - 22}{20}\right) \times 20 = 125 + 12 = 137 \text{ units.}$$

Mean : Take a = 135, h = 20

Monthly consumption (in units)	Number of consumers (f_i)	Class mark (x_i)	$d_i = x_i - 135$	$u_i = \frac{x_i - 135}{20}$	$f_i u_i$
65 – 85	4	75	– 60	– 3	– 12
85 – 105	5	95	– 40	– 2	– 10
105 – 125	13	115	– 20	– 1	– 13
125 – 145	20	135	0	0	0
145 – 165	14	155	20	1	14
165 – 185	8	175	40	2	16
185 – 205	4	195	60	3	12
Total	$\Sigma f_i = 68$				$\Sigma f_i u_i = 7$

Using the step-deviation method,

$$\bar{x} = a + \left(\frac{\Sigma f_i u_i}{\Sigma f_i}\right) \times h = 135 + \left(\frac{7}{68}\right) \times 20$$

$$= 135 + \frac{35}{17} = 135 + 2.06 = 137.06$$

Mode : Since the maximum number of consumers have their monthly consumption (in units) in the interval 125–145, the modal class is 125 – 145. Therefore,

$l = 125,\quad h = 20,\quad f_1 = 20,\quad f_0 = 13,\quad f_2 = 14$

$$\therefore \quad \text{Mode} = l + \left(\frac{f_1 - f_0}{2f_1 - f_0 - f_2}\right) \times h$$

$$= 125 + \left(\frac{20 - 13}{2 \times 20 - 13 - 14}\right) \times 20$$

$$= 125 + \frac{7}{13} \times 20 = 125 + \frac{140}{13}$$

$= 125 + 10.77 = 135.77$ units.

Comparison. On comparison, we find that the three measures are approximately the same in this case.

Q.7 If the median of the distribution given below is 28.5, find the values of x and y.

Class Interval	Frequency
0 – 10	5
10 – 20	x
20 – 30	20
30 – 40	15
40 – 50	y
50 – 60	5
Total	60

Sol.

Class Interval	Frequency (F_i)	Cumulative frequency (C.F.)
0 – 10	5	5
10 – 20	x	5 + x
20 – 30	20	25 + x
30 – 40	15	40 + x
40 – 50	y	40 + x + y
50 – 60	5	45 + x + y
Total	$\Sigma f_i = 60$	

$n = 60$ (Given)

$\Rightarrow \quad 45 + x + y = 60$

$\Rightarrow \quad x + y = 60 - 45$

$\Rightarrow \quad x + y = 15 \quad ....(1)$

The median is 28.5, which lies in the class 20–30.

So, $l = 20 \quad f = 20 \quad cf = 5 + x \quad h = 10$

$$\therefore \quad \text{Median} = l + \left(\frac{\frac{n}{2} - cf}{f}\right) \times h$$

$$\Rightarrow \quad 28.5 = 20 + \left\{\frac{\frac{60}{2} - (5 + x)}{20}\right\} \times 10$$

$$\Rightarrow \quad 28.5 = 20 + \frac{25 - x}{2}$$

$$\Rightarrow \quad \frac{25 - x}{2} = 28.5 - 20$$

$\Rightarrow \quad 25 - x = 8.5 \times 2$

$\Rightarrow \quad 25 - x = 17$

$\Rightarrow \quad x = 25 - 17 = 8 \quad ......(2)$

From (1) and (2),

$8 + y = 15$

$\Rightarrow \quad y = 15 - 8 = 7$

Hence, the values of x and y are 8 and 7 respectively.

Q.8 The length of 40 leaves of a plant are measured correct to the nearest millimetre and the data obtained is represented in the following table :

Length (in mm)	Number of leaves
118 – 126	3
127 – 135	5
136 – 144	9
145 – 153	12
154 – 162	5
163 – 171	4
172 – 180	2

Find the median length of the leaves.

(Hints : The data needs to be converted to continuous class for finding the median, since the formula assumes continuous classes. The classes then change to 117.5 – 126.5, 126.5–135.5, ..., 171.5 – 180.5)

Sol. We shall first convert the given data to continuous classes. Then, the data become

Length (in mm)	Number of leaves	Cumulative frequency
117.5 – 126.5	3	3
126.5 – 135.5	5	8
135.5 – 144.5	9	17
144.5 – 153.5	12	29
153.5 – 162.5	5	34
162.5 – 171.5	4	38
171.5 – 180.5	2	40

Now, $n = 40$

So, $\frac{n}{2} = \frac{40}{2} = 20$

This observation lies in the class 144.5–153.5. So, 144.5–153.5 is the median class.

Therefore, $l = 144.5$

$h = 9$

$cf = 17$

$f = 12$

$$\therefore \quad \text{Median} = l + \left(\frac{\frac{n}{2} - cf}{f}\right) \times h = 144.5 + \left(\frac{20-17}{12}\right) \times 9$$

$$= 144.5 + 2.25 = 146.75 \text{ mm}$$

Hence, the median length of the leaves is 146.75 mm.

Q.9 The following distribution gives the daily income of 50 workers of a factory.

Daily income (in Rs.)	100—120	120—140	140—160	160—180	180—200
Number of workers	12	14	8	6	10

Convert the distribution above to a less than type cumulative frequency distribution, and draw its ogive.

Sol. Less than type cumulative frequency distribution :

Daily income (in Rs.)	Number of workers
Less than 120	12
Less than 140	26
Less than 160	34
Less than 180	40
Less than 200	50

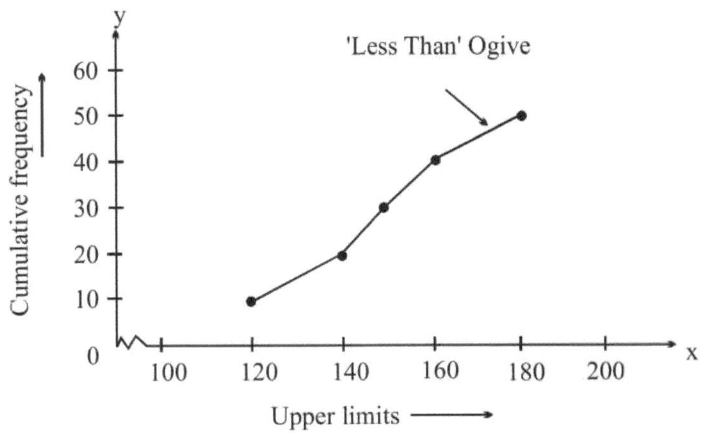

Q.10 During the medical check up of 35 students of a class, their weights are recorded as follows :

Weight(in kg)	Number of students
Less than 38	0
Less than 40	3
Less than 42	5
Less than 44	9
Less than 46	14
Less than 48	28
Less than 50	32
Less than 52	35

Draw a less than type ogive for the given data. Hence obtain the median weight from the graph and verify the result by using the formula.

Sol. Here, $\frac{n}{2}=\frac{35}{2}=17.5$

Locate 17.5 on the y-axis. From this point, draw a line parallel to the x-axis cutting the curve at a point. From this point draw a perpendicular to the x-axis. The point of intersection of this perpendicular with the x-axis determines the median of the given data as 46.4kg.

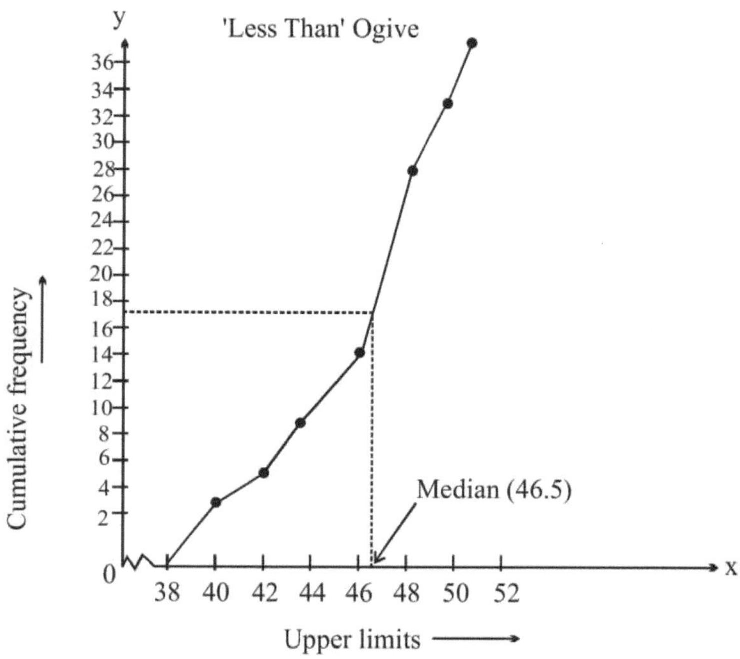

Median Weight by using the Formula :

Weight(in kg)	Number of students	Cumulative frequency
0 – 38	0	0
38 – 40	3	3
40 – 42	2	5
42 – 44	4	9
44 – 46	5	14
46 – 48	14	28
48 – 50	4	32
50 – 52	3	35

Now, $n = 35$

So, $\frac{n}{2} = \frac{35}{2} = 17.5$

This observation lies in the class 46 – 48.

So, 46 – 48 is the median class.

Therefore, $l = 46$

$h = 2$

$f = 14$

$cf = 14$

∴ Median (by using the formula)

$$= l + \left(\frac{\frac{n}{2} - cf}{f}\right) \times h = 46 + \left(\frac{17.5 - 14}{14}\right) \times 2 = 46 + \frac{1}{2} = 46.5 \text{ kg.}$$

Verification. We find that the median weight obtained from graph is the same as the median weight obtained by using the formula.

Q.11 The following table gives production yield per hectare of wheat of 100 farms of a village.

Production yield (in kg/ha)	50—55	55—60	60—65	65—70	70—75	75—80
Number of farms	2	8	12	24	38	16

Change the distribution to a more than type distribution, and draw its ogive.

Sol. More than type distribution :

Production yield (in kg/ha)	Number of farms
More than 50	100
More than 55	98
More than 60	90
More than 65	78
More than 70	54
More than 75	16

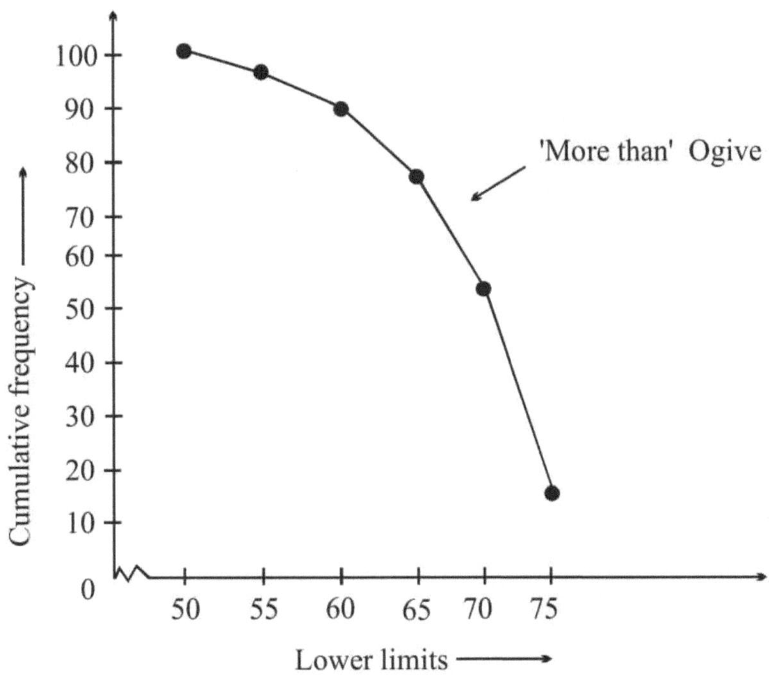

CONCEPT APPLICATION LEVEL - II [Previous Year Questions]

Q.1 The median and mode of a frequency distribution are 525 and 500 then mean of same frequency distribution is : **[NTSE-2013]**

(A) 75 (B) 107.5 (C) 527.5 (D) 537.5

Q.2 Find the mean of the data given below : **[IOM-11]**

2, 4, 10, 12, 18, 16, 14, 20

(A) 12 (B) 14.2 (C) 15 (D) 8.96

Q.3 The score of 10 students of a class test is given as 44, 54, 46, 63, 55, 42, 34, 48, 70, 38 calculate the median : **[IOM-11]**

(A) 48 (B) 46 (C) 47 (D) 49

Q.4 The clustering of data around a central value is known as : **[IOM-11]**

(A) mean (B) mode (C) median (D) central tendency

Q.5 The median from the ogive curve can be determined by the point on : **[IOM-11]**

(A) x-axis (B) origin (C) y-axis (D) none of these

Q.6 A set of numbers consists of four 5′s, six 7′s, ten 9′s, eleven 12′s, three 13′s, two 14′s. The approximate difference between mean and median of this set of numbers is : **[5th IOM]**

(A) 1 (B) 2 (C) 5 (D) 4

Q.7 The following table shows the ages of the patients admitted in a hospital during a year. Find the mode of the given data

Age (in years)	5—15	15—25	25—35	35—45	45—55	55—65
Number of students	6	11	21	23	14	5

(A) 36.8 years (B) 37.2 years (C) 35.4 years (D) 34.3 years

Q.8 Median of a data set is a number which has an equal number of observations between and above it. The median of the data 1, 9, 4, 3, 7, 6, 8, 8, 12, 15 is **[NTSE-2013]**

(A) 7.5 (B) 7

(C) 8 (D) any number between 7 and 8

Q.9 If the classes of a distribution are 1–10, 11–20, ... the upper boundary of class 1 – 10 is :

(A) 9.5 (B) 10 (C) 11.5 (D) 10.5

Q.10 Formula for the median of grouped data is :

(A) $l+\left(\dfrac{\frac{n}{2}-F}{F}\right)\times h$ (B) $l+\left(\dfrac{\frac{n}{2}-F}{f}\right)\times h$ (C) $l+\left(\dfrac{\frac{3n}{2}-F}{f}\right)\times h$ (D) $l+\left(\dfrac{\frac{n}{2}-f}{F}\right)\times h$

where,

l = lower limit of median class

F = cumulative frequency of the class preceding the median class.

f = frequency of median class

n = number of observation = Σf_i

h = width of the median class

Q.11 One of the properties of mode is :
(A) not easy to calculate (B) it is not affected by greatest and least values
(C) Difference of greatest and least values (D) None of these

Q.12 If the median is 20 and each item is increased by 2, the new median will be :
(A) 40 (B) 10 (C) 22 (D) No change

Q.13 Mean temperature of last week of September was 24°C. If mean temperature of Monday, Tuesday, Wednesday and Thursday was 22°C and that of Thursday, Friday, Saturday and Sunday was 25° then temperature of Thursday is **[Tamilnadu NTSE Stage-1_2006]**
(A) 24°C (B) 23°C (C) 22°C (D) 20°C

Q.14 A cricketer has a certain average run for 10 inning, in the 11th inning, he scores 100 runs and now his average run is increased by 9 runs. Then average of 11 inning is **[MP NTSE Stage-1_2008]**
(A) 10 runs (B) 20 runs (C) 11 runs (D) 21 runs

Q.15 The mean of six numbers is 15. If 2 is taken away from every number, the new mean would be **[Bihar NTSE Stage-1_2009]**
(A) 13 (B) 4 (C) 17 (D) 8

Q.16 Out of 50 observations the mean of 25 observation is 30 and mean of rest 25 observation is 32. Then mean of 50 observation is **[Raj. NTSE Stage-1_2010]**
(A) 34 (B) 33 (C) 32 (D) 31

Q.17 The median and mode of a frequency distribution are 525 and 500 then mean of same frequency distribution is [Raj. NTSE Stage-1_2013]

(A) 75 (B) 107.5 (C) 527.5 (D) 537.5

Q.18 For the distribution [Delhi NTSE Stage-1_2013]

Marks	Number of students
Below 5	10
Below 10	25
Below 15	37
Below 20	57
Below 25	66

The sum of the lower limits of the median class and the modal class is

(A) 15 (B) 25 (C) 30 (D) 35

Q.19 If the mean of x and $\frac{1}{x}$ is M, then the mean of x^2 and $\frac{1}{x^2}$ is [MP NTSE Stage-1_2013]

(A) M^2 (B) $\frac{M^2}{4}$ (C) $2M^2 - 1$ (D) $2M^2 + 1$

Q.20 Find the mean, mode and median of the following data [IMO-2016]

x_i	58	59	60	61	62	63	64	65	66
f_i	2	3	6	15	10	5	4	3	2

(A) 60.72, 61, 61 (B) 60.72, 62, 61 (C) 61.72, 61, 62 (D) 61.72, 61, 61

Q.21 If mode of any series is 5 and median is 3 then mean of that series is [NTSE-2016]

(A) 1 (B) 2 (C) 3 (D) 4

CONCEPT APPLICATION LEVEL - III

SECTION-A

- **Multiple choice questions with one correct answer**

Q.1 The cumulative frequency distribution is represented by:

(A) Ogive (B) Bar diagram (C) Logistic curve (D) Histogram

Q.2 If a set of data has zero as an observation, then which one of the following is NOT an appropriate measure of central tendency?

(A) Arithmetic mean (B) Geometric mean (C) Median (D) Mode

Q.3 A, B, C are three sets of values of x:

A; 2, 3, 7, 1, 3, 2,3 B: 7, 5, 9, 12, 5, 3, 8 C: 4, 4, 11, 7, 2, 3, 4

Select the correct statement among the following

(A) Mean of A is equal to Mode of C (B) Mean of C is equal to Median of B

(C) Median of B is equal to Mode of A (D) Mean, Median and Mode of A are same

Q.4 The mean of the values of 1, 2, 3,...............n with respective frequencies x, 2x, 3x....., nx is:

(A) $\frac{n+1}{2}$ (B) $\frac{2n+1}{6}$ (C) $\frac{n}{2}$ (D) $\frac{2n+1}{3}$

Q.5 If the variate is of discrete type, then the frequency distribution can be respresented by:

(A) A scatter diagram (B) A bar diagram (C) A histrogram (D) A pie diagram

Q.6 Find the simple and weighted mean of the first 'n' natural numbers, the weights being the corresponding numbers:

(A) $\frac{n-1}{2}, \frac{2n+1}{3}$ (B) $\frac{n+1}{2}, \frac{2n-1}{3}$ (C) $\left\{\frac{n+1}{2}, \frac{2n+1}{3}\right\}$ (D) $\frac{n-1}{2}, \frac{2n-1}{3}$

Q.7 The number of observations in a group is 40. If the average of first 10 is 4.5 and that of the remaining 30 is 3.5, then the average of the whole group is:

(A) $\frac{1}{5}$ (B) $\frac{15}{4}$ (C) 4 (D) 8

Q.8 The median of a set of 9 distinct obervations is 20.5. If each of the largest 4 observation of the set is increased by2, then the median of the new set:

(A) Is increased by 2 (B) Is decreased by 2

(C) Is two times the original median (D) Remains the same as that of the original set

Q.9 If the mean of x_1 and x_2 is M_1, and that of x_1, x_2, x_3, x_4 is M_2, the mean of ax_1, ax_1. x_3/a, x_4/a is

(A) $\frac{M_1+M_2}{2}$ (B) $\frac{aM_1+(M_2/a)}{2}$

(C) $\frac{1}{2a}\{(a^2-1)M_1+2M_2\}$ (D) $\frac{1}{2a}\{2(a^2-1)M_1+2M_2\}$

Q.10 If a frequency distribution for the number of persons x in a household is prepared with class intervals as (1-4), (5-8), (9-12), etc., then the number of persons x belonging to class interval (5-8) satisfies.

(A) $5 < x < 8$ (B) $5 \leq x < 8$ (C) $5 < x \leq 8$ (D) $5 \leq x \leq 8$

Q.11 In a histogram heights of rectangles are:

(A) Always proportional to the frequencies of the classes

(B) Proportional to the frequency densities if the classes of distributions are not of equal size

(C) Always proportional to the cumulative frequencies of the classes

(D) Prportional to the cumulative frequencies only when classes of distribution are of equal size

Q.12 Arithmetic mean of n observations is m. If two observations 0 and m are added, then the new mean will be:

(A) m (B) $\frac{m}{n+1}$ (C) $\frac{nm}{n+1}$ (D) $\frac{(n+1)m}{n+2}$

Q.13 For a symmetric distribution, the empirical relationship between mean, median and mode is:

(A) Mean > Median > Mode (B) Mean = Median + Mode

(C) Mode - Mean = 3 (Median - Mean) (D) Mean - Mode = 3 (Mean- Median)

Q.14 In a histogram with equal class intervals, heights of bars are proportional to:

(A) Mid - value of the classes (B) Frequencies of respective classes

(C) Cumulative frequency of the classes (D) Class interval of the classes

Q.15 The median of the following incomplete frequency distribution is 4

x	1	2	3	4	5	6	7	8
Frequency	2	3	4	1	2	4	2	-

The frequency of 8 is:

(A) 1 (B) 2 (C) 3 (D) 4

Q.16 The mid value of a class interval is 42. If the class size is 10, then the upper and lower limits of the class are:

(A) 47 and 37 (B) 37 and 47 (C) 37.5 and 47.5 (D) 47.5 and 37.5

Q.17 The mode of the given distribution is:

Weight (in kg)	40	43	46	49	52	55
Number of children	5	8	16	9	7	3

(A) 40 (B) 46 (C) 55 (D) None of these

Q.18 If the first five elements of a set replaced by $(x_i + 5)$, where $i = 1, 2, 3, ...5$ and the next five elements are replaced by $(x_j - 5)$, where $j = 6 .... 10$ then the mean will change by

(A) 25 (B) 10 (C) 5 (D) 0

SECTION-B

- **Assertion & Reason**

Instructions: In the following questions as Assertion (A) is given followed by a Reason (R). Mark your responses from the following options.

(A) Both Assertion and Reason are true and Reason is the correct explanation of 'Assertion'

(B) Both Assertion and Reason are true and Reason is not the correct explanation of 'Assertion'

(C) Assertion is true but Reason is false

(D) Assertion is false but Reason is true

Q.1 **Assertion:** The monthly salaries of four persons are Rs. 10,000, Rs. 10,500, Rs. 11,000 and Rs. 12,000. The arithmetic mean is typical of their salaries.

Reason: Arithmetic mean is strongly affected by extreme values.

Q.2. **Assertion:** The most accurate graphical representation of statistical data is by means of ogives.

Reason: Because cumulative frequencies are represented in it.

Q.3 **Assertion:** The mean of $x_1, x_2, x_3, x_4, x_5, x_6, x_7, x_8$, and x_9 which are in an arithmetic progression is x_5.

Reason: Mean is always the middle most observation if the data are in an arithmetic progression.

SECTION-C

- **Match the following (one to one)**

  Column-I and **column-II** contains **four** entries each. Entries of column-I are to be matched with some entries of column-II. Only One entry of column-I may have the matching with the one entry of column-II and one entry of column-II may have only one matching with one entry of column-I

Q.1

	Column I		Column II
(A)	The direct method	(P)	$\overline{X} = a + \frac{\sum f_i u_i}{\sum f_i} h$
(B)	Step deviation method	(Q)	$l + \left(\frac{f_1 - f_0}{2f_1 - f_0 - f_2}\right) xh$
(C)	Mode	(R)	$l + \left(\frac{\frac{N}{2} - c.f}{f}\right) \times h$
(D)	Median	(S)	$\overline{X} = \frac{\sum f_i x_i}{\sum f_i}$

Q.2

Class Interval	Frequency
30-34	7
35-39	10
40-44	12
45-49	13
50-54	8
55-59	4

	Column I		Column II
(A)	The actual class limits of the fourth class	(P)	5
(B)	The class boundries of the sixth class	(Q)	44.5 - 49.5
(C)	The class mark of the third class	(R)	54.5 - 59.5
(D)	The size of the third class	(S)	42

ANSWER KEY

CONCEPT APPLICATION LEVEL - II

Q.1	D	Q.2	A	Q.3	C	Q.4	D	Q.5	A	Q.6	A	Q.7	A
Q.8	A	Q.9	D	Q.10	B	Q.11	B	Q.12	C	Q.13	D	Q.14	A
Q.15	A	Q.16	D	Q.17	D	Q.18	B	Q.19	C	Q.20	D	Q.21	B

CONCEPT APPLICATION LEVEL - III

SECTION-A

Q.1	A	Q.2	D	Q.3	D	Q.4	D	Q.5	B	Q.6	C	Q.7	B
Q.8	D	Q.9	D	Q.10	B	Q.11	A	Q.12	D	Q.13	C	Q.14	B
Q.15	A	Q.16	A	Q.17	B	Q.18	D						

SECTION-B

Q.1 C 2. A 3. C

SECTION-C

Q.1 A - (S), B - (P), C - (Q), D - (R) Q.2. A - (Q), B - (R), C - (S), D - (P)

Printed by Libri Plureos GmbH in Hamburg,
Germany

9 798890 025388